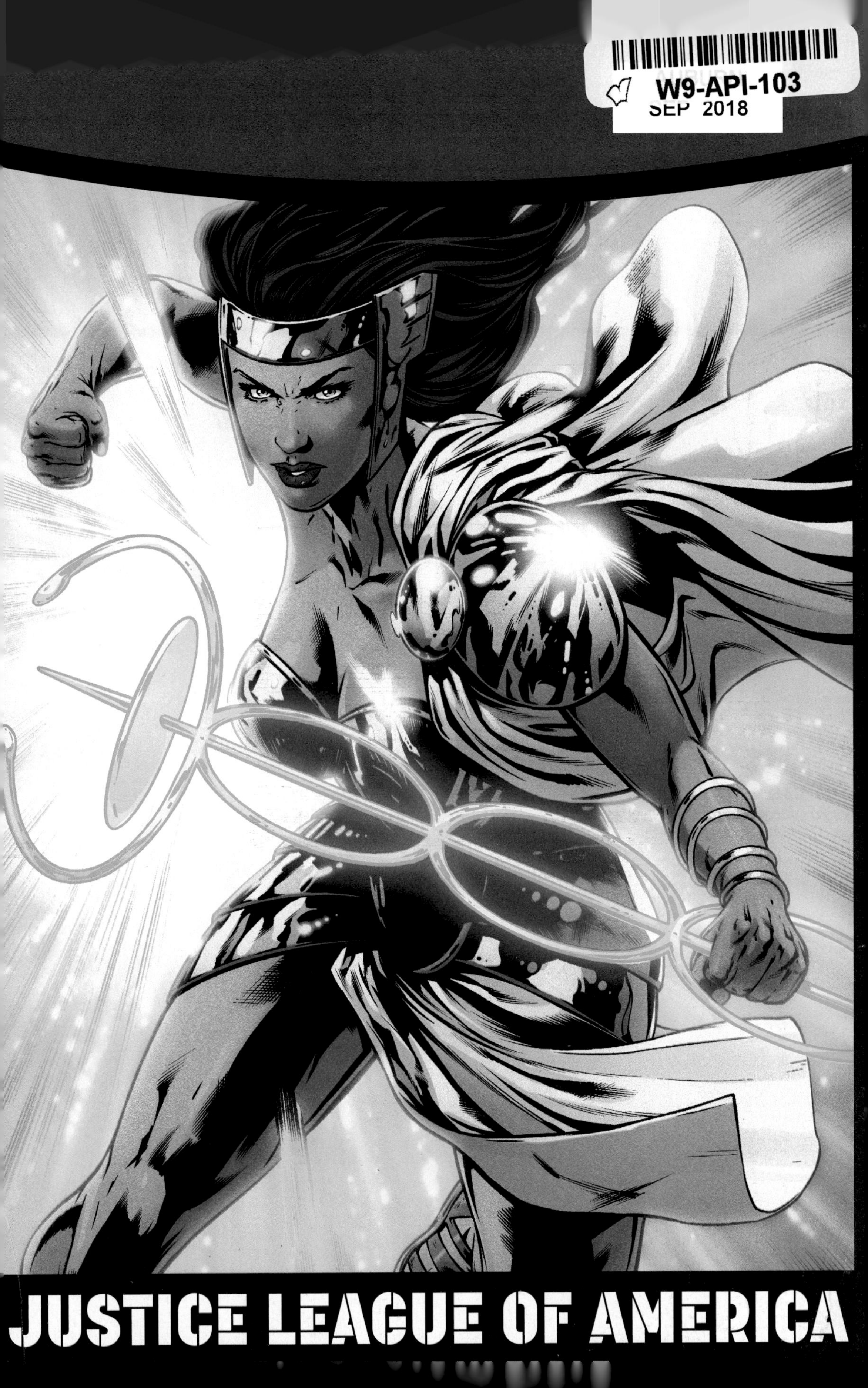

JUSTICE LEAGUE OF AMERICA

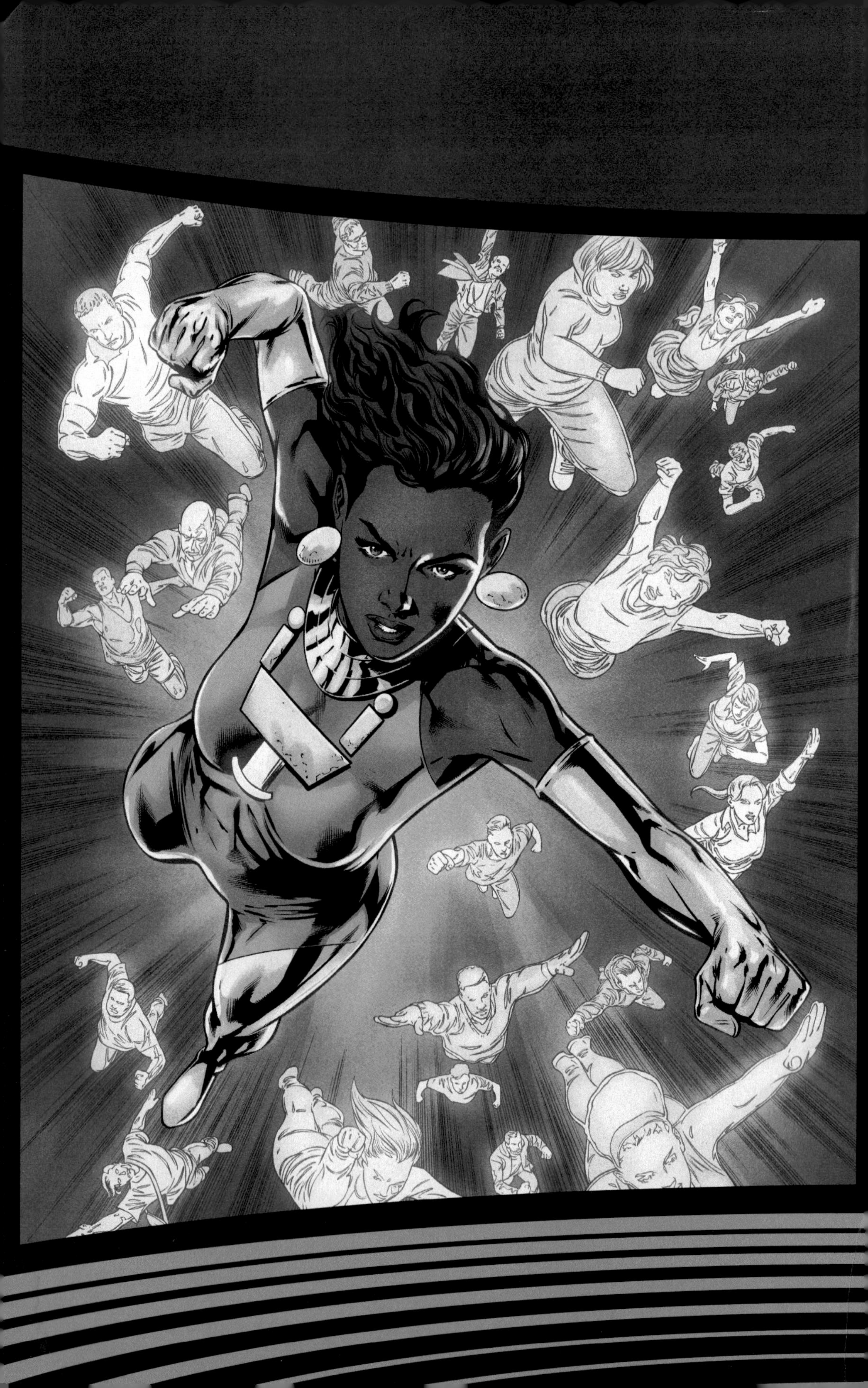

JUSTICE LEAGUE OF AMERICA
VOL.5 DEADLY FABLE

STEVE ORLANDO
writer

HUGO PETRUS * **NEIL EDWARDS**
MIGUEL MENDONÇA * **MINKYU JUNG**
pencillers

HUGO PETRUS * **DANIEL HENRIQUES**
DEXTER VINES * **ANDY OWENS** * **WAYNE FAUCHER**
inkers

HI-FI * **CHRIS SOTOMAYOR**
colorists

CLAYTON COWLES
letterer

DOUG MAHNKE and WIL QUINTANA
collection cover artists

PROMETHEA created by JOHN FRANCIS MOORE and PAUL GUINAN

BRIAN CUNNINGHAM Editor – Original Series ✷ **DAVE WIELGOSZ** Assistant Editor – Original Series
JEB WOODARD Group Editor – Collected Editions ✷ **ERIKA ROTHBERG** Editor – Collected Edition
STEVE COOK Design Director – Books ✷ **SHANNON STEWART** Publication Design

BOB HARRAS Senior VP – Editor-in-Chief, DC Comics
PAT McCALLUM Executive Editor, DC Comics

DAN DiDIO Publisher ✷ **JIM LEE** Publisher & Chief Creative Officer
AMIT DESAI Executive VP – Business & Marketing Strategy, Direct to Consumer & Global Franchise Management
BOBBIE CHASE VP & Executive Editor, Young Reader & Talent Development ✷ **MARK CHIARELLO** Senior VP – Art, Design & Collected Editions
JOHN CUNNINGHAM Senior VP – Sales & Trade Marketing ✷ **BRIAR DARDEN** VP – Business Affairs
ANNE DePIES Senior VP – Business Strategy, Finance & Administration ✷ **DON FALLETTI** VP – Manufacturing Operations
LAWRENCE GANEM VP – Editorial Administration & Talent Relations ✷ **ALISON GILL** Senior VP – Manufacturing & Operations
HANK KANALZ Senior VP – Editorial Strategy & Administration ✷ **JAY KOGAN** Senior VP – Legal Affairs ✷ **JACK MAHAN** VP – Business Affairs
NICK J. NAPOLITANO VP – Manufacturing Administration ✷ **LISETTE OSTERLOH** VP – Digital Marketing & Events
EDDIE SCANNELL VP – Consumer Marketing ✷ **COURTNEY SIMMONS** Senior VP – Publicity & Communications
JIM (SKI) SOKOLOWSKI VP – Comic Book Specialty Sales & Trade Marketing
NANCY SPEARS VP – Mass, Book, Digital Sales & Trade Marketing ✷ **MICHELE R. WELLS** VP – Content Strategy

JUSTICE LEAGUE OF AMERICA VOL. 5: DEADLY FABLE

Published by DC Comics. Compilation and all new material Copyright © 2018 DC Comics. All Rights Reserved.
Originally published in single magazine form in JUSTICE LEAGUE OF AMERICA 22-29. Copyright © 2018 DC Comics. All Rights Reserved.
All characters, their distinctive likenesses and related elements featured in this publication are trademarks of DC Comics.
The stories, characters and incidents featured in this publication are entirely fictional.
DC Comics does not read or accept unsolicited submissions of ideas, stories or artwork.

DC Comics, 2900 West Alameda Ave., Burbank, CA 91505
Printed by LSC Communications, Owensville, MO, USA. 8/24/18. First Printing.
ISBN: 978-1-4012-8449-7

Library of Congress Cataloging-in-Publication Data is available.

PEFC Certified

Printed on paper from
sustainably managed
forests, controlled
sources

PEFC™

PEFC/29-31-337   www.pefc.org

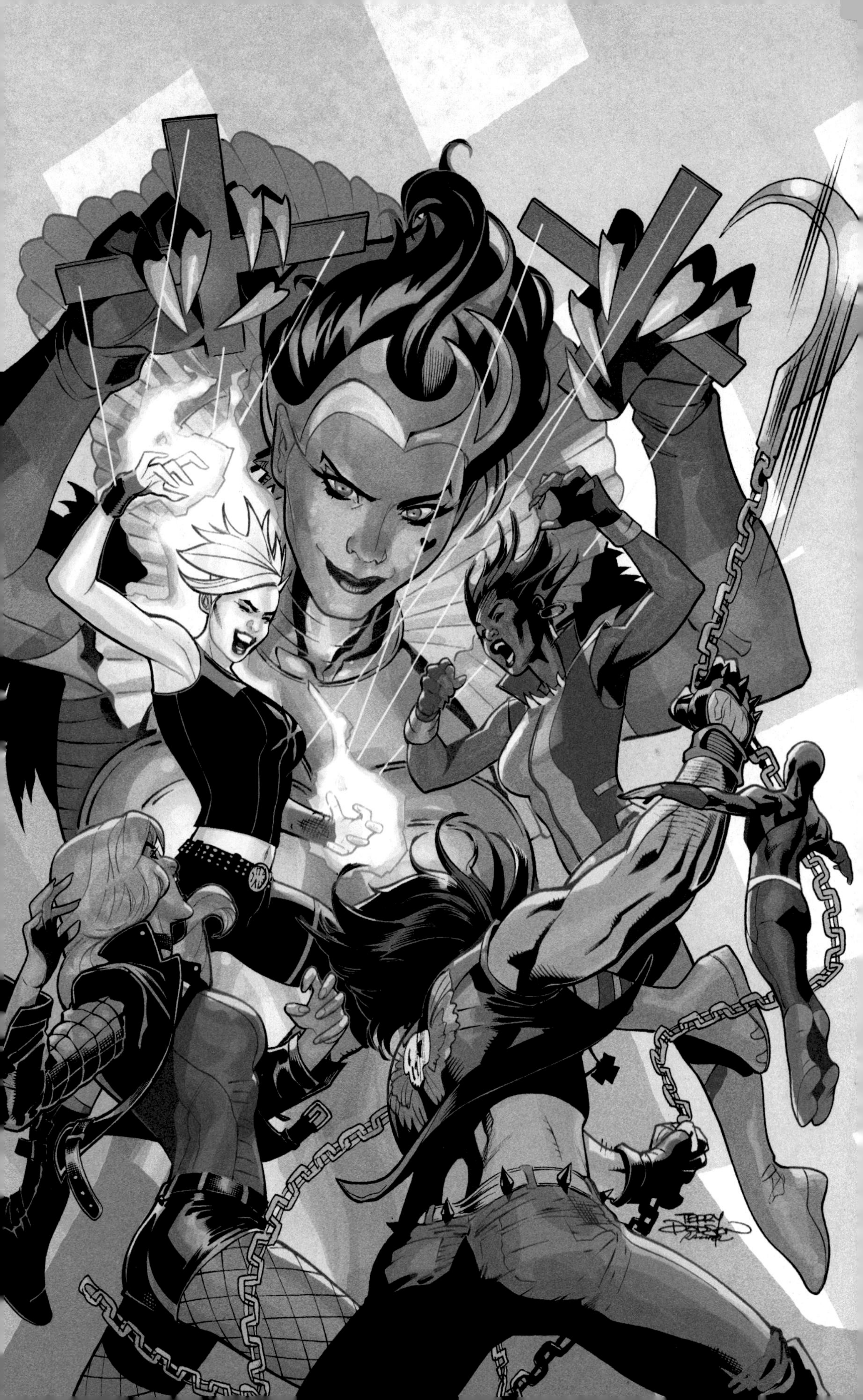

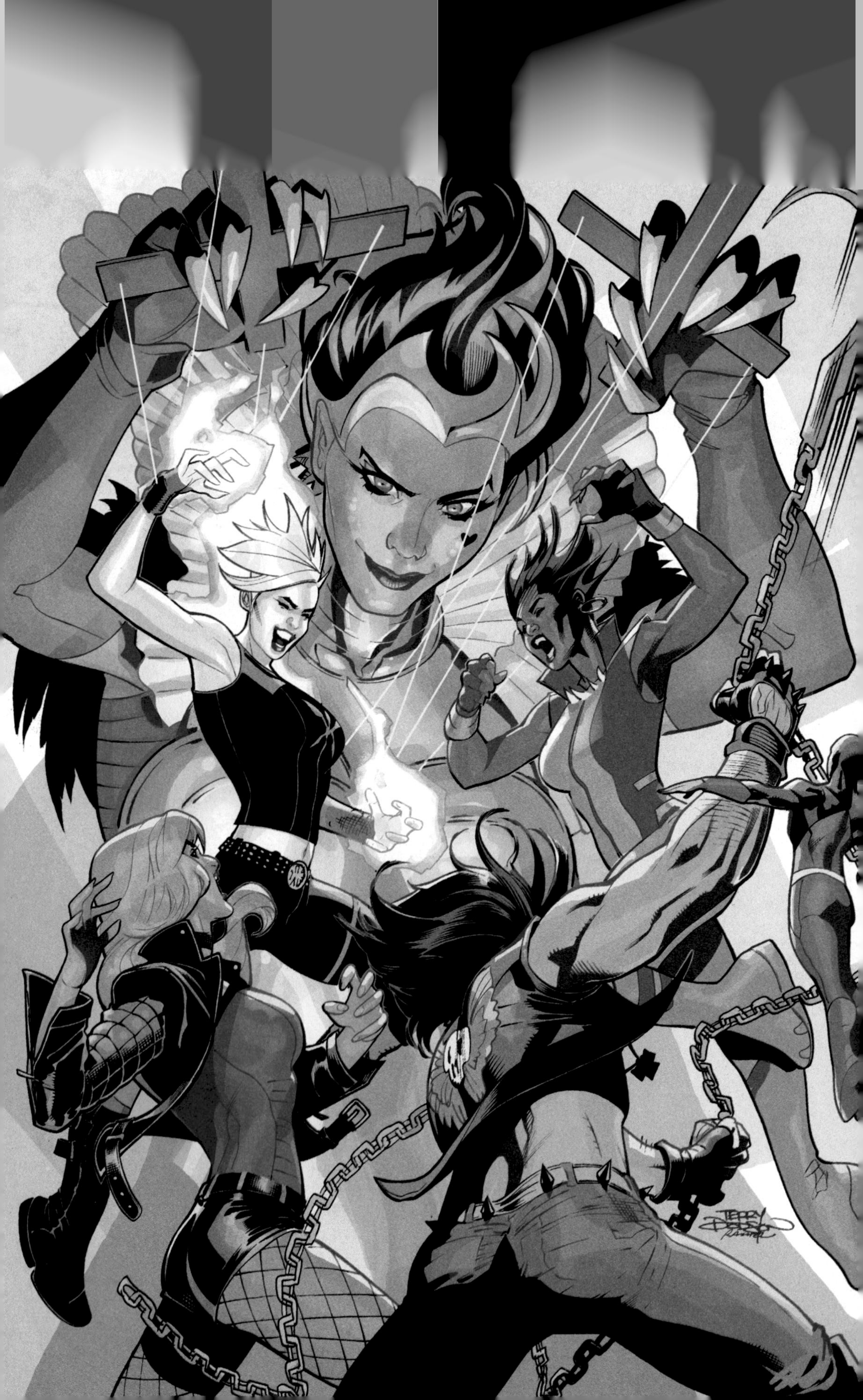

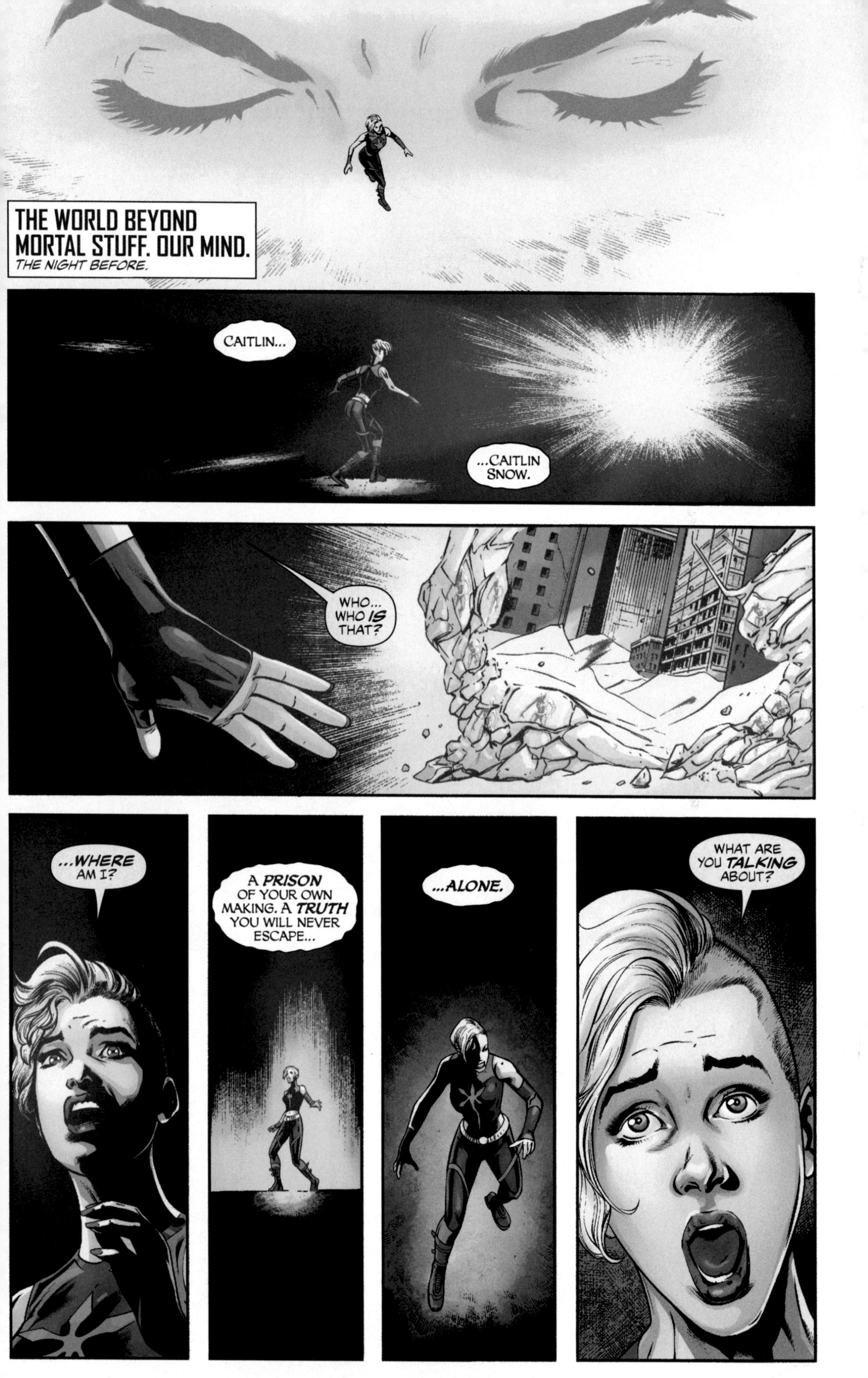
THE WORLD BEYOND MORTAL STUFF. OUR MIND.
THE NIGHT BEFORE.
CAITLIN...
...CAITLIN SNOW.
WHO... WHO IS THAT?
...WHERE AM I?
A PRISON OF YOUR OWN MAKING. A TRUTH YOU WILL NEVER ESCAPE...
...ALONE.
WHAT ARE YOU TALKING ABOUT?

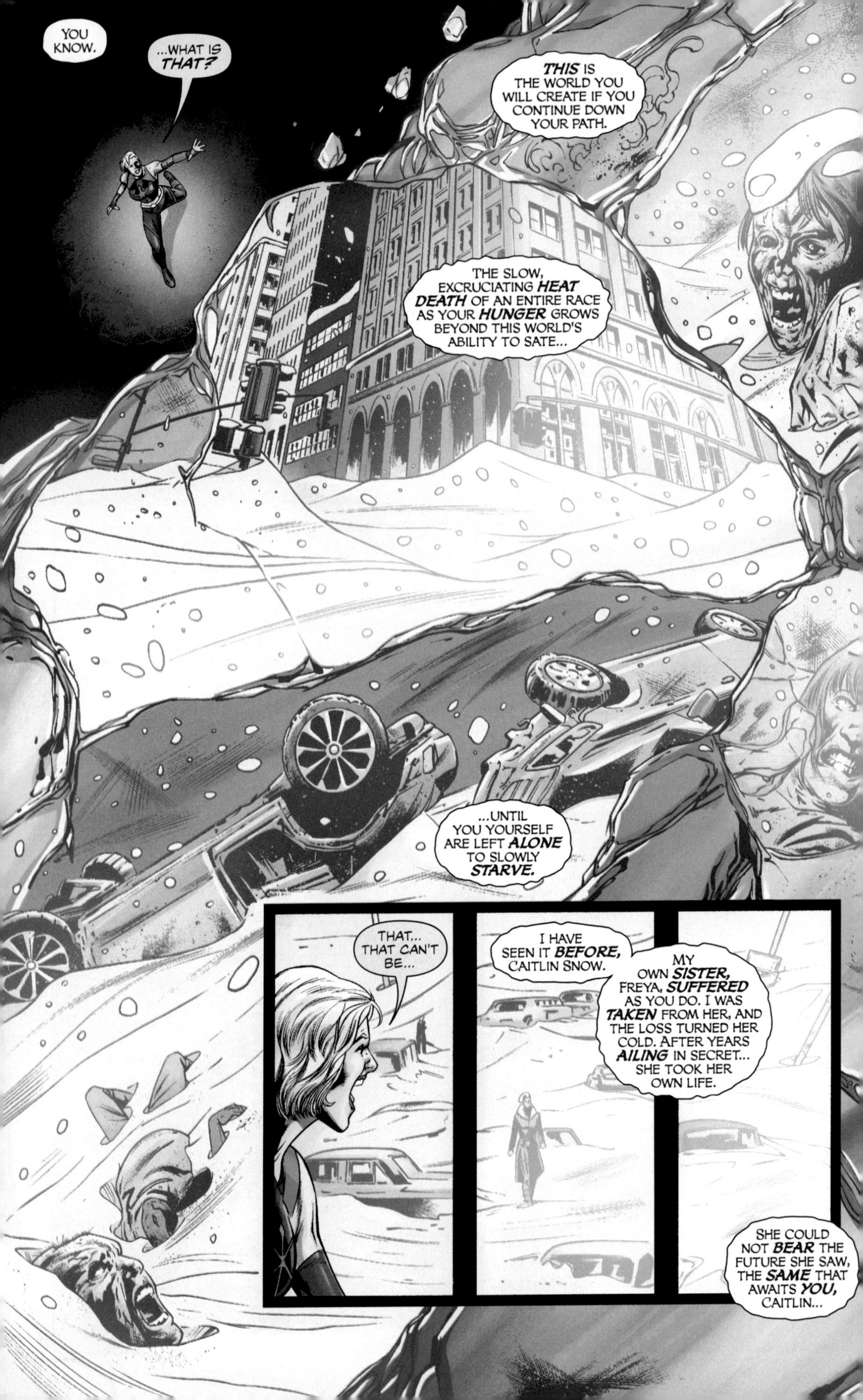
YOU KNOW.
...WHAT IS THAT?
THIS IS THE WORLD YOU WILL CREATE IF YOU CONTINUE DOWN YOUR PATH.
THE SLOW, EXCRUCIATING HEAT DEATH OF AN ENTIRE RACE AS YOUR HUNGER GROWS BEYOND THIS WORLD'S ABILITY TO SATE...
...UNTIL YOU YOURSELF ARE LEFT ALONE TO SLOWLY STARVE.
THAT... THAT CAN'T BE...
I HAVE SEEN IT BEFORE, CAITLIN SNOW.
MY OWN SISTER, FREYA, SUFFERED AS YOU DO. I WAS TAKEN FROM HER, AND THE LOSS TURNED HER COLD. AFTER YEARS AILING IN SECRET... SHE TOOK HER OWN LIFE.
SHE COULD NOT BEAR THE FUTURE SHE SAW, THE SAME THAT AWAITS YOU, CAITLIN...

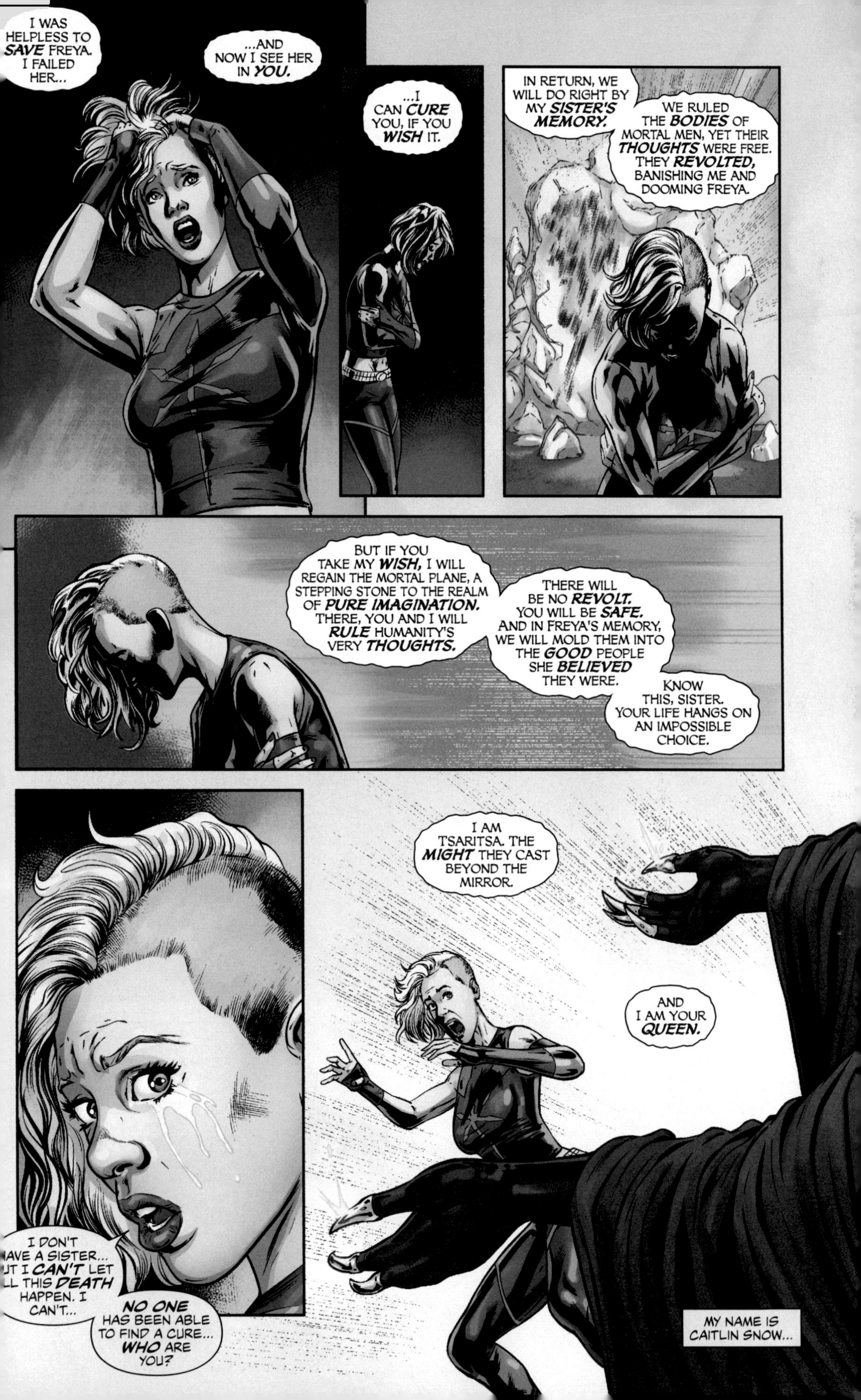

I WAS HELPLESS TO SAVE FREYA. I FAILED HER...
...AND NOW I SEE HER IN YOU.
...I CAN CURE YOU, IF YOU WISH IT.
IN RETURN, WE WILL DO RIGHT BY MY SISTER'S MEMORY.
WE RULED THE BODIES OF MORTAL MEN, YET THEIR THOUGHTS WERE FREE. THEY REVOLTED, BANISHING ME AND DOOMING FREYA.
BUT IF YOU TAKE MY WISH, I WILL REGAIN THE MORTAL PLANE, A STEPPING STONE TO THE REALM OF PURE IMAGINATION. THERE, YOU AND I WILL RULE HUMANITY'S VERY THOUGHTS.
THERE WILL BE NO REVOLT. YOU WILL BE SAFE. AND IN FREYA'S MEMORY, WE WILL MOLD THEM INTO THE GOOD PEOPLE SHE BELIEVED THEY WERE.
KNOW THIS, SISTER. YOUR LIFE HANGS ON AN IMPOSSIBLE CHOICE.
I DON'T AVE A SISTER... UT I CAN'T LET LL THIS DEATH HAPPEN. I CAN'T...
NO ONE HAS BEEN ABLE TO FIND A CURE... WHO ARE YOU?
I AM TSARITSA. THE MIGHT THEY CAST BEYOND THE MIRROR.
AND I AM YOUR QUEEN.
MY NAME IS CAITLIN SNOW...

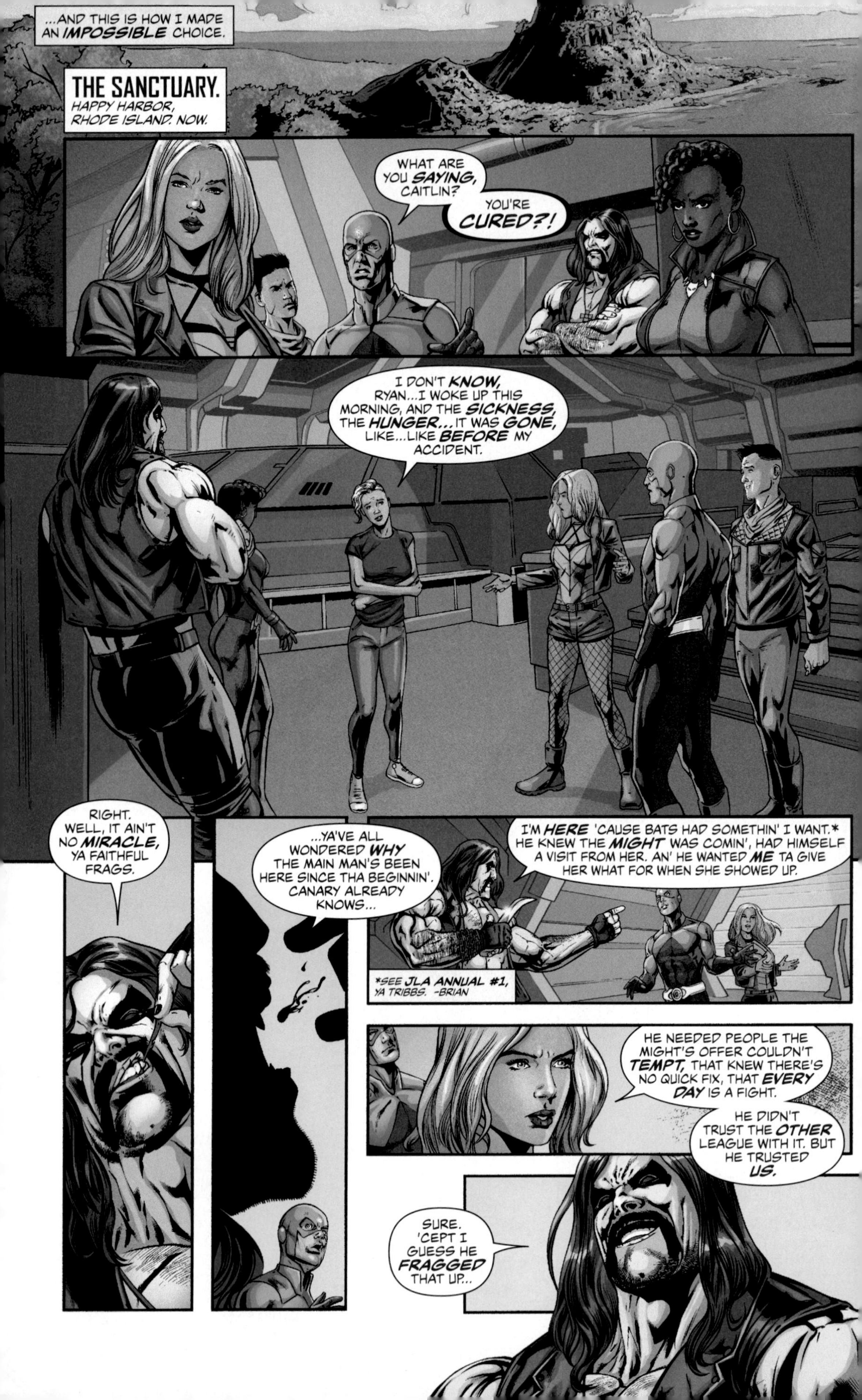
...AND THIS IS HOW I MADE AN IMPOSSIBLE CHOICE.
THE SANCTUARY. HAPPY HARBOR, RHODE ISLAND. NOW.
WHAT ARE YOU SAYING, CAITLIN?
YOU'RE CURED?!
I DON'T KNOW, RYAN...I WOKE UP THIS MORNING, AND THE SICKNESS, THE HUNGER... IT WAS GONE, LIKE...LIKE BEFORE MY ACCIDENT.
RIGHT. WELL, IT AIN'T NO MIRACLE, YA FAITHFUL FRAGS.
...YA'VE ALL WONDERED WHY THE MAIN MAN'S BEEN HERE SINCE THA BEGINNIN'. CANARY ALREADY KNOWS...
I'M HERE 'CAUSE BATS HAD SOMETHIN' I WANT.* HE KNEW THE MIGHT WAS COMIN', HAD HIMSELF A VISIT FROM HER. AN' HE WANTED ME TA GIVE HER WHAT FOR WHEN SHE SHOWED UP.
*SEE JLA ANNUAL #1, YA TRIBBS. -BRIAN
HE NEEDED PEOPLE THE MIGHT'S OFFER COULDN'T TEMPT, THAT KNEW THERE'S NO QUICK FIX, THAT EVERY DAY IS A FIGHT.
HE DIDN'T TRUST THE OTHER LEAGUE WITH IT. BUT HE TRUSTED US.
SURE. 'CEPT I GUESS HE FRAGGED THAT UP...

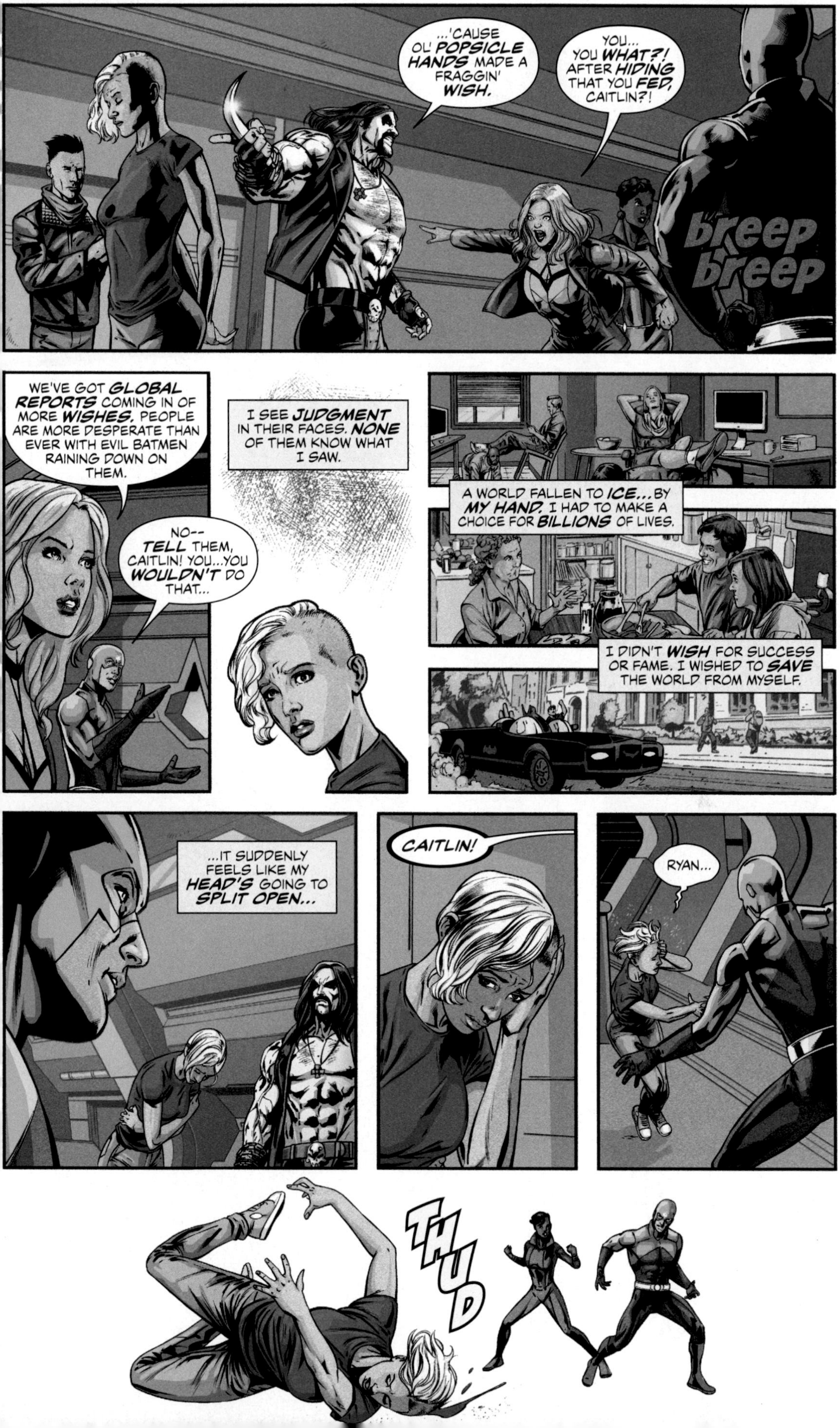
...'CAUSE OL' POPSICLE HANDS MADE A FRAGGIN' WISH.
YOU... YOU WHAT?! AFTER HIDING THAT YOU FED, CAITLIN?!
breep breep
WE'VE GOT GLOBAL REPORTS COMING IN OF MORE WISHES. PEOPLE ARE MORE DESPERATE THAN EVER WITH EVIL BATMEN RAINING DOWN ON THEM.
NO-- TELL THEM, CAITLIN! YOU...YOU WOULDN'T DO THAT...
I SEE JUDGMENT IN THEIR FACES. NONE OF THEM KNOW WHAT I SAW.
A WORLD FALLEN TO ICE...BY MY HAND. I HAD TO MAKE A CHOICE FOR BILLIONS OF LIVES.
I DIDN'T WISH FOR SUCCESS OR FAME. I WISHED TO SAVE THE WORLD FROM MYSELF.
...IT SUDDENLY FEELS LIKE MY HEAD'S GOING TO SPLIT OPEN...
CAITLIN!
RYAN...
THUD

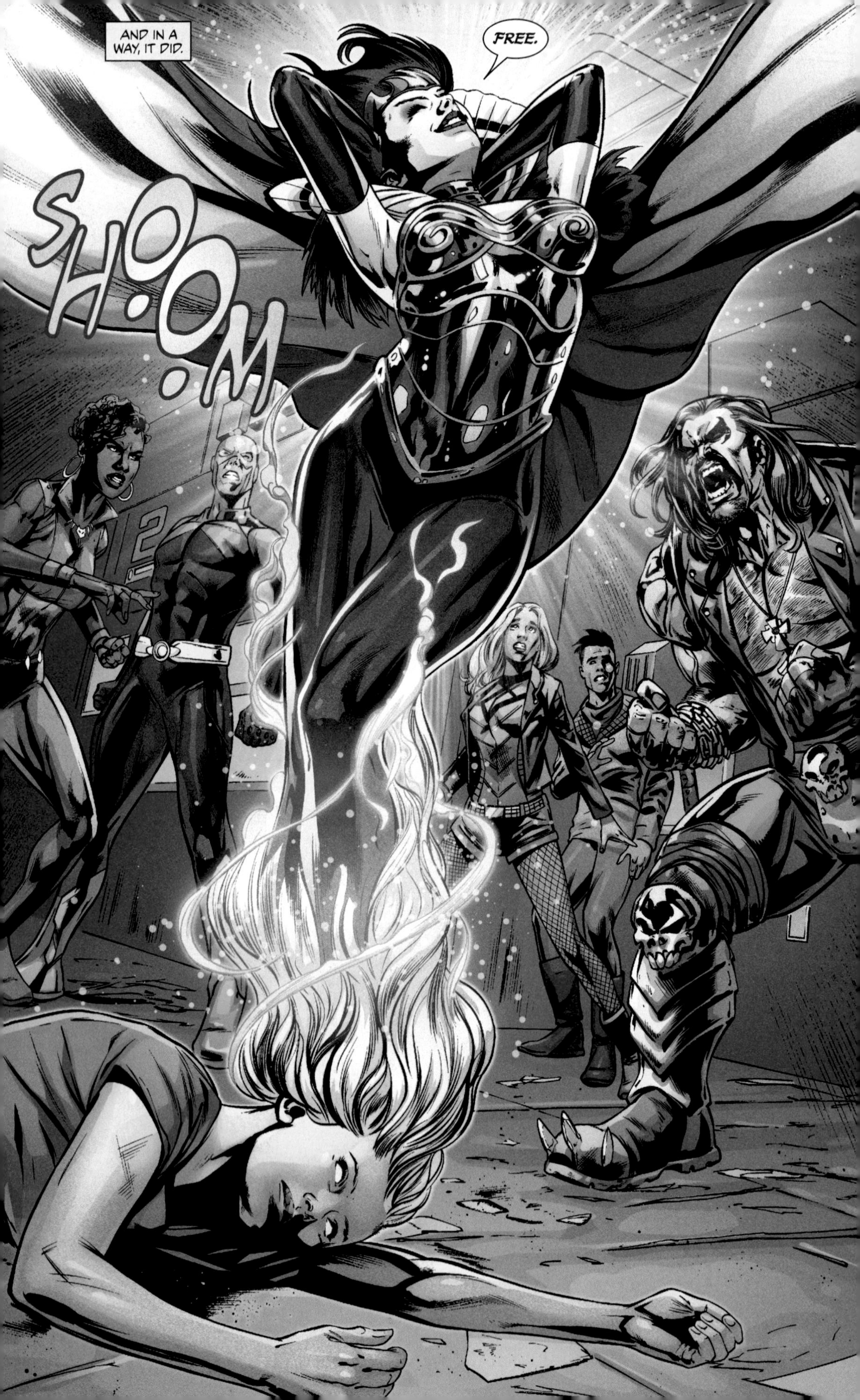
AND IN A WAY, IT DID.
FREE.
SHOOOM

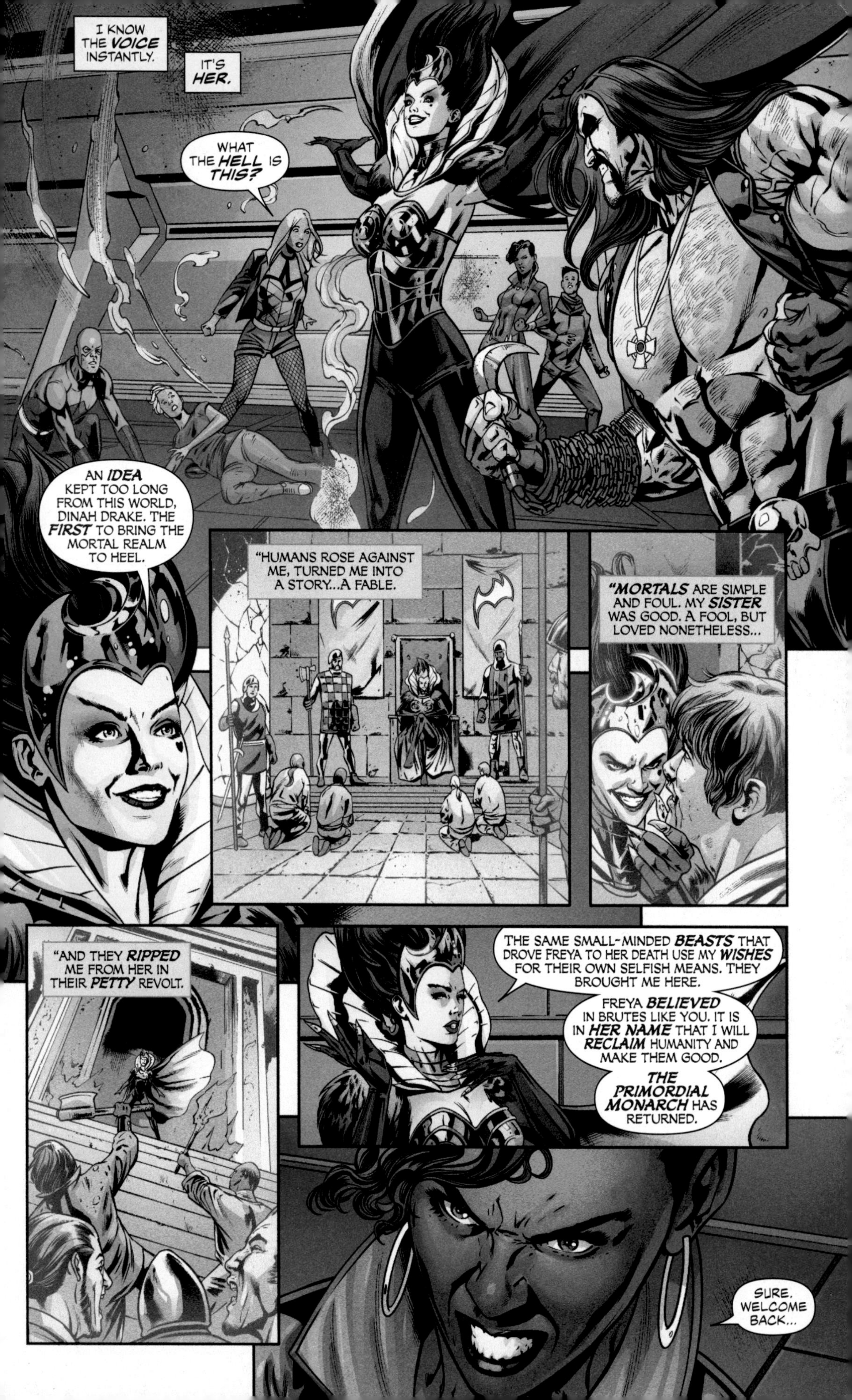
I KNOW THE VOICE INSTANTLY.
IT'S HER.
WHAT THE HELL IS THIS?
AN IDEA KEPT TOO LONG FROM THIS WORLD, DINAH DRAKE. THE FIRST TO BRING THE MORTAL REALM TO HEEL.
"HUMANS ROSE AGAINST ME, TURNED ME INTO A STORY...A FABLE.
"MORTALS ARE SIMPLE AND FOUL. MY SISTER WAS GOOD. A FOOL, BUT LOVED NONETHELESS...
"AND THEY RIPPED ME FROM HER IN THEIR PETTY REVOLT.
THE SAME SMALL-MINDED BEASTS THAT DROVE FREYA TO HER DEATH USE MY WISHES FOR THEIR OWN SELFISH MEANS. THEY BROUGHT ME HERE.
FREYA BELIEVED IN BRUTES LIKE YOU. IT IS IN HER NAME THAT I WILL RECLAIM HUMANITY AND MAKE THEM GOOD.
THE PRIMORDIAL MONARCH HAS RETURNED.
SURE. WELCOME BACK...

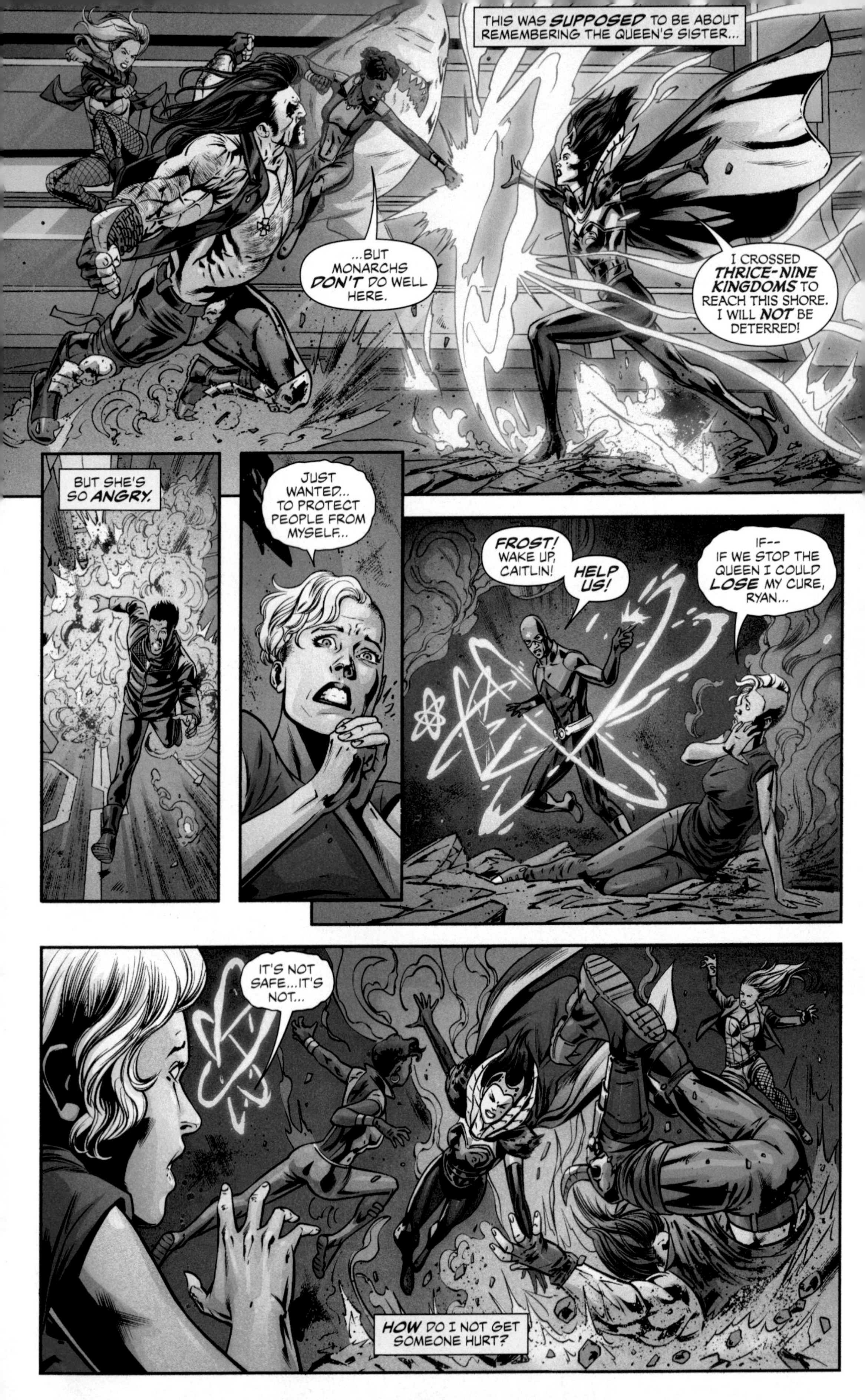
THIS WAS SUPPOSED TO BE ABOUT REMEMBERING THE QUEEN'S SISTER...
...BUT MONARCHS DON'T DO WELL HERE.
I CROSSED THRICE-NINE KINGDOMS TO REACH THIS SHORE. I WILL NOT BE DETERRED!
BUT SHE'S SO ANGRY.
JUST WANTED... TO PROTECT PEOPLE FROM MYSELF...
FROST! WAKE UP, CAITLIN!
HELP US!
IF-- IF WE STOP THE QUEEN I COULD LOSE MY CURE, RYAN...
IT'S NOT SAFE...IT'S NOT...
HOW DO I NOT GET SOMEONE HURT?

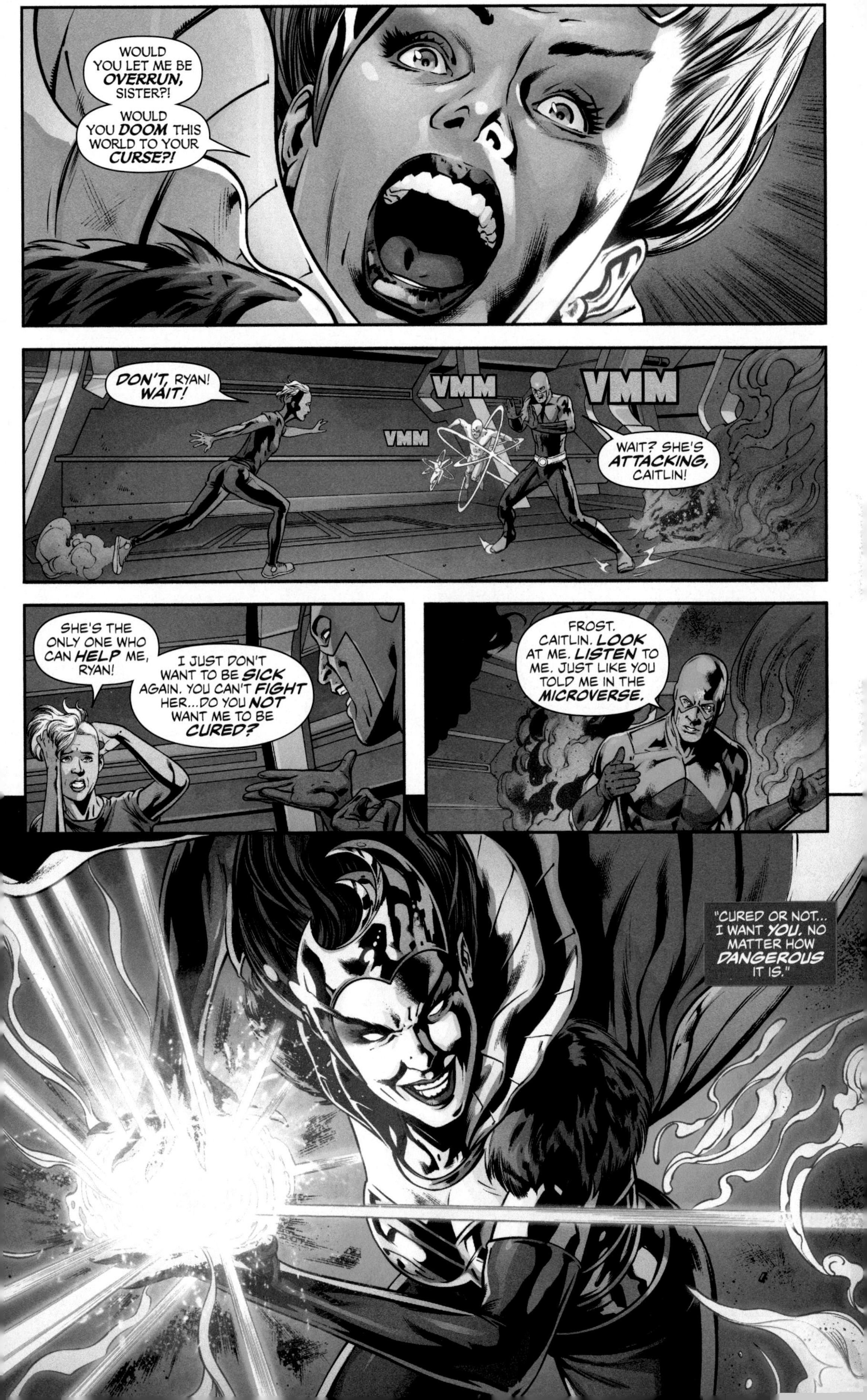
WOULD YOU LET ME BE OVERRUN, SISTER?!
WOULD YOU DOOM THIS WORLD TO YOUR CURSE?!
DON'T, RYAN! WAIT!
VMM
VMM
VMM
WAIT? SHE'S ATTACKING, CAITLIN!
SHE'S THE ONLY ONE WHO CAN HELP ME, RYAN!
I JUST DON'T WANT TO BE SICK AGAIN. YOU CAN'T FIGHT HER...DO YOU NOT WANT ME TO BE CURED?
FROST. CAITLIN. LOOK AT ME. LISTEN TO ME. JUST LIKE YOU TOLD ME IN THE MICROVERSE.
"CURED OR NOT... I WANT YOU. NO MATTER HOW DANGEROUS IT IS."

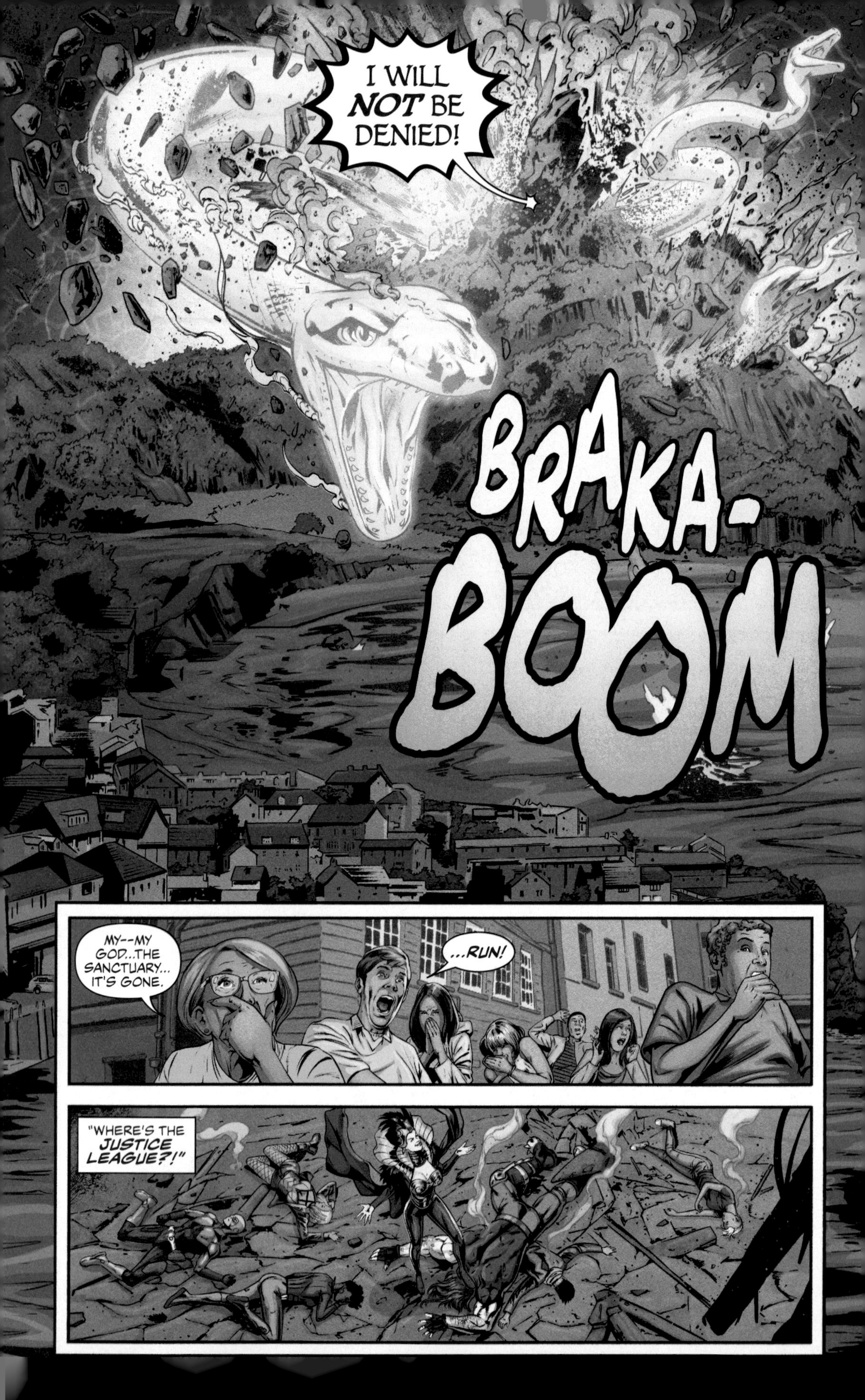
I WILL NOT BE DENIED!
BRAKA-BOOM
MY--MY GOD...THE SANCTUARY... IT'S GONE.
...RUN!
"WHERE'S THE JUSTICE LEAGUE?!"

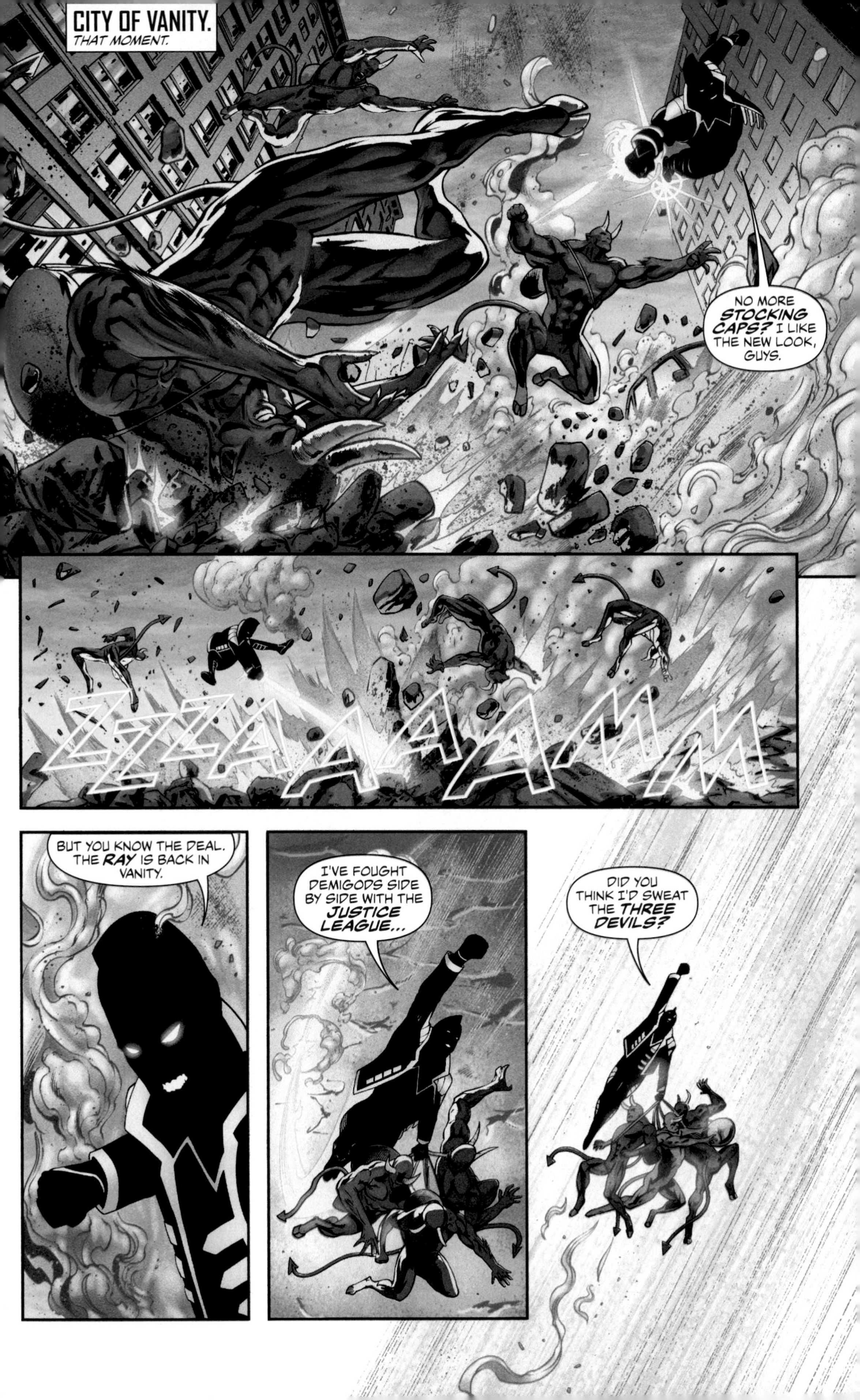
CITY OF VANITY.
THAT MOMENT.
NO MORE STOCKING CAPS? I LIKE THE NEW LOOK, GUYS.
ZZZAAAAMM
BUT YOU KNOW THE DEAL. THE RAY IS BACK IN VANITY.
I'VE FOUGHT DEMIGODS SIDE BY SIDE WITH THE JUSTICE LEAGUE...
DID YOU THINK I'D SWEAT THE THREE DEVILS?

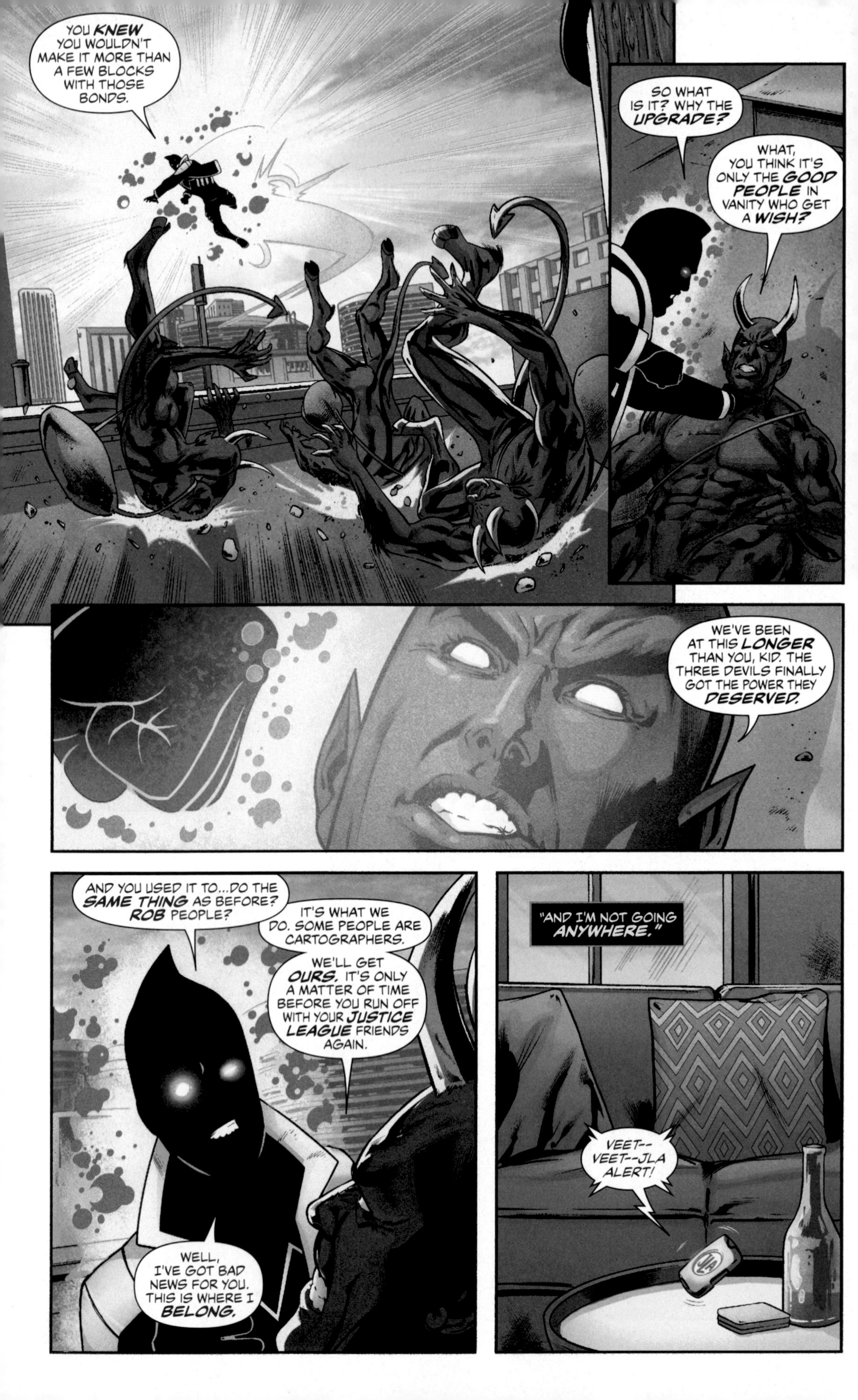
YOU KNEW YOU WOULDN'T MAKE IT MORE THAN A FEW BLOCKS WITH THOSE BONDS.
SO WHAT IS IT? WHY THE UPGRADE?
WHAT, YOU THINK IT'S ONLY THE GOOD PEOPLE IN VANITY WHO GET A WISH?
WE'VE BEEN AT THIS LONGER THAN YOU, KID. THE THREE DEVILS FINALLY GOT THE POWER THEY DESERVED.
AND YOU USED IT TO...DO THE SAME THING AS BEFORE? ROB PEOPLE?
IT'S WHAT WE DO. SOME PEOPLE ARE CARTOGRAPHERS.
WE'LL GET OURS. IT'S ONLY A MATTER OF TIME BEFORE YOU RUN OFF WITH YOUR JUSTICE LEAGUE FRIENDS AGAIN.
WELL, I'VE GOT BAD NEWS FOR YOU. THIS IS WHERE I BELONG.
"AND I'M NOT GOING ANYWHERE."
VEET-- VEET--JLA ALERT!
JLA

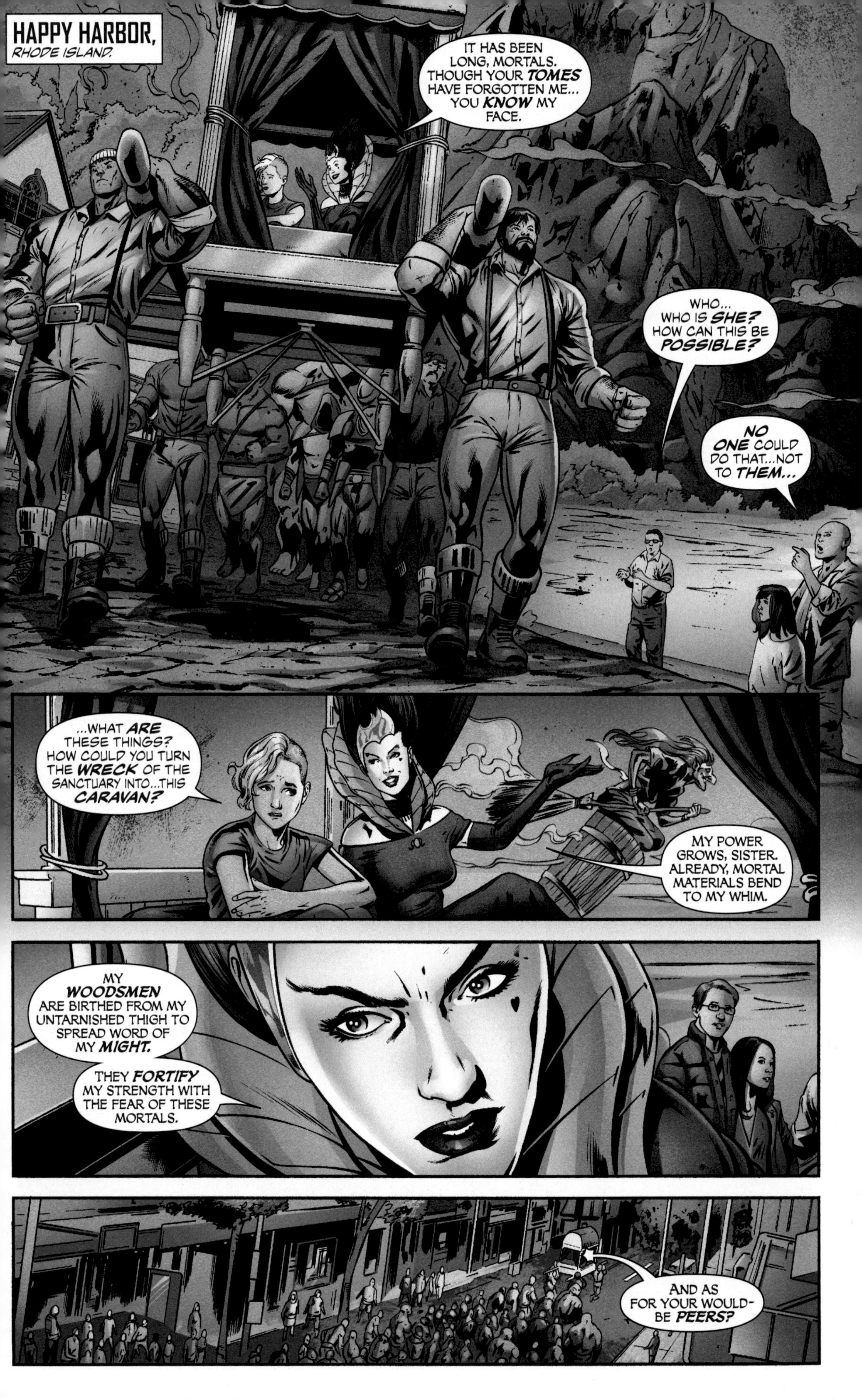
HAPPY HARBOR, RHODE ISLAND.
IT HAS BEEN LONG, MORTALS. THOUGH YOUR TOMES HAVE FORGOTTEN ME... YOU KNOW MY FACE.
WHO... WHO IS SHE? HOW CAN THIS BE POSSIBLE?
NO ONE COULD DO THAT...NOT TO THEM...
...WHAT ARE THESE THINGS? HOW COULD YOU TURN THE WRECK OF THE SANCTUARY INTO...THIS CARAVAN?
MY POWER GROWS, SISTER. ALREADY, MORTAL MATERIALS BEND TO MY WHIM.
MY WOODSMEN ARE BIRTHED FROM MY UNTARNISHED THIGH TO SPREAD WORD OF MY MIGHT.
THEY FORTIFY MY STRENGTH WITH THE FEAR OF THESE MORTALS.
AND AS FOR YOUR WOULD-BE PEERS?

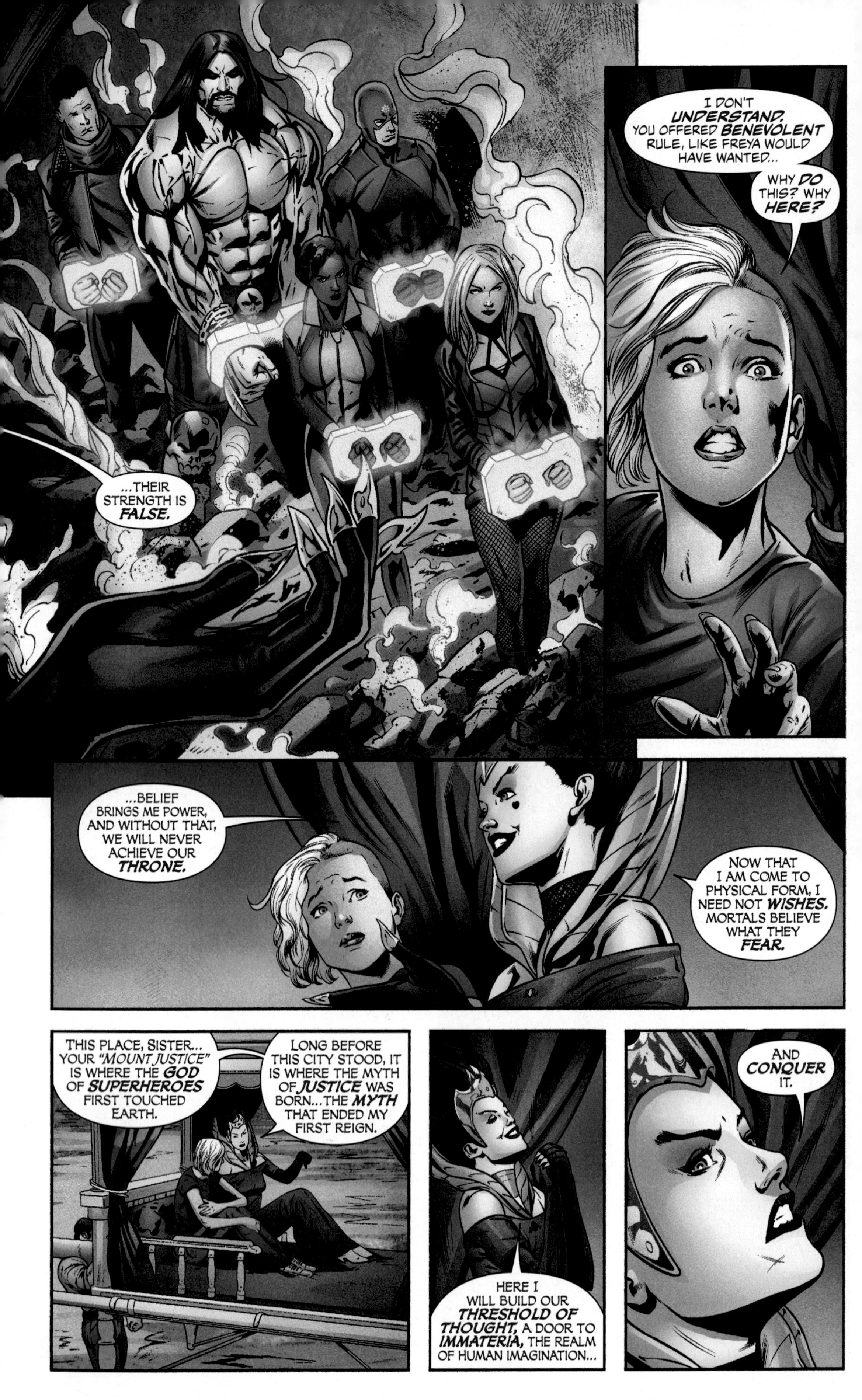

...THEIR STRENGTH IS FALSE.
I DON'T UNDERSTAND. YOU OFFERED BENEVOLENT RULE, LIKE FREYA WOULD HAVE WANTED...
WHY DO THIS? WHY HERE?
...BELIEF BRINGS ME POWER, AND WITHOUT THAT, WE WILL NEVER ACHIEVE OUR THRONE.
NOW THAT I AM COME TO PHYSICAL FORM, I NEED NOT WISHES. MORTALS BELIEVE WHAT THEY FEAR.
THIS PLACE, SISTER... YOUR "MOUNT JUSTICE" IS WHERE THE GOD OF SUPERHEROES FIRST TOUCHED EARTH.
LONG BEFORE THIS CITY STOOD, IT IS WHERE THE MYTH OF JUSTICE WAS BORN...THE MYTH THAT ENDED MY FIRST REIGN.
HERE I WILL BUILD OUR THRESHOLD OF THOUGHT, A DOOR TO IMMATERIA, THE REALM OF HUMAN IMAGINATION...
AND CONQUER IT.

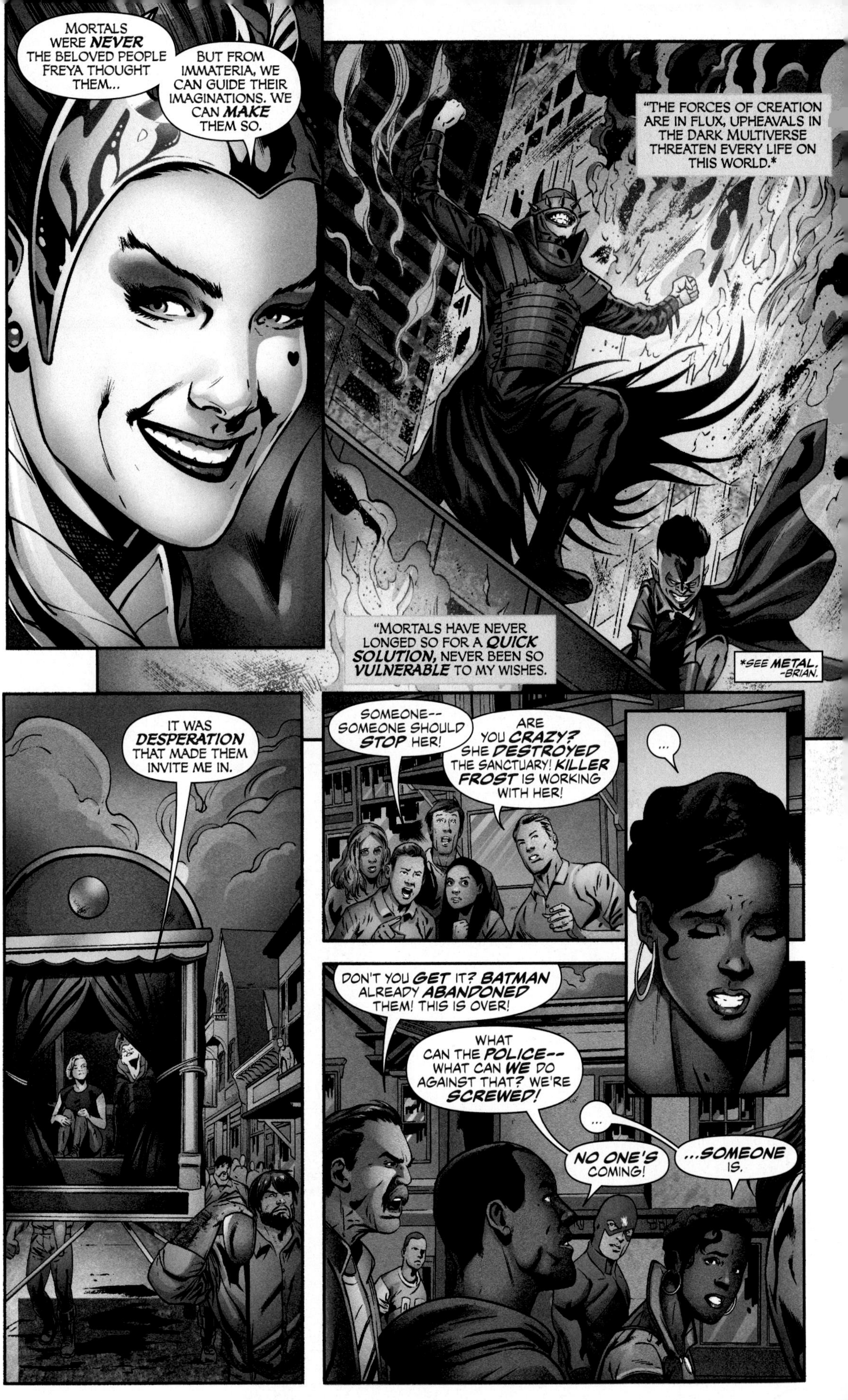
MORTALS WERE NEVER THE BELOVED PEOPLE FREYA THOUGHT THEM...
BUT FROM IMMATERIA, WE CAN GUIDE THEIR IMAGINATIONS. WE CAN MAKE THEM SO.
"THE FORCES OF CREATION ARE IN FLUX, UPHEAVALS IN THE DARK MULTIVERSE THREATEN EVERY LIFE ON THIS WORLD.*
"MORTALS HAVE NEVER LONGED SO FOR A QUICK SOLUTION, NEVER BEEN SO VULNERABLE TO MY WISHES.
*SEE METAL. -BRIAN.
IT WAS DESPERATION THAT MADE THEM INVITE ME IN.
SOMEONE-- SOMEONE SHOULD STOP HER!
ARE YOU CRAZY? SHE DESTROYED THE SANCTUARY! KILLER FROST IS WORKING WITH HER!
...
DON'T YOU GET IT? BATMAN ALREADY ABANDONED THEM! THIS IS OVER!
WHAT CAN THE POLICE-- WHAT CAN WE DO AGAINST THAT? WE'RE SCREWED!
...
NO ONE'S COMING!
...SOMEONE IS.

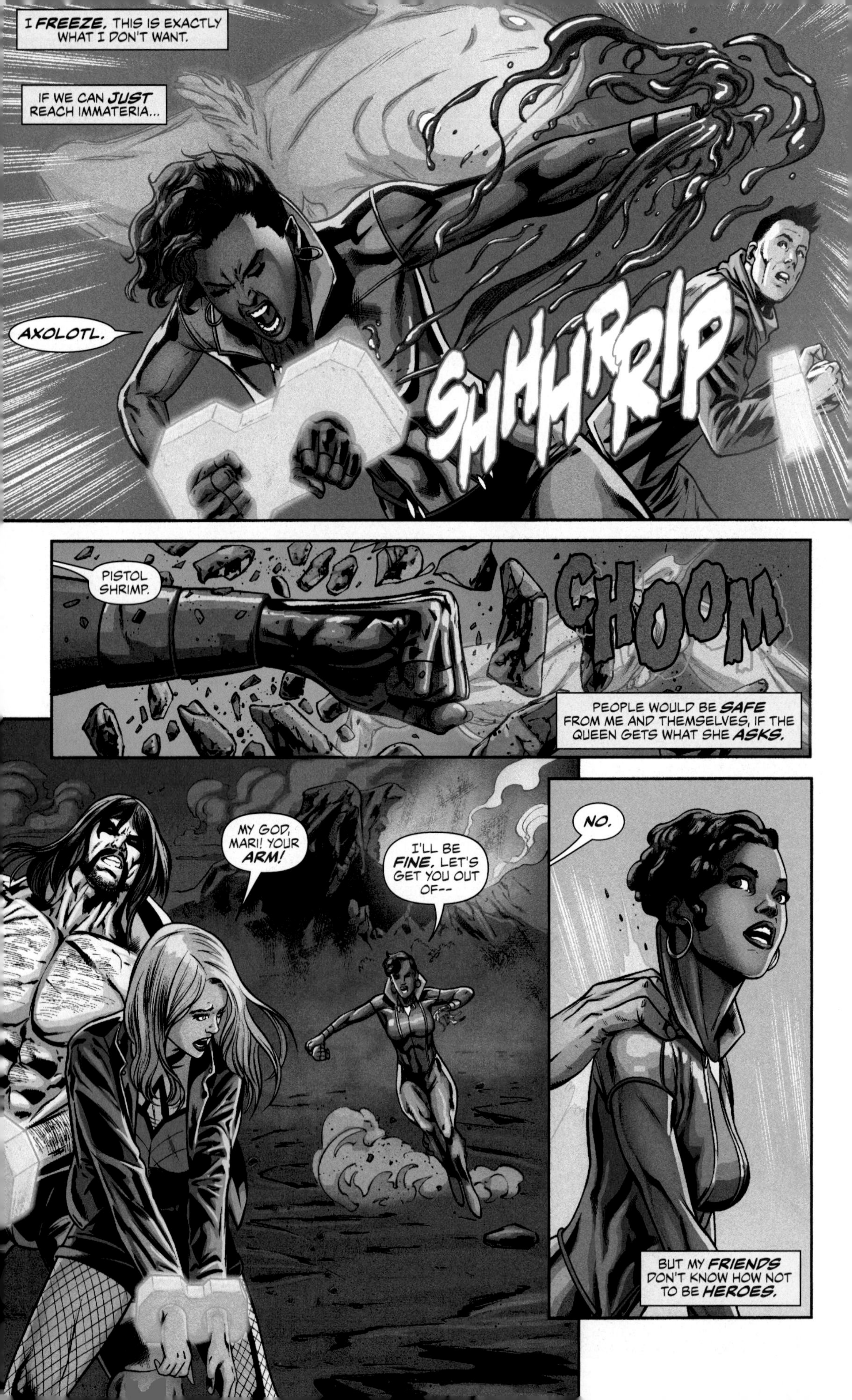

I FREEZE. THIS IS EXACTLY WHAT I DON'T WANT.
IF WE CAN JUST REACH IMMATERIA...
AXOLOTL.
SHHHRRIP
PISTOL SHRIMP.
CHOOM
PEOPLE WOULD BE SAFE FROM ME AND THEMSELVES, IF THE QUEEN GETS WHAT SHE ASKS.
MY GOD, MARI! YOUR ARM!
I'LL BE FINE. LET'S GET YOU OUT OF--
NO.
BUT MY FRIENDS DON'T KNOW HOW NOT TO BE HEROES.

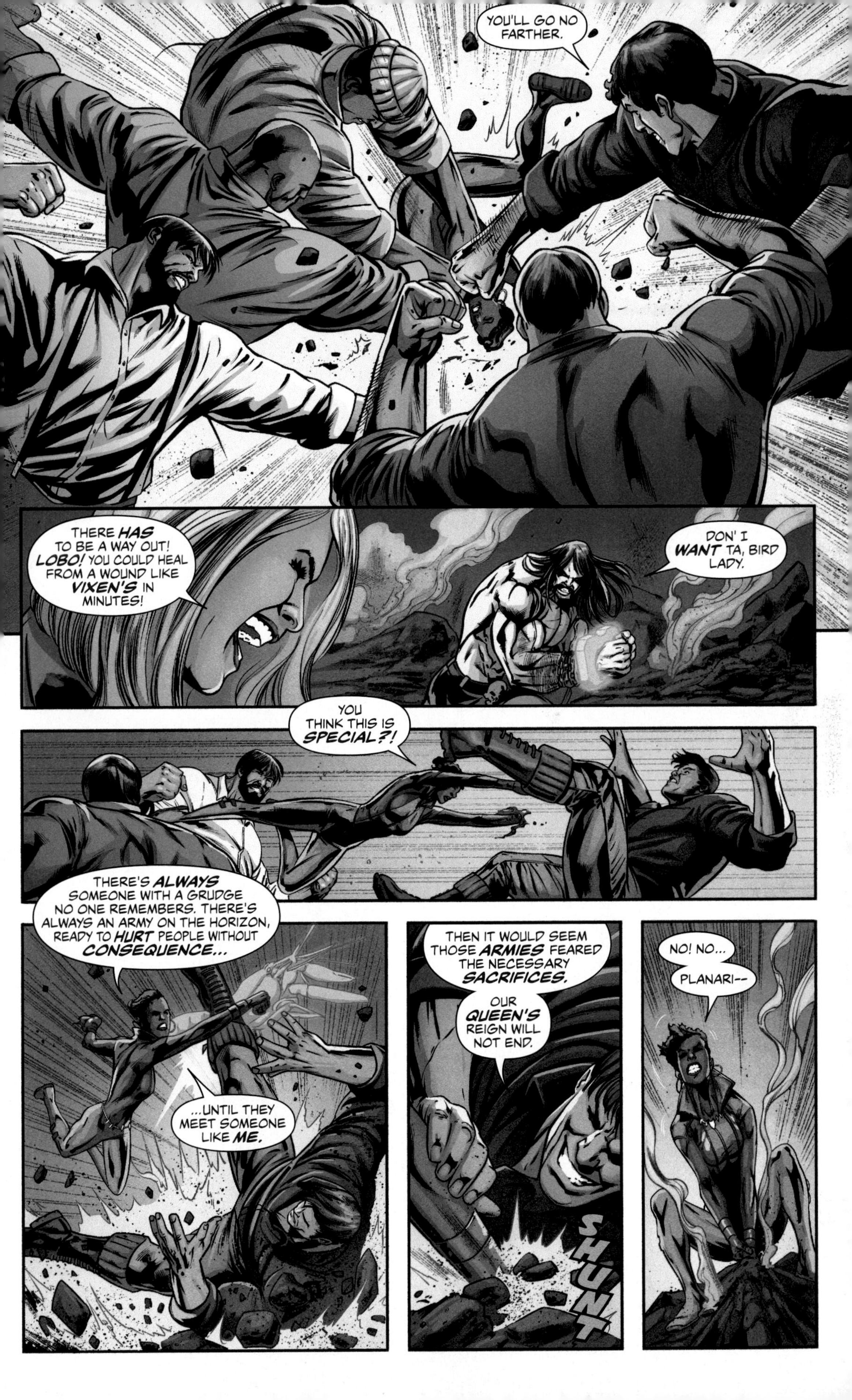
YOU'LL GO NO FARTHER.
THERE HAS TO BE A WAY OUT! LOBO! YOU COULD HEAL FROM A WOUND LIKE VIXEN'S IN MINUTES!
DON' I WANT TA, BIRD LADY.
YOU THINK THIS IS SPECIAL?!
THERE'S ALWAYS SOMEONE WITH A GRUDGE NO ONE REMEMBERS. THERE'S ALWAYS AN ARMY ON THE HORIZON, READY TO HURT PEOPLE WITHOUT CONSEQUENCE...
...UNTIL THEY MEET SOMEONE LIKE ME.
THEN IT WOULD SEEM THOSE ARMIES FEARED THE NECESSARY SACRIFICES.
OUR QUEEN'S REIGN WILL NOT END.
SHUNT
NO! NO...
PLANARI--

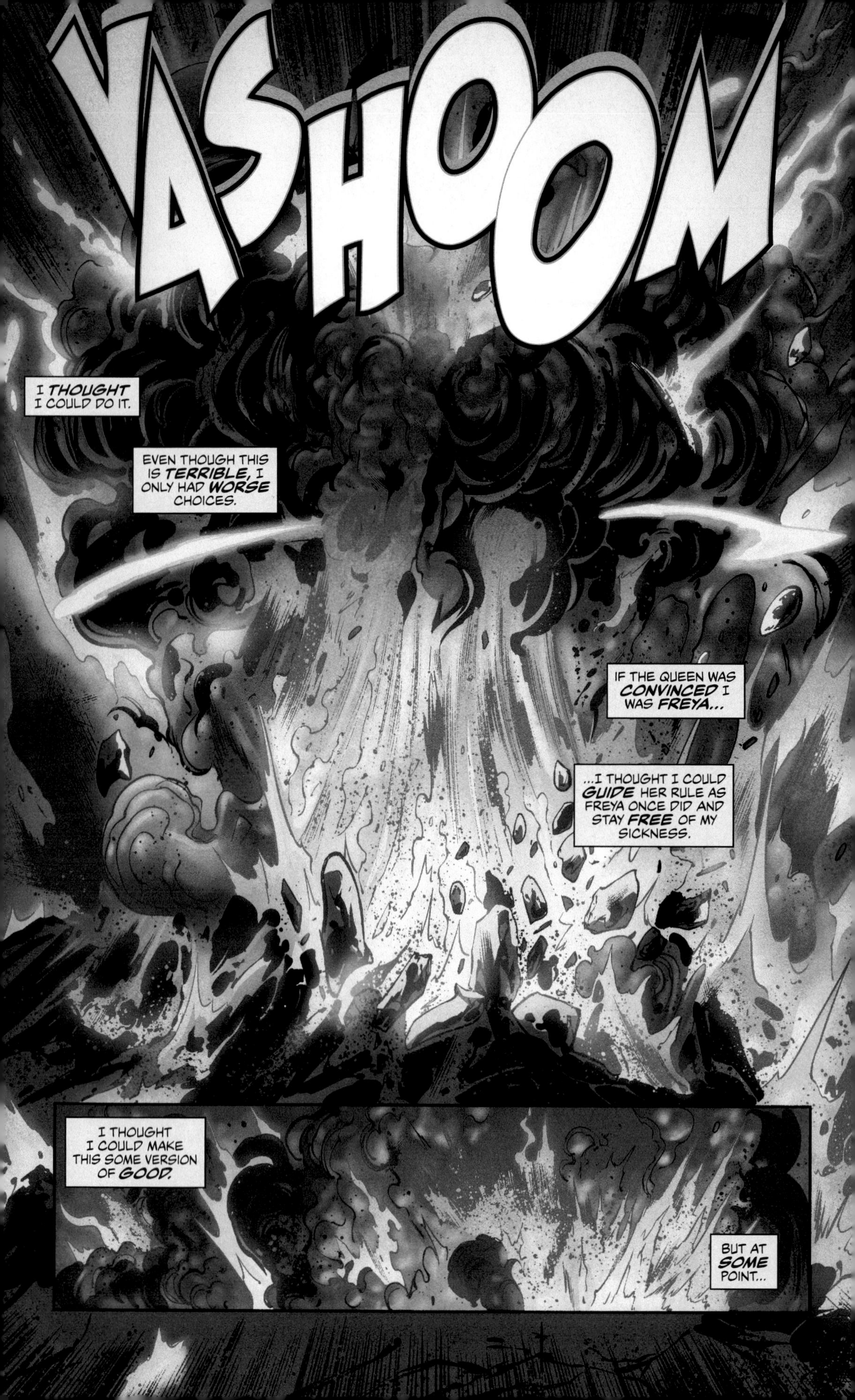
VASHOOOM
I THOUGHT I COULD DO IT.
EVEN THOUGH THIS IS TERRIBLE, I ONLY HAD WORSE CHOICES.
IF THE QUEEN WAS CONVINCED I WAS FREYA...
...I THOUGHT I COULD GUIDE HER RULE AS FREYA ONCE DID AND STAY FREE OF MY SICKNESS.
I THOUGHT I COULD MAKE THIS SOME VERSION OF GOOD.
BUT AT SOME POINT...

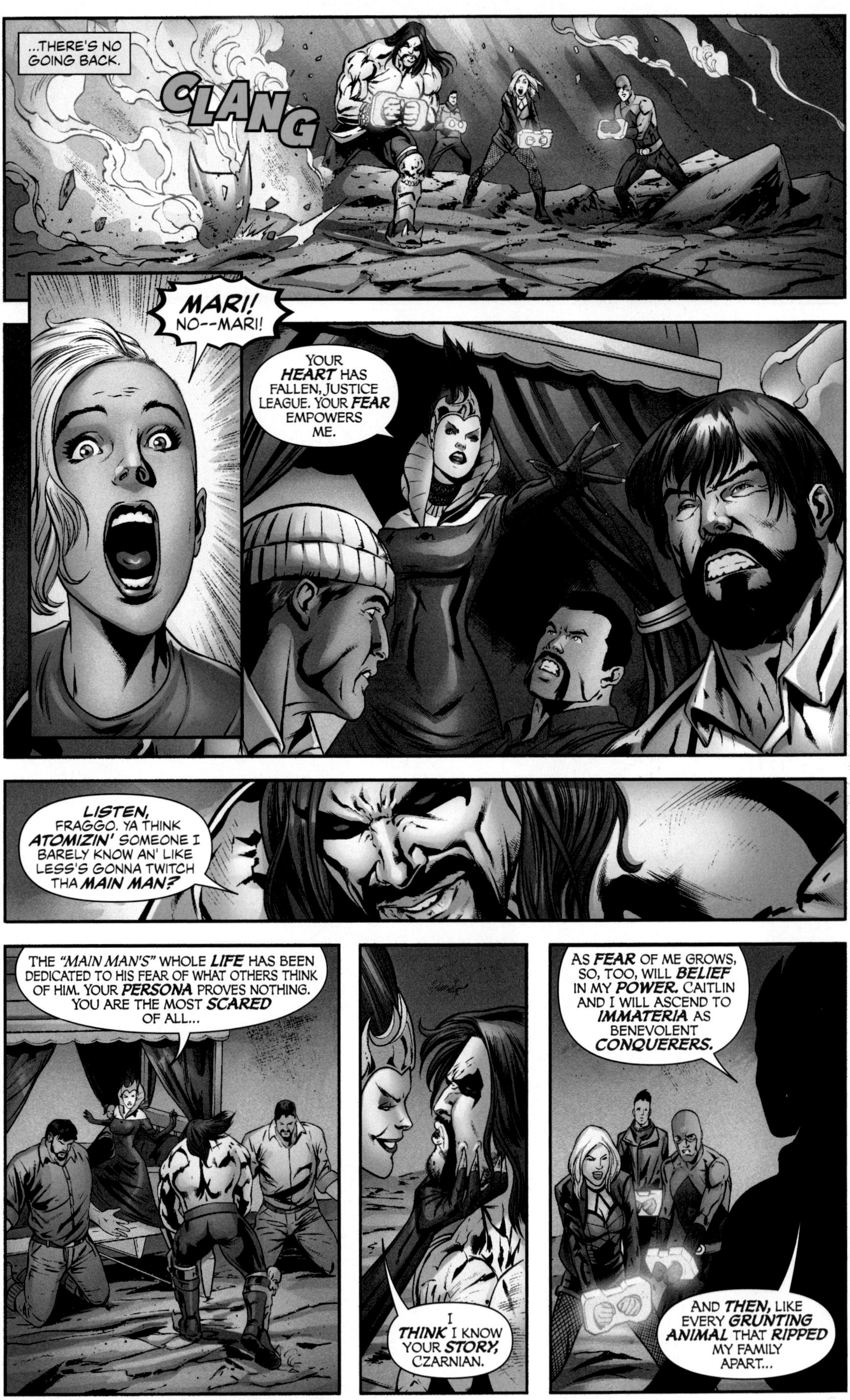

...THERE'S NO GOING BACK.
CLANG
MARI! NO--MARI!
YOUR HEART HAS FALLEN, JUSTICE LEAGUE. YOUR FEAR EMPOWERS ME.
LISTEN, FRAGGO. YA THINK ATOMIZIN' SOMEONE I BARELY KNOW AN' LIKE LESS'S GONNA TWITCH THA MAIN MAN?
THE "MAIN MAN'S" WHOLE LIFE HAS BEEN DEDICATED TO HIS FEAR OF WHAT OTHERS THINK OF HIM. YOUR PERSONA PROVES NOTHING. YOU ARE THE MOST SCARED OF ALL...
I THINK I KNOW YOUR STORY, CZARNIAN.
AS FEAR OF ME GROWS, SO, TOO, WILL BELIEF IN MY POWER. CAITLIN AND I WILL ASCEND TO IMMATERIA AS BENEVOLENT CONQUERERS.
AND THEN, LIKE EVERY GRUNTING ANIMAL THAT RIPPED MY FAMILY APART...

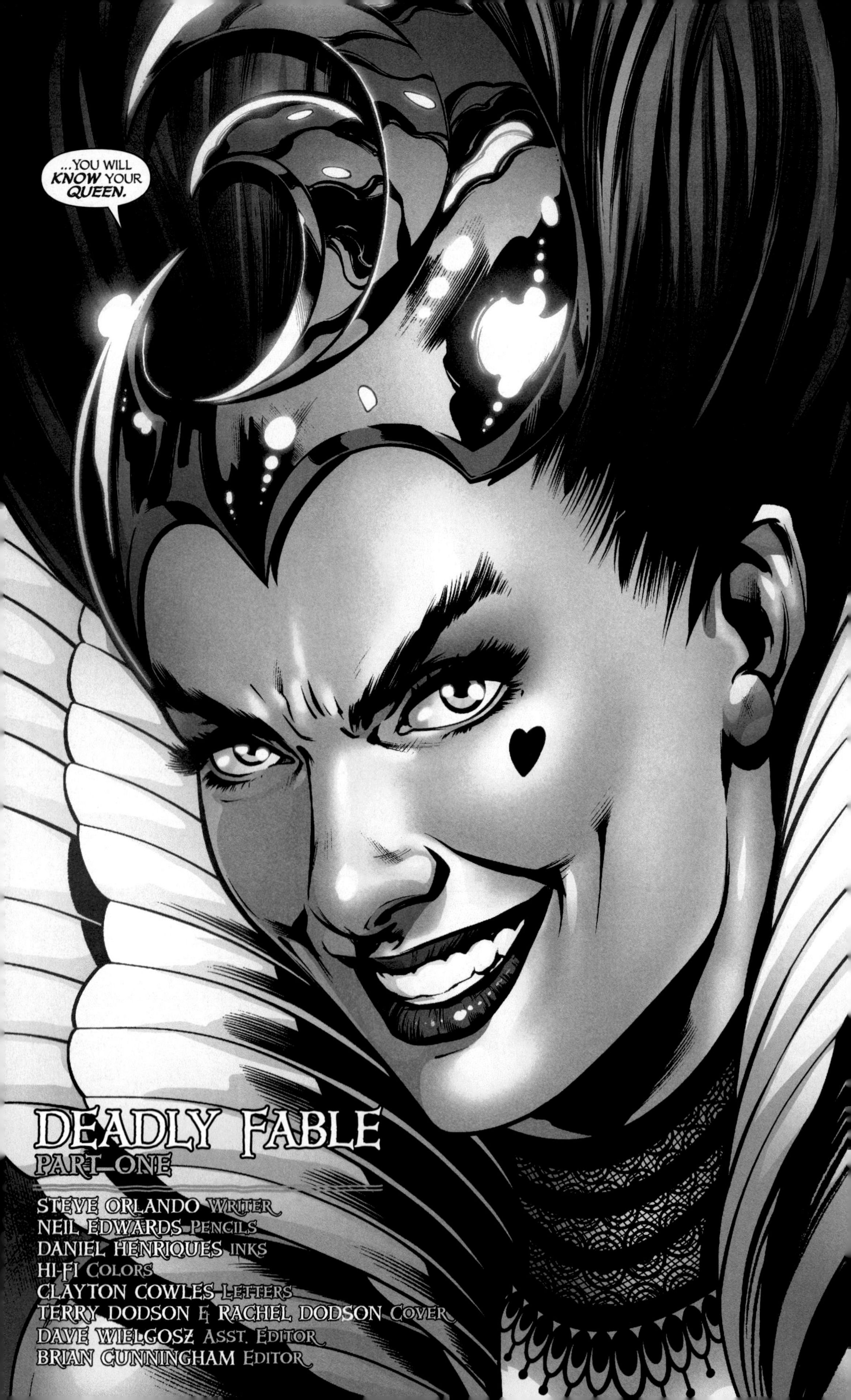
...YOU WILL KNOW YOUR QUEEN.
DEADLY FABLE
PART ONE
STEVE ORLANDO WRITER
NEIL EDWARDS PENCILS
DANIEL HENRIQUES INKS
HI-FI COLORS
CLAYTON COWLES LETTERS
TERRY DODSON & RACHEL DODSON COVER
DAVE WIELGOSZ ASST. EDITOR
BRIAN CUNNINGHAM EDITOR

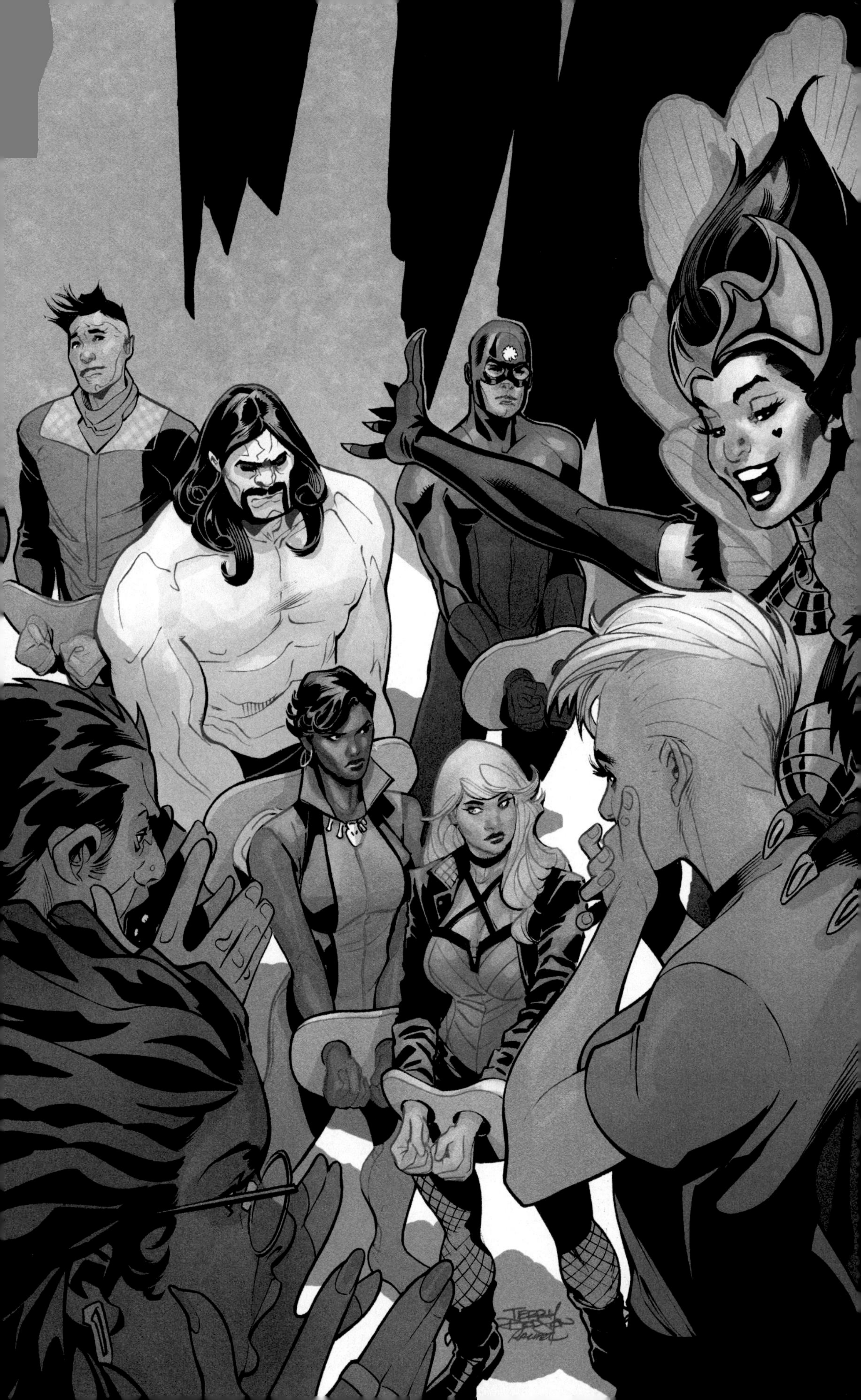

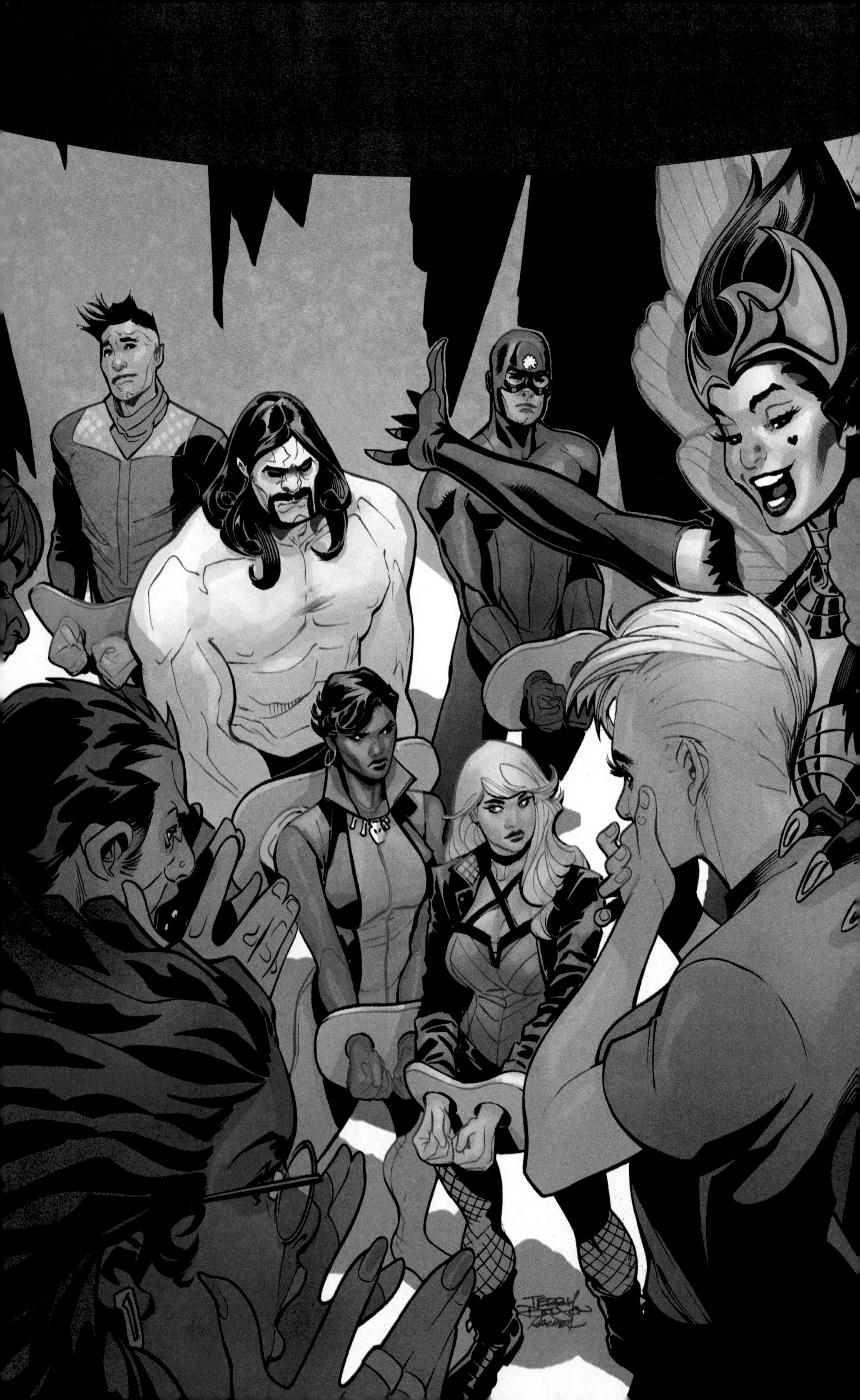

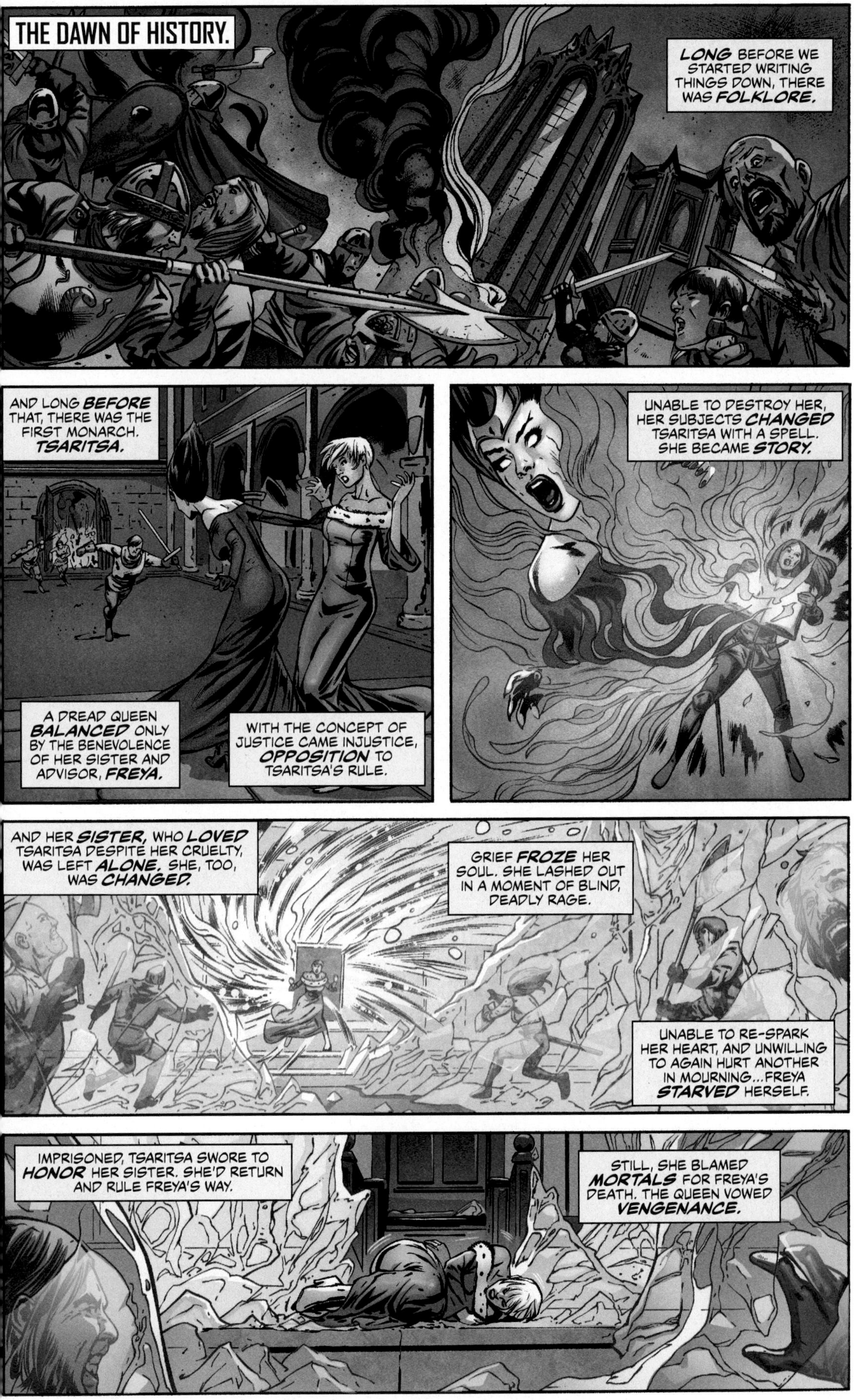
THE DAWN OF HISTORY.
LONG BEFORE WE STARTED WRITING THINGS DOWN, THERE WAS FOLKLORE.
AND LONG BEFORE THAT, THERE WAS THE FIRST MONARCH. TSARITSA.
A DREAD QUEEN BALANCED ONLY BY THE BENEVOLENCE OF HER SISTER AND ADVISOR, FREYA.
WITH THE CONCEPT OF JUSTICE CAME INJUSTICE, OPPOSITION TO TSARITSA'S RULE.
UNABLE TO DESTROY HER, HER SUBJECTS CHANGED TSARITSA WITH A SPELL. SHE BECAME STORY.
AND HER SISTER, WHO LOVED TSARITSA DESPITE HER CRUELTY, WAS LEFT ALONE. SHE, TOO, WAS CHANGED.
GRIEF FROZE HER SOUL. SHE LASHED OUT IN A MOMENT OF BLIND, DEADLY RAGE.
UNABLE TO RE-SPARK HER HEART, AND UNWILLING TO AGAIN HURT ANOTHER IN MOURNING...FREYA STARVED HERSELF.
IMPRISONED, TSARITSA SWORE TO HONOR HER SISTER. SHE'D RETURN AND RULE FREYA'S WAY.
STILL, SHE BLAMED MORTALS FOR FREYA'S DEATH. THE QUEEN VOWED VENGENANCE.

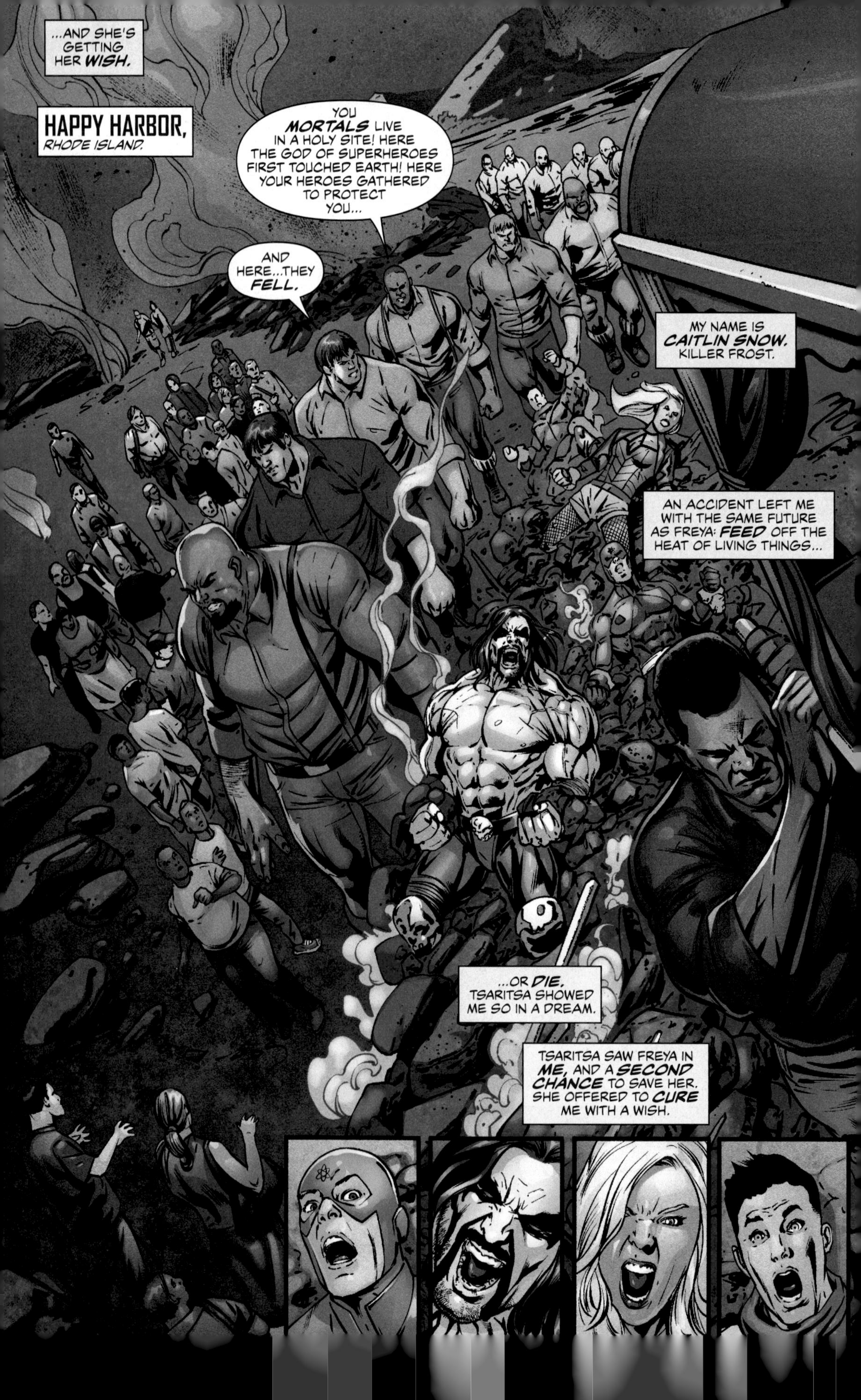

...AND SHE'S GETTING HER WISH.
HAPPY HARBOR, RHODE ISLAND.
YOU MORTALS LIVE IN A HOLY SITE! HERE THE GOD OF SUPERHEROES FIRST TOUCHED EARTH! HERE YOUR HEROES GATHERED TO PROTECT YOU...
AND HERE...THEY FELL.
MY NAME IS CAITLIN SNOW. KILLER FROST.
AN ACCIDENT LEFT ME WITH THE SAME FUTURE AS FREYA: FEED OFF THE HEAT OF LIVING THINGS...
...OR DIE. TSARITSA SHOWED ME SO IN A DREAM.
TSARITSA SAW FREYA IN ME, AND A SECOND CHANCE TO SAVE HER. SHE OFFERED TO CURE ME WITH A WISH.

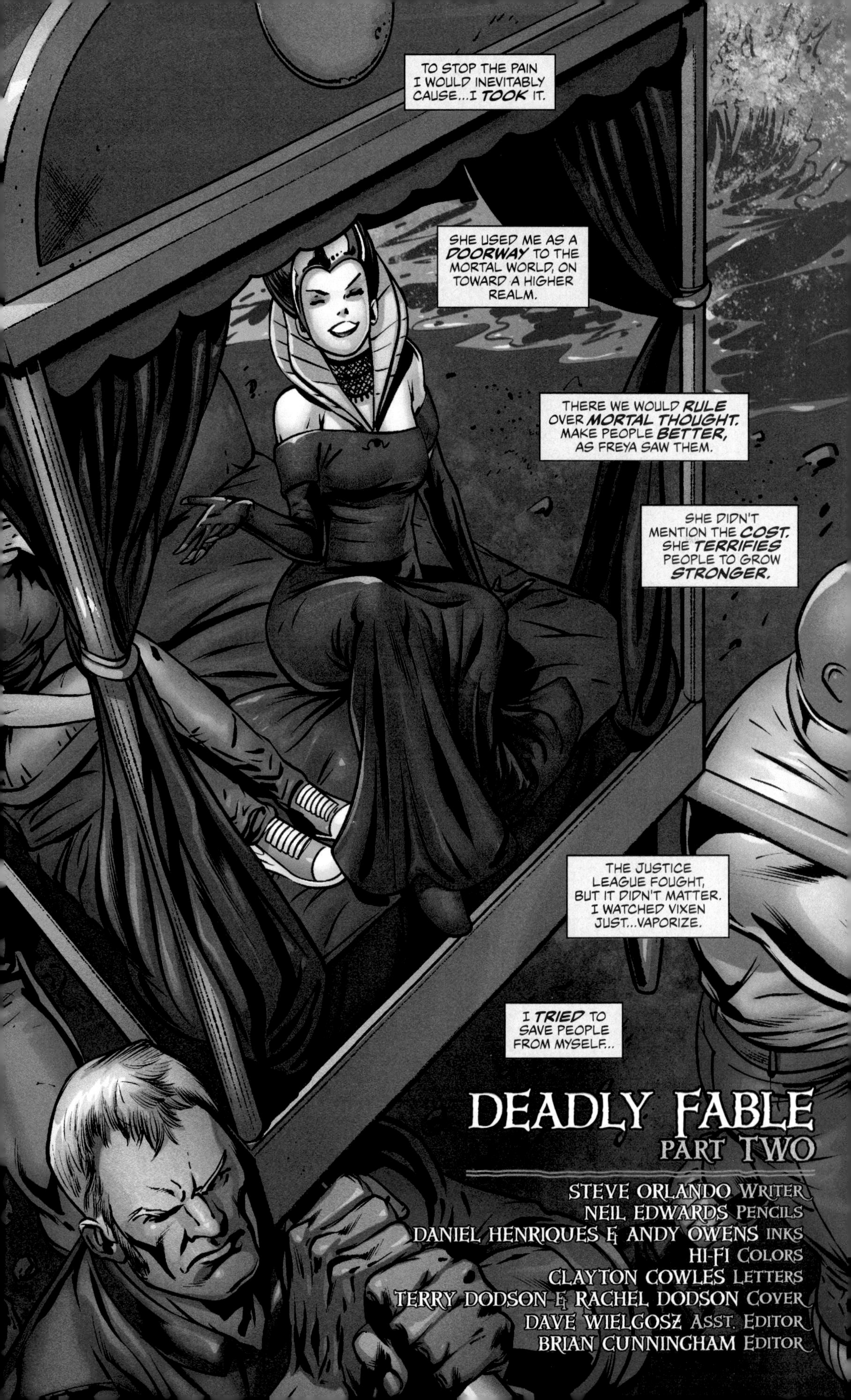

TO STOP THE PAIN I WOULD INEVITABLY CAUSE...I TOOK IT.
SHE USED ME AS A DOORWAY TO THE MORTAL WORLD, ON TOWARD A HIGHER REALM.
THERE WE WOULD RULE OVER MORTAL THOUGHT. MAKE PEOPLE BETTER, AS FREYA SAW THEM.
SHE DIDN'T MENTION THE COST. SHE TERRIFIES PEOPLE TO GROW STRONGER.
THE JUSTICE LEAGUE FOUGHT, BUT IT DIDN'T MATTER. I WATCHED VIXEN JUST...VAPORIZE.
I TRIED TO SAVE PEOPLE FROM MYSELF...
DEADLY FABLE
PART TWO
STEVE ORLANDO WRITER
NEIL EDWARDS PENCILS
DANIEL HENRIQUES & ANDY OWENS INKS
HI-FI COLORS
CLAYTON COWLES LETTERS
TERRY DODSON & RACHEL DODSON COVER
DAVE WIELGOSZ ASST. EDITOR
BRIAN CUNNINGHAM EDITOR

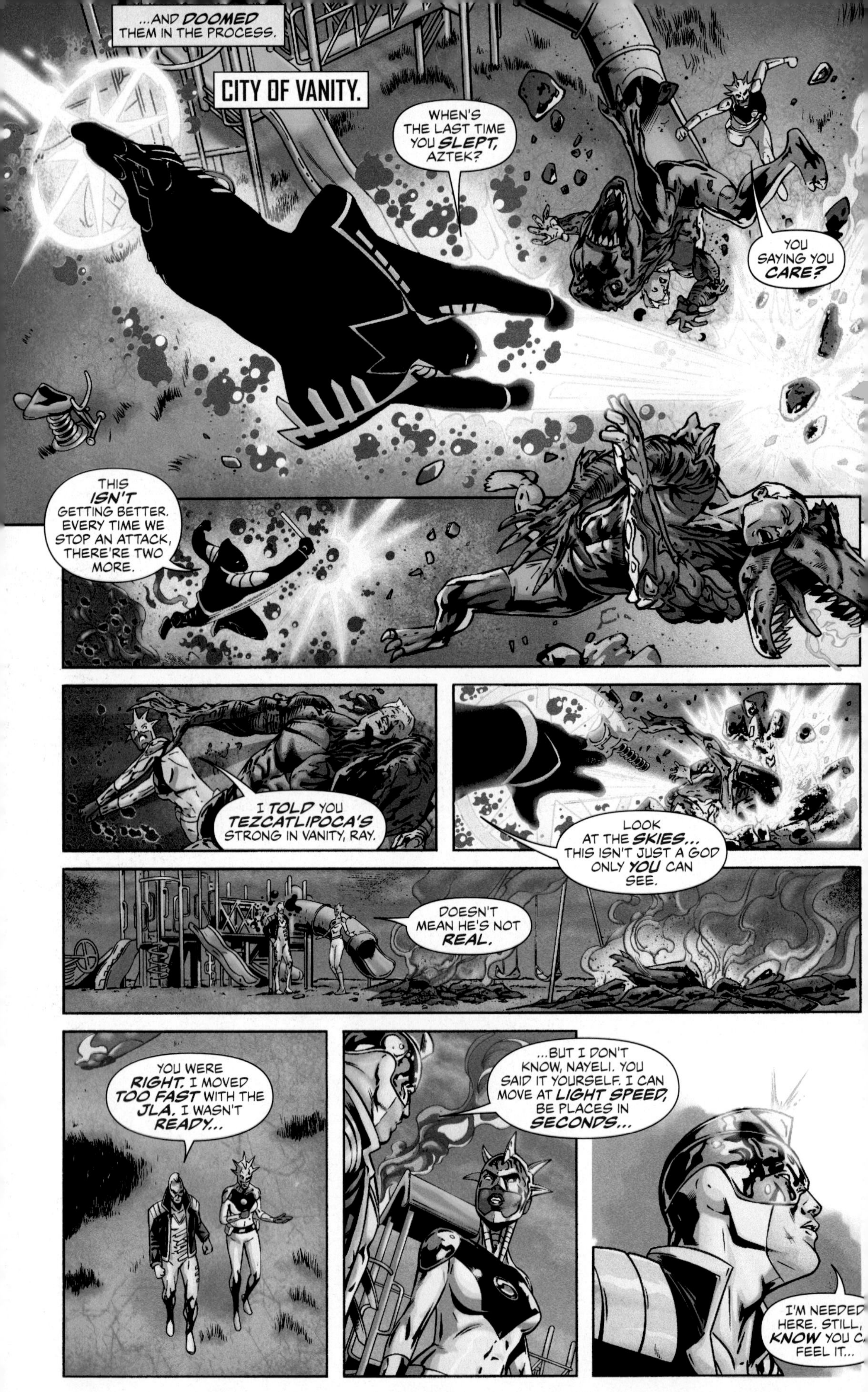

...AND DOOMED THEM IN THE PROCESS.
CITY OF VANITY.
WHEN'S THE LAST TIME YOU SLEPT, AZTEK?
YOU SAYING YOU CARE?
THIS ISN'T GETTING BETTER. EVERY TIME WE STOP AN ATTACK, THERE'RE TWO MORE.
I TOLD YOU TEZCATLIPOCA'S STRONG IN VANITY, RAY.
LOOK AT THE SKIES... THIS ISN'T JUST A GOD ONLY YOU CAN SEE.
DOESN'T MEAN HE'S NOT REAL.
YOU WERE RIGHT. I MOVED TOO FAST WITH THE JLA. I WASN'T READY...
...BUT I DON'T KNOW, NAYELI. YOU SAID IT YOURSELF. I CAN MOVE AT LIGHT SPEED, BE PLACES IN SECONDS...
I'M NEEDED HERE. STILL, I KNOW YOU CA FEEL IT...

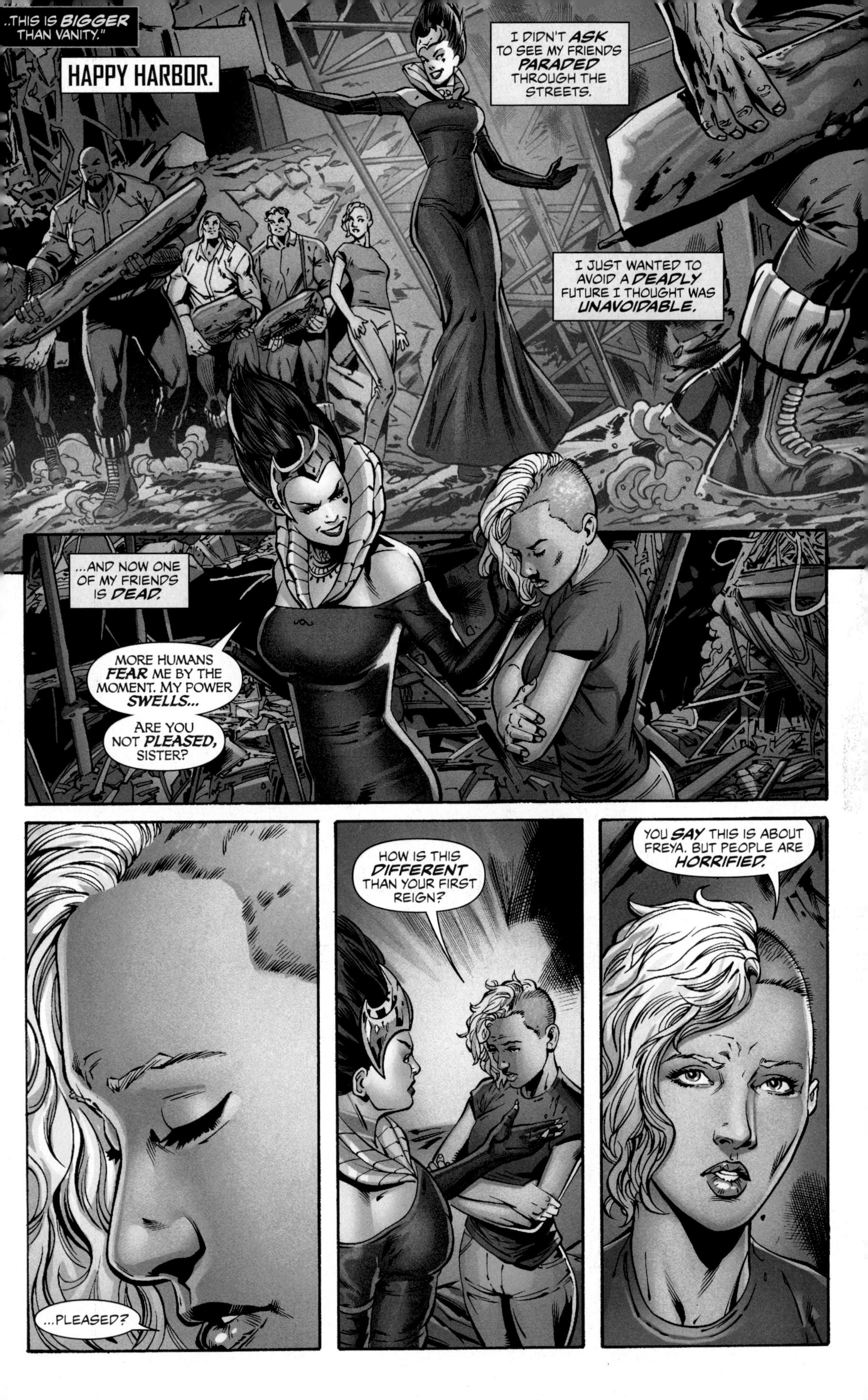

"...THIS IS BIGGER THAN VANITY."
HAPPY HARBOR.
I DIDN'T ASK TO SEE MY FRIENDS PARADED THROUGH THE STREETS.
I JUST WANTED TO AVOID A DEADLY FUTURE I THOUGHT WAS UNAVOIDABLE.
...AND NOW ONE OF MY FRIENDS IS DEAD.
MORE HUMANS FEAR ME BY THE MOMENT. MY POWER SWELLS...
ARE YOU NOT PLEASED, SISTER?
...PLEASED?
HOW IS THIS DIFFERENT THAN YOUR FIRST REIGN?
YOU SAY THIS IS ABOUT FREYA, BUT PEOPLE ARE HORRIFIED.

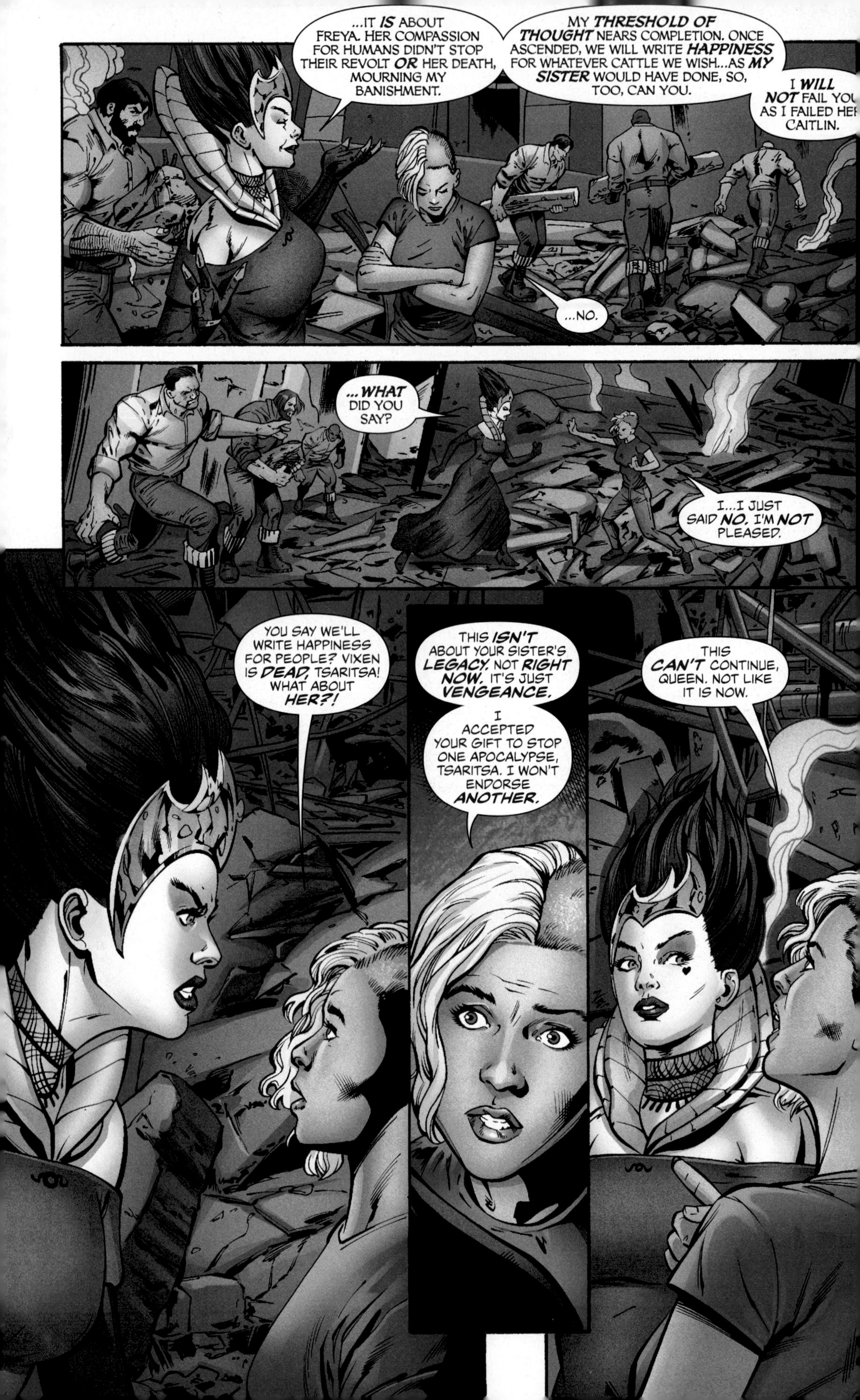
...IT IS ABOUT FREYA. HER COMPASSION FOR HUMANS DIDN'T STOP THEIR REVOLT OR HER DEATH, MOURNING MY BANISHMENT.
MY THRESHOLD OF THOUGHT NEARS COMPLETION. ONCE ASCENDED, WE WILL WRITE HAPPINESS FOR WHATEVER CATTLE WE WISH...AS MY SISTER WOULD HAVE DONE, SO, TOO, CAN YOU.
I WILL NOT FAIL YOU AS I FAILED HER CAITLIN.
...NO.
...WHAT DID YOU SAY?
I...I JUST SAID NO. I'M NOT PLEASED.
YOU SAY WE'LL WRITE HAPPINESS FOR PEOPLE? VIXEN IS DEAD, TSARITSA! WHAT ABOUT HER?!
THIS ISN'T ABOUT YOUR SISTER'S LEGACY. NOT RIGHT NOW. IT'S JUST VENGEANCE.
I ACCEPTED YOUR GIFT TO STOP ONE APOCALYPSE, TSARITSA. I WON'T ENDORSE ANOTHER.
THIS CAN'T CONTINUE, QUEEN. NOT LIKE IT IS NOW.

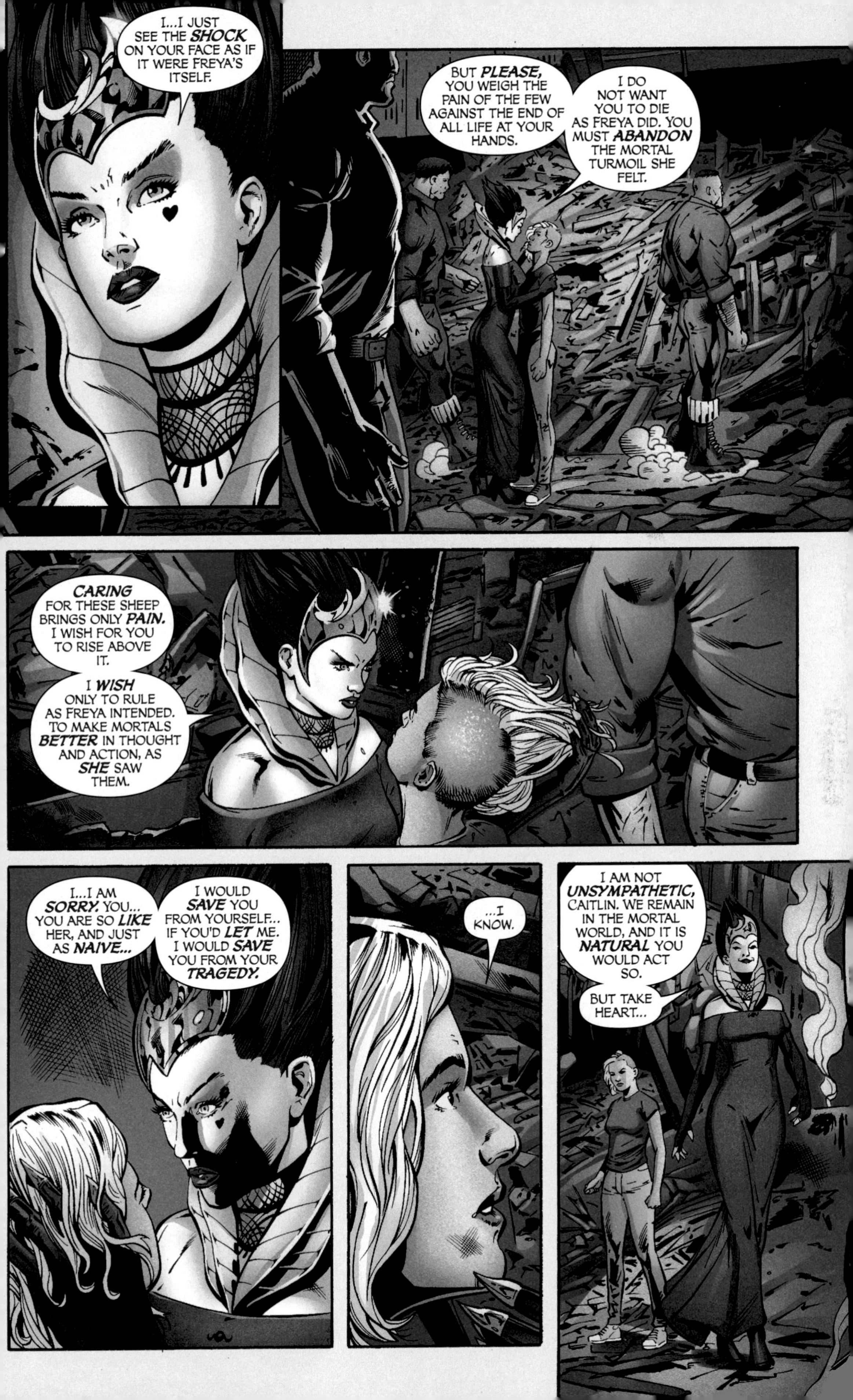
I...I JUST SEE THE SHOCK ON YOUR FACE AS IF IT WERE FREYA'S ITSELF.
BUT PLEASE, YOU WEIGH THE PAIN OF THE FEW AGAINST THE END OF ALL LIFE AT YOUR HANDS.
I DO NOT WANT YOU TO DIE AS FREYA DID. YOU MUST ABANDON THE MORTAL TURMOIL SHE FELT.
CARING FOR THESE SHEEP BRINGS ONLY PAIN. I WISH FOR YOU TO RISE ABOVE IT.
I WISH ONLY TO RULE AS FREYA INTENDED. TO MAKE MORTALS BETTER IN THOUGHT AND ACTION, AS SHE SAW THEM.
I...I AM SORRY. YOU... YOU ARE SO LIKE HER, AND JUST AS NAIVE...
I WOULD SAVE YOU FROM YOURSELF... IF YOU'D LET ME. I WOULD SAVE YOU FROM YOUR TRAGEDY.
...I KNOW.
I AM NOT UNSYMPATHETIC, CAITLIN. WE REMAIN IN THE MORTAL WORLD, AND IT IS NATURAL YOU WOULD ACT SO.
BUT TAKE HEART...

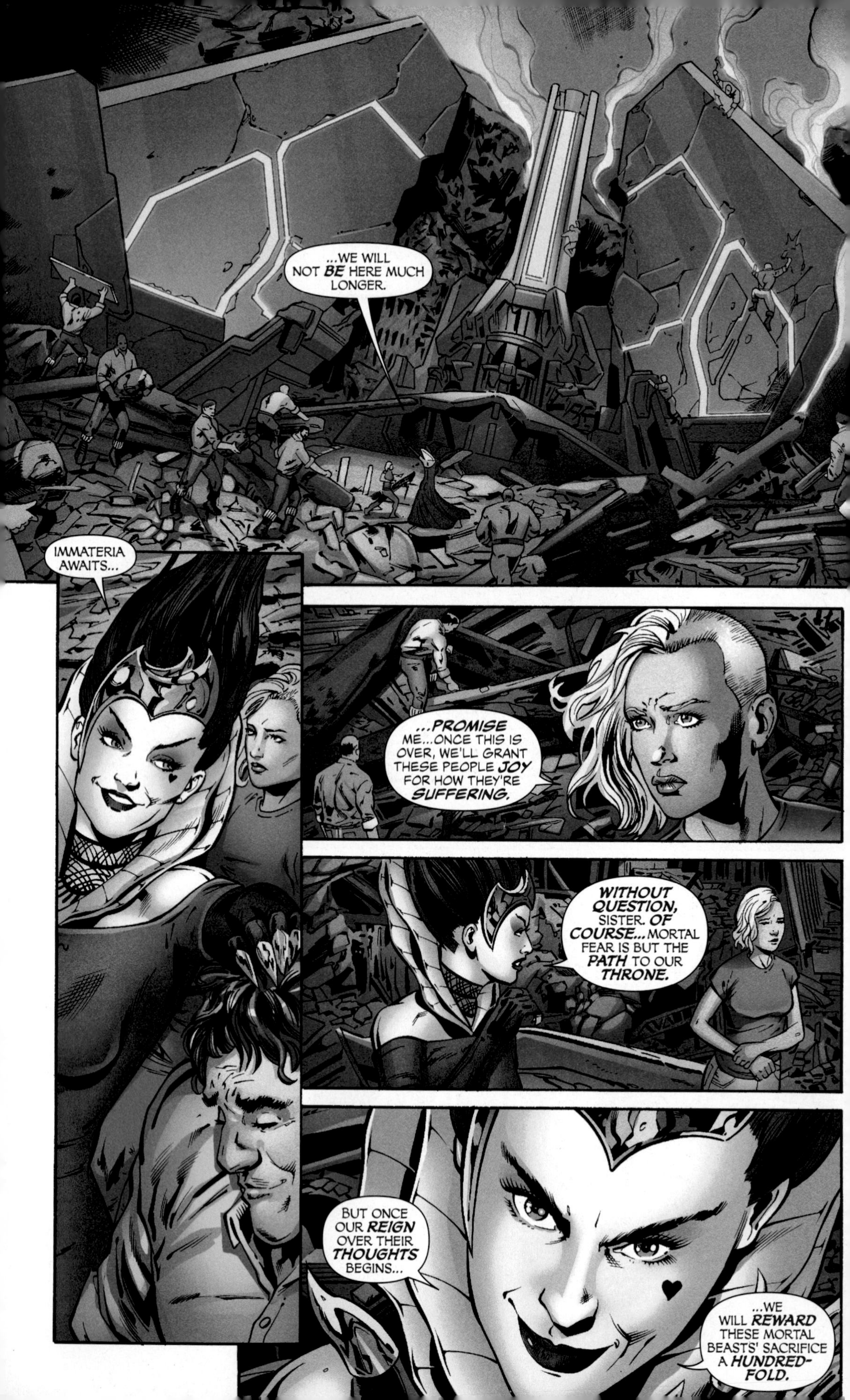
...WE WILL NOT BE HERE MUCH LONGER.
IMMATERIA AWAITS...
...PROMISE ME...ONCE THIS IS OVER, WE'LL GRANT THESE PEOPLE JOY FOR HOW THEY'RE SUFFERING.
WITHOUT QUESTION, SISTER. OF COURSE...MORTAL FEAR IS BUT THE PATH TO OUR THRONE.
BUT ONCE OUR REIGN OVER THEIR THOUGHTS BEGINS...
...WE WILL REWARD THESE MORTAL BEASTS' SACRIFICE A HUNDRED-FOLD.

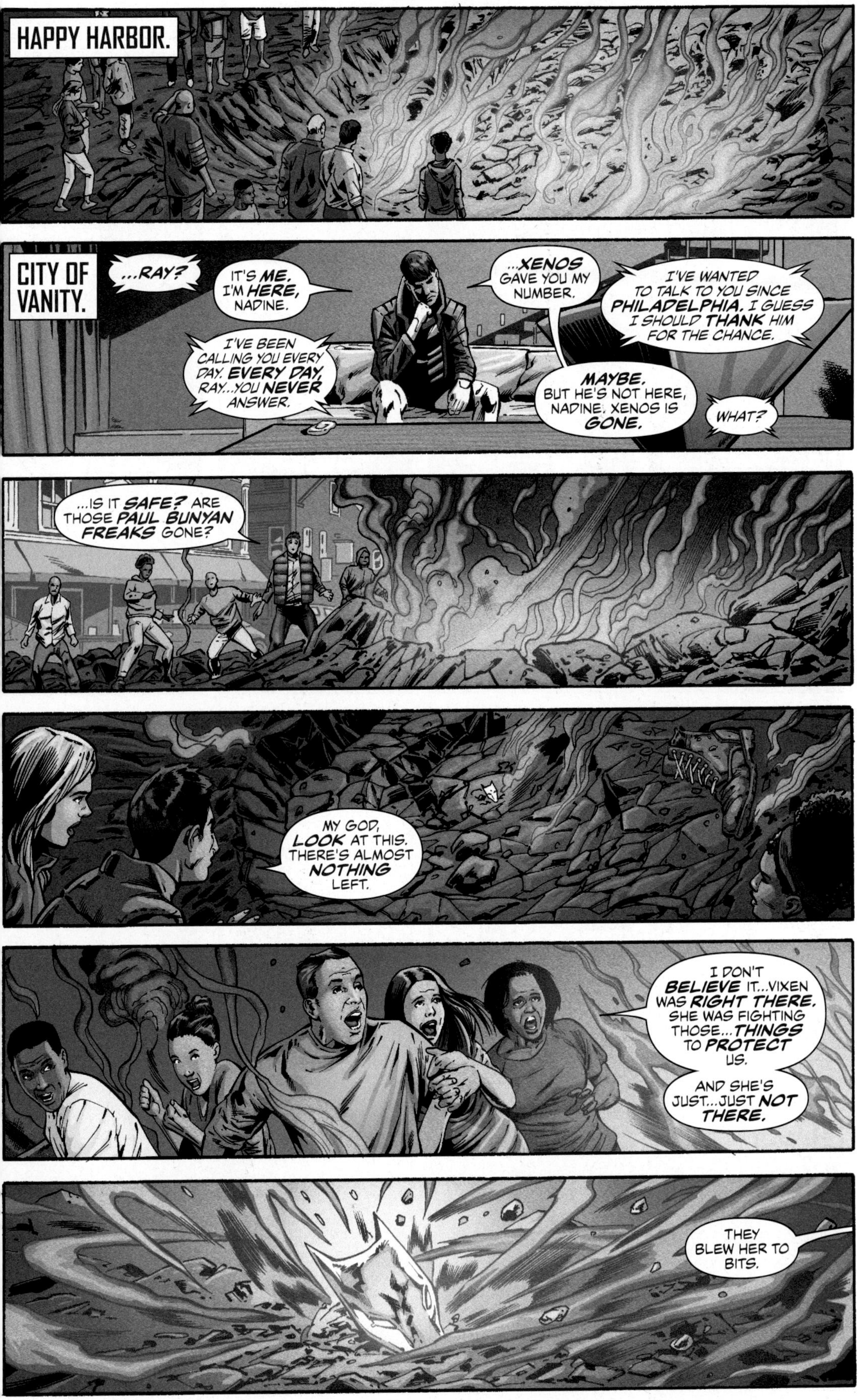
HAPPY HARBOR.
CITY OF VANITY.
...RAY?
IT'S ME. I'M HERE, NADINE.
I'VE BEEN CALLING YOU EVERY DAY. EVERY DAY, RAY...YOU NEVER ANSWER.
...XENOS GAVE YOU MY NUMBER.
I'VE WANTED TO TALK TO YOU SINCE PHILADELPHIA. I GUESS I SHOULD THANK HIM FOR THE CHANCE.
MAYBE. BUT HE'S NOT HERE, NADINE. XENOS IS GONE.
WHAT?
...IS IT SAFE? ARE THOSE PAUL BUNYAN FREAKS GONE?
MY GOD, LOOK AT THIS. THERE'S ALMOST NOTHING LEFT.
I DON'T BELIEVE IT...VIXEN WAS RIGHT THERE. SHE WAS FIGHTING THOSE...THINGS TO PROTECT US.
AND SHE'S JUST...JUST NOT THERE.
THEY BLEW HER TO BITS.

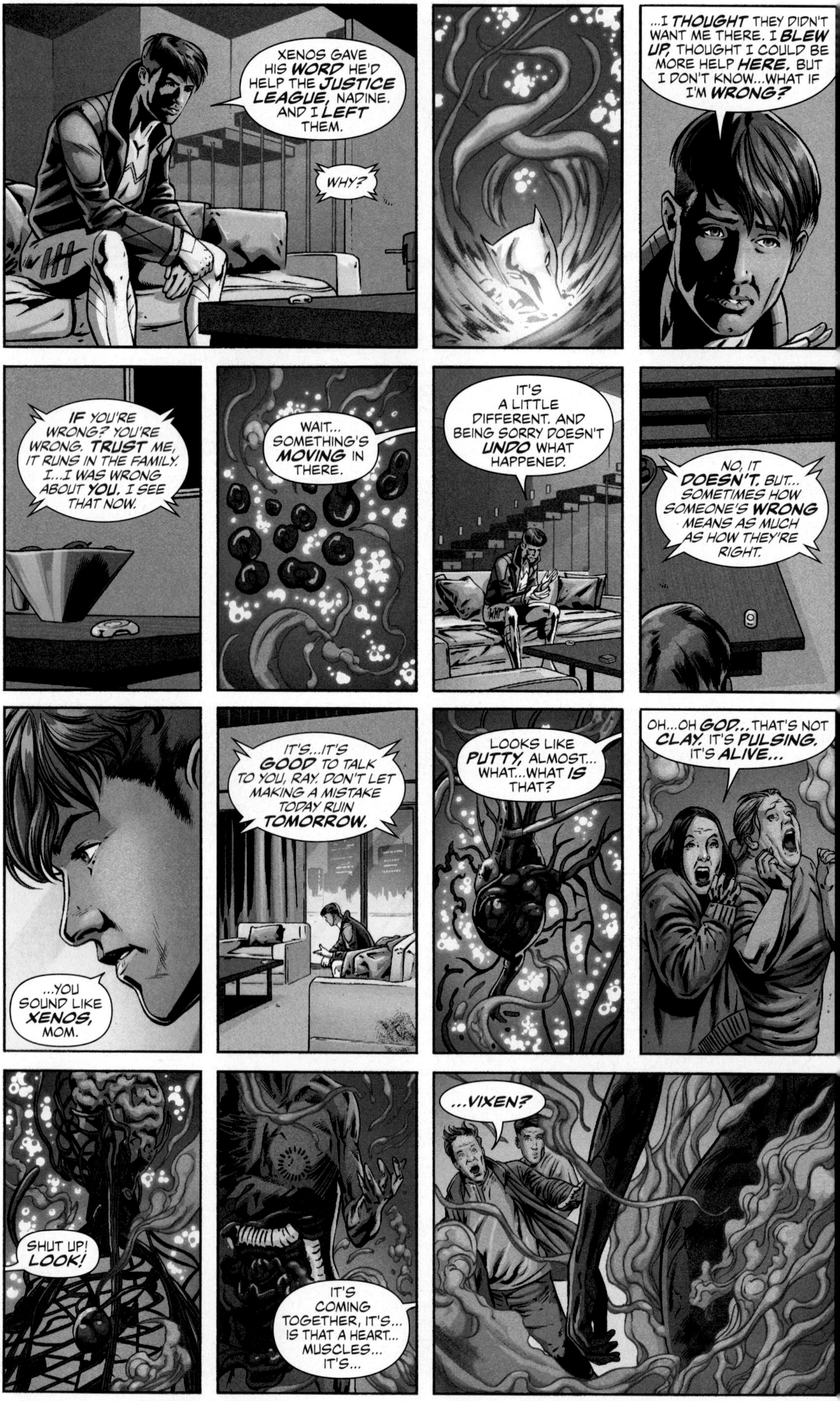
XENOS GAVE HIS WORD HE'D HELP THE JUSTICE LEAGUE, NADINE. AND I LEFT THEM.
WHY?
...I THOUGHT THEY DIDN'T WANT ME THERE. I BLEW UP, THOUGHT I COULD BE MORE HELP HERE. BUT I DON'T KNOW...WHAT IF I'M WRONG?
IF YOU'RE WRONG? YOU'RE WRONG. TRUST ME, IT RUNS IN THE FAMILY. I...I WAS WRONG ABOUT YOU. I SEE THAT NOW.
WAIT... SOMETHING'S MOVING IN THERE.
IT'S A LITTLE DIFFERENT. AND BEING SORRY DOESN'T UNDO WHAT HAPPENED.
NO, IT DOESN'T. BUT... SOMETIMES HOW SOMEONE'S WRONG MEANS AS MUCH AS HOW THEY'RE RIGHT.
...YOU SOUND LIKE XENOS, MOM.
IT'S...IT'S GOOD TO TALK TO YOU, RAY. DON'T LET MAKING A MISTAKE TODAY RUIN TOMORROW.
LOOKS LIKE PUTTY, ALMOST... WHAT...WHAT IS THAT?
OH...OH GOD...THAT'S NOT CLAY. IT'S PULSING. IT'S ALIVE...
SHUT UP! LOOK!
IT'S COMING TOGETHER, IT'S... IS THAT A HEART... MUSCLES... IT'S...
...VIXEN?

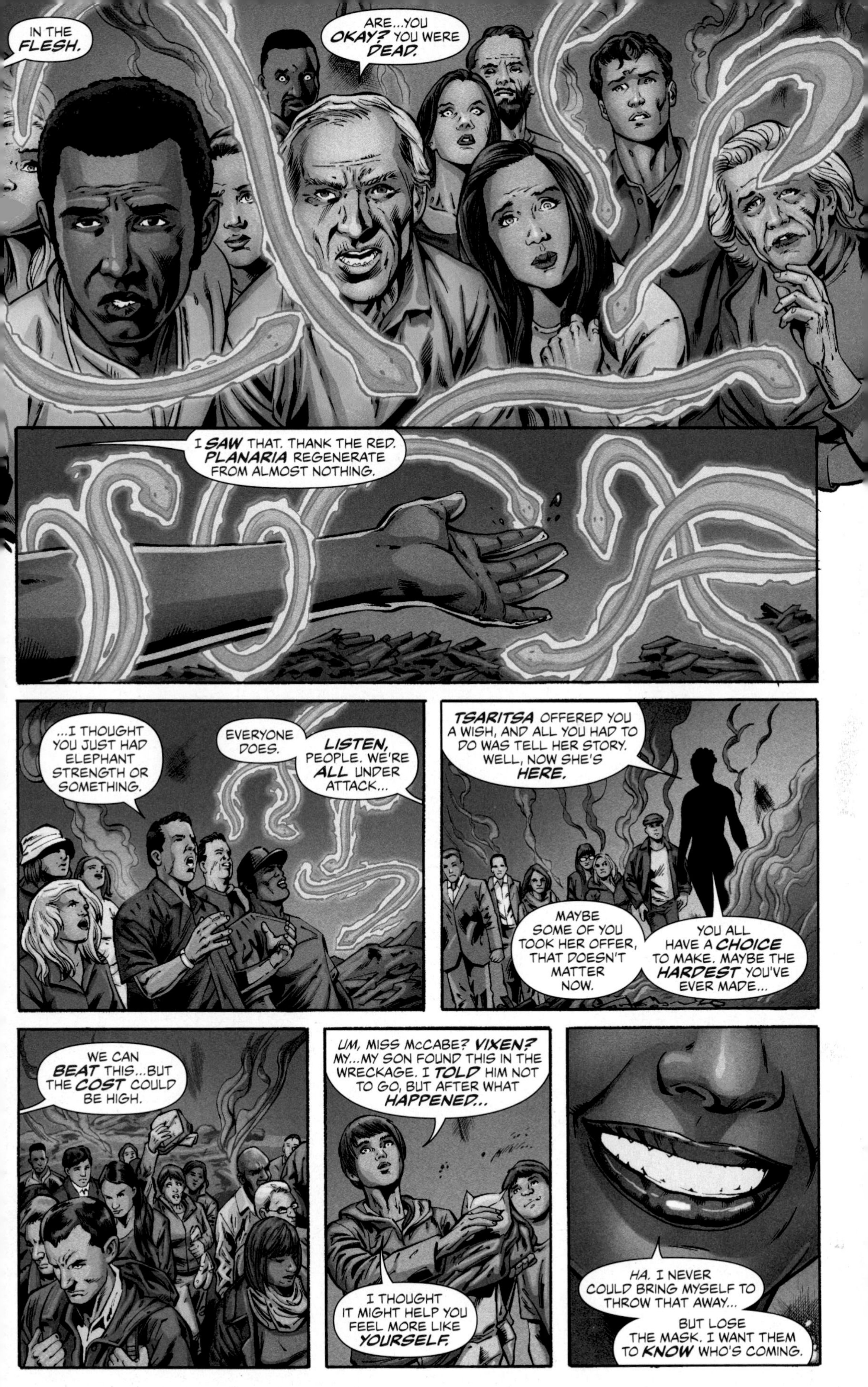
IN THE FLESH.
ARE...YOU OKAY? YOU WERE DEAD.
I SAW THAT. THANK THE RED. PLANARIA REGENERATE FROM ALMOST NOTHING.
...I THOUGHT YOU JUST HAD ELEPHANT STRENGTH OR SOMETHING.
EVERYONE DOES.
LISTEN, PEOPLE. WE'RE ALL UNDER ATTACK...
TSARITSA OFFERED YOU A WISH, AND ALL YOU HAD TO DO WAS TELL HER STORY. WELL, NOW SHE'S HERE.
MAYBE SOME OF YOU TOOK HER OFFER, THAT DOESN'T MATTER NOW.
YOU ALL HAVE A CHOICE TO MAKE. MAYBE THE HARDEST YOU'VE EVER MADE...
WE CAN BEAT THIS...BUT THE COST COULD BE HIGH.
UM, MISS McCABE? VIXEN? MY...MY SON FOUND THIS IN THE WRECKAGE. I TOLD HIM NOT TO GO, BUT AFTER WHAT HAPPENED...
I THOUGHT IT MIGHT HELP YOU FEEL MORE LIKE YOURSELF.
HA. I NEVER COULD BRING MYSELF TO THROW THAT AWAY...
BUT LOSE THE MASK. I WANT THEM TO KNOW WHO'S COMING.

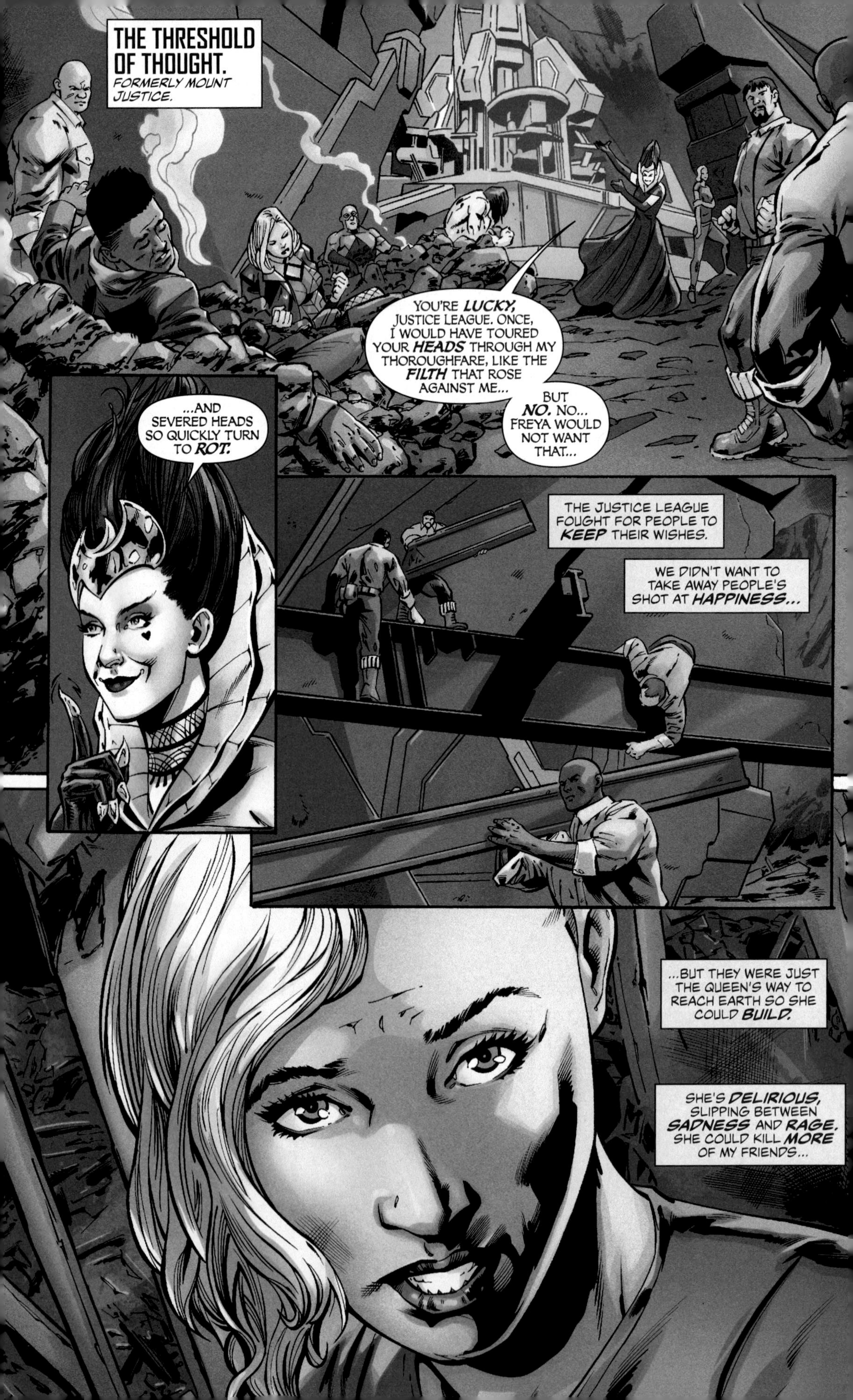
THE THRESHOLD OF THOUGHT.
FORMERLY MOUNT JUSTICE.
YOU'RE LUCKY, JUSTICE LEAGUE. ONCE, I WOULD HAVE TOURED YOUR HEADS THROUGH MY THOROUGHFARE, LIKE THE FILTH THAT ROSE AGAINST ME...
BUT NO. NO... FREYA WOULD NOT WANT THAT...
...AND SEVERED HEADS SO QUICKLY TURN TO ROT.
THE JUSTICE LEAGUE FOUGHT FOR PEOPLE TO KEEP THEIR WISHES.
WE DIDN'T WANT TO TAKE AWAY PEOPLE'S SHOT AT HAPPINESS...
...BUT THEY WERE JUST THE QUEEN'S WAY TO REACH EARTH SO SHE COULD BUILD.
SHE'S DELIRIOUS, SLIPPING BETWEEN SADNESS AND RAGE. SHE COULD KILL MORE OF MY FRIENDS...

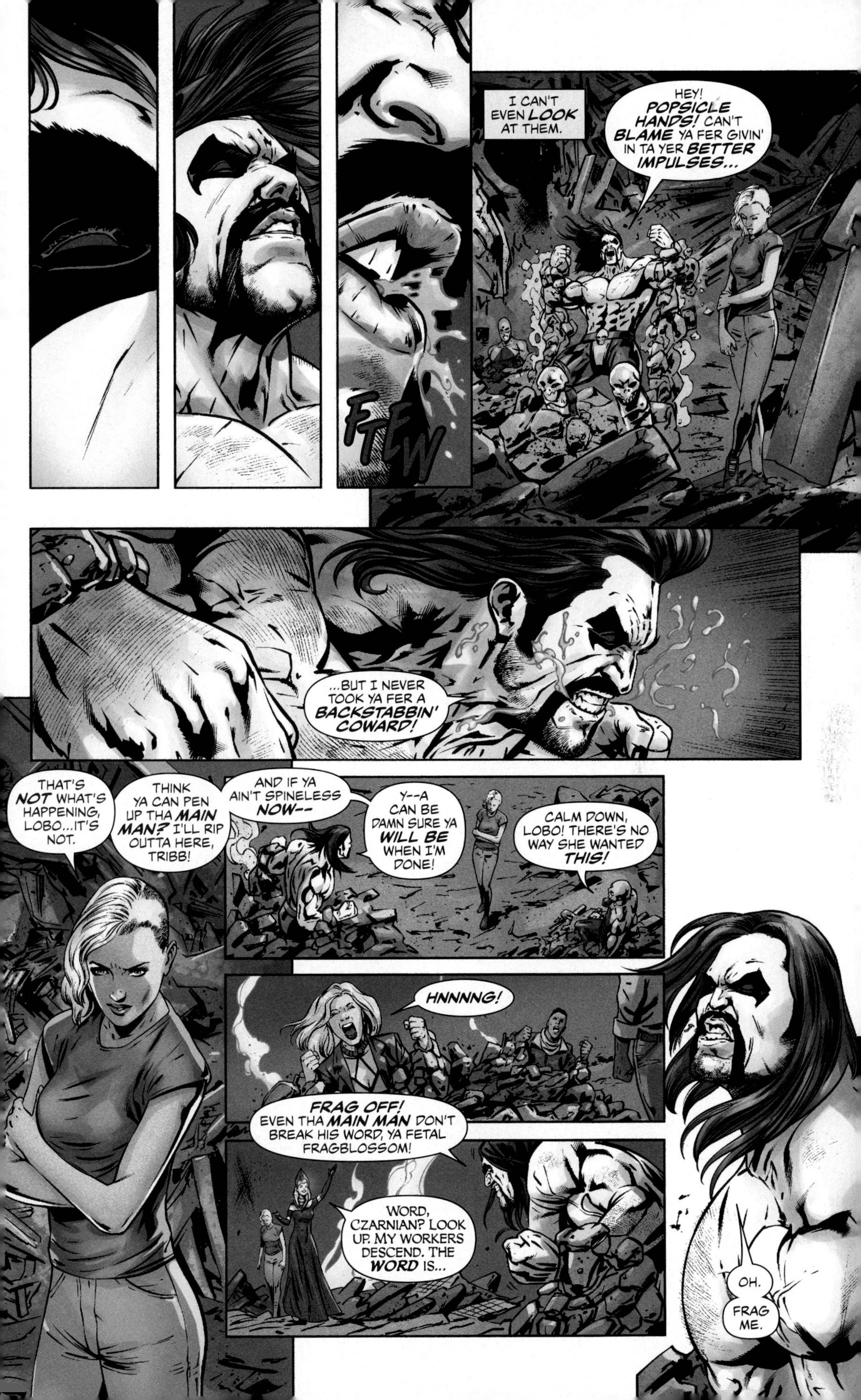
I CAN'T EVEN LOOK AT THEM.
HEY! POPSICLE HANDS! CAN'T BLAME YA FER GIVIN' IN TA YER BETTER IMPULSES...
FTEW
...BUT I NEVER TOOK YA FER A BACKSTABBIN' COWARD!
THAT'S NOT WHAT'S HAPPENING, LOBO...IT'S NOT.
THINK YA CAN PEN UP THA MAIN MAN? I'LL RIP OUTTA HERE, TRIBB!
AND IF YA AIN'T SPINELESS NOW--
Y--A CAN BE DAMN SURE YA WILL BE WHEN I'M DONE!
CALM DOWN, LOBO! THERE'S NO WAY SHE WANTED THIS!
HNNNNG!
FRAG OFF! EVEN THA MAIN MAN DON'T BREAK HIS WORD, YA FETAL FRAGBLOSSOM!
WORD, CZARNIAN? LOOK UP. MY WORKERS DESCEND. THE WORD IS...
OH.
FRAG ME.

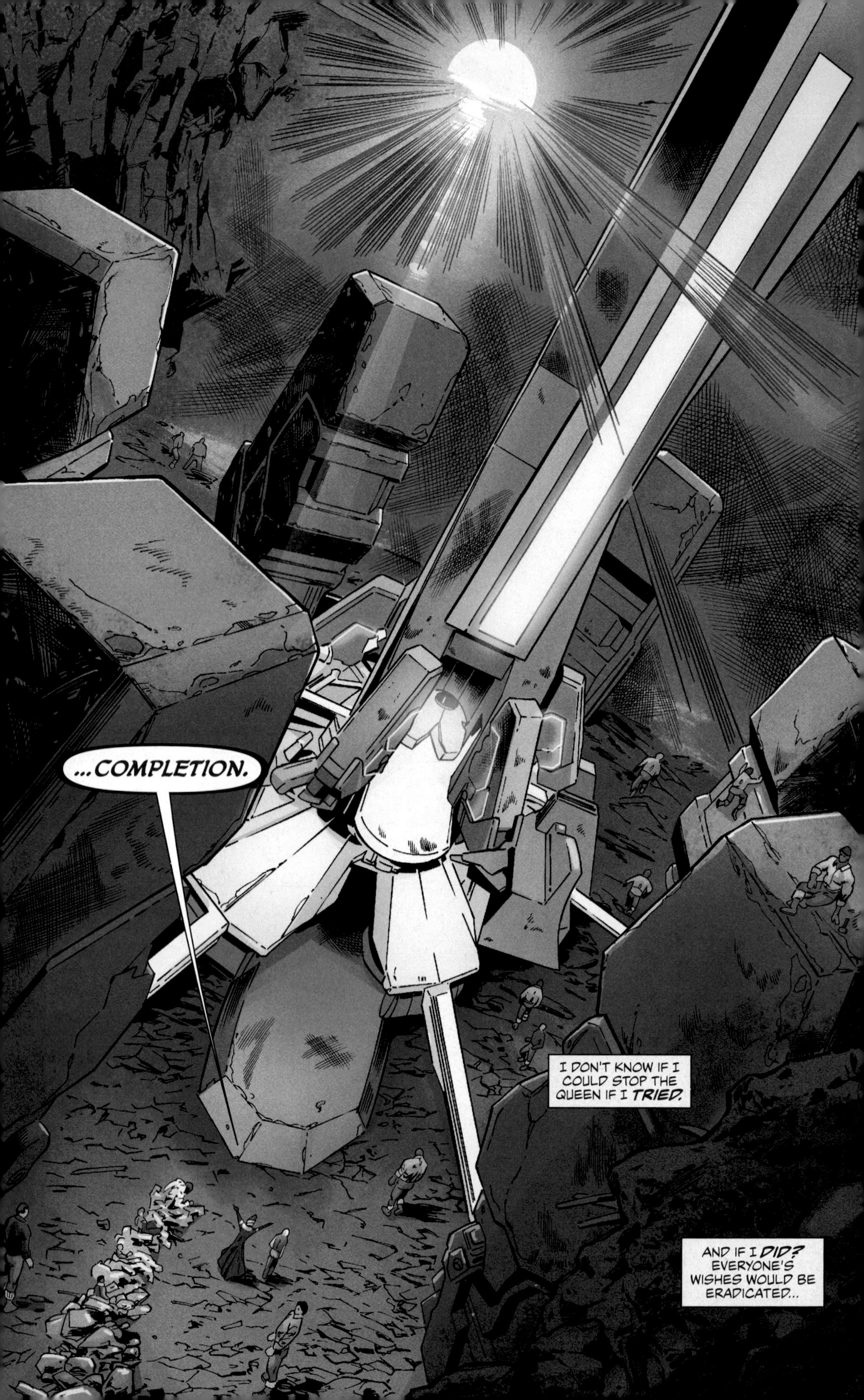
...COMPLETION.
I DON'T KNOW IF I COULD STOP THE QUEEN IF I TRIED.
AND IF I DID? EVERYONE'S WISHES WOULD BE ERADICATED...

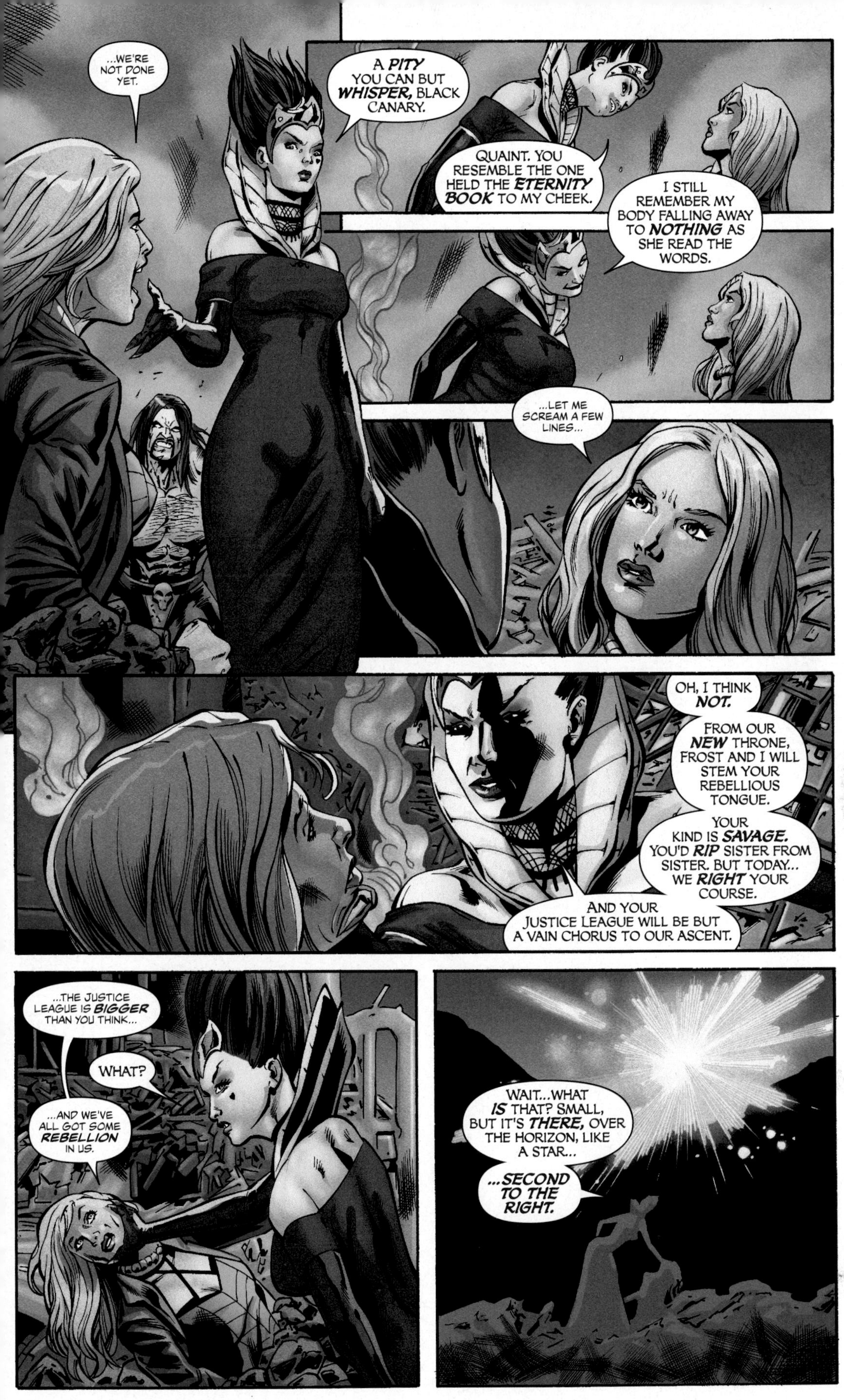
...WE'RE NOT DONE YET.
A PITY YOU CAN BUT WHISPER, BLACK CANARY.
QUAINT. YOU RESEMBLE THE ONE HELD THE ETERNITY BOOK TO MY CHEEK.
I STILL REMEMBER MY BODY FALLING AWAY TO NOTHING AS SHE READ THE WORDS.
...LET ME SCREAM A FEW LINES...
OH, I THINK NOT.
FROM OUR NEW THRONE, FROST AND I WILL STEM YOUR REBELLIOUS TONGUE.
YOUR KIND IS SAVAGE. YOU'D RIP SISTER FROM SISTER. BUT TODAY... WE RIGHT YOUR COURSE.
AND YOUR JUSTICE LEAGUE WILL BE BUT A VAIN CHORUS TO OUR ASCENT.
...THE JUSTICE LEAGUE IS BIGGER THAN YOU THINK...
WHAT?
...AND WE'VE ALL GOT SOME REBELLION IN US.
WAIT...WHAT IS THAT? SMALL, BUT IT'S THERE, OVER THE HORIZON, LIKE A STAR...
...SECOND TO THE RIGHT.

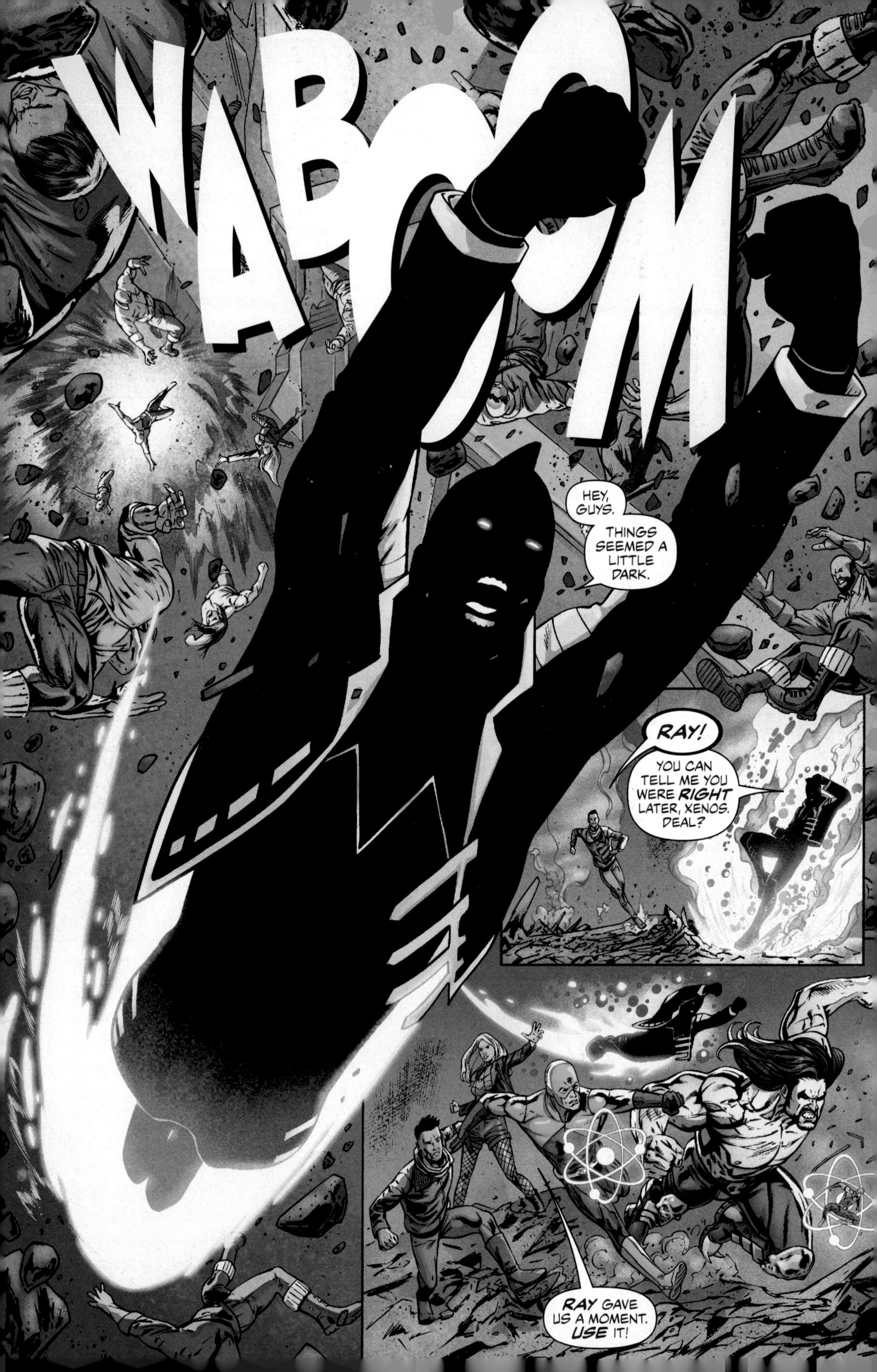
WABOOM
HEY, GUYS.
THINGS SEEMED A LITTLE DARK.
RAY!
YOU CAN TELL ME YOU WERE RIGHT LATER, XENOS. DEAL?
RAY GAVE US A MOMENT. USE IT!

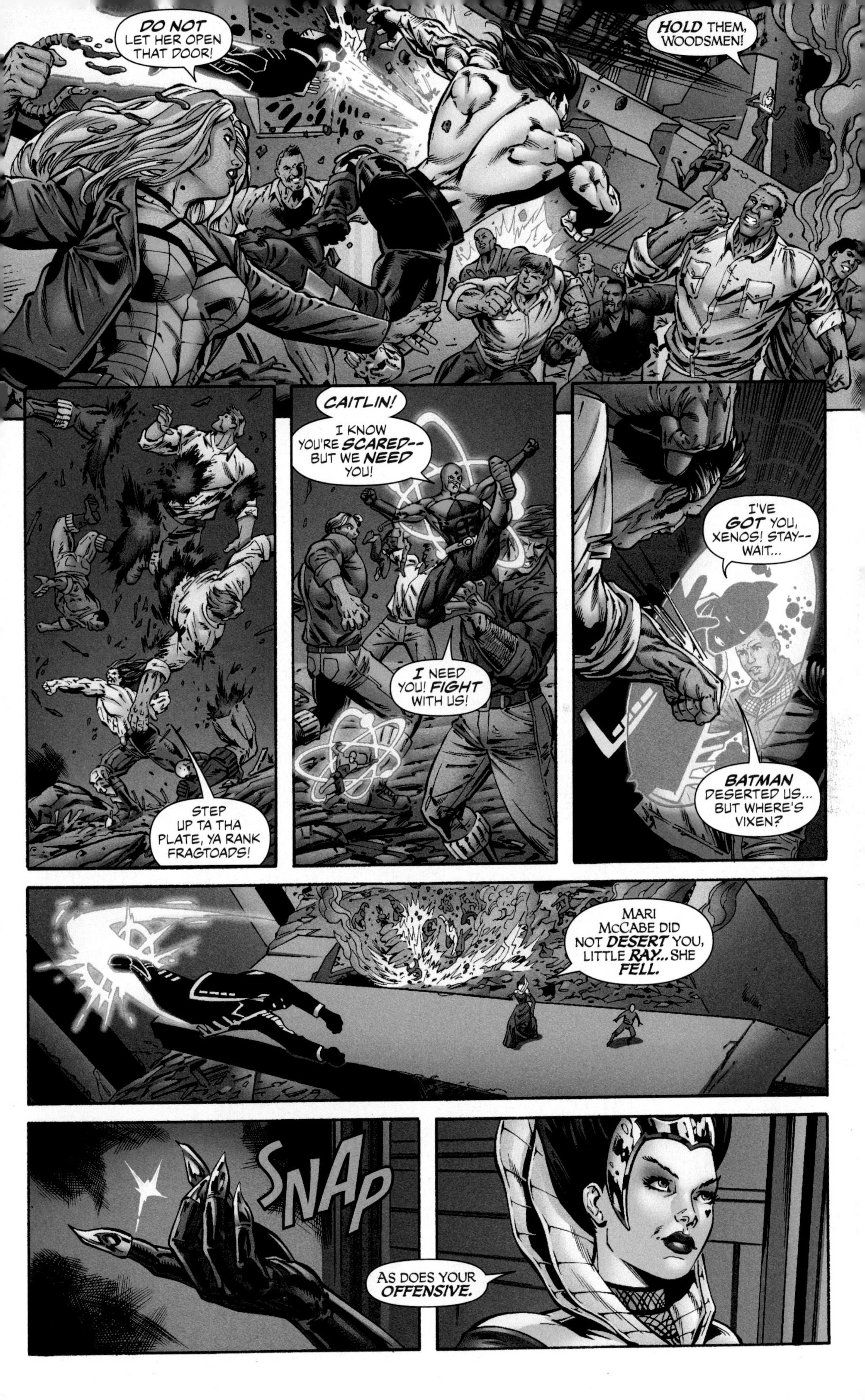
DO NOT LET HER OPEN THAT DOOR!
HOLD THEM, WOODSMEN!
STEP UP TA THA PLATE, YA RANK FRAGTOADS!
CAITLIN!
I KNOW YOU'RE SCARED-- BUT WE NEED YOU!
I NEED YOU! FIGHT WITH US!
I'VE GOT YOU, XENOS! STAY-- WAIT...
BATMAN DESERTED US... BUT WHERE'S VIXEN?
MARI McCABE DID NOT DESERT YOU, LITTLE RAY... SHE FELL.
SNAP
AS DOES YOUR OFFENSIVE.

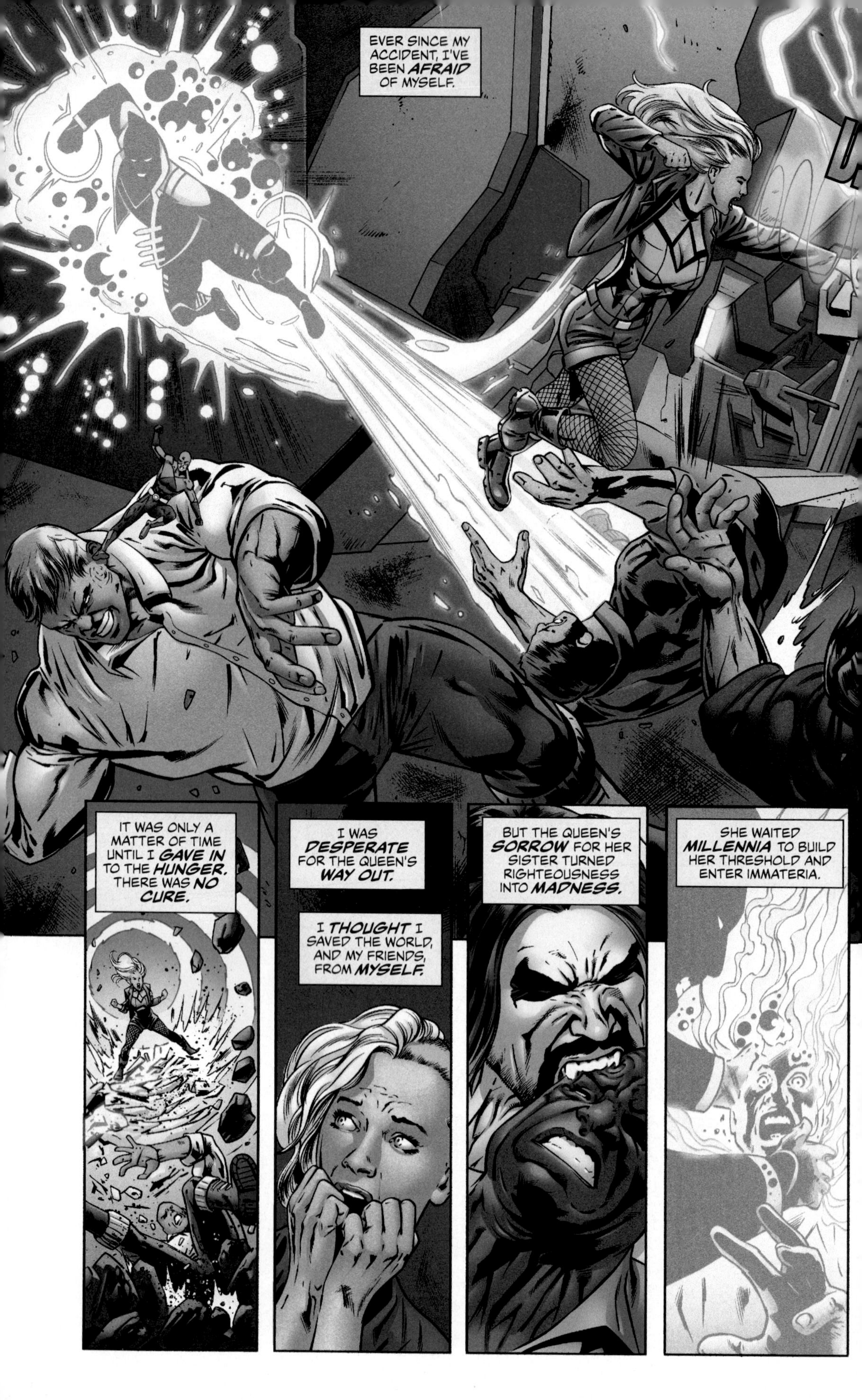
EVER SINCE MY ACCIDENT, I'VE BEEN AFRAID OF MYSELF.
IT WAS ONLY A MATTER OF TIME UNTIL I GAVE IN TO THE HUNGER. THERE WAS NO CURE.
I WAS DESPERATE FOR THE QUEEN'S WAY OUT.
I THOUGHT I SAVED THE WORLD, AND MY FRIENDS, FROM MYSELF.
BUT THE QUEEN'S SORROW FOR HER SISTER TURNED RIGHTEOUSNESS INTO MADNESS.
SHE WAITED MILLENNIA TO BUILD HER THRESHOLD AND ENTER IMMATERIA.

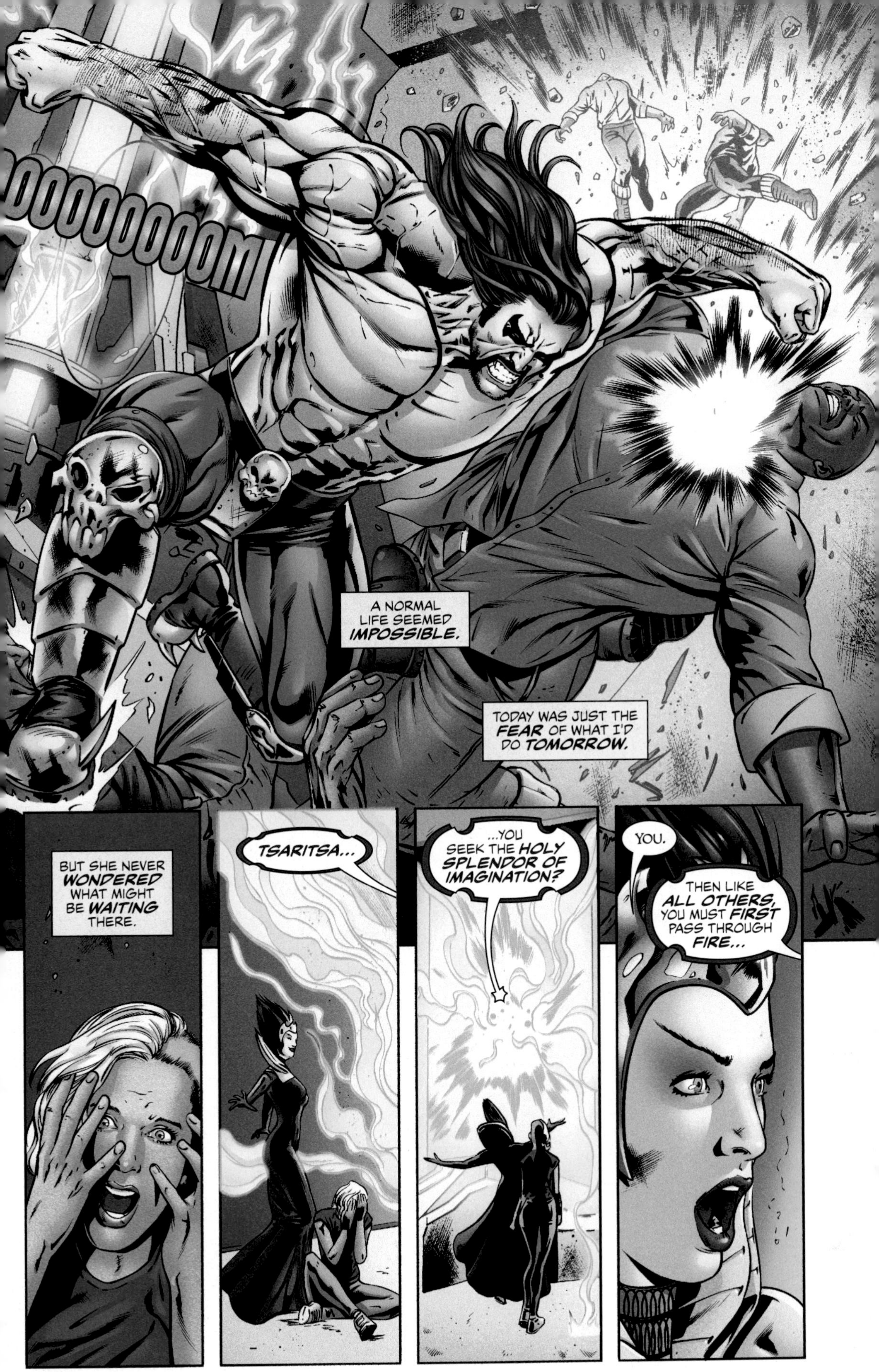
BOOOOOOOOOM
A NORMAL LIFE SEEMED IMPOSSIBLE.
TODAY WAS JUST THE FEAR OF WHAT I'D DO TOMORROW.
BUT SHE NEVER WONDERED WHAT MIGHT BE WAITING THERE.
TSARITSA...
...YOU SEEK THE HOLY SPLENDOR OF IMAGINATION?
YOU.
THEN LIKE ALL OTHERS, YOU MUST FIRST PASS THROUGH FIRE...

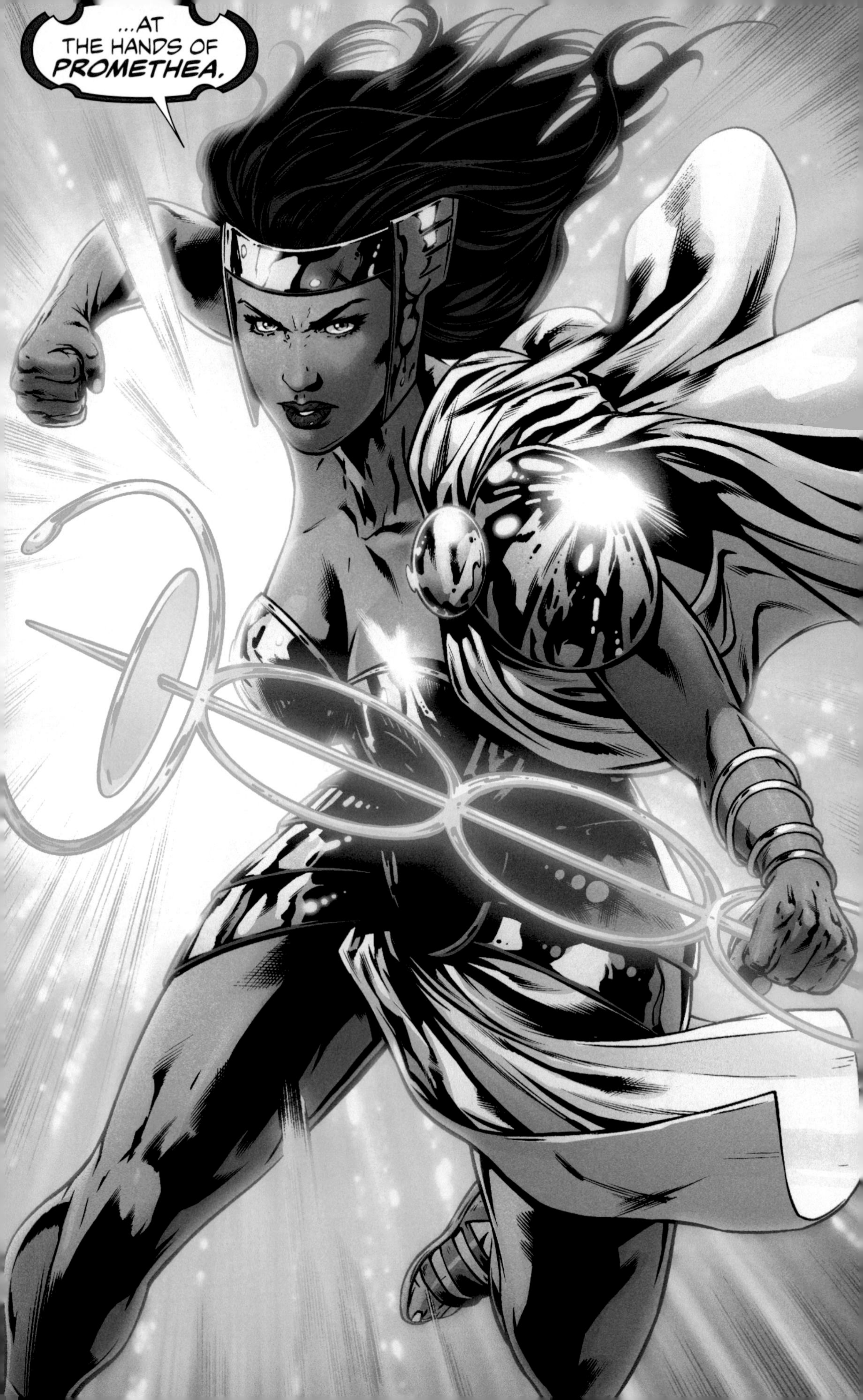
...AT THE HANDS OF PROMETHEA.

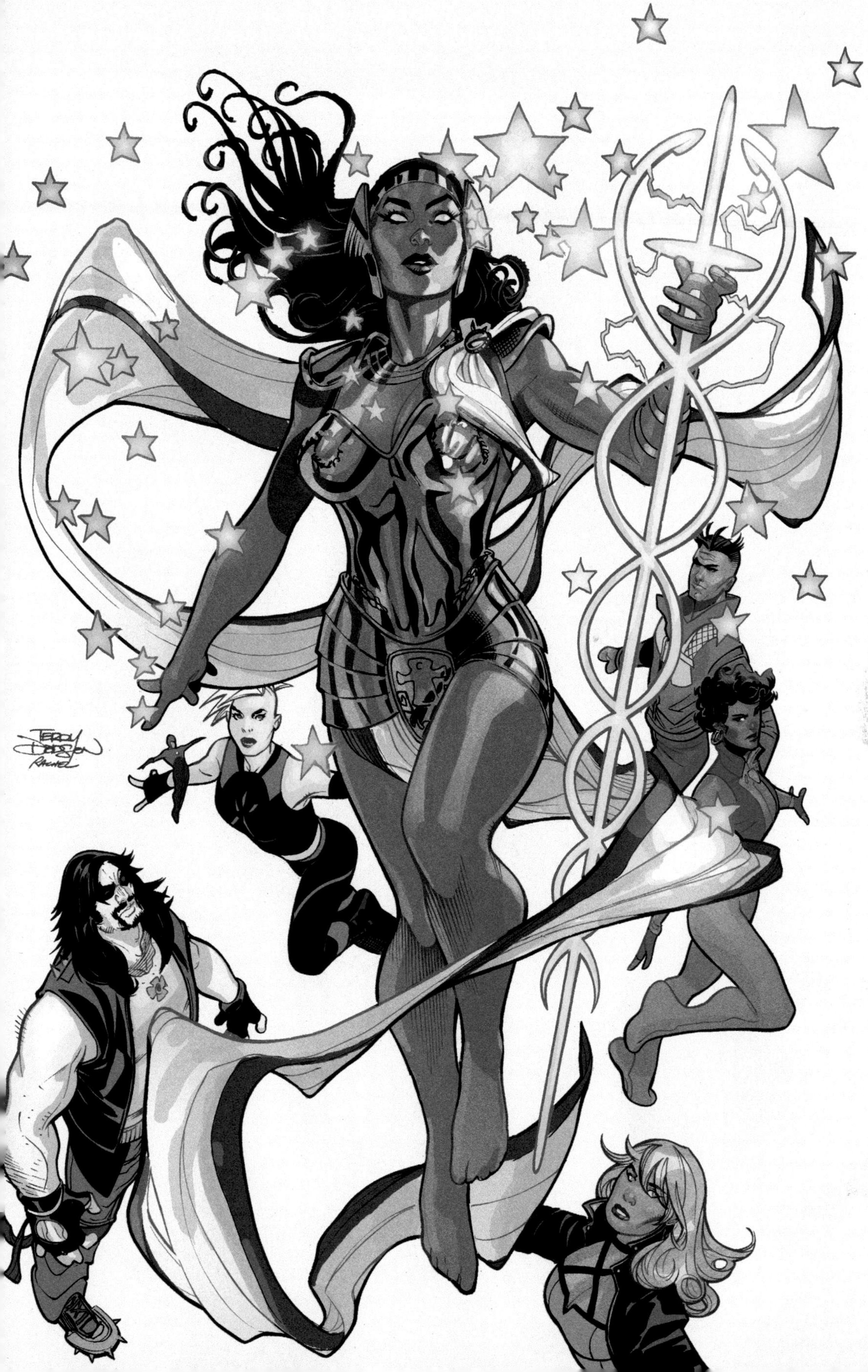
TERRY DODSON
RACHEL

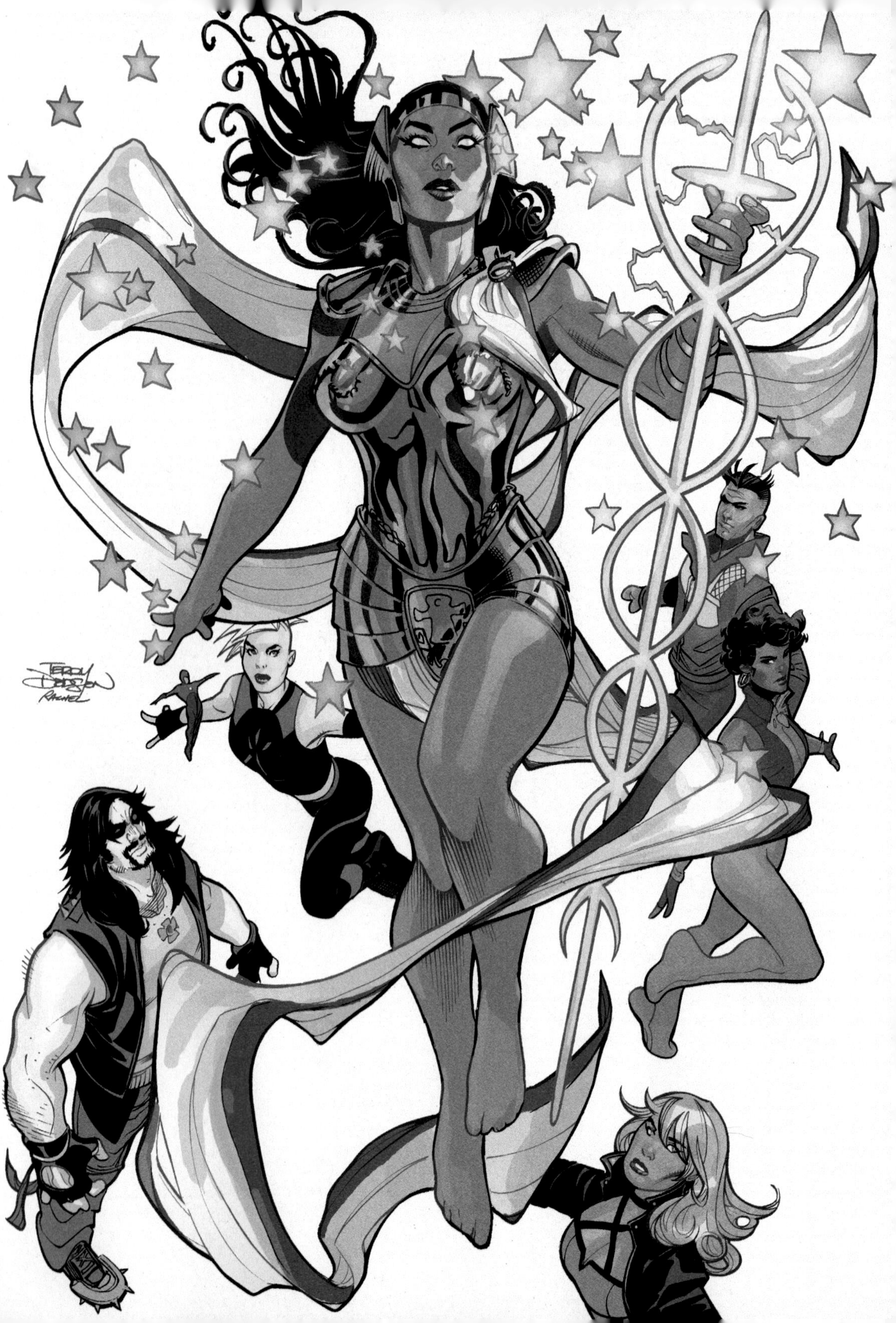
TERRY DODSON
RACHEL

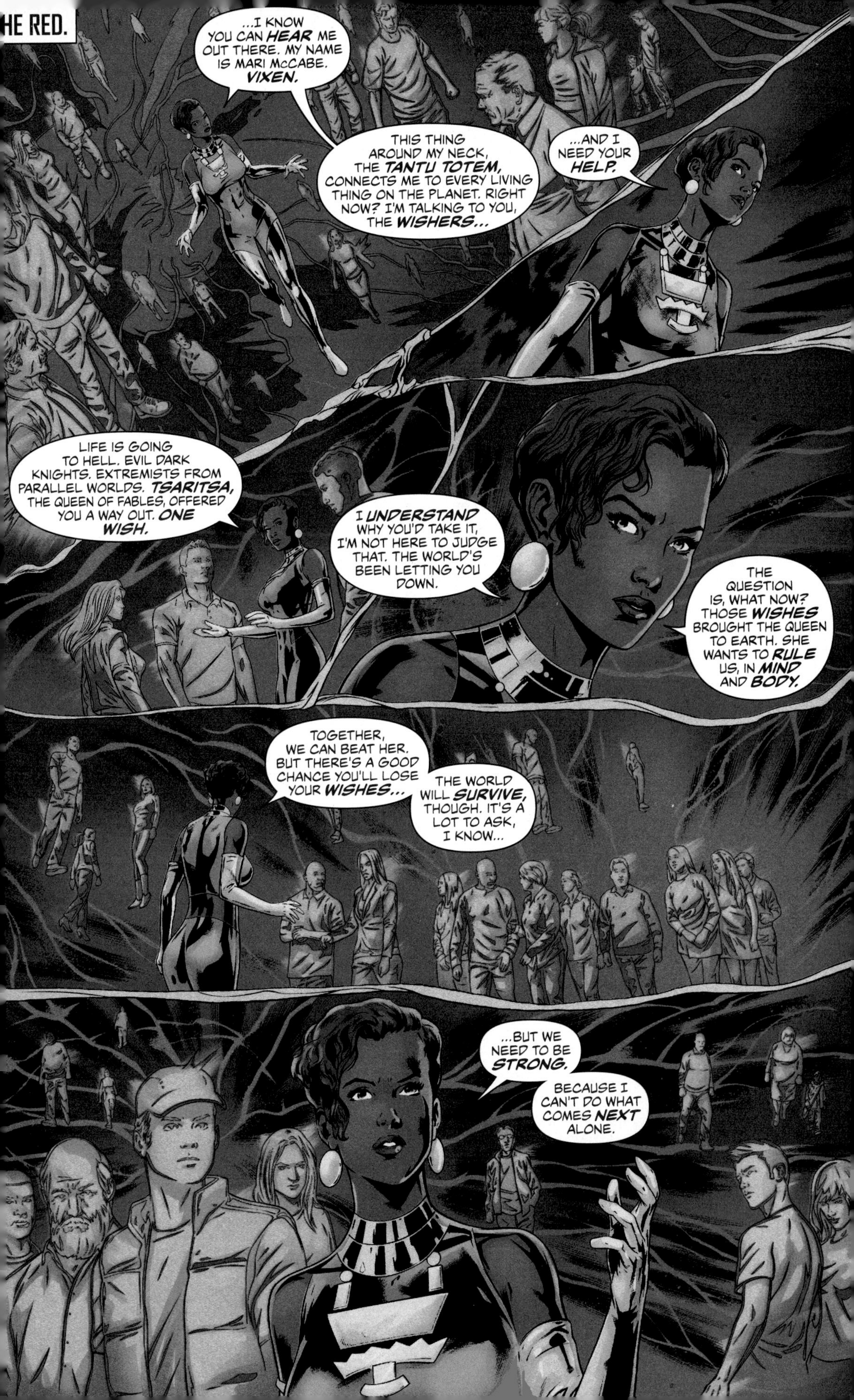
HE RED.
...I KNOW YOU CAN HEAR ME OUT THERE. MY NAME IS MARI McCABE. VIXEN.
THIS THING AROUND MY NECK, THE TANTU TOTEM, CONNECTS ME TO EVERY LIVING THING ON THE PLANET. RIGHT NOW? I'M TALKING TO YOU, THE WISHERS...
...AND I NEED YOUR HELP.
LIFE IS GOING TO HELL. EVIL DARK KNIGHTS. EXTREMISTS FROM PARALLEL WORLDS. TSARITSA, THE QUEEN OF FABLES, OFFERED YOU A WAY OUT. ONE WISH.
I UNDERSTAND WHY YOU'D TAKE IT, I'M NOT HERE TO JUDGE THAT. THE WORLD'S BEEN LETTING YOU DOWN.
THE QUESTION IS, WHAT NOW? THOSE WISHES BROUGHT THE QUEEN TO EARTH. SHE WANTS TO RULE US, IN MIND AND BODY.
TOGETHER, WE CAN BEAT HER. BUT THERE'S A GOOD CHANCE YOU'LL LOSE YOUR WISHES...
THE WORLD WILL SURVIVE, THOUGH. IT'S A LOT TO ASK, I KNOW...
...BUT WE NEED TO BE STRONG.
BECAUSE I CAN'T DO WHAT COMES NEXT ALONE.

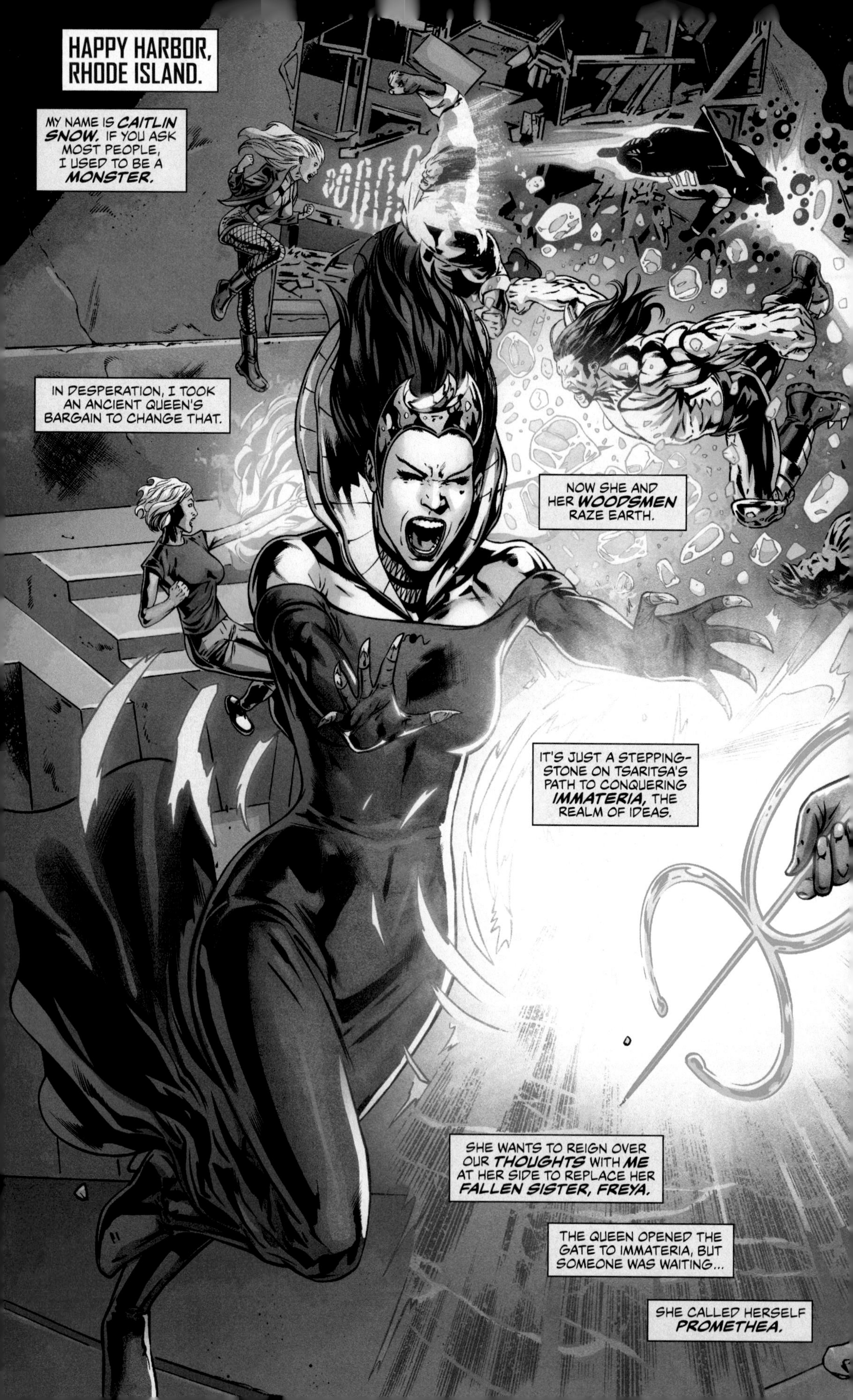
HAPPY HARBOR, RHODE ISLAND.
MY NAME IS CAITLIN SNOW. IF YOU ASK MOST PEOPLE, I USED TO BE A MONSTER.
IN DESPERATION, I TOOK AN ANCIENT QUEEN'S BARGAIN TO CHANGE THAT.
NOW SHE AND HER WOODSMEN RAZE EARTH.
IT'S JUST A STEPPING-STONE ON TSARITSA'S PATH TO CONQUERING IMMATERIA, THE REALM OF IDEAS.
SHE WANTS TO REIGN OVER OUR THOUGHTS WITH ME AT HER SIDE TO REPLACE HER FALLEN SISTER, FREYA.
THE QUEEN OPENED THE GATE TO IMMATERIA, BUT SOMEONE WAS WAITING...
SHE CALLED HERSELF PROMETHEA.

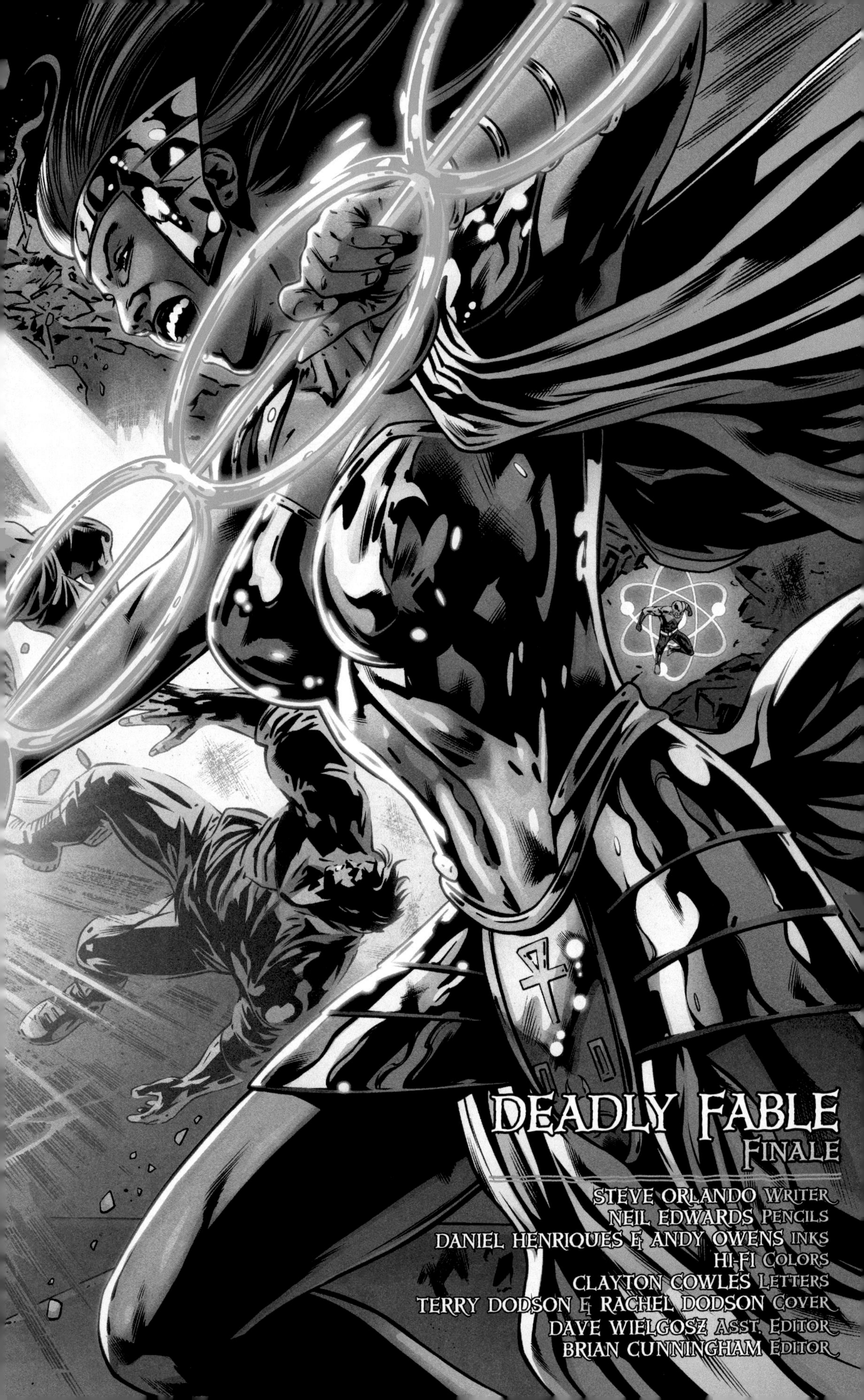
DEADLY FABLE
FINALE
STEVE ORLANDO WRITER
NEIL EDWARDS PENCILS
DANIEL HENRIQUES & ANDY OWENS INKS
HI-FI COLORS
CLAYTON COWLES LETTERS
TERRY DODSON & RACHEL DODSON COVER
DAVE WIELGOSZ ASST. EDITOR
BRIAN CUNNINGHAM EDITOR

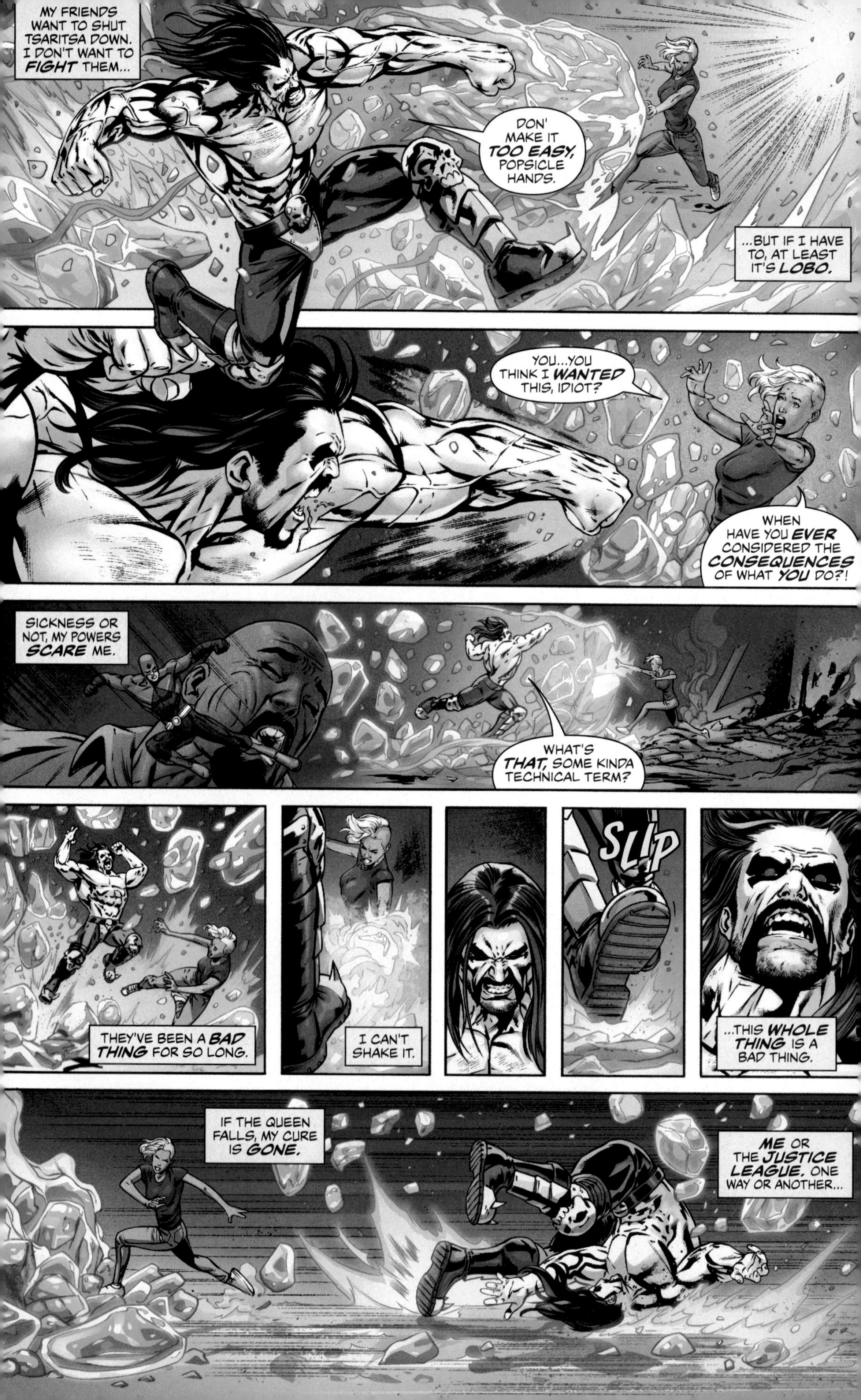
MY FRIENDS WANT TO SHUT TSARITSA DOWN. I DON'T WANT TO FIGHT THEM...
DON' MAKE IT TOO EASY, POPSICLE HANDS.
...BUT IF I HAVE TO, AT LEAST IT'S LOBO.
YOU...YOU THINK I WANTED THIS, IDIOT?
WHEN HAVE YOU EVER CONSIDERED THE CONSEQUENCES OF WHAT YOU DO?!
SICKNESS OR NOT, MY POWERS SCARE ME.
WHAT'S THAT, SOME KINDA TECHNICAL TERM?
THEY'VE BEEN A BAD THING FOR SO LONG.
I CAN'T SHAKE IT.
SLIP
...THIS WHOLE THING IS A BAD THING.
IF THE QUEEN FALLS, MY CURE IS GONE.
ME OR THE JUSTICE LEAGUE. ONE WAY OR ANOTHER...

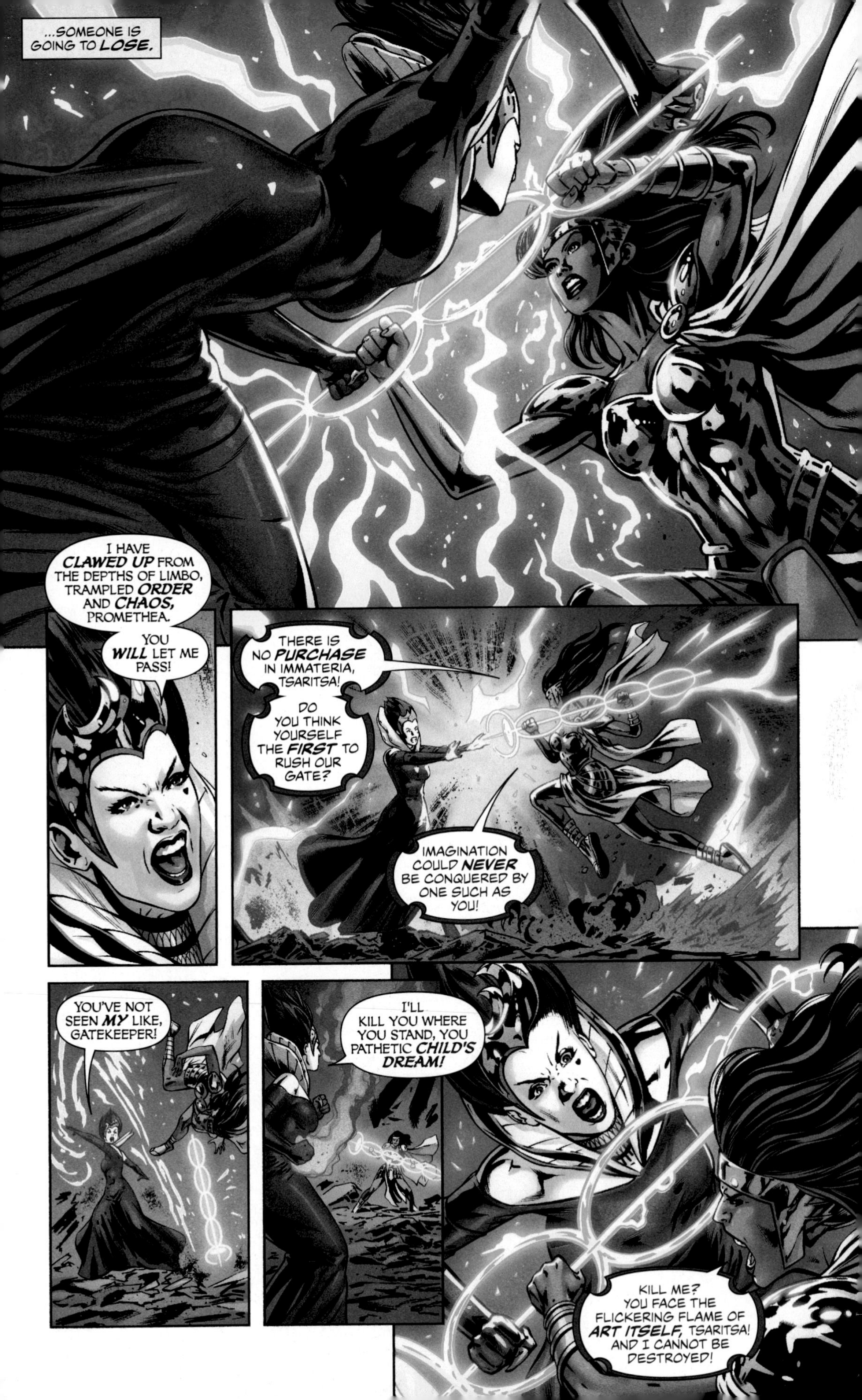
...SOMEONE IS GOING TO LOSE.
I HAVE CLAWED UP FROM THE DEPTHS OF LIMBO, TRAMPLED ORDER AND CHAOS, PROMETHEA.
YOU WILL LET ME PASS!
THERE IS NO PURCHASE IN IMMATERIA, TSARITSA!
DO YOU THINK YOURSELF THE FIRST TO RUSH OUR GATE?
IMAGINATION COULD NEVER BE CONQUERED BY ONE SUCH AS YOU!
YOU'VE NOT SEEN MY LIKE, GATEKEEPER!
I'LL KILL YOU WHERE YOU STAND, YOU PATHETIC CHILD'S DREAM!
KILL ME? YOU FACE THE FLICKERING FLAME OF ART ITSELF, TSARITSA! AND I CANNOT BE DESTROYED!

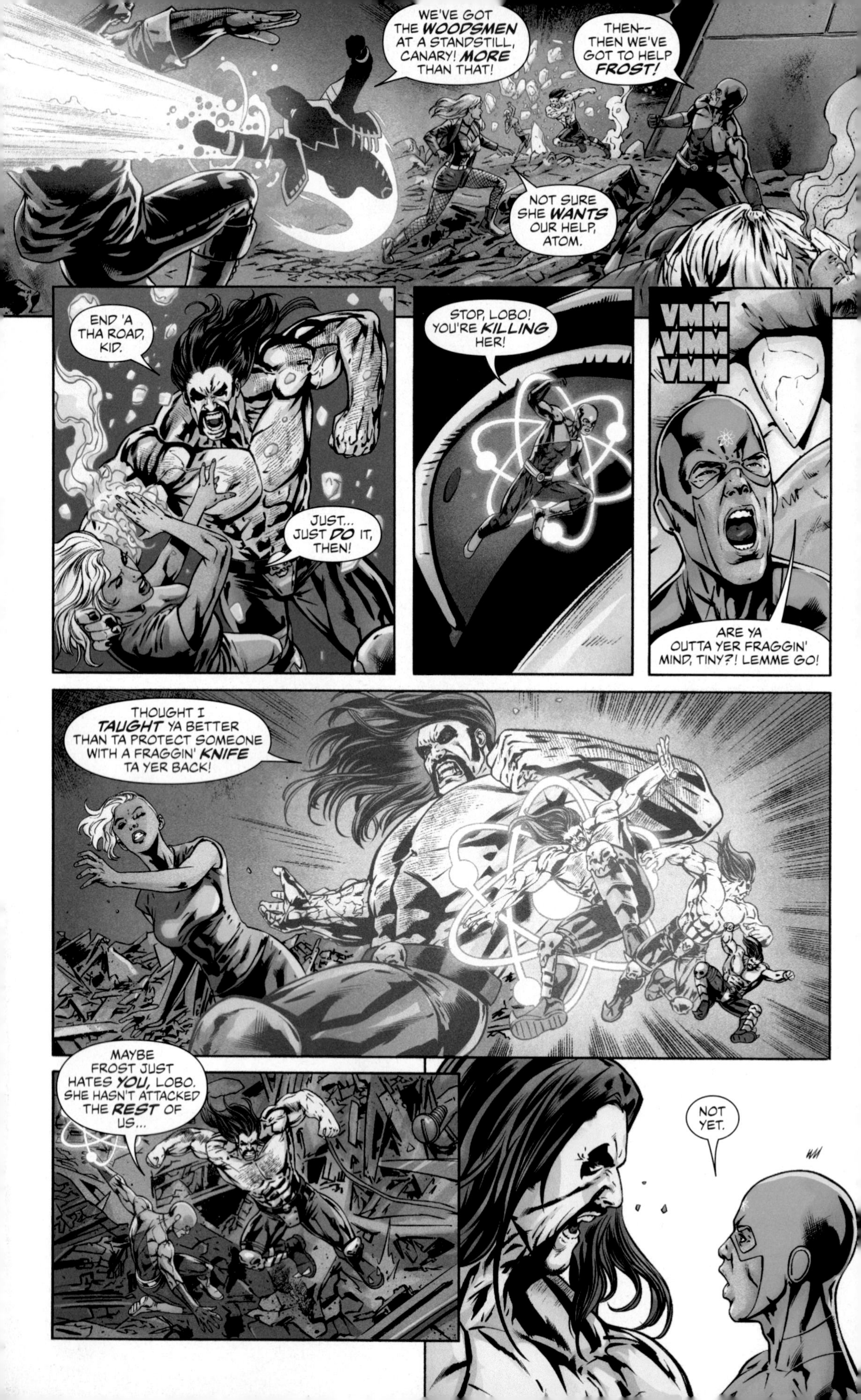
WE'VE GOT THE WOODSMEN AT A STANDSTILL, CANARY! MORE THAN THAT!
THEN-- THEN WE'VE GOT TO HELP FROST!
NOT SURE SHE WANTS OUR HELP, ATOM.
END 'A THA ROAD, KID.
JUST... JUST DO IT, THEN!
STOP, LOBO! YOU'RE KILLING HER!
VMM VMM VMM
ARE YA OUTTA YER FRAGGIN' MIND, TINY?! LEMME GO!
THOUGHT I TAUGHT YA BETTER THAN TA PROTECT SOMEONE WITH A FRAGGIN' KNIFE TA YER BACK!
MAYBE FROST JUST HATES YOU, LOBO. SHE HASN'T ATTACKED THE REST OF US...
NOT YET.

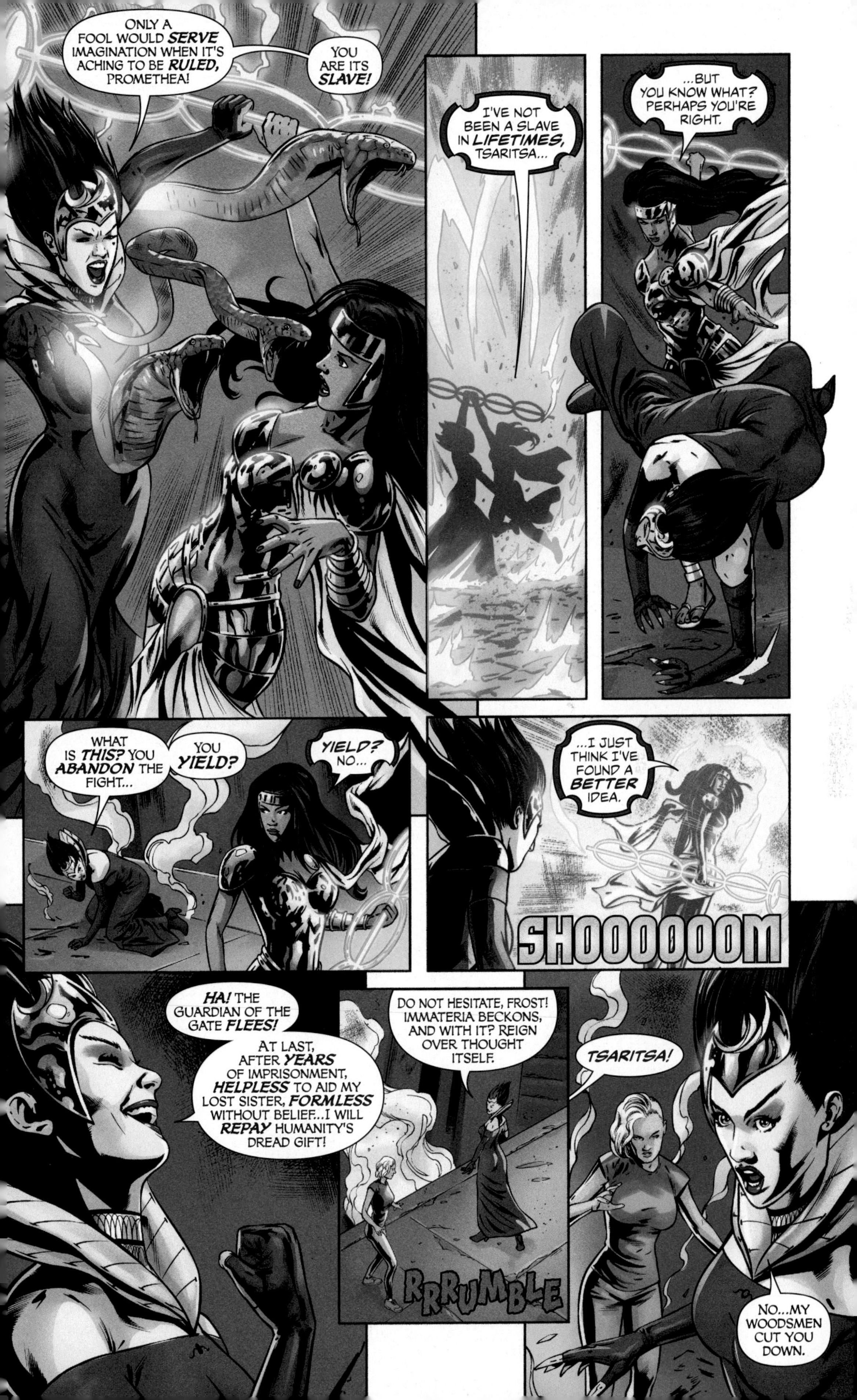
ONLY A FOOL WOULD SERVE IMAGINATION WHEN IT'S ACHING TO BE RULED, PROMETHEA!
YOU ARE ITS SLAVE!
I'VE NOT BEEN A SLAVE IN LIFETIMES, TSARITSA...
...BUT YOU KNOW WHAT? PERHAPS YOU'RE RIGHT.
WHAT IS THIS? YOU ABANDON THE FIGHT...
YOU YIELD?
YIELD? NO...
...I JUST THINK I'VE FOUND A BETTER IDEA.
SHOOOOOOM
HA! THE GUARDIAN OF THE GATE FLEES!
AT LAST, AFTER YEARS OF IMPRISONMENT, HELPLESS TO AID MY LOST SISTER, FORMLESS WITHOUT BELIEF...I WILL REPAY HUMANITY'S DREAD GIFT!
DO NOT HESITATE, FROST! IMMATERIA BECKONS, AND WITH IT? REIGN OVER THOUGHT ITSELF.
RRRUMBLE
TSARITSA!
NO...MY WOODSMEN CUT YOU DOWN.

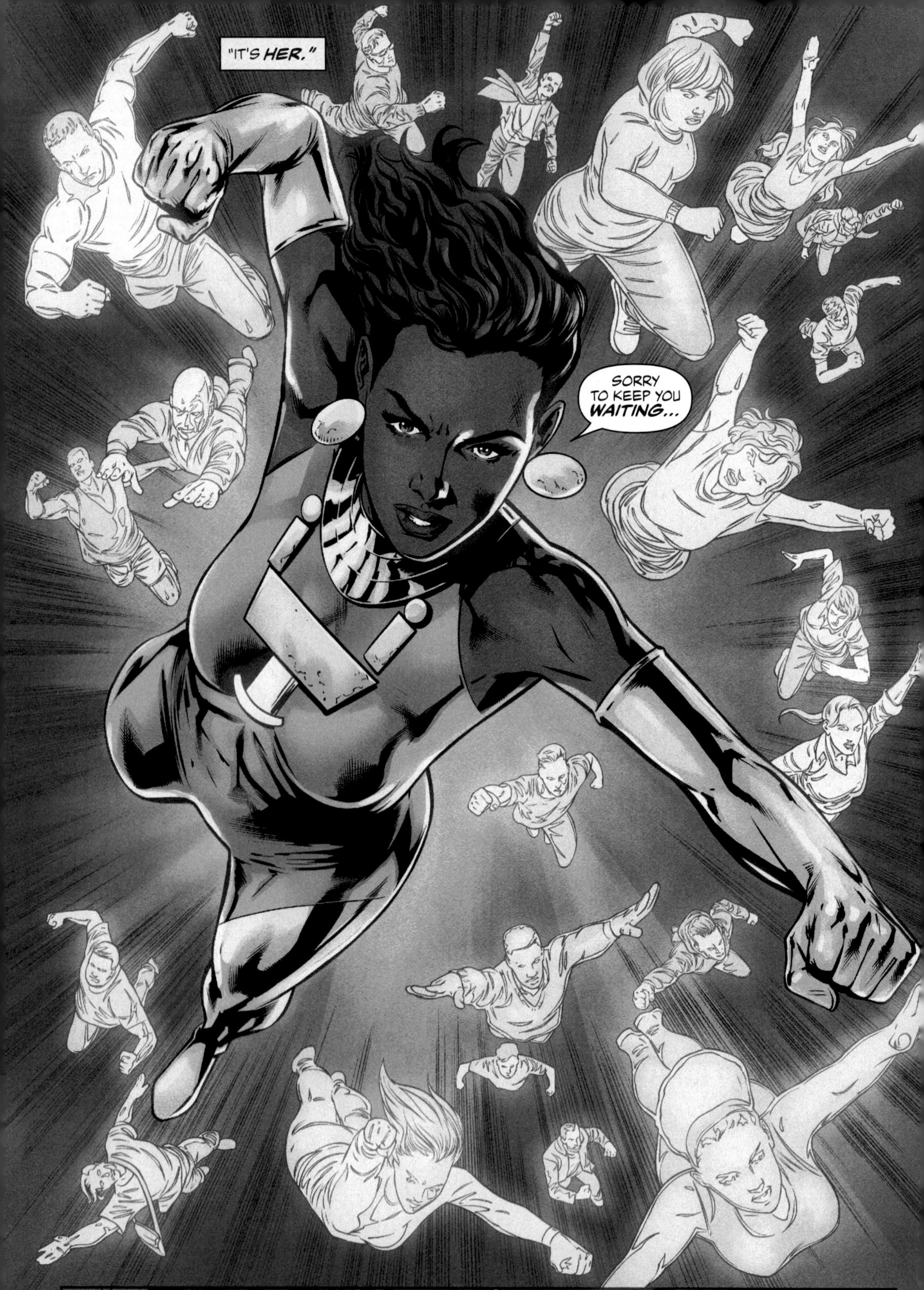
"IT'S HER."
SORRY TO KEEP YOU WAITING...
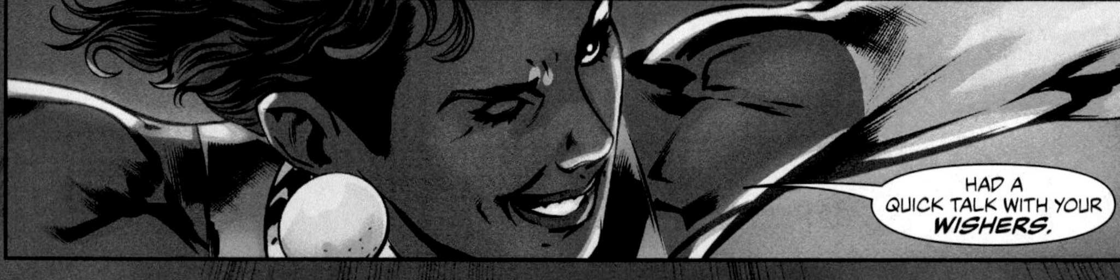
HAD A QUICK TALK WITH YOUR WISHERS.

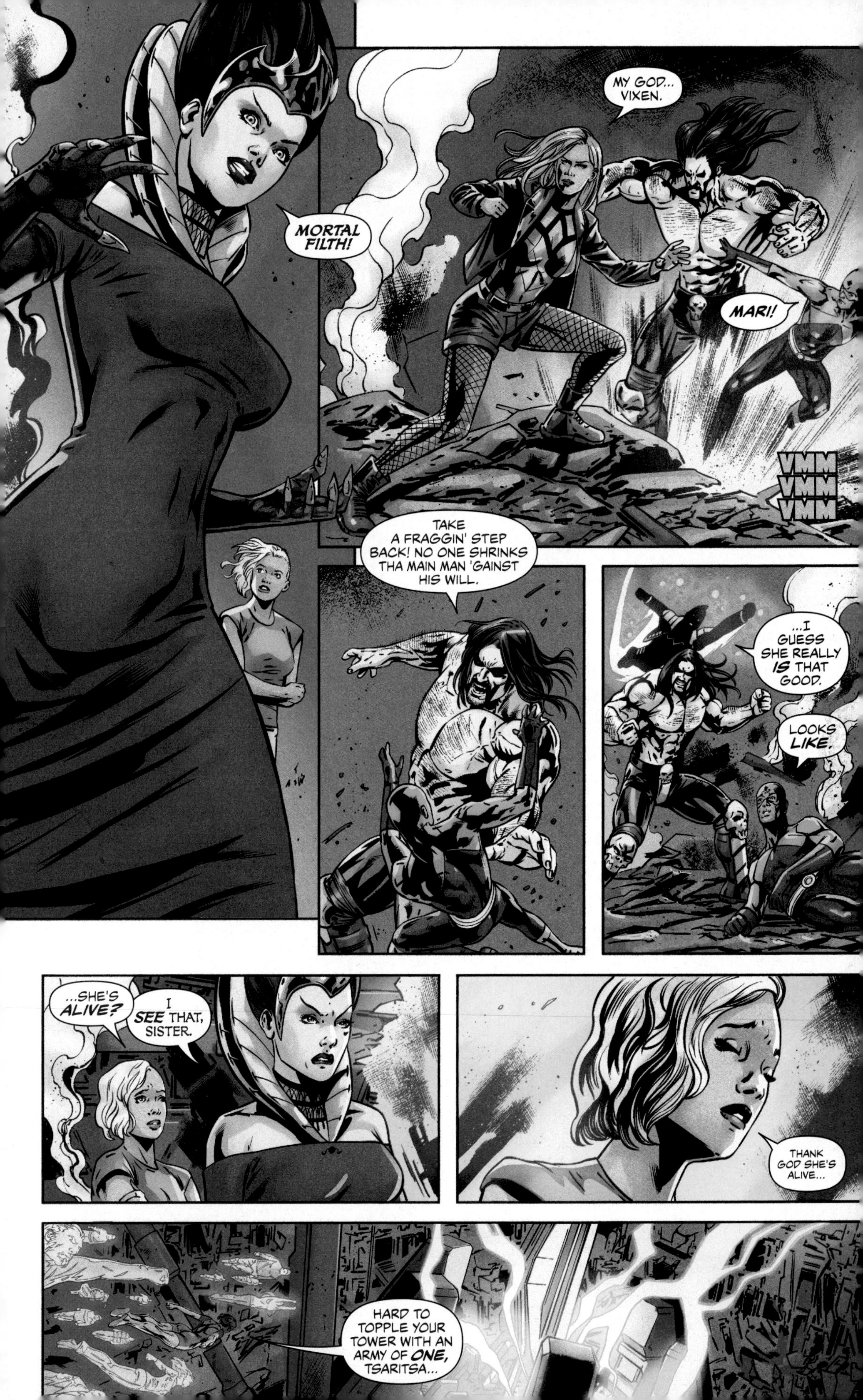
MORTAL FILTH!
MY GOD... VIXEN.
MARI!
VMM VMM VMM
TAKE A FRAGGIN' STEP BACK! NO ONE SHRINKS THA MAIN MAN 'GAINST HIS WILL.
...I GUESS SHE REALLY IS THAT GOOD.
LOOKS LIKE.
...SHE'S ALIVE?
I SEE THAT, SISTER.
THANK GOD SHE'S ALIVE...
HARD TO TOPPLE YOUR TOWER WITH AN ARMY OF ONE, TSARITSA...

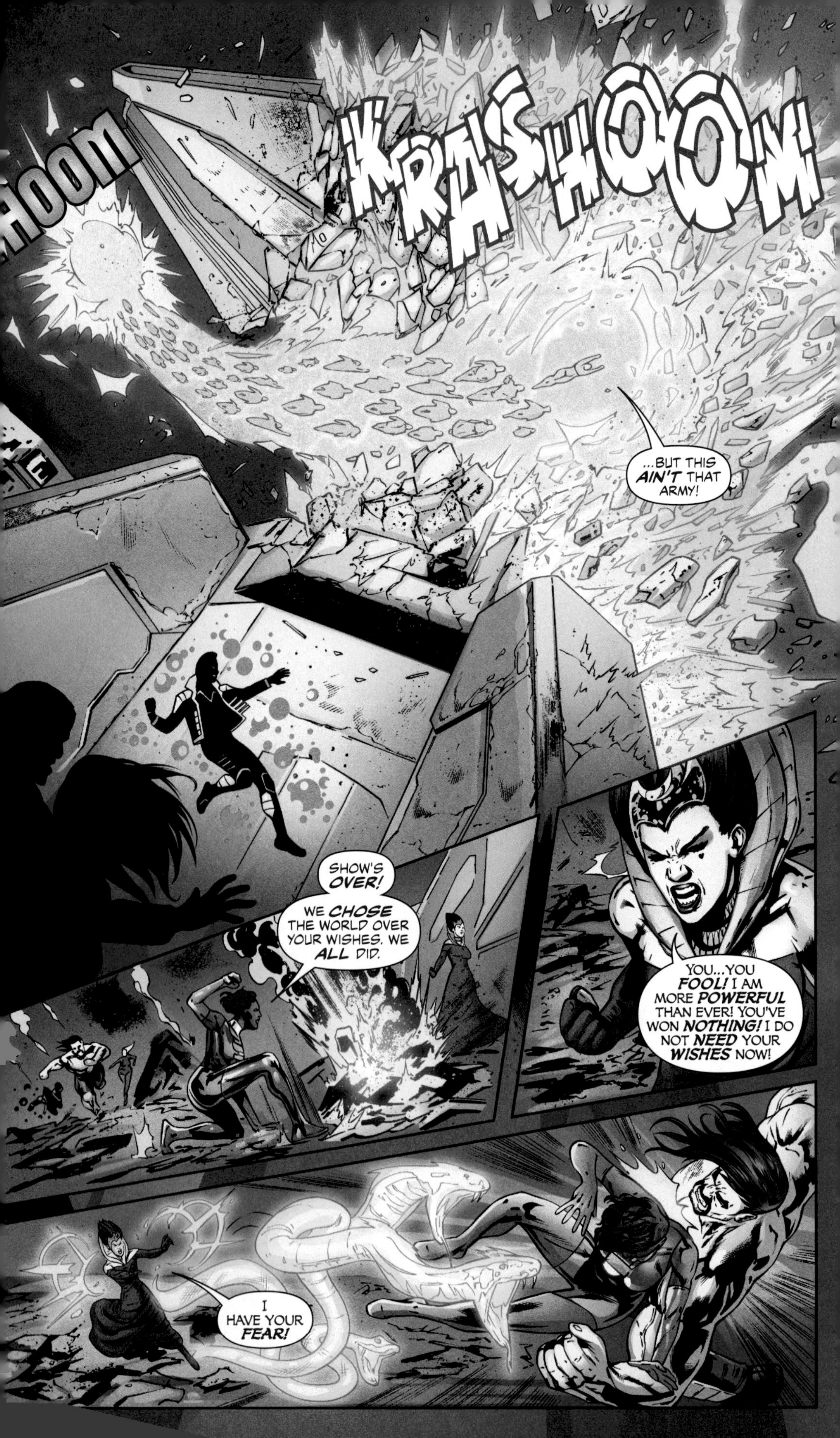
HOOM
KRASHOOOM
...BUT THIS AIN'T THAT ARMY!
SHOW'S OVER!
WE CHOSE THE WORLD OVER YOUR WISHES. WE ALL DID.
YOU...YOU FOOL! I AM MORE POWERFUL THAN EVER! YOU'VE WON NOTHING! I DO NOT NEED YOUR WISHES NOW!
I HAVE YOUR FEAR!

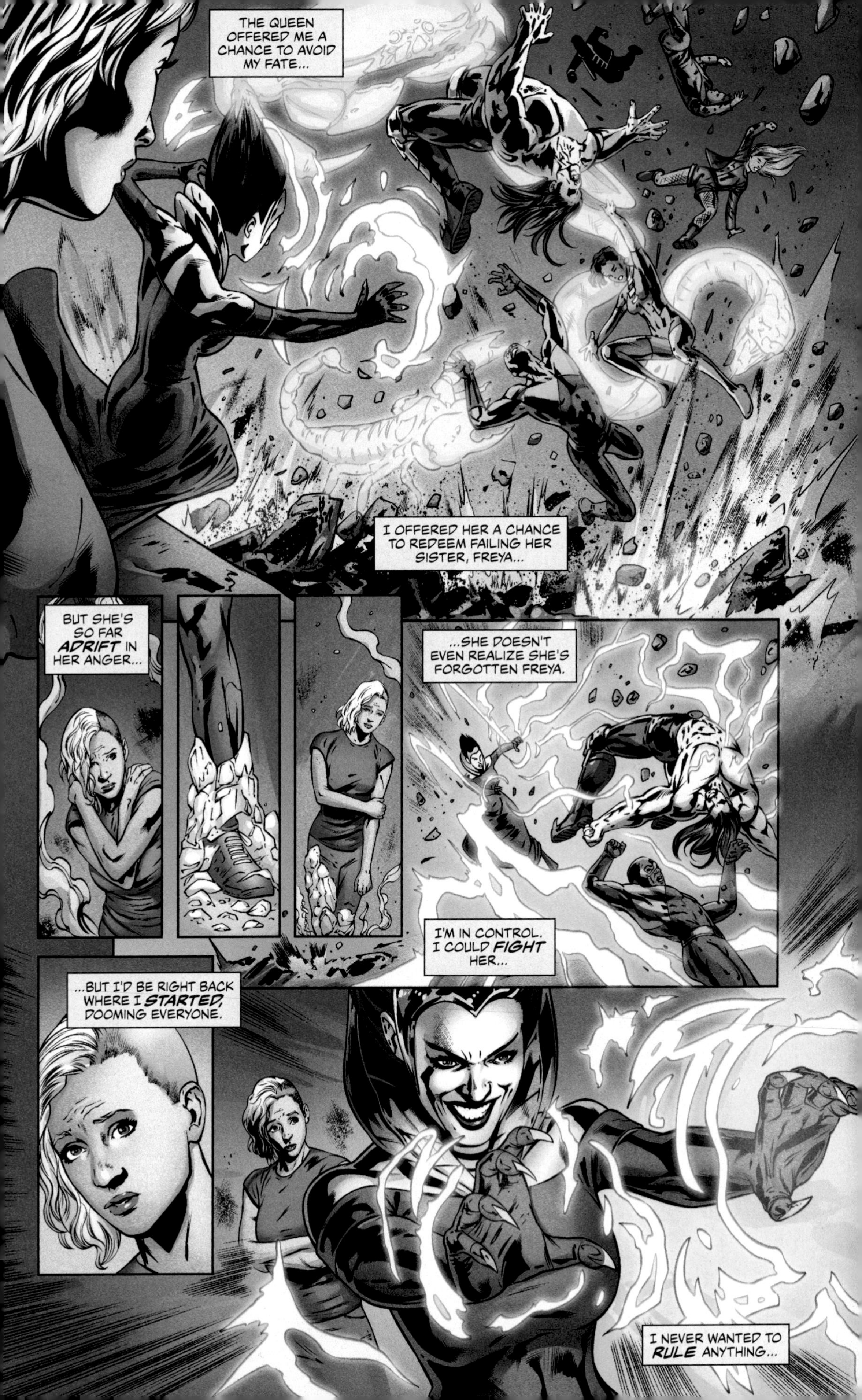
THE QUEEN OFFERED ME A CHANCE TO AVOID MY FATE...
I OFFERED HER A CHANCE TO REDEEM FAILING HER SISTER, FREYA...
BUT SHE'S SO FAR ADRIFT IN HER ANGER...
...SHE DOESN'T EVEN REALIZE SHE'S FORGOTTEN FREYA.
I'M IN CONTROL. I COULD FIGHT HER...
...BUT I'D BE RIGHT BACK WHERE I STARTED, DOOMING EVERYONE.
I NEVER WANTED TO RULE ANYTHING...

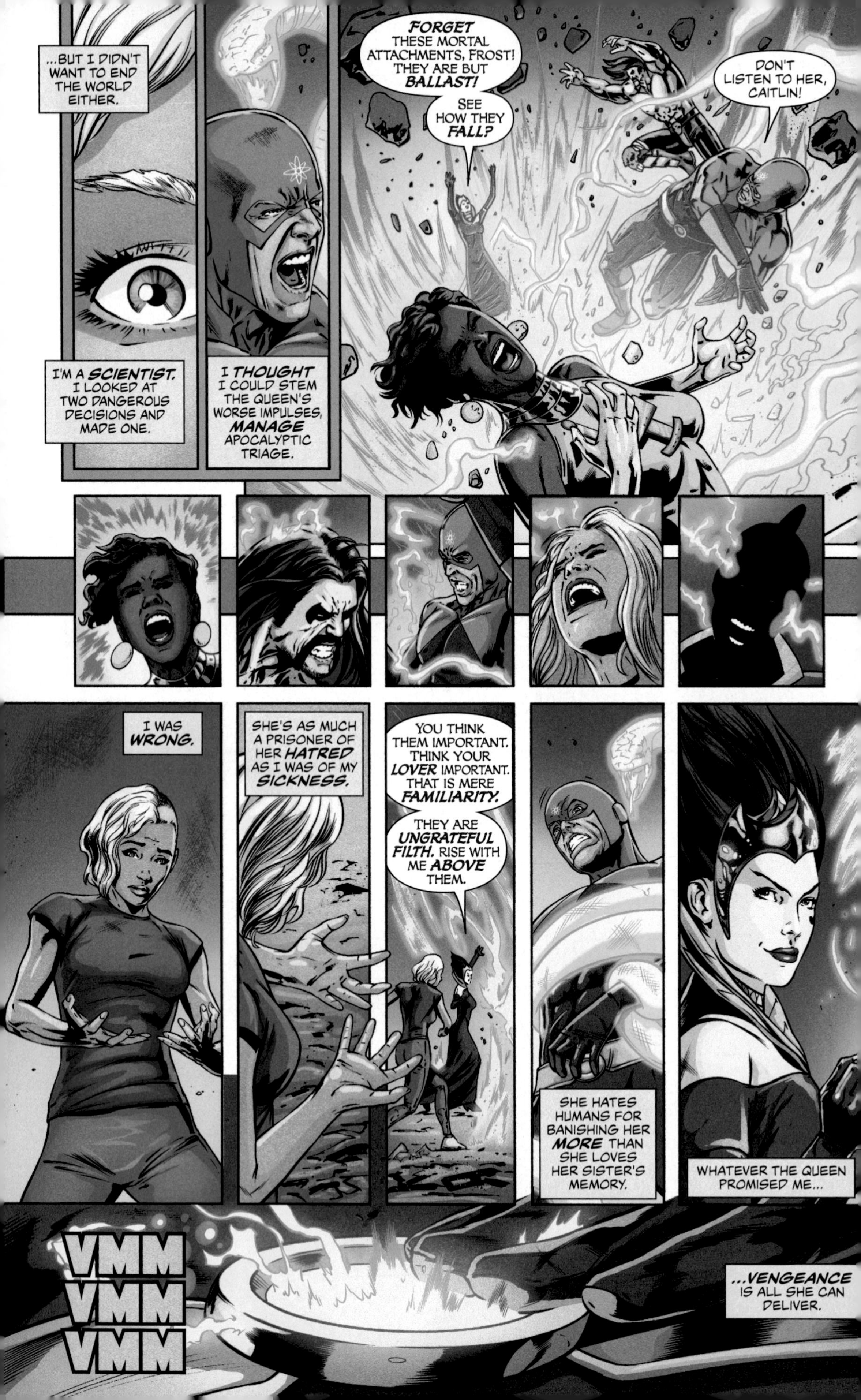
...BUT I DIDN'T WANT TO END THE WORLD EITHER.
I'M A SCIENTIST. I LOOKED AT TWO DANGEROUS DECISIONS AND MADE ONE.
I THOUGHT I COULD STEM THE QUEEN'S WORSE IMPULSES, MANAGE APOCALYPTIC TRIAGE.
FORGET THESE MORTAL ATTACHMENTS, FROST! THEY ARE BUT BALLAST!
SEE HOW THEY FALL?
DON'T LISTEN TO HER, CAITLIN!
I WAS WRONG.
SHE'S AS MUCH A PRISONER OF HER HATRED AS I WAS OF MY SICKNESS.
YOU THINK THEM IMPORTANT. THINK YOUR LOVER IMPORTANT. THAT IS MERE FAMILIARITY.
THEY ARE UNGRATEFUL FILTH. RISE WITH ME ABOVE THEM.
SHE HATES HUMANS FOR BANISHING HER MORE THAN SHE LOVES HER SISTER'S MEMORY.
WHATEVER THE QUEEN PROMISED ME...
VMM VMM VMM
...VENGEANCE IS ALL SHE CAN DELIVER.

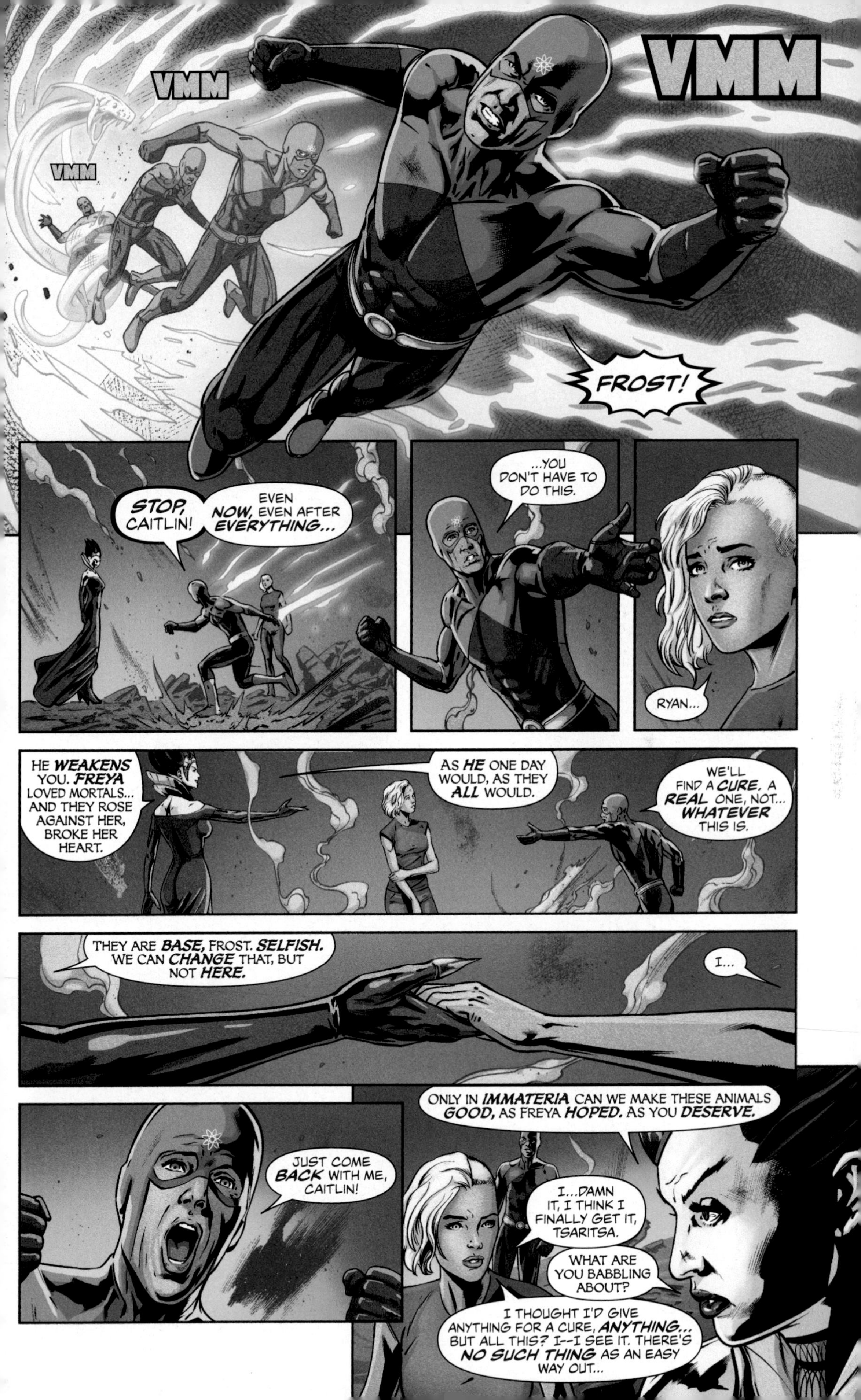
VMM
VMM
VMM
FROST!
STOP, CAITLIN!
EVEN NOW, EVEN AFTER EVERYTHING...
...YOU DON'T HAVE TO DO THIS.
RYAN...
HE WEAKENS YOU. FREYA LOVED MORTALS... AND THEY ROSE AGAINST HER, BROKE HER HEART.
AS HE ONE DAY WOULD, AS THEY ALL WOULD.
WE'LL FIND A CURE. A REAL ONE, NOT... WHATEVER THIS IS.
THEY ARE BASE, FROST. SELFISH. WE CAN CHANGE THAT, BUT NOT HERE.
I...
ONLY IN IMMATERIA CAN WE MAKE THESE ANIMALS GOOD, AS FREYA HOPED. AS YOU DESERVE.
JUST COME BACK WITH ME, CAITLIN!
I...DAMN IT, I THINK I FINALLY GET IT, TSARITSA.
WHAT ARE YOU BABBLING ABOUT?
I THOUGHT I'D GIVE ANYTHING FOR A CURE, ANYTHING... BUT ALL THIS? I--I SEE IT. THERE'S NO SUCH THING AS AN EASY WAY OUT...

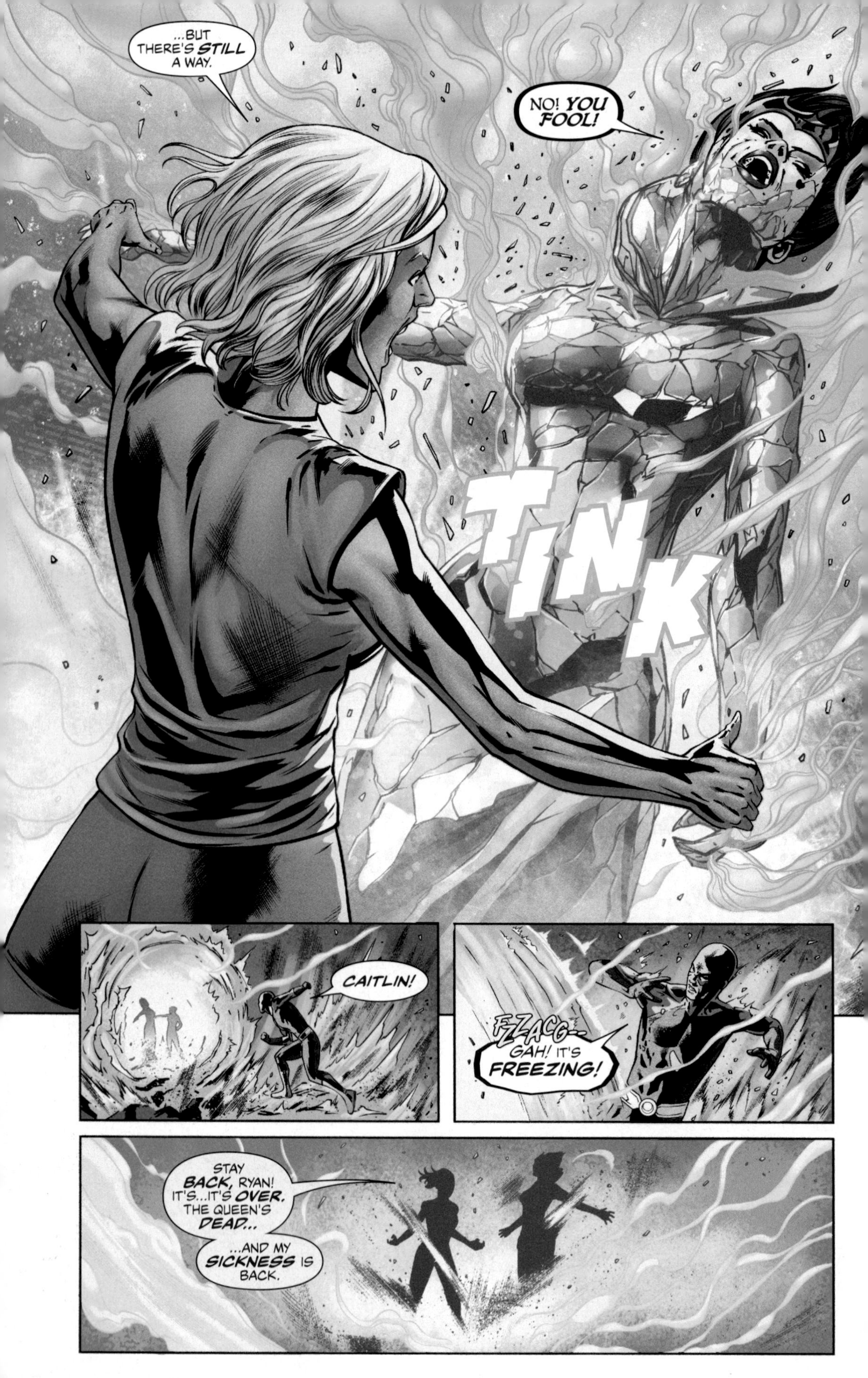
...BUT THERE'S STILL A WAY.
NO! YOU FOOL!
TINK
CAITLIN!
FZZACG--
GAH! IT'S FREEZING!
STAY BACK, RYAN! IT'S...IT'S OVER. THE QUEEN'S DEAD...
...AND MY SICKNESS IS BACK.

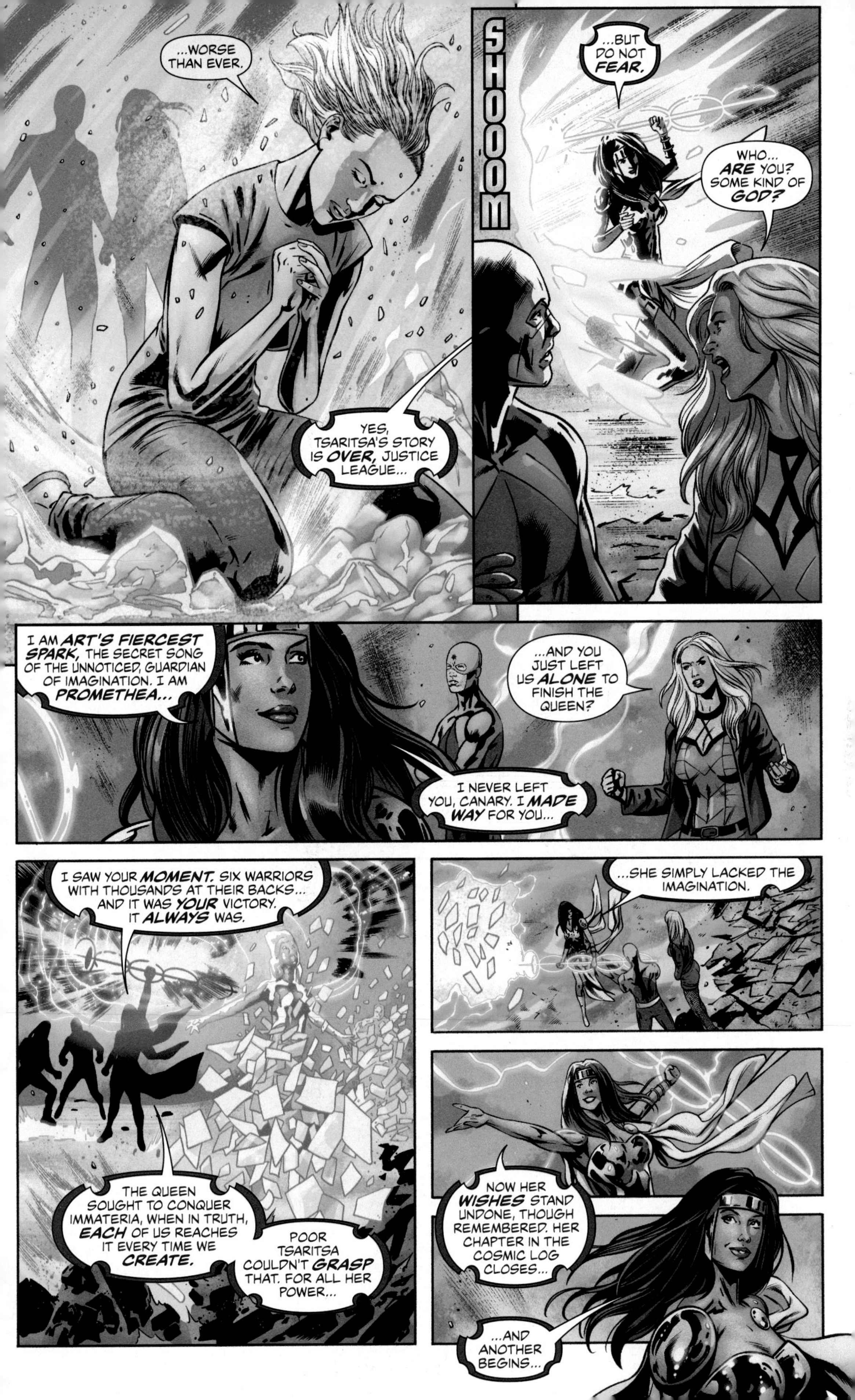
...WORSE THAN EVER.
YES, TSARITSA'S STORY IS OVER, JUSTICE LEAGUE...
SHOOOM
...BUT DO NOT FEAR.
WHO... ARE YOU? SOME KIND OF GOD?
I AM ART'S FIERCEST SPARK, THE SECRET SONG OF THE UNNOTICED, GUARDIAN OF IMAGINATION. I AM PROMETHEA...
...AND YOU JUST LEFT US ALONE TO FINISH THE QUEEN?
I NEVER LEFT YOU, CANARY. I MADE WAY FOR YOU...
I SAW YOUR MOMENT. SIX WARRIORS WITH THOUSANDS AT THEIR BACKS... AND IT WAS YOUR VICTORY. IT ALWAYS WAS.
THE QUEEN SOUGHT TO CONQUER IMMATERIA, WHEN IN TRUTH, EACH OF US REACHES IT EVERY TIME WE CREATE.
POOR TSARITSA COULDN'T GRASP THAT. FOR ALL HER POWER...
...SHE SIMPLY LACKED THE IMAGINATION.
NOW HER WISHES STAND UNDONE, THOUGH REMEMBERED. HER CHAPTER IN THE COSMIC LOG CLOSES...
...AND ANOTHER BEGINS...

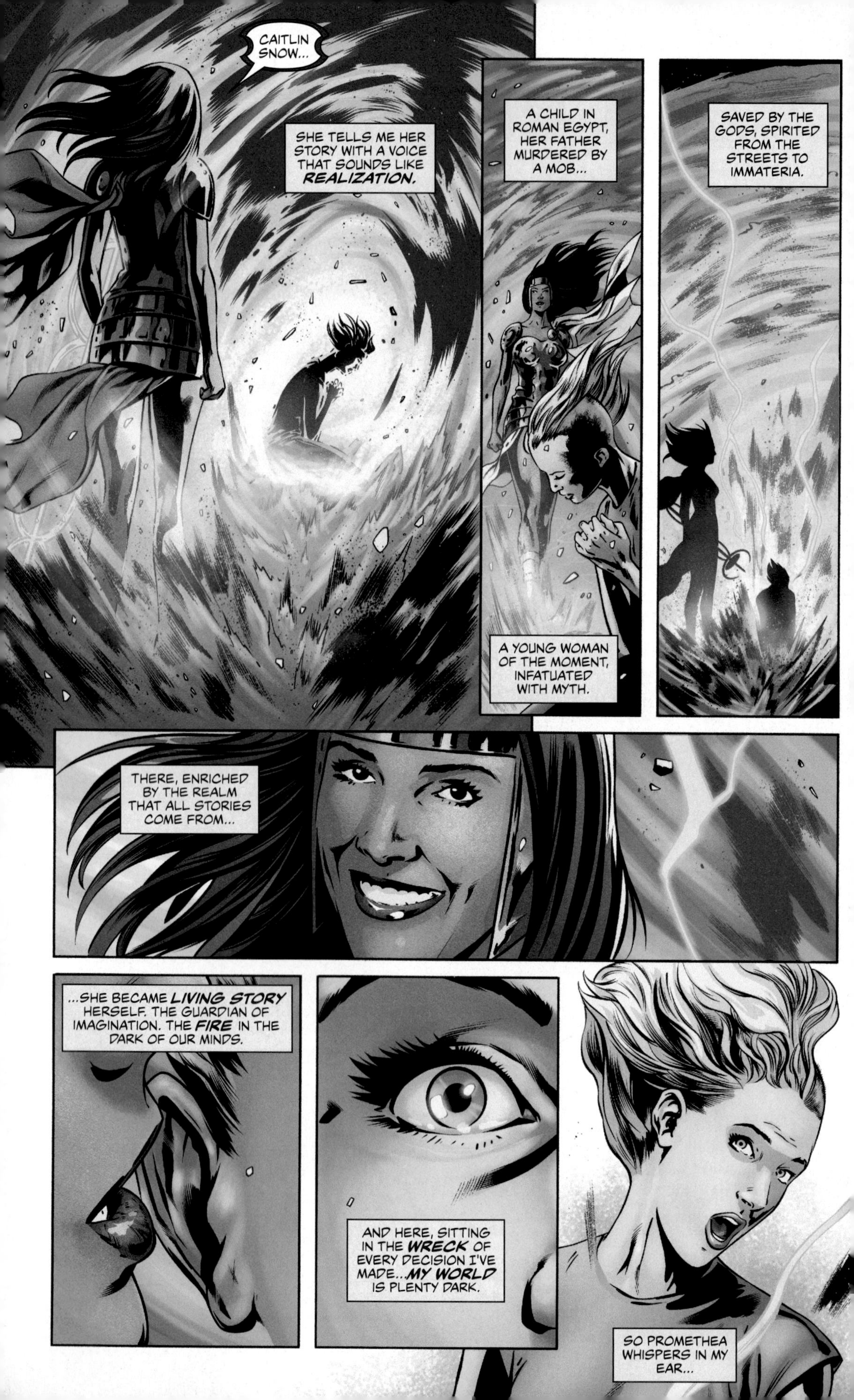
CAITLIN SNOW...
SHE TELLS ME HER STORY WITH A VOICE THAT SOUNDS LIKE REALIZATION.
A CHILD IN ROMAN EGYPT, HER FATHER MURDERED BY A MOB...
A YOUNG WOMAN OF THE MOMENT, INFATUATED WITH MYTH.
SAVED BY THE GODS, SPIRITED FROM THE STREETS TO IMMATERIA.
THERE, ENRICHED BY THE REALM THAT ALL STORIES COME FROM...
...SHE BECAME LIVING STORY HERSELF. THE GUARDIAN OF IMAGINATION. THE FIRE IN THE DARK OF OUR MINDS.
AND HERE, SITTING IN THE WRECK OF EVERY DECISION I'VE MADE...MY WORLD IS PLENTY DARK.
SO PROMETHEA WHISPERS IN MY EAR...

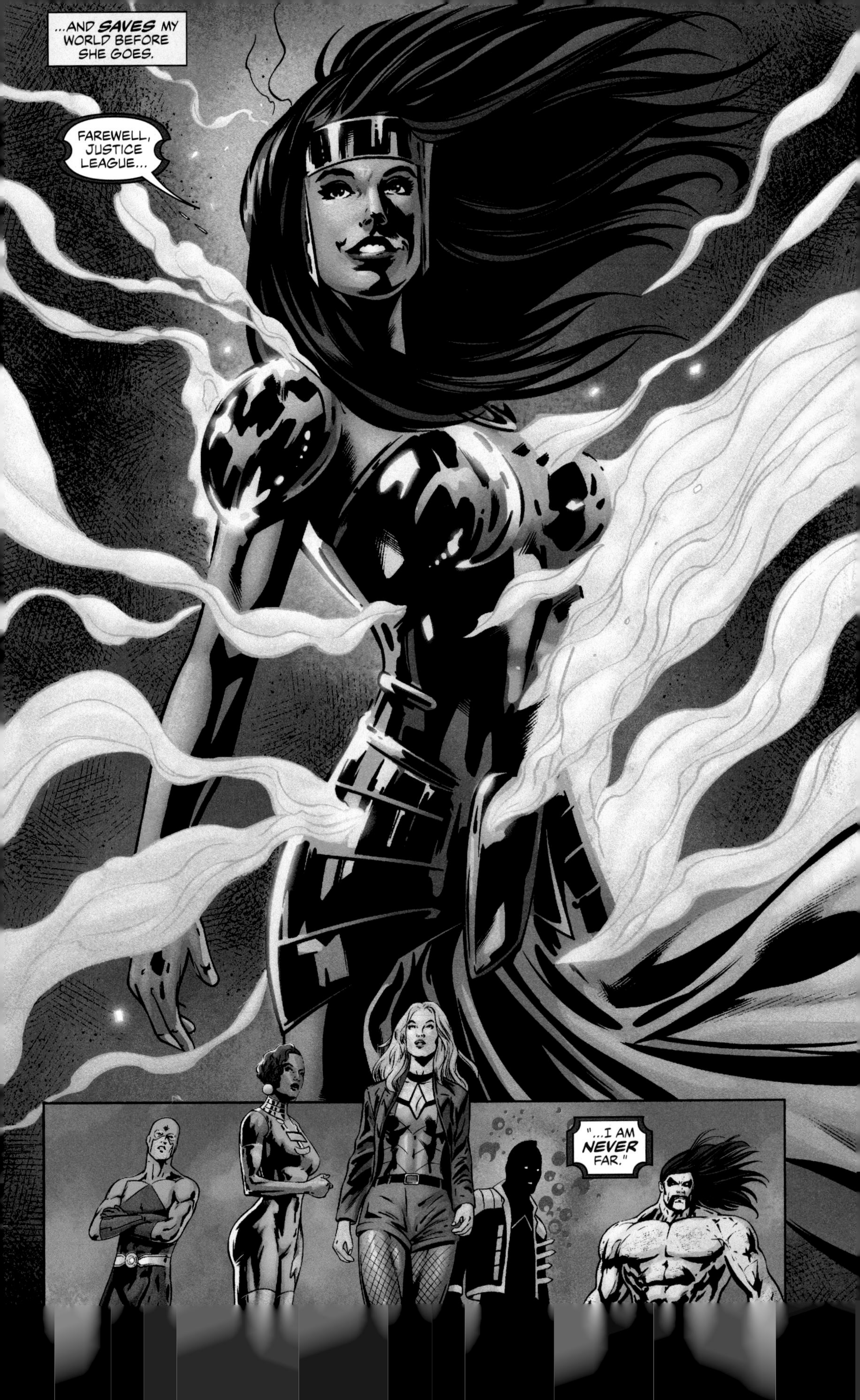
...AND SAVES MY WORLD BEFORE SHE GOES.
FAREWELL, JUSTICE LEAGUE...
"...I AM NEVER FAR."

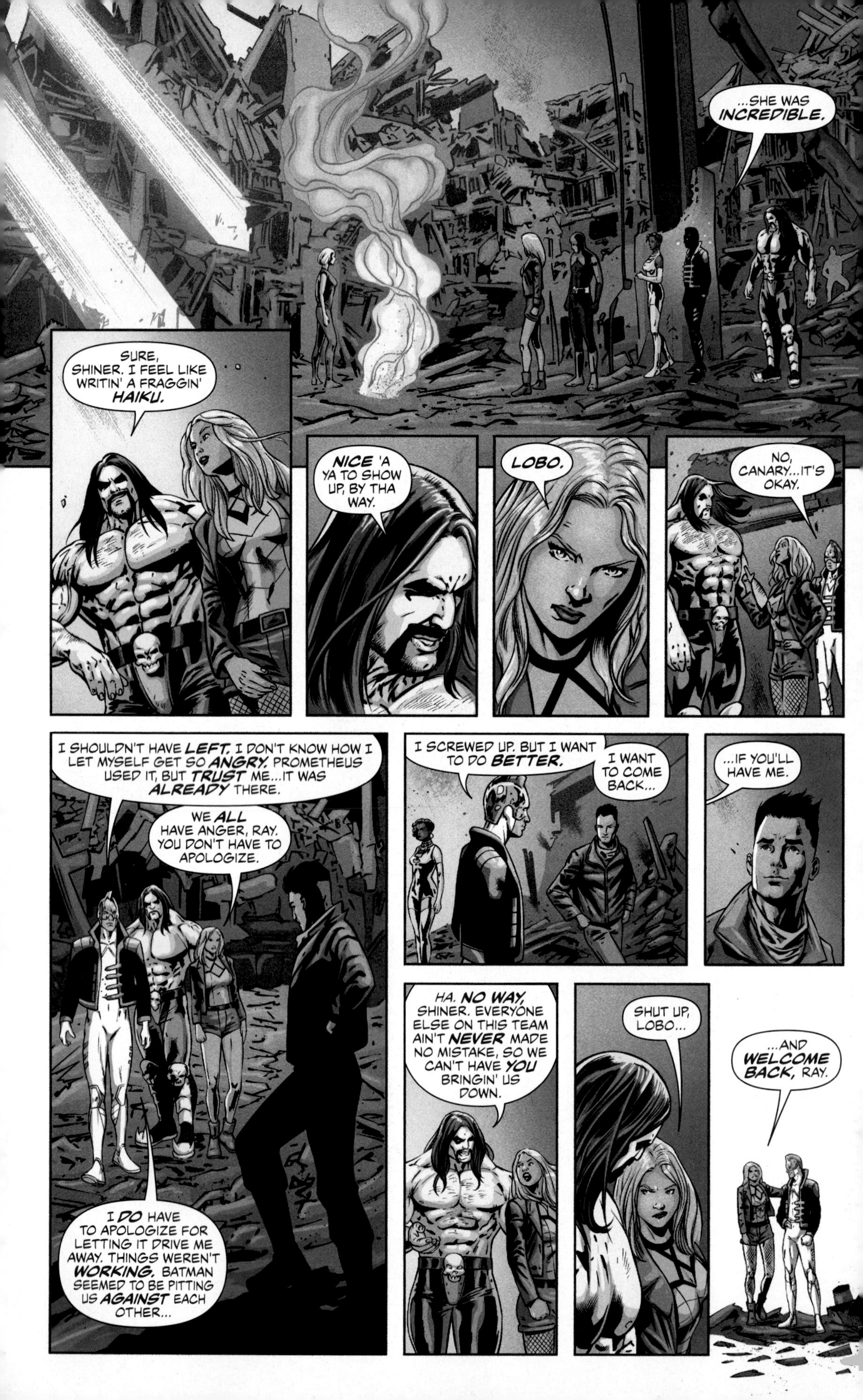
...SHE WAS INCREDIBLE.
SURE, SHINER. I FEEL LIKE WRITIN' A FRAGGIN' HAIKU.
NICE 'A YA TO SHOW UP, BY THA WAY.
LOBO.
NO, CANARY...IT'S OKAY.
I SHOULDN'T HAVE LEFT. I DON'T KNOW HOW I LET MYSELF GET SO ANGRY. PROMETHEUS USED IT, BUT TRUST ME...IT WAS ALREADY THERE.
WE ALL HAVE ANGER, RAY. YOU DON'T HAVE TO APOLOGIZE.
I DO HAVE TO APOLOGIZE FOR LETTING IT DRIVE ME AWAY. THINGS WEREN'T WORKING. BATMAN SEEMED TO BE PITTING US AGAINST EACH OTHER...
I SCREWED UP. BUT I WANT TO DO BETTER.
I WANT TO COME BACK...
...IF YOU'LL HAVE ME.
HA. NO WAY, SHINER. EVERYONE ELSE ON THIS TEAM AIN'T NEVER MADE NO MISTAKE, SO WE CAN'T HAVE YOU BRINGIN' US DOWN.
SHUT UP, LOBO...
...AND WELCOME BACK, RAY.

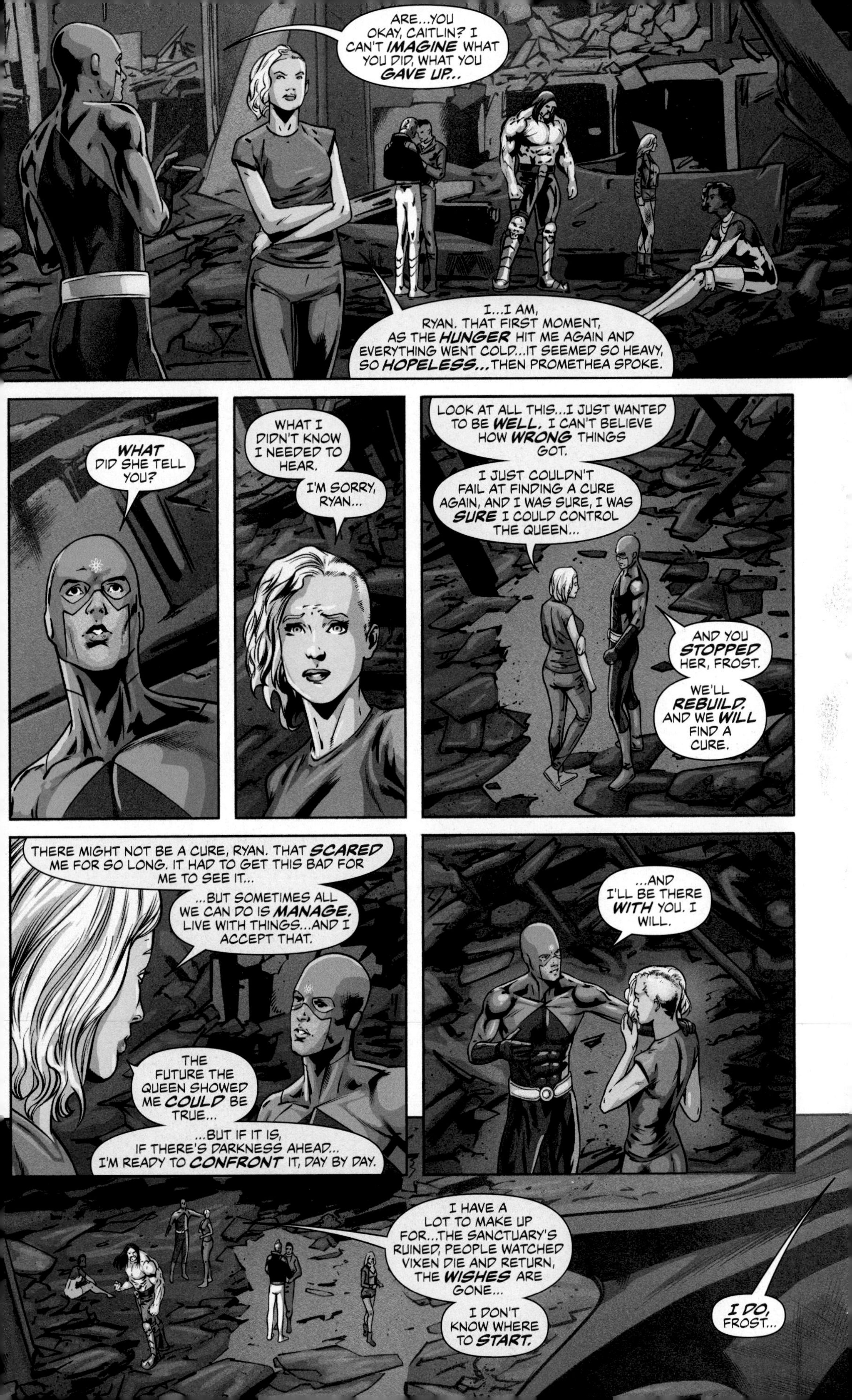
ARE...YOU OKAY, CAITLIN? I CAN'T IMAGINE WHAT YOU DID, WHAT YOU GAVE UP...
I...I AM, RYAN. THAT FIRST MOMENT, AS THE HUNGER HIT ME AGAIN AND EVERYTHING WENT COLD...IT SEEMED SO HEAVY, SO HOPELESS...THEN PROMETHEA SPOKE.
WHAT DID SHE TELL YOU?
WHAT I DIDN'T KNOW I NEEDED TO HEAR.
I'M SORRY, RYAN...
LOOK AT ALL THIS...I JUST WANTED TO BE WELL. I CAN'T BELIEVE HOW WRONG THINGS GOT.
I JUST COULDN'T FAIL AT FINDING A CURE AGAIN, AND I WAS SURE, I WAS SURE I COULD CONTROL THE QUEEN...
AND YOU STOPPED HER, FROST.
WE'LL REBUILD, AND WE WILL FIND A CURE.
THERE MIGHT NOT BE A CURE, RYAN. THAT SCARED ME FOR SO LONG. IT HAD TO GET THIS BAD FOR ME TO SEE IT...
...BUT SOMETIMES ALL WE CAN DO IS MANAGE. LIVE WITH THINGS...AND I ACCEPT THAT.
THE FUTURE THE QUEEN SHOWED ME COULD BE TRUE...
...BUT IF IT IS, IF THERE'S DARKNESS AHEAD... I'M READY TO CONFRONT IT, DAY BY DAY.
...AND I'LL BE THERE WITH YOU. I WILL.
I HAVE A LOT TO MAKE UP FOR...THE SANCTUARY'S RUINED, PEOPLE WATCHED VIXEN DIE AND RETURN, THE WISHES ARE GONE...
I DON'T KNOW WHERE TO START.
I DO, FROST...

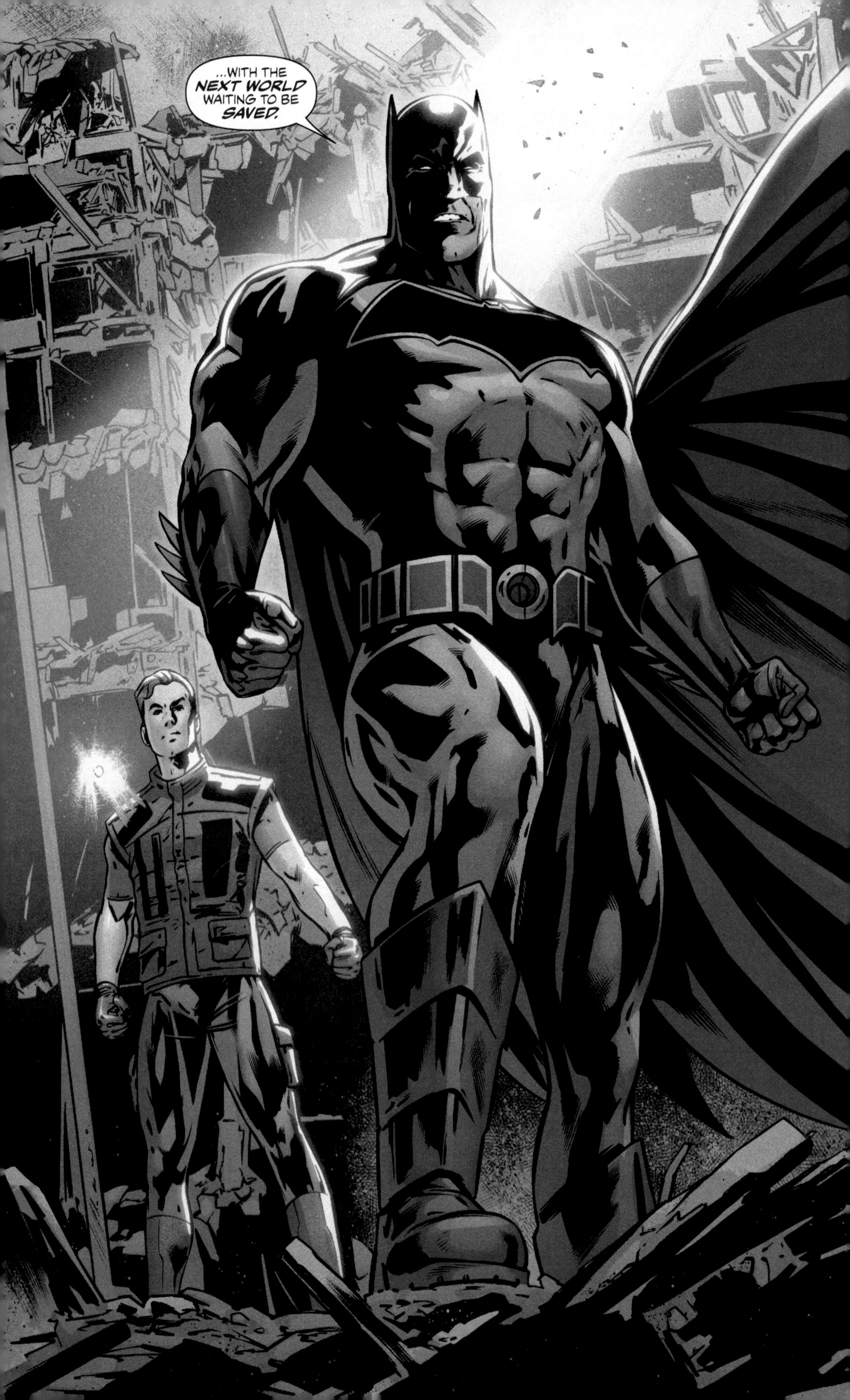
...WITH THE NEXT WORLD WAITING TO BE SAVED.

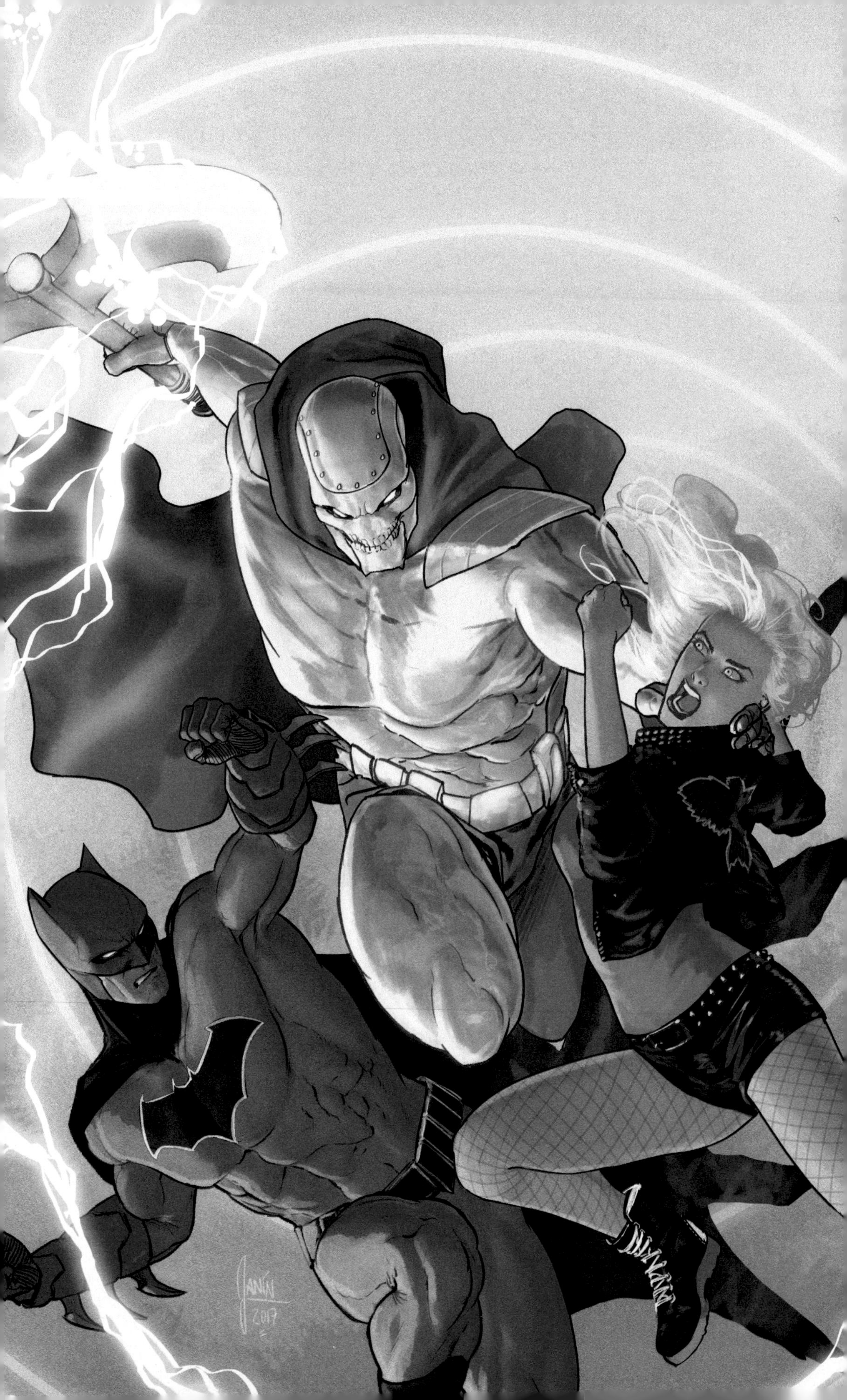

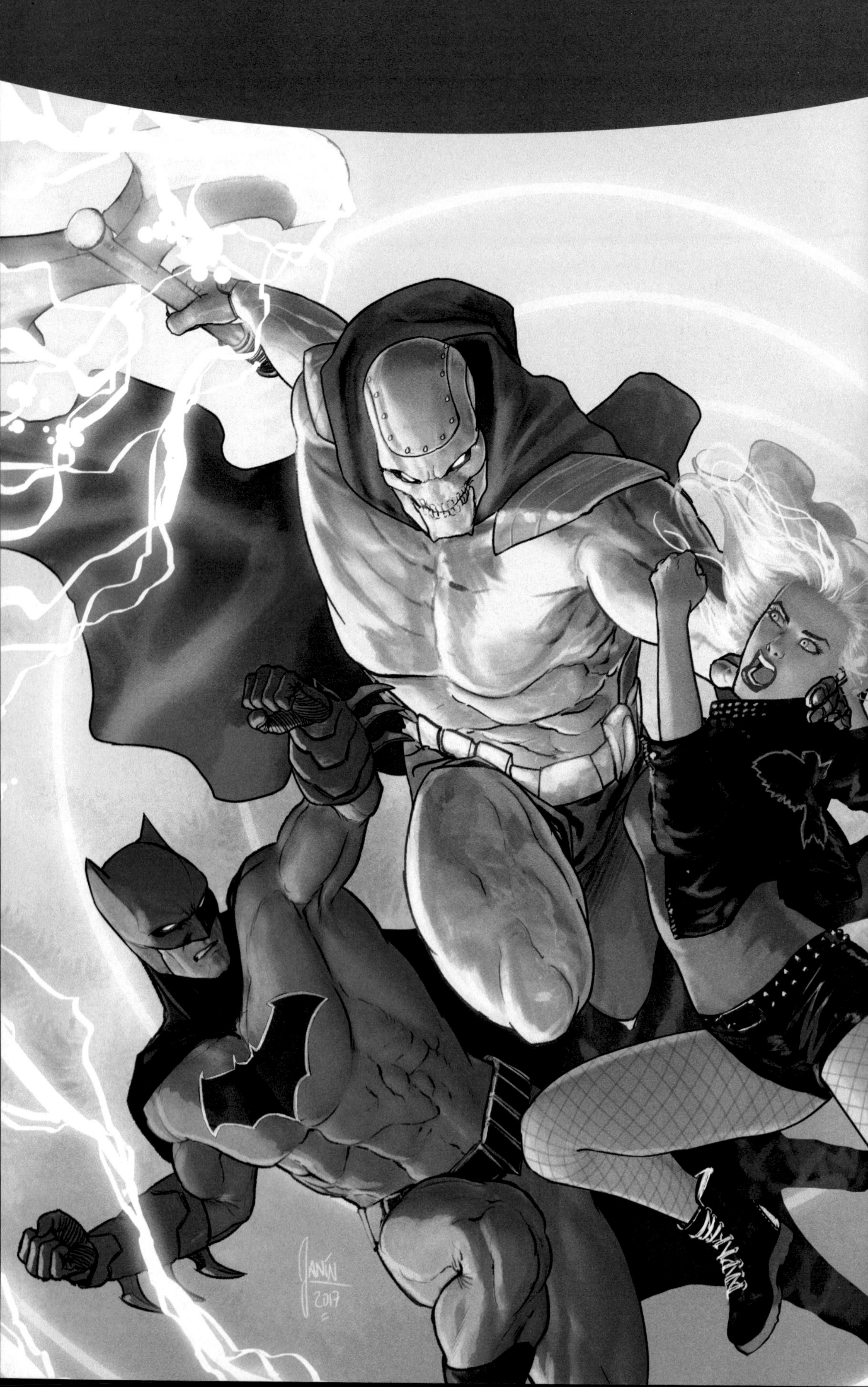

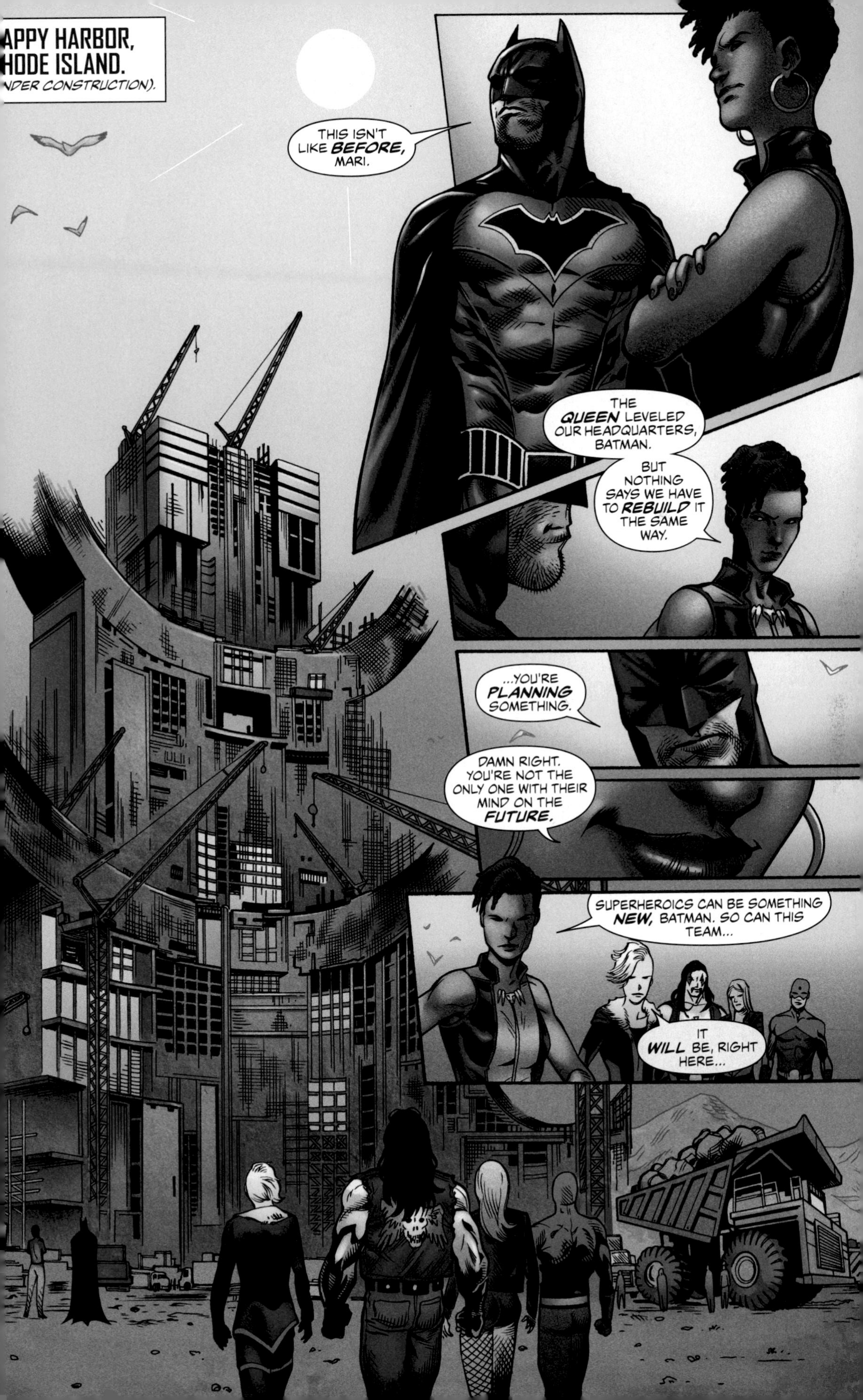
APPY HARBOR,
HODE ISLAND.
NDER CONSTRUCTION).
THIS ISN'T LIKE BEFORE, MARI.
THE QUEEN LEVELED OUR HEADQUARTERS, BATMAN.
BUT NOTHING SAYS WE HAVE TO REBUILD IT THE SAME WAY.
...YOU'RE PLANNING SOMETHING.
DAMN RIGHT. YOU'RE NOT THE ONLY ONE WITH THEIR MIND ON THE FUTURE.
SUPERHEROICS CAN BE SOMETHING NEW, BATMAN. SO CAN THIS TEAM...
IT WILL BE, RIGHT HERE...

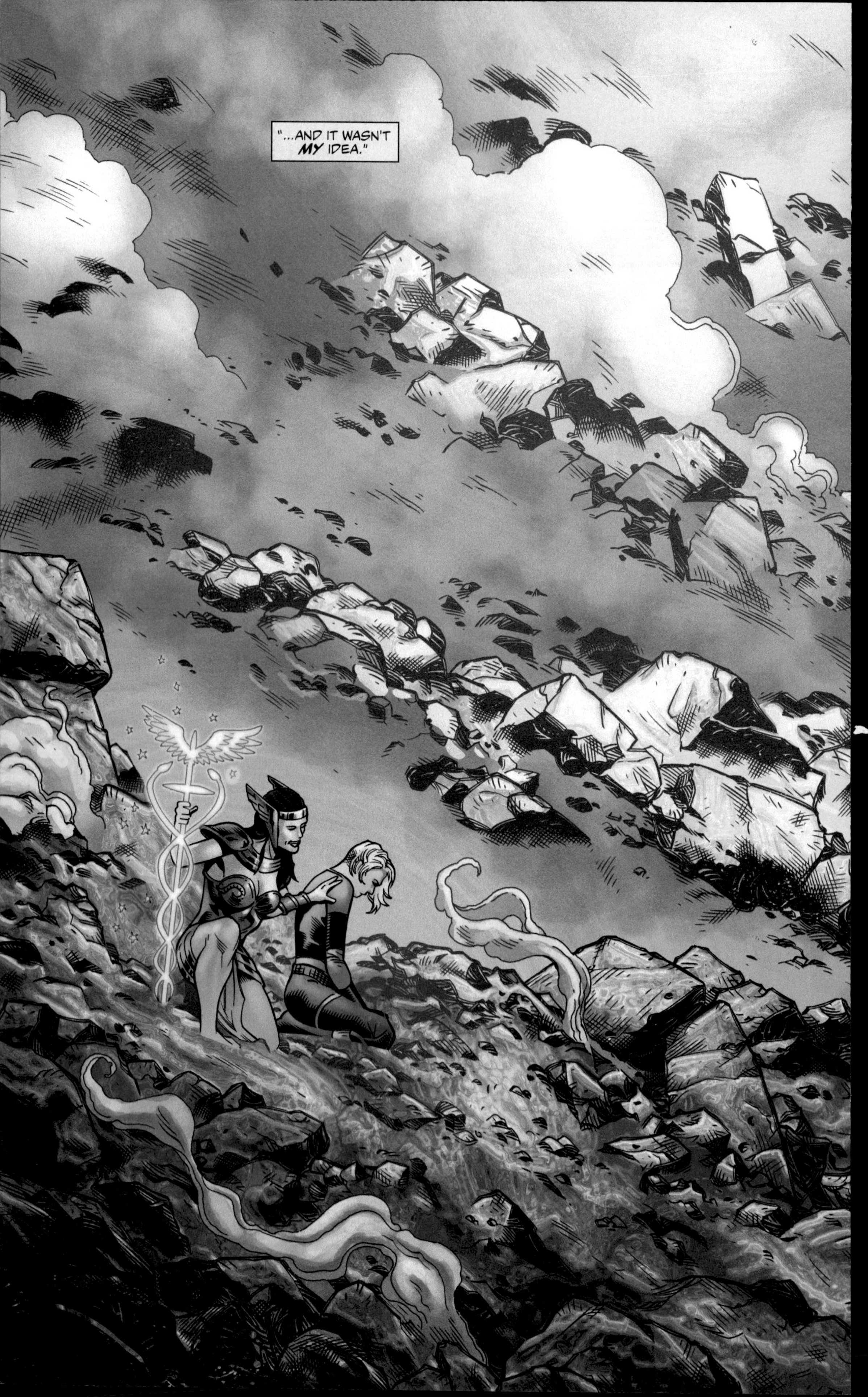
"...AND IT WASN'T MY IDEA."

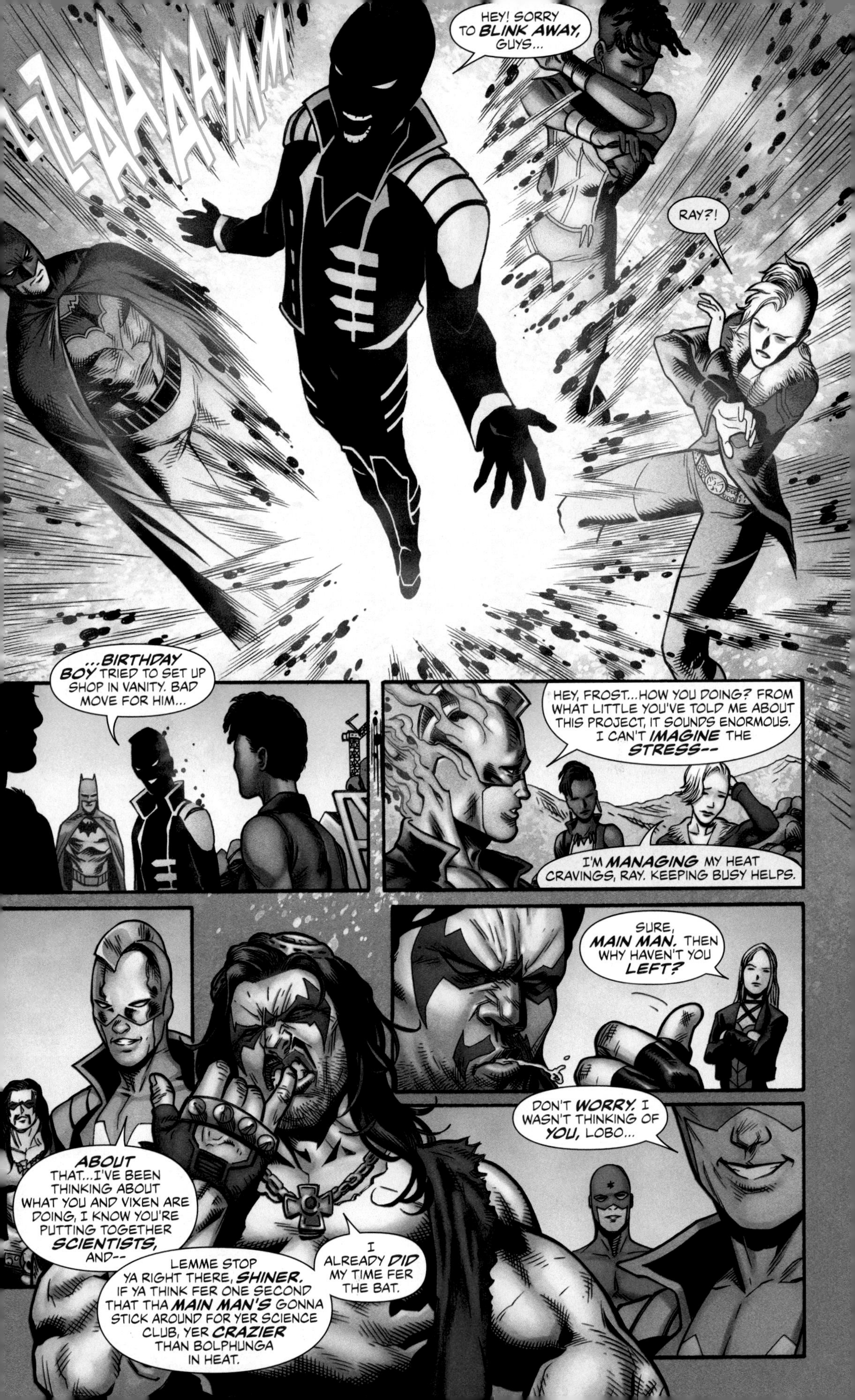
ZZAAAAMM
HEY! SORRY TO BLINK AWAY, GUYS...
RAY?!
...BIRTHDAY BOY TRIED TO SET UP SHOP IN VANITY. BAD MOVE FOR HIM...
HEY, FROST...HOW YOU DOING? FROM WHAT LITTLE YOU'VE TOLD ME ABOUT THIS PROJECT, IT SOUNDS ENORMOUS. I CAN'T IMAGINE THE STRESS--
I'M MANAGING MY HEAT CRAVINGS, RAY. KEEPING BUSY HELPS.
ABOUT THAT...I'VE BEEN THINKING ABOUT WHAT YOU AND VIXEN ARE DOING. I KNOW YOU'RE PUTTING TOGETHER SCIENTISTS, AND--
LEMME STOP YA RIGHT THERE, SHINER. IF YA THINK FER ONE SECOND THAT THA MAIN MAN'S GONNA STICK AROUND FOR YER SCIENCE CLUB, YER CRAZIER THAN BOLPHUNGA IN HEAT.
I ALREADY DID MY TIME FER THE BAT.
SURE, MAIN MAN. THEN WHY HAVEN'T YOU LEFT?
DON'T WORRY. I WASN'T THINKING OF YOU, LOBO...

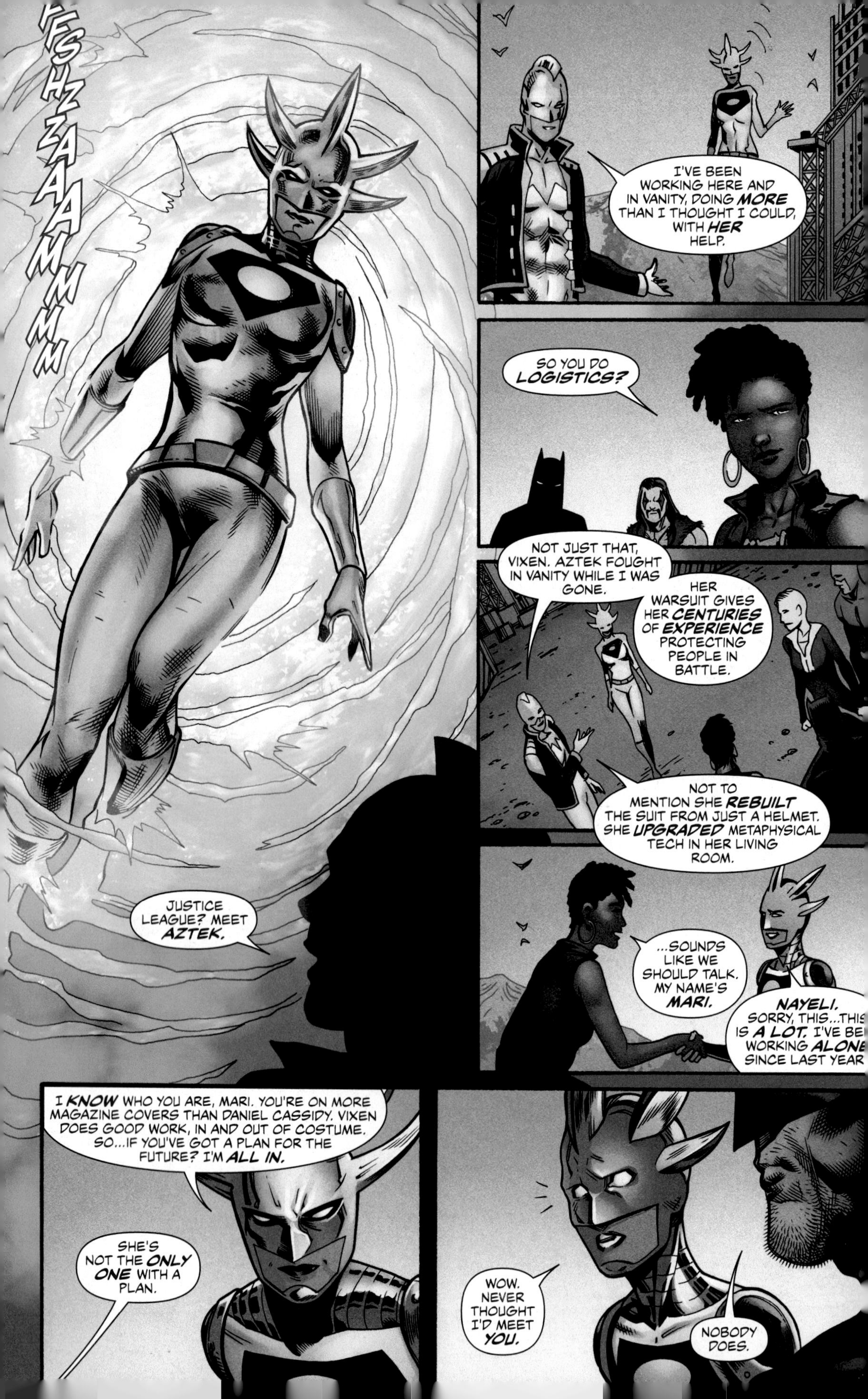
FSHZZAAAMMMMM
JUSTICE LEAGUE? MEET AZTEK.
I'VE BEEN WORKING HERE AND IN VANITY, DOING MORE THAN I THOUGHT I COULD, WITH HER HELP.
SO YOU DO LOGISTICS?
NOT JUST THAT, VIXEN. AZTEK FOUGHT IN VANITY WHILE I WAS GONE.
HER WARSUIT GIVES HER CENTURIES OF EXPERIENCE PROTECTING PEOPLE IN BATTLE.
NOT TO MENTION SHE REBUILT THE SUIT FROM JUST A HELMET. SHE UPGRADED METAPHYSICAL TECH IN HER LIVING ROOM.
...SOUNDS LIKE WE SHOULD TALK. MY NAME'S MARI.
NAYELI. SORRY, THIS...THIS IS A LOT. I'VE BEEN WORKING ALONE SINCE LAST YEAR
I KNOW WHO YOU ARE, MARI. YOU'RE ON MORE MAGAZINE COVERS THAN DANIEL CASSIDY. VIXEN DOES GOOD WORK, IN AND OUT OF COSTUME. SO...IF YOU'VE GOT A PLAN FOR THE FUTURE? I'M ALL IN.
SHE'S NOT THE ONLY ONE WITH A PLAN.
WOW. NEVER THOUGHT I'D MEET YOU.
NOBODY DOES.

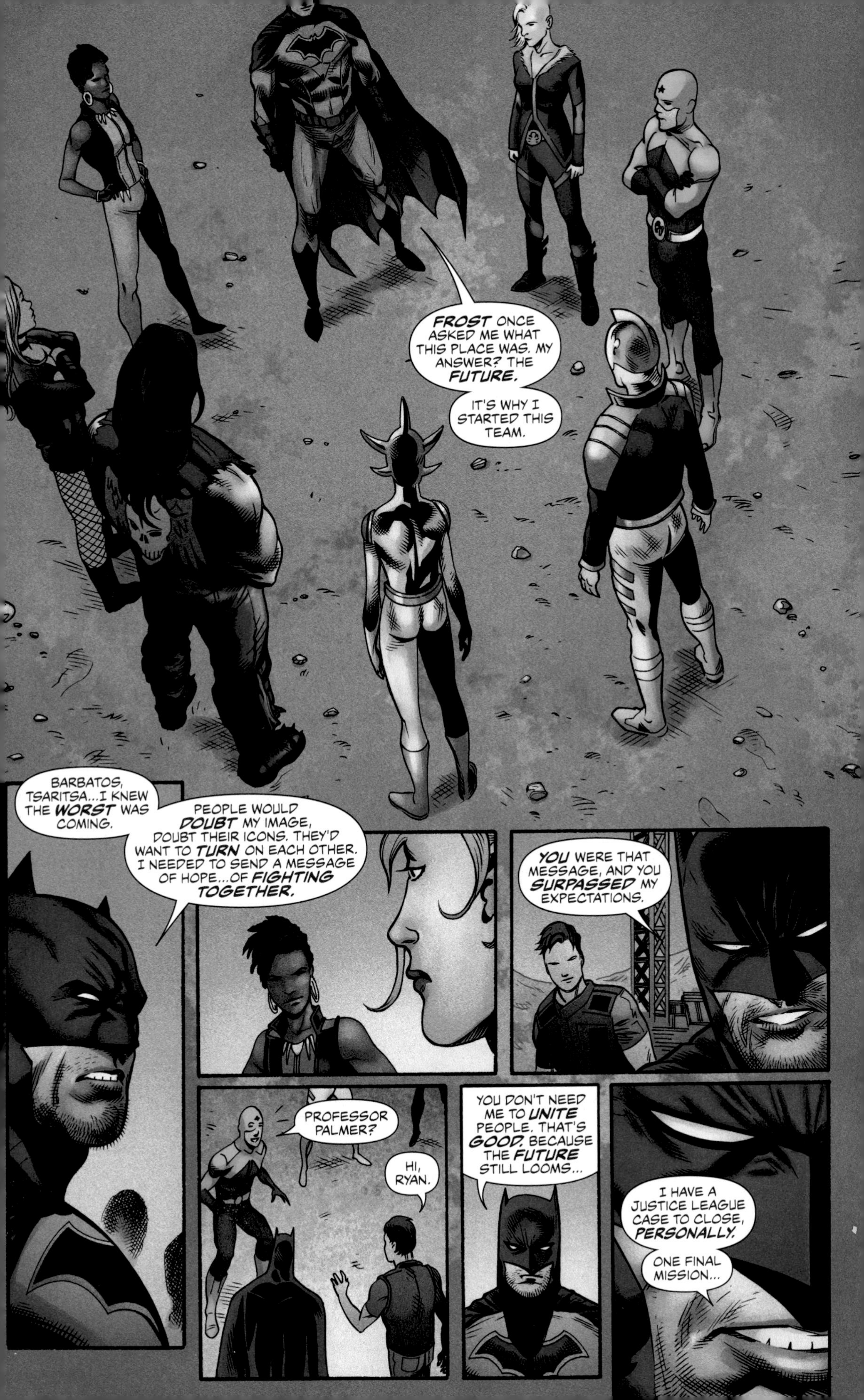
FROST ONCE ASKED ME WHAT THIS PLACE WAS. MY ANSWER? THE FUTURE.
IT'S WHY I STARTED THIS TEAM.
BARBATOS, TSARITSA...I KNEW THE WORST WAS COMING.
PEOPLE WOULD DOUBT MY IMAGE, DOUBT THEIR ICONS. THEY'D WANT TO TURN ON EACH OTHER. I NEEDED TO SEND A MESSAGE OF HOPE...OF FIGHTING TOGETHER.
YOU WERE THAT MESSAGE, AND YOU SURPASSED MY EXPECTATIONS.
PROFESSOR PALMER?
HI, RYAN.
YOU DON'T NEED ME TO UNITE PEOPLE. THAT'S GOOD, BECAUSE THE FUTURE STILL LOOMS...
I HAVE A JUSTICE LEAGUE CASE TO CLOSE, PERSONALLY.
ONE FINAL MISSION...

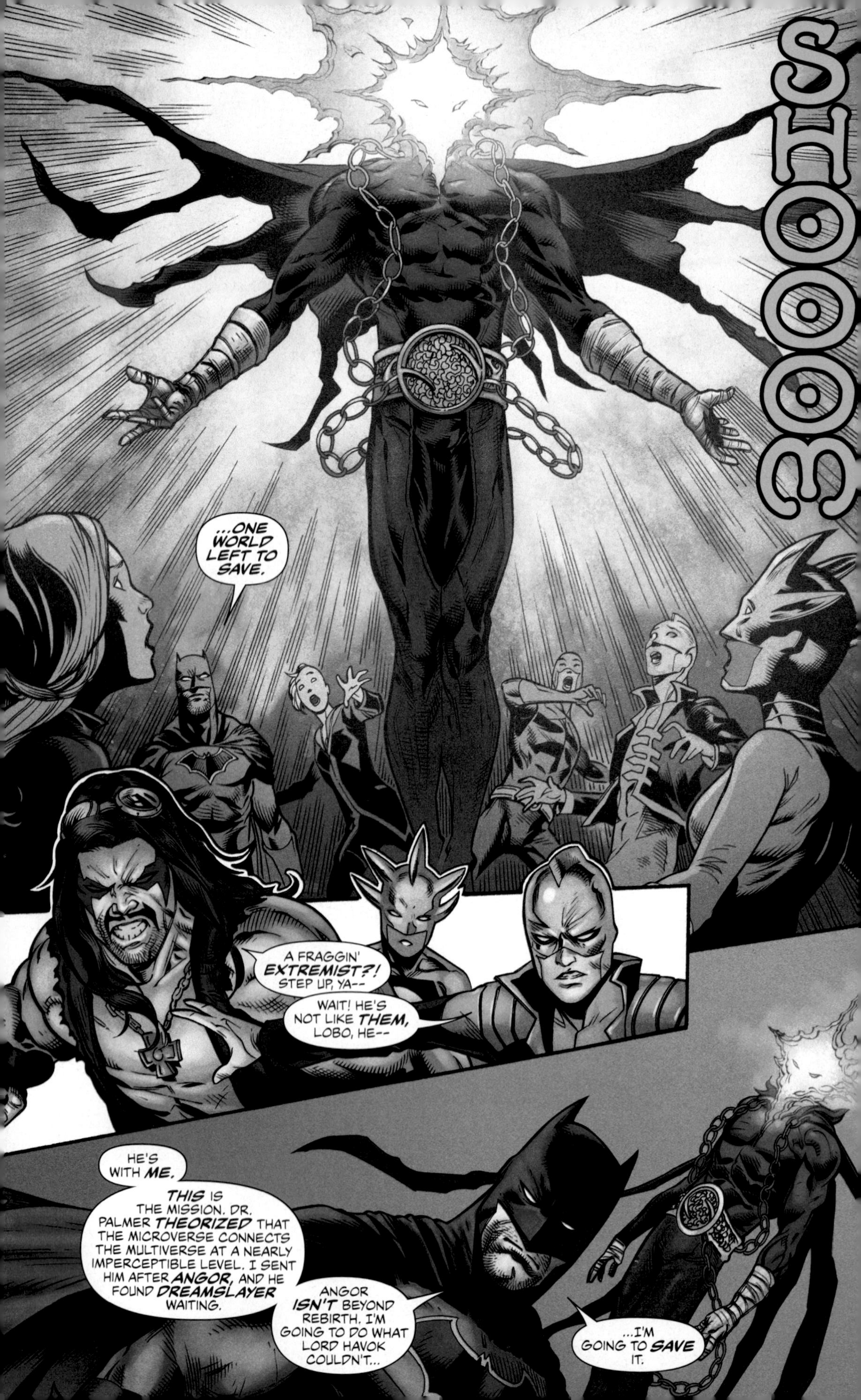
SHOOOOOM
...ONE WORLD LEFT TO SAVE.
A FRAGGIN' EXTREMIST?! STEP UP, YA--
WAIT! HE'S NOT LIKE THEM, LOBO, HE--
HE'S WITH ME.
THIS IS THE MISSION. DR. PALMER THEORIZED THAT THE MICROVERSE CONNECTS THE MULTIVERSE AT A NEARLY IMPERCEPTIBLE LEVEL. I SENT HIM AFTER ANGOR, AND HE FOUND DREAMSLAYER WAITING.
ANGOR ISN'T BEYOND REBIRTH. I'M GOING TO DO WHAT LORD HAVOK COULDN'T...
...I'M GOING TO SAVE IT.

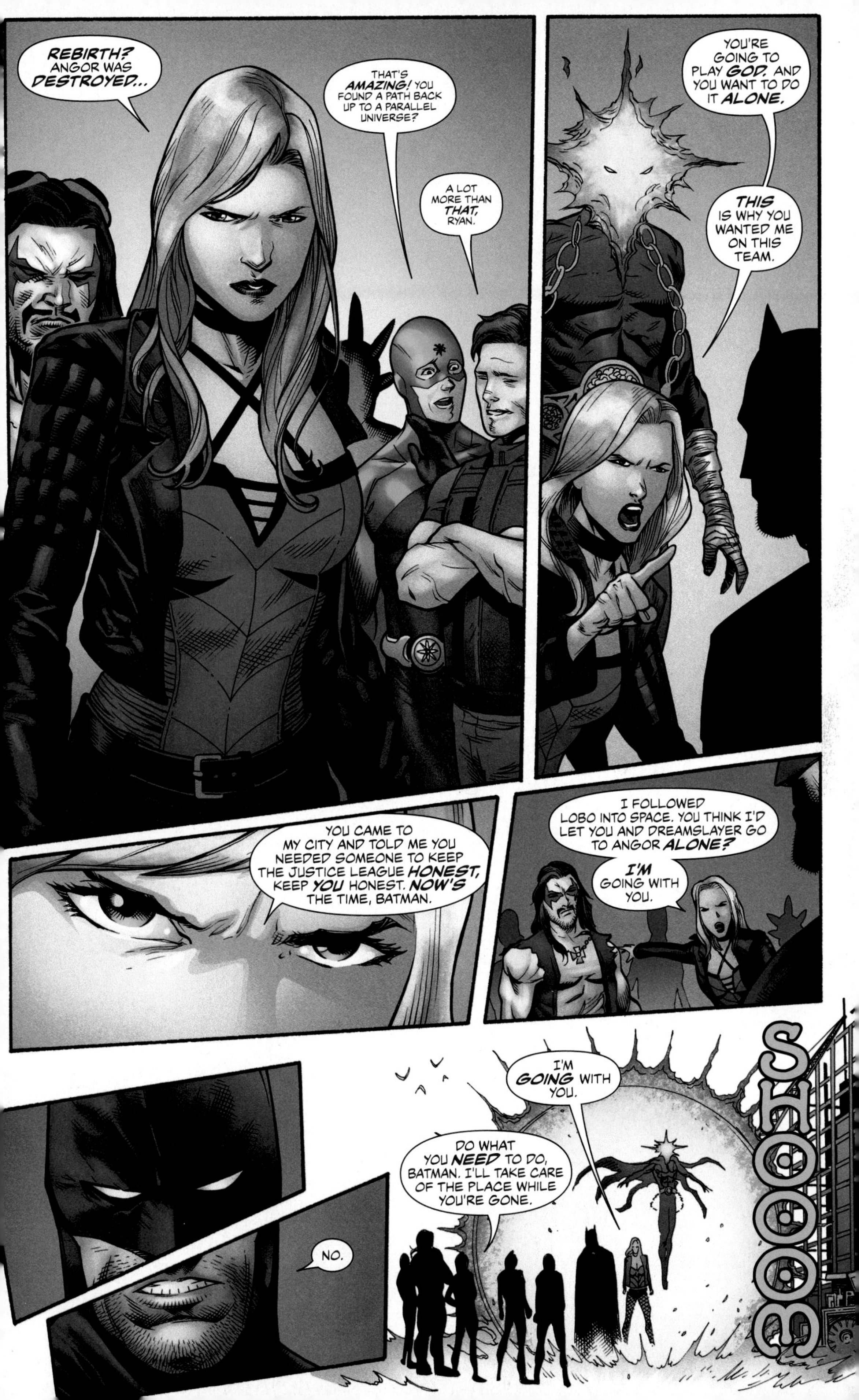
REBIRTH? ANGOR WAS DESTROYED...
THAT'S AMAZING! YOU FOUND A PATH BACK UP TO A PARALLEL UNIVERSE?
A LOT MORE THAN THAT, RYAN.
YOU'RE GOING TO PLAY GOD. AND YOU WANT TO DO IT ALONE.
THIS IS WHY YOU WANTED ME ON THIS TEAM.
YOU CAME TO MY CITY AND TOLD ME YOU NEEDED SOMEONE TO KEEP THE JUSTICE LEAGUE HONEST, KEEP YOU HONEST. NOW'S THE TIME, BATMAN.
I FOLLOWED LOBO INTO SPACE. YOU THINK I'D LET YOU AND DREAMSLAYER GO TO ANGOR ALONE?
I'M GOING WITH YOU.
NO.
I'M GOING WITH YOU.
DO WHAT YOU NEED TO DO, BATMAN. I'LL TAKE CARE OF THE PLACE WHILE YOU'RE GONE.
SHOOOOM

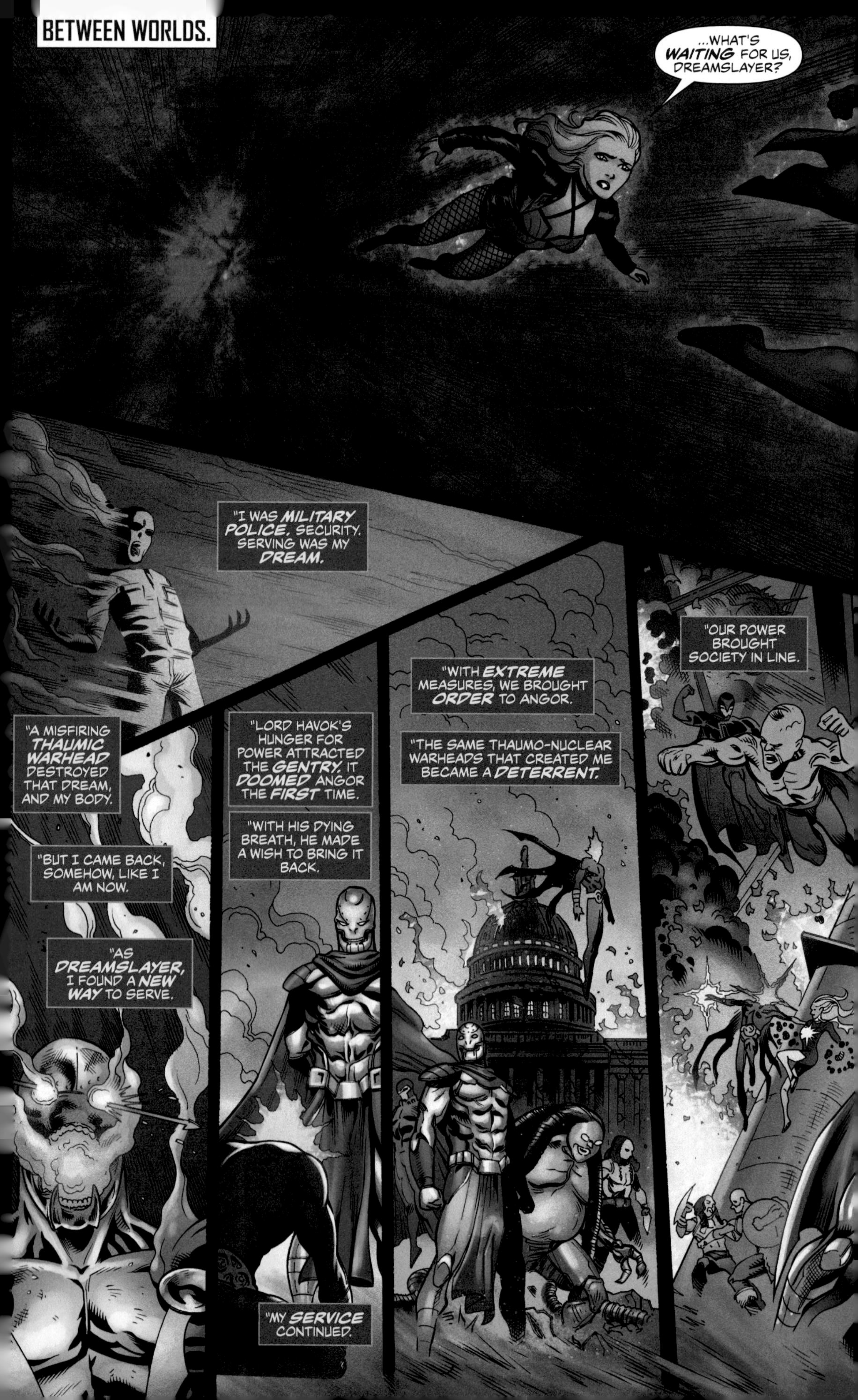
BETWEEN WORLDS.
...WHAT'S WAITING FOR US, DREAMSLAYER?
"I WAS MILITARY POLICE. SECURITY. SERVING WAS MY DREAM.
"A MISFIRING THAUMIC WARHEAD DESTROYED THAT DREAM, AND MY BODY.
"BUT I CAME BACK, SOMEHOW, LIKE I AM NOW.
"AS DREAMSLAYER, I FOUND A NEW WAY TO SERVE.
"LORD HAVOK'S HUNGER FOR POWER ATTRACTED THE GENTRY. IT DOOMED ANGOR THE FIRST TIME.
"WITH HIS DYING BREATH, HE MADE A WISH TO BRING IT BACK.
"MY SERVICE CONTINUED.
"WITH EXTREME MEASURES, WE BROUGHT ORDER TO ANGOR.
"THE SAME THAUMO-NUCLEAR WARHEADS THAT CREATED ME BECAME A DETERRENT.
"OUR POWER BROUGHT SOCIETY IN LINE.

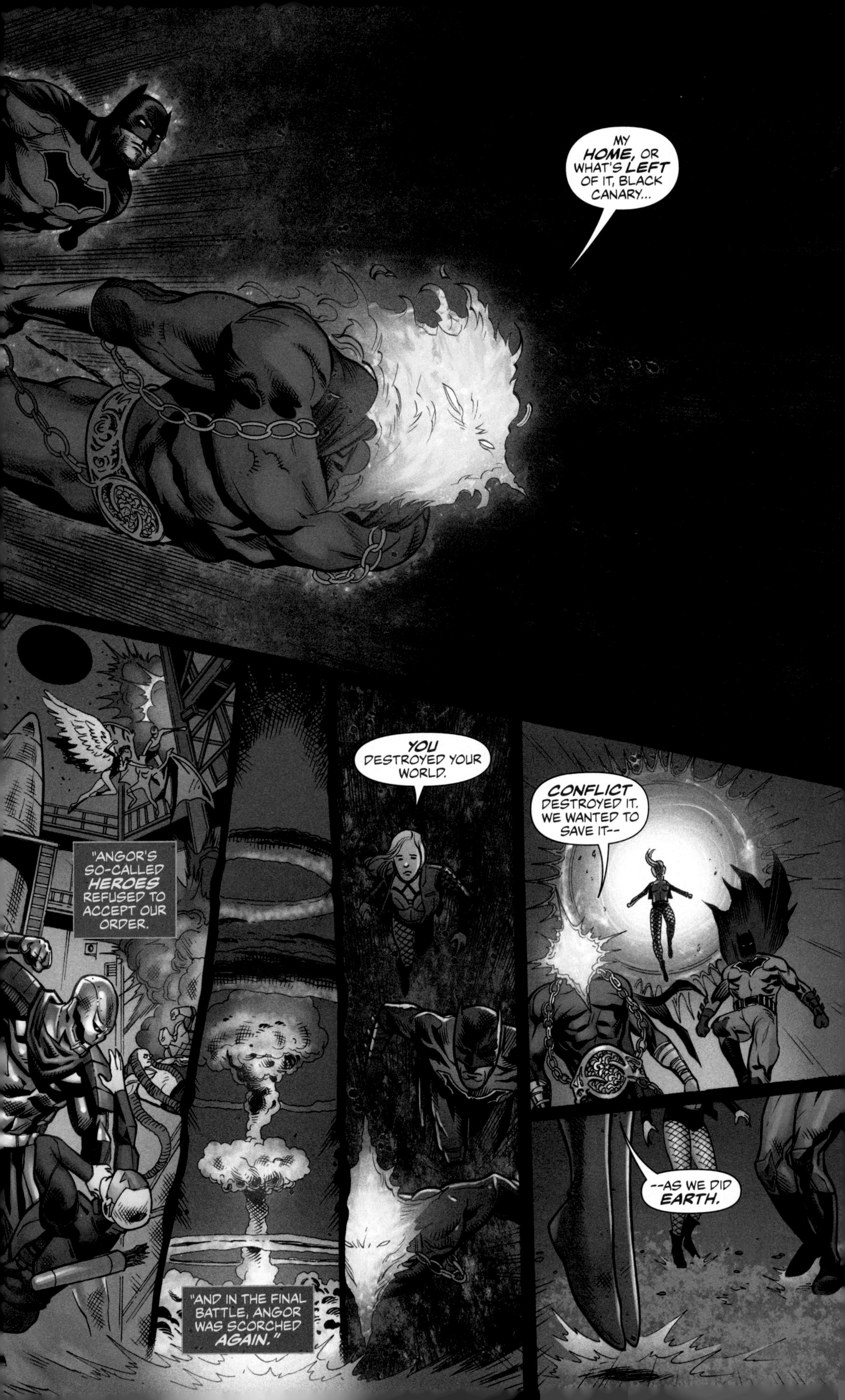

MY HOME, OR WHAT'S LEFT OF IT, BLACK CANARY...
"ANGOR'S SO-CALLED HEROES REFUSED TO ACCEPT OUR ORDER.
"AND IN THE FINAL BATTLE, ANGOR WAS SCORCHED AGAIN."
YOU DESTROYED YOUR WORLD.
CONFLICT DESTROYED IT. WE WANTED TO SAVE IT--
--AS WE DID EARTH.

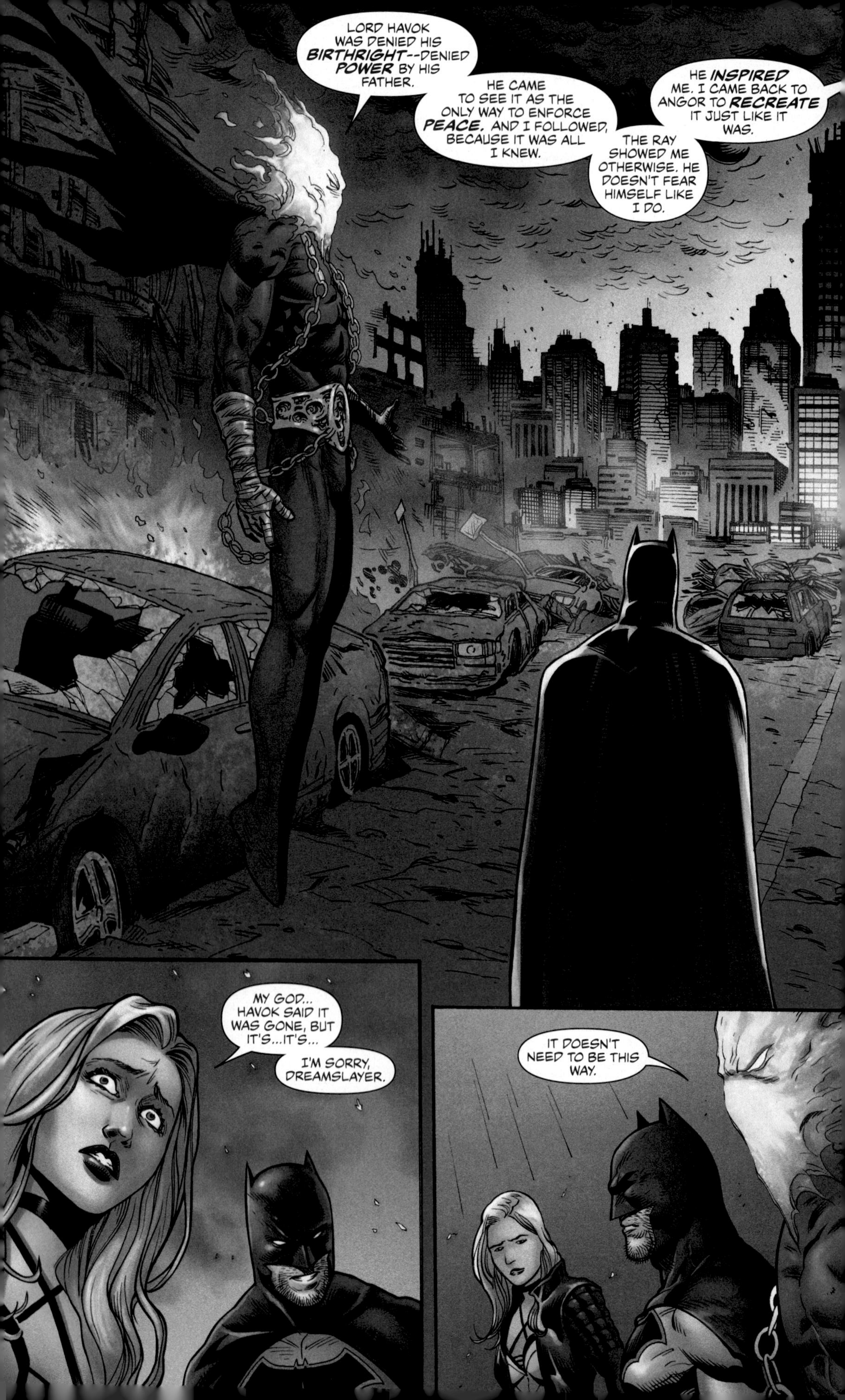
LORD HAVOK WAS DENIED HIS BIRTHRIGHT--DENIED POWER BY HIS FATHER.
HE CAME TO SEE IT AS THE ONLY WAY TO ENFORCE PEACE. AND I FOLLOWED, BECAUSE IT WAS ALL I KNEW.
THE RAY SHOWED ME OTHERWISE. HE DOESN'T FEAR HIMSELF LIKE I DO.
HE INSPIRED ME. I CAME BACK TO ANGOR TO RECREATE IT JUST LIKE IT WAS.
MY GOD... HAVOK SAID IT WAS GONE, BUT IT'S...IT'S...
I'M SORRY, DREAMSLAYER.
IT DOESN'T NEED TO BE THIS WAY.

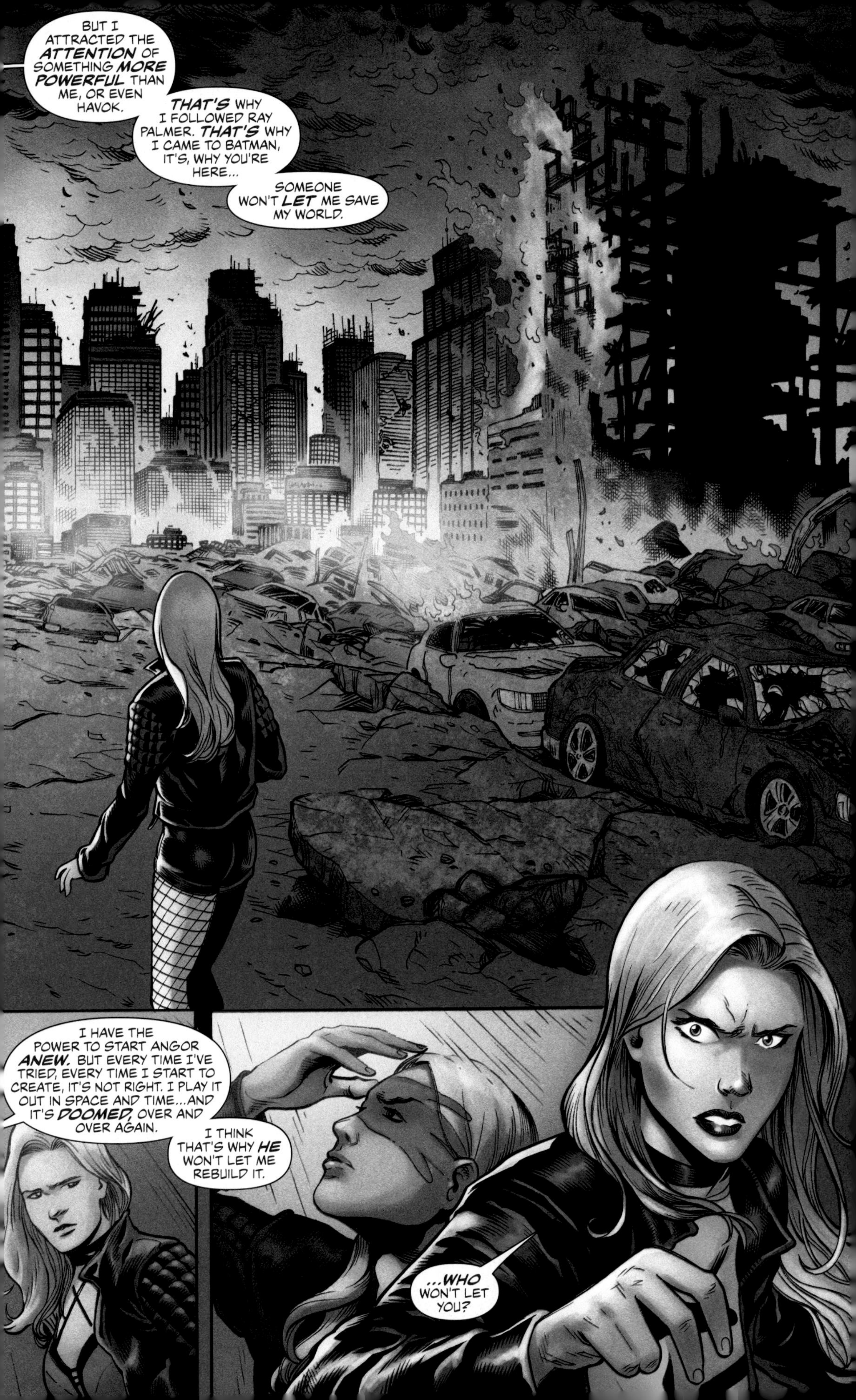
BUT I ATTRACTED THE ATTENTION OF SOMETHING MORE POWERFUL THAN ME, OR EVEN HAVOK.
THAT'S WHY I FOLLOWED RAY PALMER. THAT'S WHY I CAME TO BATMAN, IT'S, WHY YOU'RE HERE...
SOMEONE WON'T LET ME SAVE MY WORLD.
I HAVE THE POWER TO START ANGOR ANEW. BUT EVERY TIME I'VE TRIED, EVERY TIME I START TO CREATE, IT'S NOT RIGHT. I PLAY IT OUT IN SPACE AND TIME...AND IT'S DOOMED, OVER AND OVER AGAIN.
I THINK THAT'S WHY HE WON'T LET ME REBUILD IT.
...WHO WON'T LET YOU?

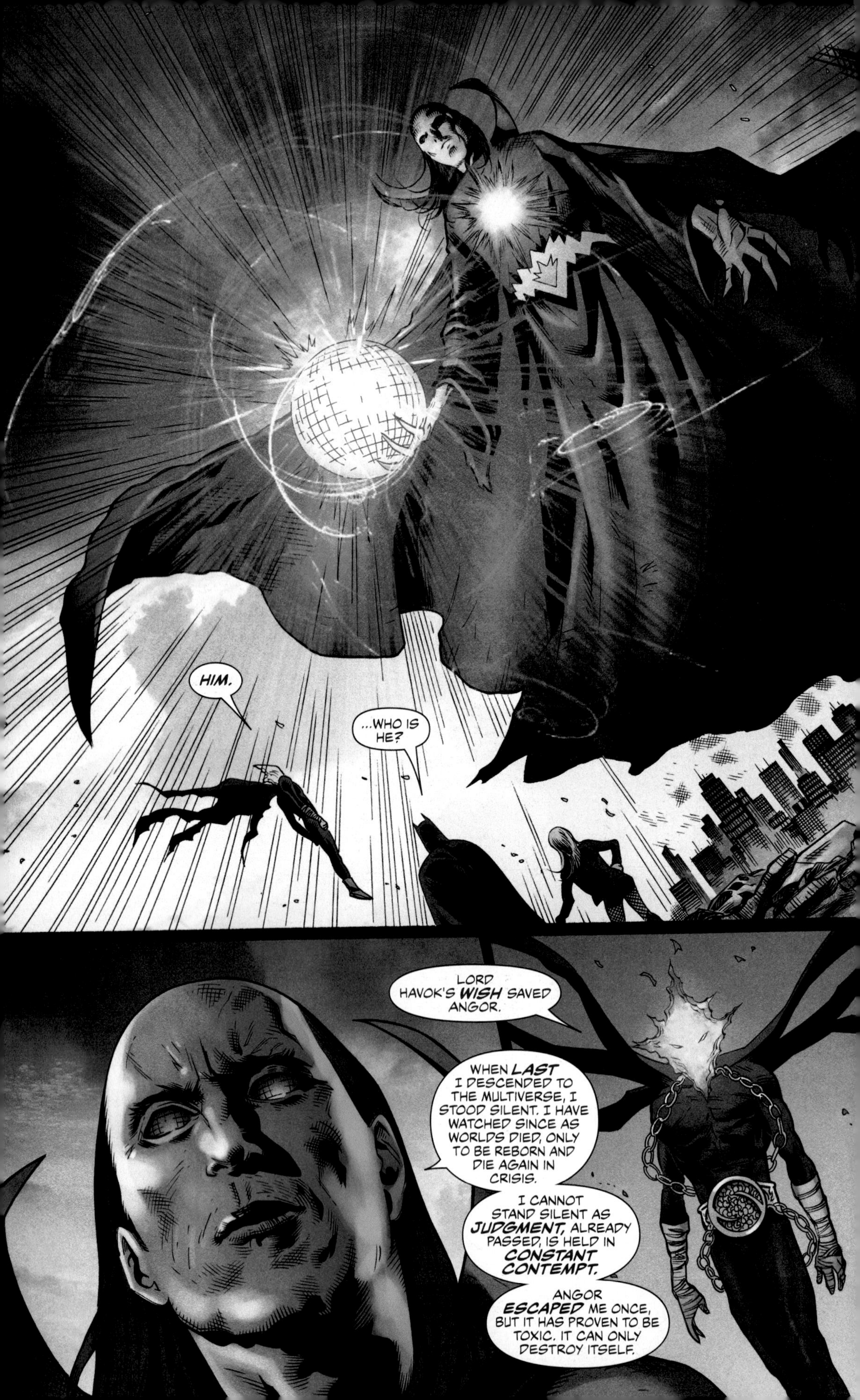
HIM.
...WHO IS HE?
LORD HAVOK'S WISH SAVED ANGOR.
WHEN LAST I DESCENDED TO THE MULTIVERSE, I STOOD SILENT. I HAVE WATCHED SINCE AS WORLDS DIED, ONLY TO BE REBORN AND DIE AGAIN IN CRISIS.
I CANNOT STAND SILENT AS JUDGMENT, ALREADY PASSED, IS HELD IN CONSTANT CONTEMPT.
ANGOR ESCAPED ME ONCE, BUT IT HAS PROVEN TO BE TOXIC. IT CAN ONLY DESTROY ITSELF.

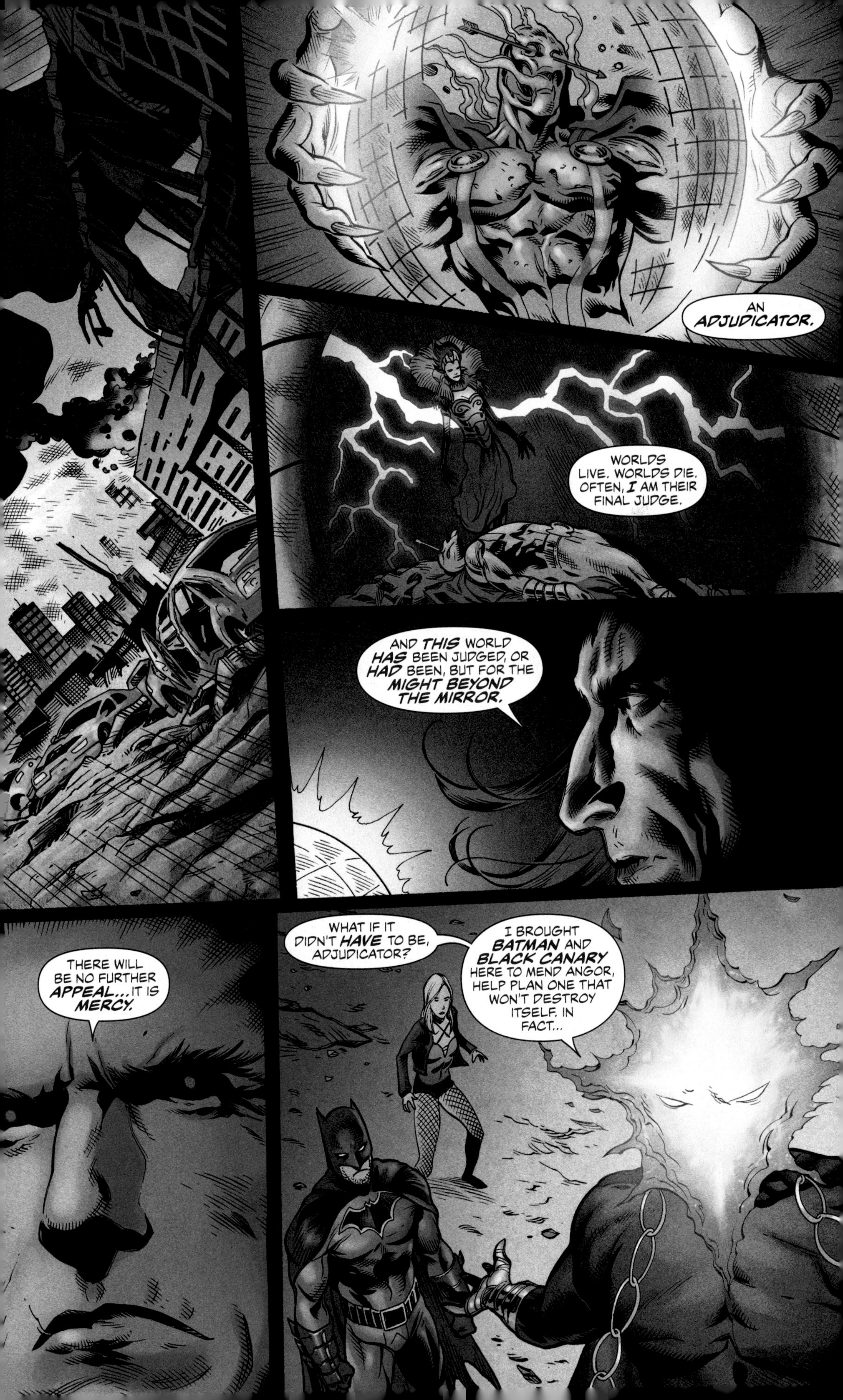
AN ADJUDICATOR.
WORLDS LIVE. WORLDS DIE. OFTEN, I AM THEIR FINAL JUDGE.
AND THIS WORLD HAS BEEN JUDGED, OR HAD BEEN, BUT FOR THE MIGHT BEYOND THE MIRROR.
THERE WILL BE NO FURTHER APPEAL... IT IS MERCY.
WHAT IF IT DIDN'T HAVE TO BE, ADJUDICATOR?
I BROUGHT BATMAN AND BLACK CANARY HERE TO MEND ANGOR, HELP PLAN ONE THAT WON'T DESTROY ITSELF. IN FACT...

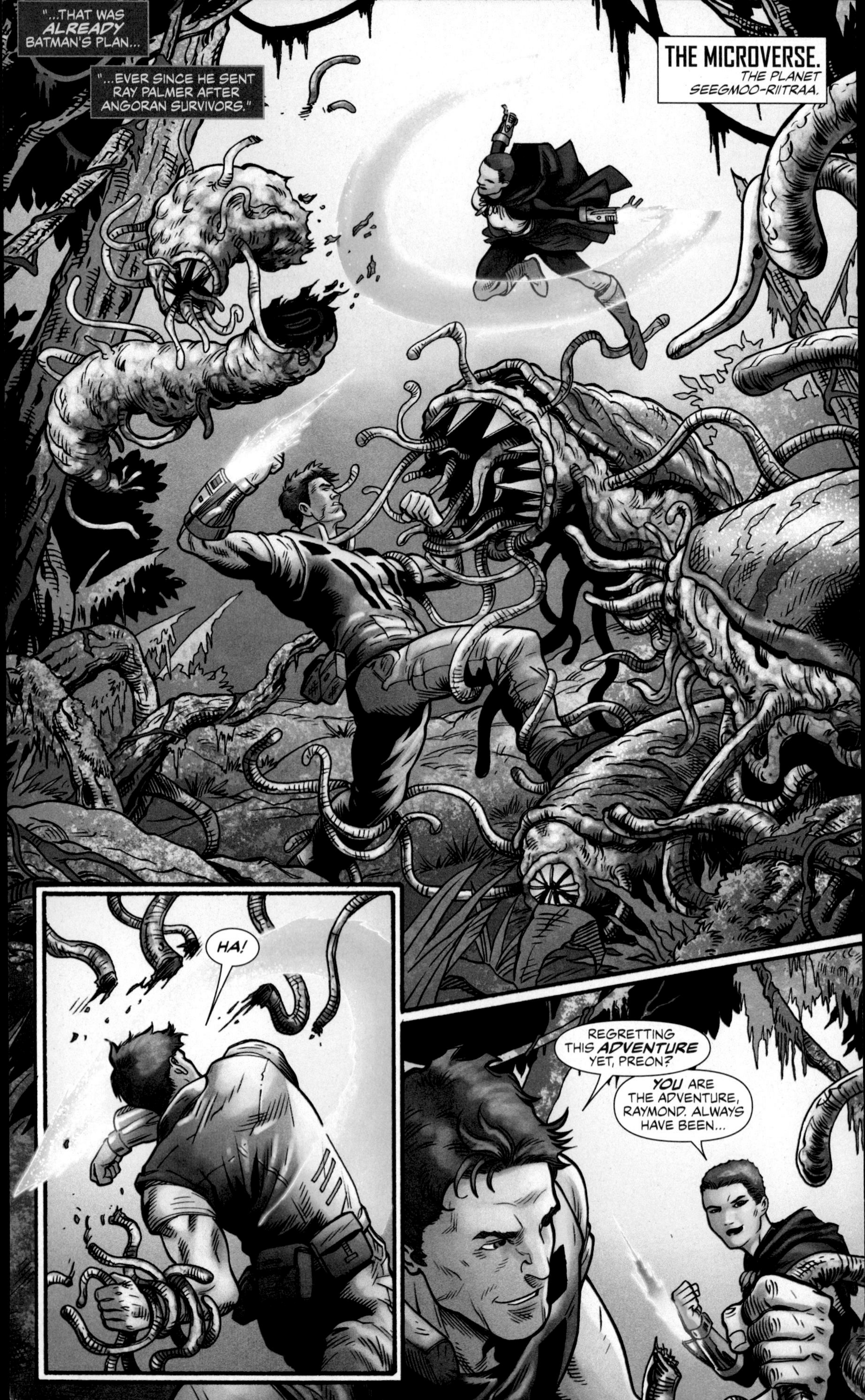
"...THAT WAS ALREADY BATMAN'S PLAN...
"...EVER SINCE HE SENT RAY PALMER AFTER ANGORAN SURVIVORS."
THE MICROVERSE. THE PLANET SEEGMOO-RIITRAA.
HA!
REGRETTING THIS ADVENTURE YET, PREON?
YOU ARE THE ADVENTURE, RAYMOND. ALWAYS HAVE BEEN...

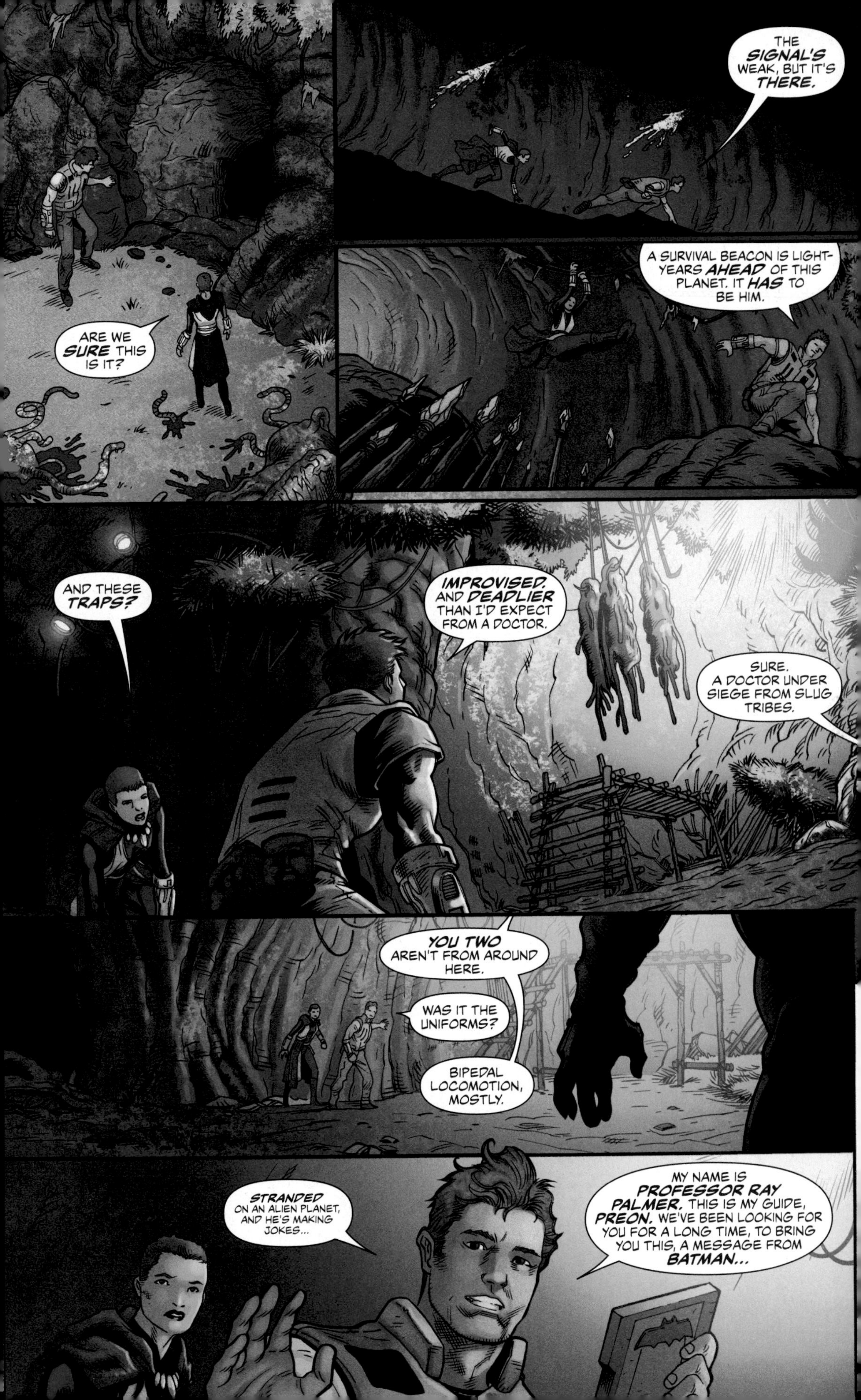
ARE WE SURE THIS IS IT?
THE SIGNAL'S WEAK, BUT IT'S THERE.
A SURVIVAL BEACON IS LIGHT-YEARS AHEAD OF THIS PLANET. IT HAS TO BE HIM.
AND THESE TRAPS?
IMPROVISED. AND DEADLIER THAN I'D EXPECT FROM A DOCTOR.
SURE. A DOCTOR UNDER SIEGE FROM SLUG TRIBES.
YOU TWO AREN'T FROM AROUND HERE.
WAS IT THE UNIFORMS?
BIPEDAL LOCOMOTION, MOSTLY.
STRANDED ON AN ALIEN PLANET, AND HE'S MAKING JOKES...
MY NAME IS PROFESSOR RAY PALMER. THIS IS MY GUIDE, PREON. WE'VE BEEN LOOKING FOR YOU FOR A LONG TIME, TO BRING YOU THIS, A MESSAGE FROM BATMAN...

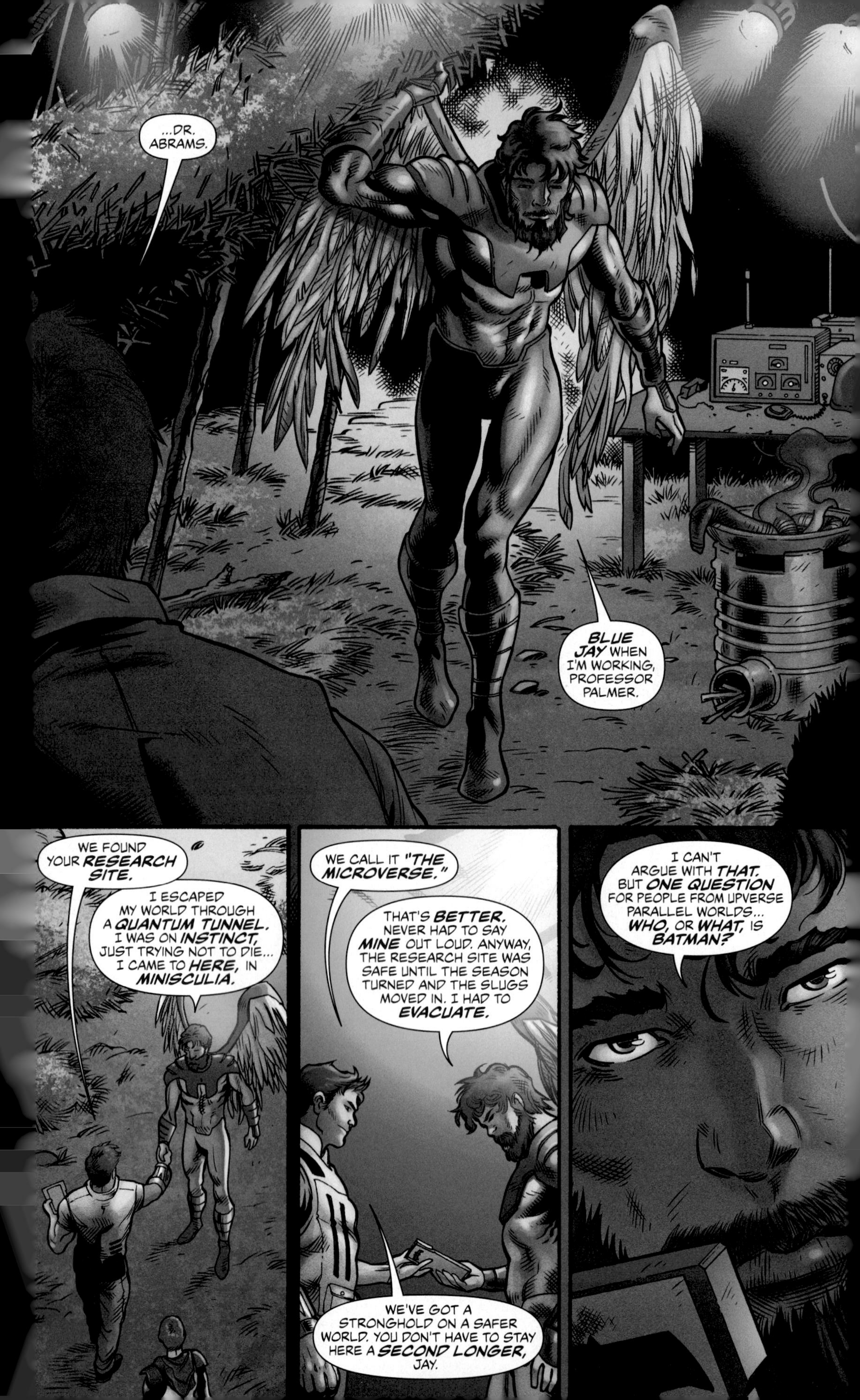
...DR. ABRAMS.
BLUE JAY WHEN I'M WORKING, PROFESSOR PALMER.
WE FOUND YOUR RESEARCH SITE.
I ESCAPED MY WORLD THROUGH A QUANTUM TUNNEL. I WAS ON INSTINCT, JUST TRYING NOT TO DIE... I CAME TO HERE, IN MINISCULIA.
WE CALL IT "THE MICROVERSE."
THAT'S BETTER. NEVER HAD TO SAY MINE OUT LOUD. ANYWAY, THE RESEARCH SITE WAS SAFE UNTIL THE SEASON TURNED AND THE SLUGS MOVED IN. I HAD TO EVACUATE.
WE'VE GOT A STRONGHOLD ON A SAFER WORLD. YOU DON'T HAVE TO STAY HERE A SECOND LONGER, JAY.
I CAN'T ARGUE WITH THAT. BUT ONE QUESTION FOR PEOPLE FROM UPVERSE PARALLEL WORLDS... WHO, OR WHAT, IS BATMAN?

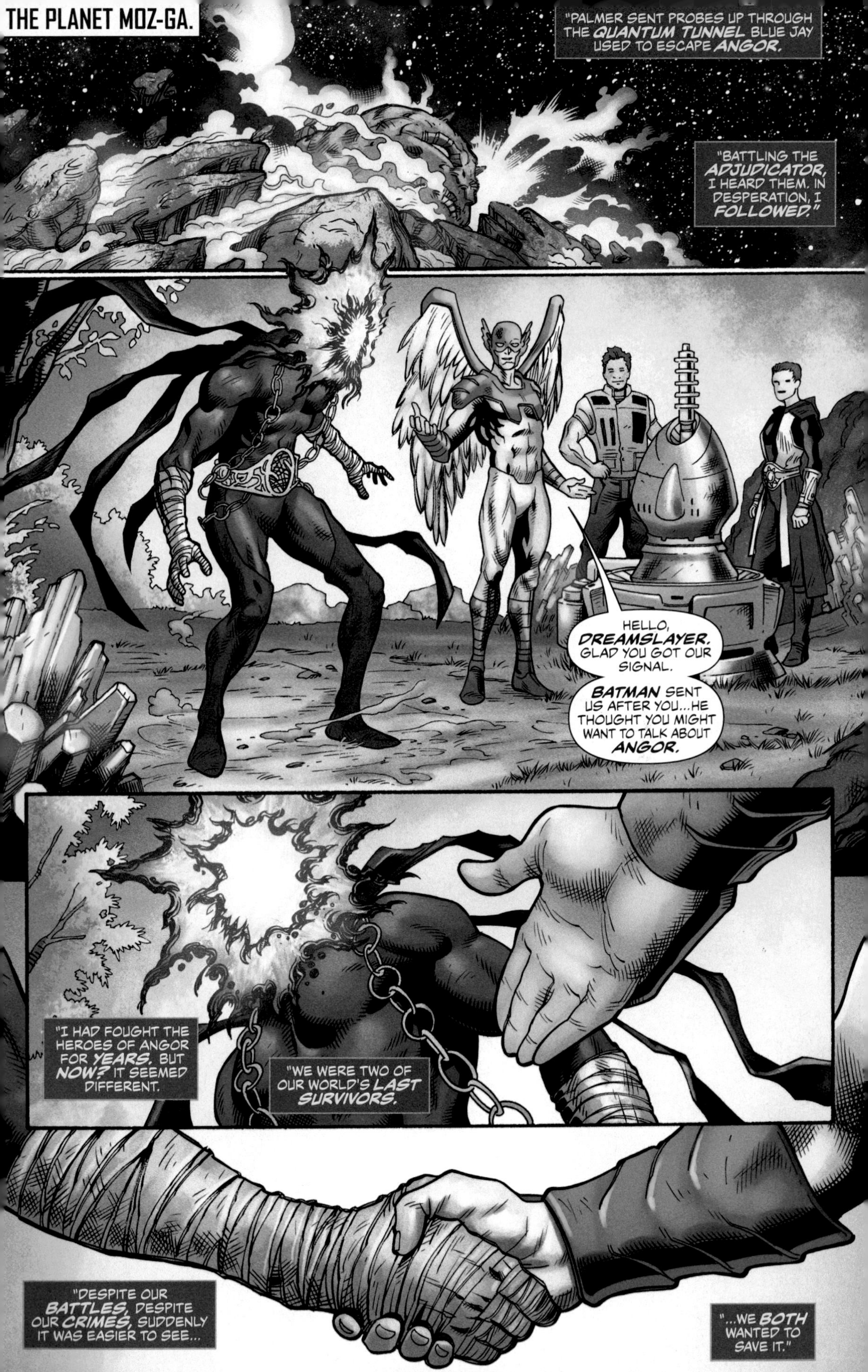
THE PLANET MOZ-GA.
"PALMER SENT PROBES UP THROUGH THE QUANTUM TUNNEL BLUE JAY USED TO ESCAPE ANGOR.
"BATTLING THE ADJUDICATOR, I HEARD THEM. IN DESPERATION, I FOLLOWED."
HELLO, DREAMSLAYER. GLAD YOU GOT OUR SIGNAL.
BATMAN SENT US AFTER YOU...HE THOUGHT YOU MIGHT WANT TO TALK ABOUT ANGOR.
"I HAD FOUGHT THE HEROES OF ANGOR FOR YEARS. BUT NOW? IT SEEMED DIFFERENT.
"WE WERE TWO OF OUR WORLD'S LAST SURVIVORS.
"DESPITE OUR BATTLES, DESPITE OUR CRIMES, SUDDENLY IT WAS EASIER TO SEE...
"...WE BOTH WANTED TO SAVE IT."

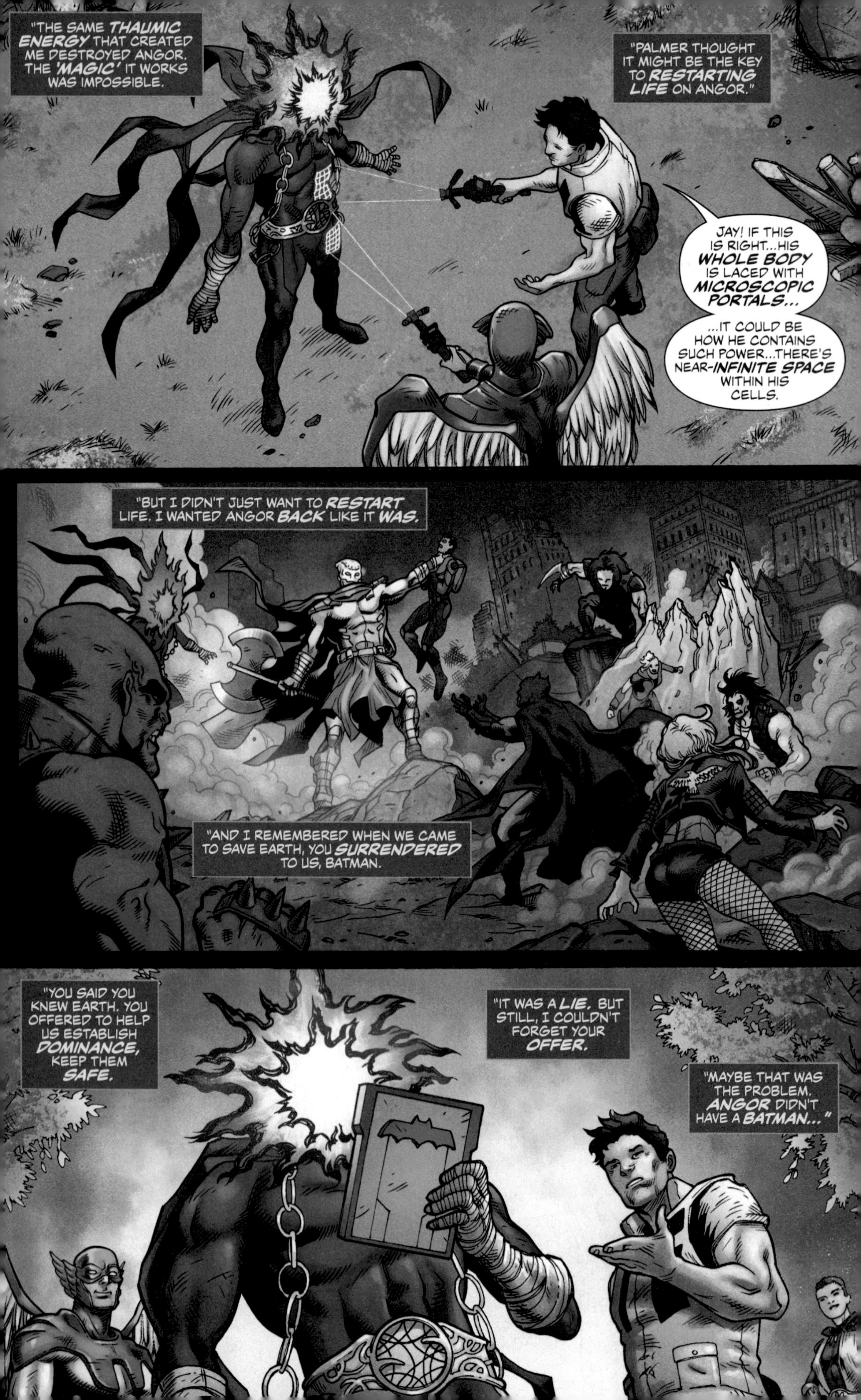
"THE SAME THAUMIC ENERGY THAT CREATED ME DESTROYED ANGOR. THE 'MAGIC' IT WORKS WAS IMPOSSIBLE.
"PALMER THOUGHT IT MIGHT BE THE KEY TO RESTARTING LIFE ON ANGOR."
JAY! IF THIS IS RIGHT...HIS WHOLE BODY IS LACED WITH MICROSCOPIC PORTALS...
...IT COULD BE HOW HE CONTAINS SUCH POWER...THERE'S NEAR-INFINITE SPACE WITHIN HIS CELLS.
"BUT I DIDN'T JUST WANT TO RESTART LIFE. I WANTED ANGOR BACK LIKE IT WAS.
"AND I REMEMBERED WHEN WE CAME TO SAVE EARTH, YOU SURRENDERED TO US, BATMAN.
"YOU SAID YOU KNEW EARTH. YOU OFFERED TO HELP US ESTABLISH DOMINANCE, KEEP THEM SAFE.
"IT WAS A LIE. BUT STILL, I COULDN'T FORGET YOUR OFFER.
"MAYBE THAT WAS THE PROBLEM. ANGOR DIDN'T HAVE A BATMAN..."

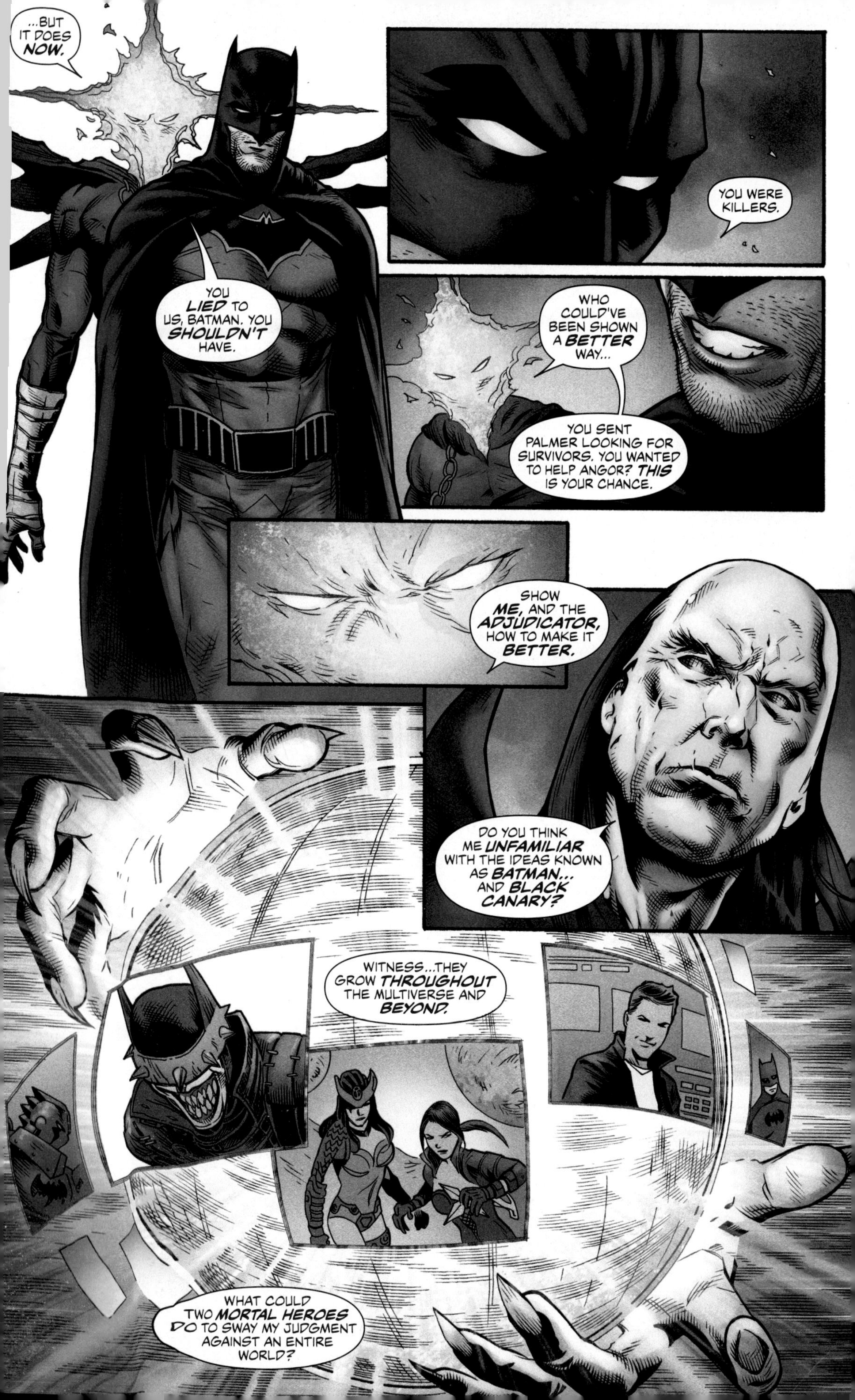
...BUT IT DOES NOW.
YOU LIED TO US, BATMAN. YOU SHOULDN'T HAVE.
YOU WERE KILLERS.
WHO COULD'VE BEEN SHOWN A BETTER WAY...
YOU SENT PALMER LOOKING FOR SURVIVORS. YOU WANTED TO HELP ANGOR? THIS IS YOUR CHANCE.
SHOW ME, AND THE ADJUDICATOR, HOW TO MAKE IT BETTER.
DO YOU THINK ME UNFAMILIAR WITH THE IDEAS KNOWN AS BATMAN... AND BLACK CANARY?
WITNESS...THEY GROW THROUGHOUT THE MULTIVERSE AND BEYOND.
WHAT COULD TWO MORTAL HEROES DO TO SWAY MY JUDGMENT AGAINST AN ENTIRE WORLD?

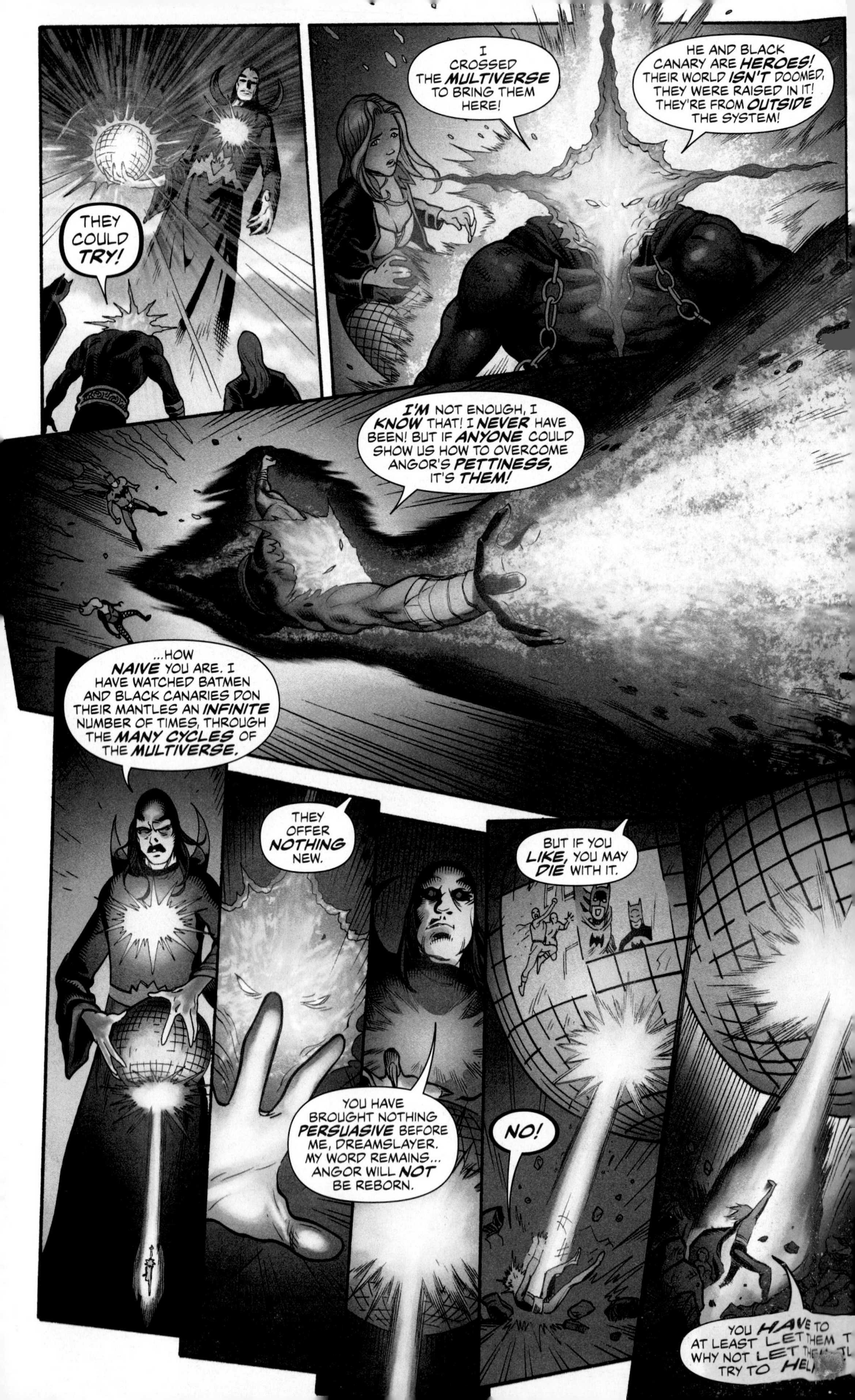
THEY COULD TRY!
I CROSSED THE MULTIVERSE TO BRING THEM HERE!
HE AND BLACK CANARY ARE HEROES! THEIR WORLD ISN'T DOOMED, THEY WERE RAISED IN IT! THEY'RE FROM OUTSIDE THE SYSTEM!
I'M NOT ENOUGH, I KNOW THAT! I NEVER HAVE BEEN! BUT IF ANYONE COULD SHOW US HOW TO OVERCOME ANGOR'S PETTINESS, IT'S THEM!
...HOW NAIVE YOU ARE. I HAVE WATCHED BATMEN AND BLACK CANARIES DON THEIR MANTLES AN INFINITE NUMBER OF TIMES, THROUGH THE MANY CYCLES OF THE MULTIVERSE.
THEY OFFER NOTHING NEW.
YOU HAVE BROUGHT NOTHING PERSUASIVE BEFORE ME, DREAMSLAYER. MY WORD REMAINS... ANGOR WILL NOT BE REBORN.
BUT IF YOU LIKE, YOU MAY DIE WITH IT.
NO!
YOU HAVE TO
AT LEAST LET THEM
WHY NOT LET
TRY TO

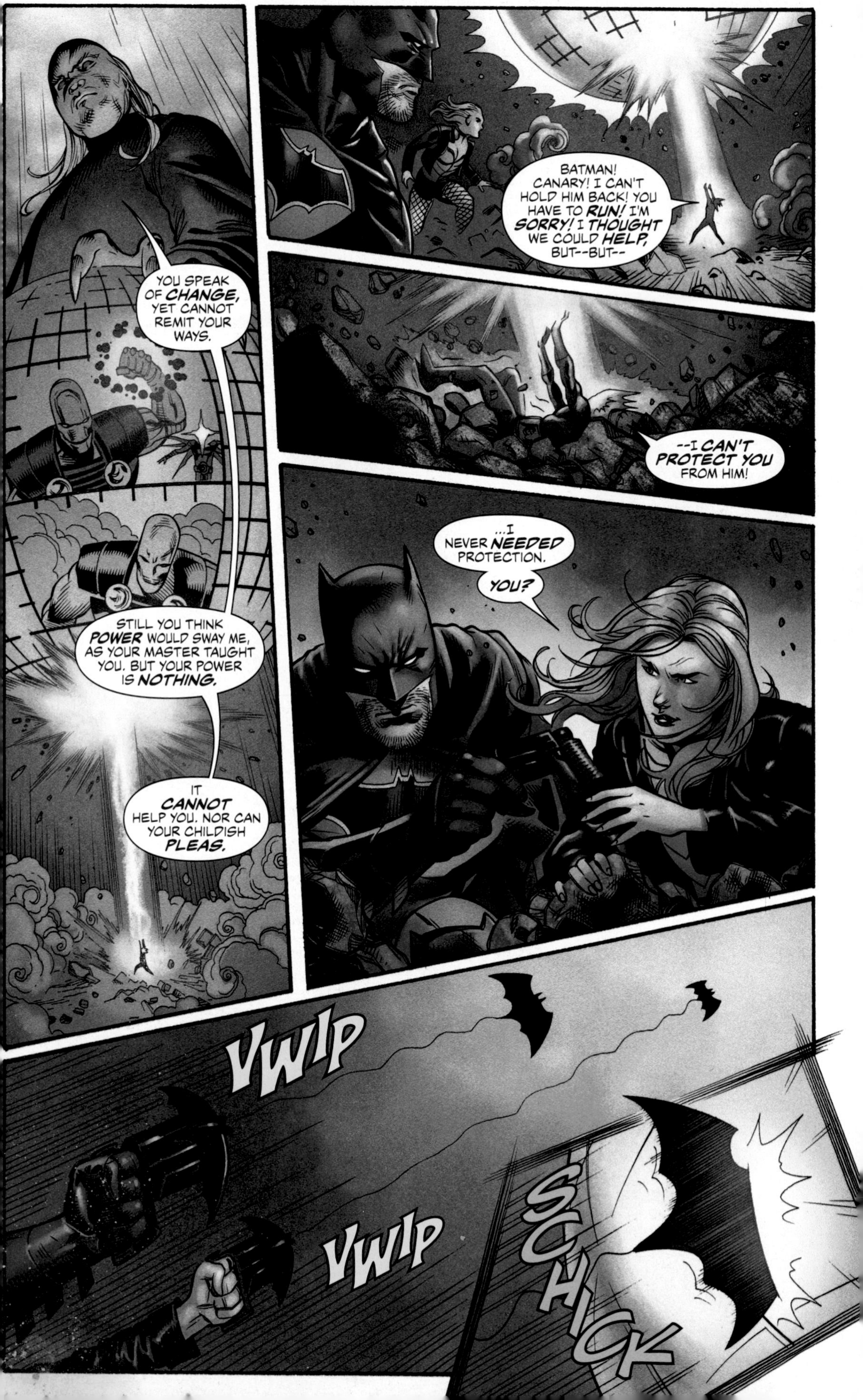
YOU SPEAK OF CHANGE, YET CANNOT REMIT YOUR WAYS.
STILL YOU THINK POWER WOULD SWAY ME, AS YOUR MASTER TAUGHT YOU. BUT YOUR POWER IS NOTHING.
IT CANNOT HELP YOU. NOR CAN YOUR CHILDISH PLEAS.
BATMAN! CANARY! I CAN'T HOLD HIM BACK! YOU HAVE TO RUN! I'M SORRY! I THOUGHT WE COULD HELP, BUT--BUT--
--I CAN'T PROTECT YOU FROM HIM!
...I NEVER NEEDED PROTECTION.
YOU?
VWIP
VWIP
SCHICK

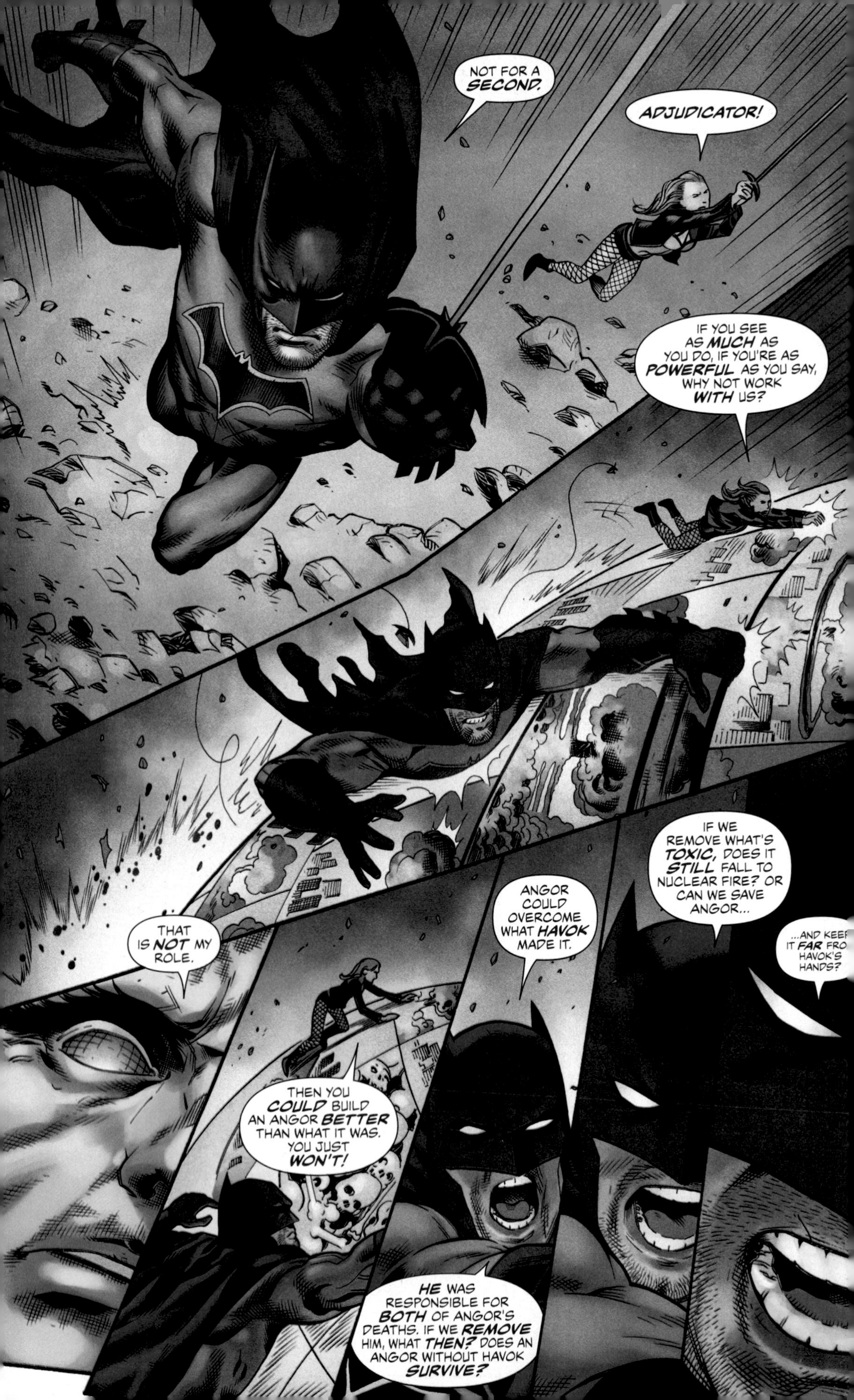
NOT FOR A SECOND.
ADJUDICATOR!
IF YOU SEE AS MUCH AS YOU DO, IF YOU'RE AS POWERFUL AS YOU SAY, WHY NOT WORK WITH US?
THAT IS NOT MY ROLE.
THEN YOU COULD BUILD AN ANGOR BETTER THAN WHAT IT WAS. YOU JUST WON'T!
ANGOR COULD OVERCOME WHAT HAVOK MADE IT.
HE WAS RESPONSIBLE FOR BOTH OF ANGOR'S DEATHS. IF WE REMOVE HIM, WHAT THEN? DOES AN ANGOR WITHOUT HAVOK SURVIVE?
IF WE REMOVE WHAT'S TOXIC, DOES IT STILL FALL TO NUCLEAR FIRE? OR CAN WE SAVE ANGOR...

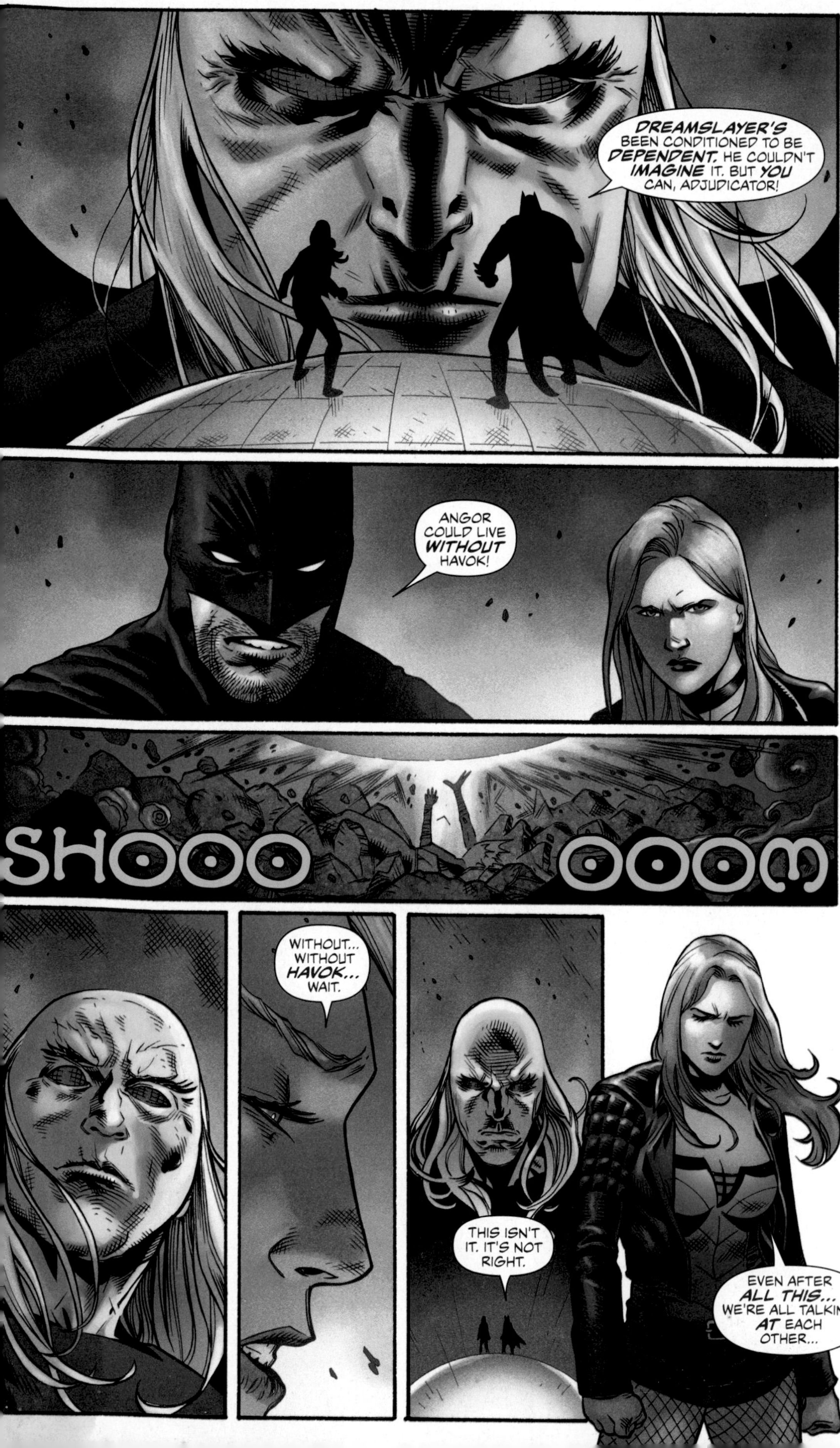
DREAMSLAYER'S BEEN CONDITIONED TO BE DEPENDENT. HE COULDN'T IMAGINE IT. BUT YOU CAN, ADJUDICATOR!
ANGOR COULD LIVE WITHOUT HAVOK!
SHOOO OOOM
WITHOUT... WITHOUT HAVOK... WAIT.
THIS ISN'T IT. IT'S NOT RIGHT.
EVEN AFTER ALL THIS... WE'RE ALL TALKING AT EACH OTHER...

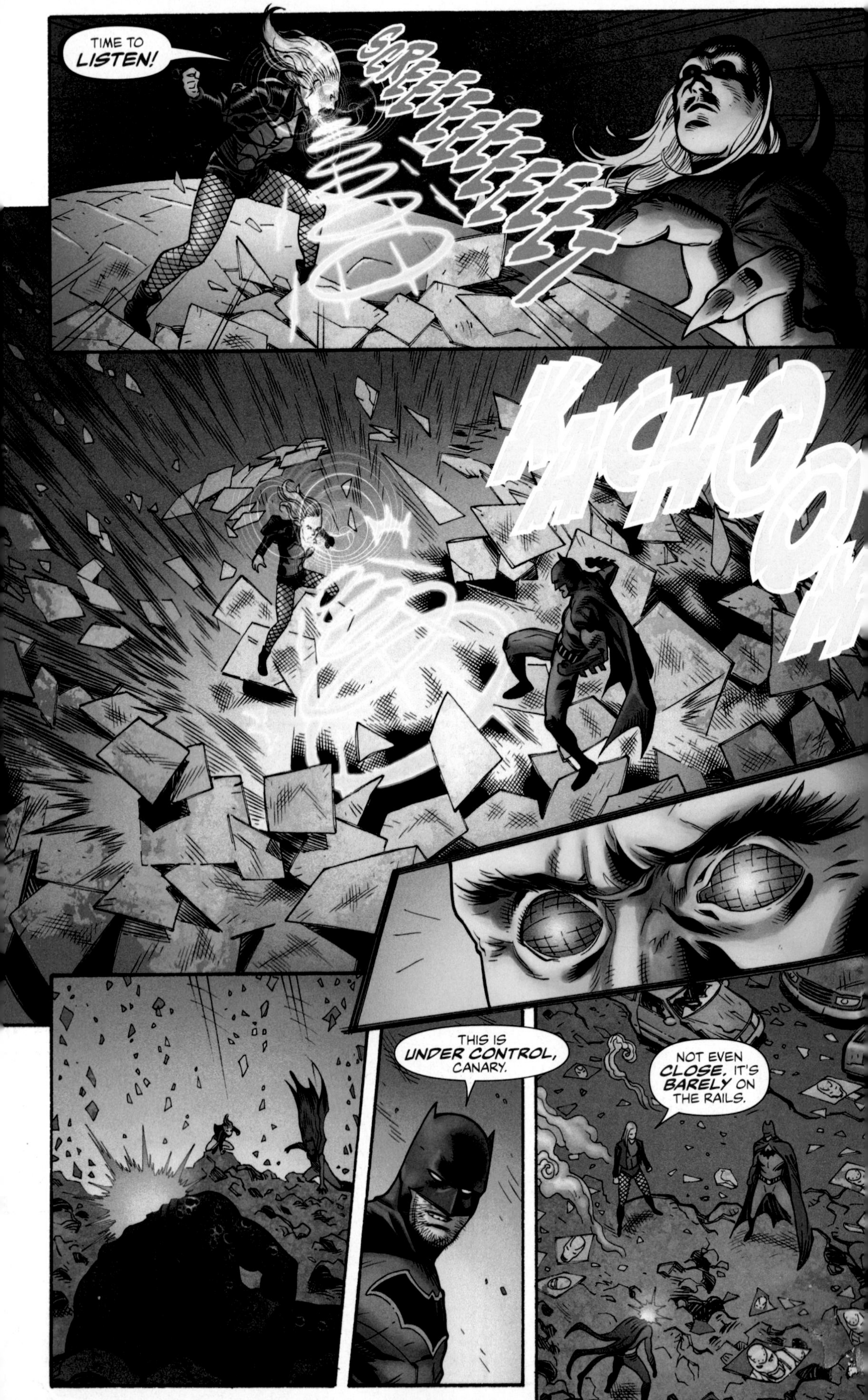
TIME TO LISTEN!
SCREEEEEEEEEEEEET
THIS IS UNDER CONTROL, CANARY.
NOT EVEN CLOSE. IT'S BARELY ON THE RAILS.

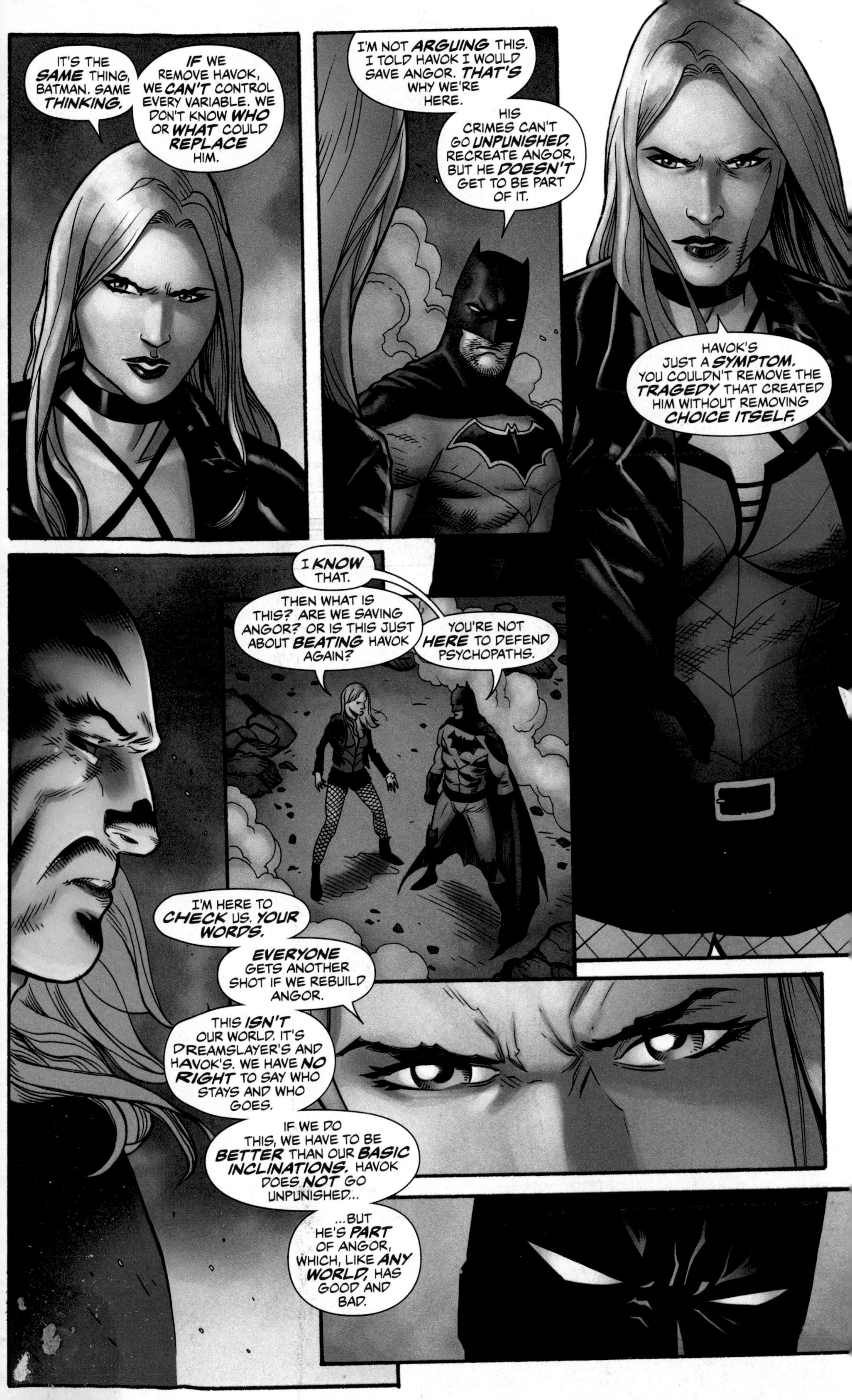
IT'S THE SAME THING, BATMAN. SAME THINKING.
IF WE REMOVE HAVOK, WE CAN'T CONTROL EVERY VARIABLE. WE DON'T KNOW WHO OR WHAT COULD REPLACE HIM.
I'M NOT ARGUING THIS. I TOLD HAVOK I WOULD SAVE ANGOR. THAT'S WHY WE'RE HERE.
HIS CRIMES CAN'T GO UNPUNISHED. RECREATE ANGOR, BUT HE DOESN'T GET TO BE PART OF IT.
HAVOK'S JUST A SYMPTOM. YOU COULDN'T REMOVE THE TRAGEDY THAT CREATED HIM WITHOUT REMOVING CHOICE ITSELF.
I KNOW THAT.
YOU'RE NOT HERE TO DEFEND PSYCHOPATHS.
THEN WHAT IS THIS? ARE WE SAVING ANGOR? OR IS THIS JUST ABOUT BEATING HAVOK AGAIN?
I'M HERE TO CHECK US. YOUR WORDS.
EVERYONE GETS ANOTHER SHOT IF WE REBUILD ANGOR.
THIS ISN'T OUR WORLD. IT'S DREAMSLAYER'S AND HAVOK'S. WE HAVE NO RIGHT TO SAY WHO STAYS AND WHO GOES.
IF WE DO THIS, WE HAVE TO BE BETTER THAN OUR BASIC INCLINATIONS. HAVOK DOES NOT GO UNPUNISHED...
...BUT HE'S PART OF ANGOR, WHICH, LIKE ANY WORLD, HAS GOOD AND BAD.

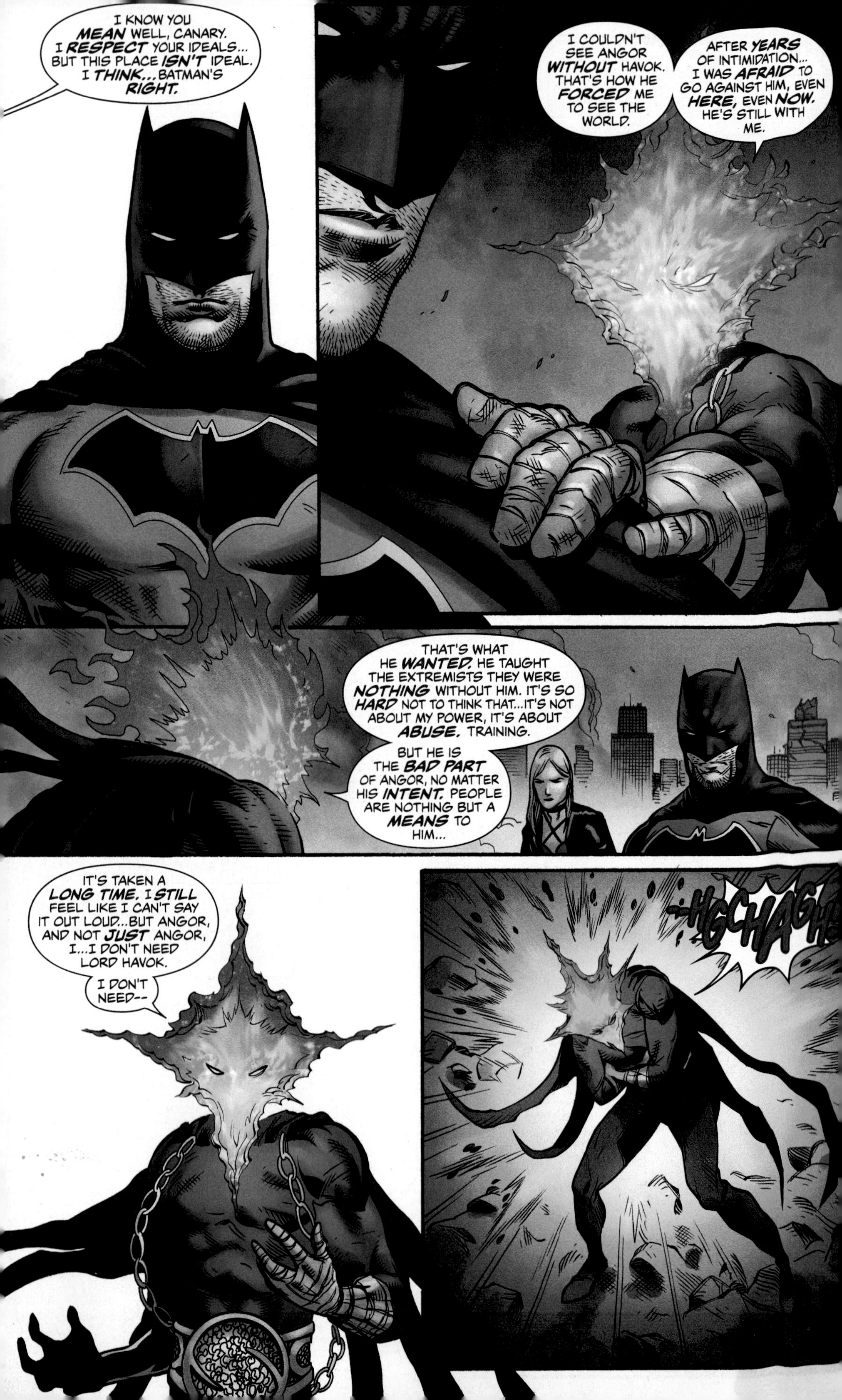
I KNOW YOU MEAN WELL, CANARY. I RESPECT YOUR IDEALS... BUT THIS PLACE ISN'T IDEAL. I THINK... BATMAN'S RIGHT.
I COULDN'T SEE ANGOR WITHOUT HAVOK. THAT'S HOW HE FORCED ME TO SEE THE WORLD.
AFTER YEARS OF INTIMIDATION... I WAS AFRAID TO GO AGAINST HIM, EVEN HERE, EVEN NOW. HE'S STILL WITH ME.
THAT'S WHAT HE WANTED. HE TAUGHT THE EXTREMISTS THEY WERE NOTHING WITHOUT HIM. IT'S SO HARD NOT TO THINK THAT...IT'S NOT ABOUT MY POWER, IT'S ABOUT ABUSE. TRAINING.
BUT HE IS THE BAD PART OF ANGOR, NO MATTER HIS INTENT. PEOPLE ARE NOTHING BUT A MEANS TO HIM...
IT'S TAKEN A LONG TIME. I STILL FEEL LIKE I CAN'T SAY IT OUT LOUD...BUT ANGOR, AND NOT JUST ANGOR, I...I DON'T NEED LORD HAVOK.
I DON'T NEED--
-HGCHAGH

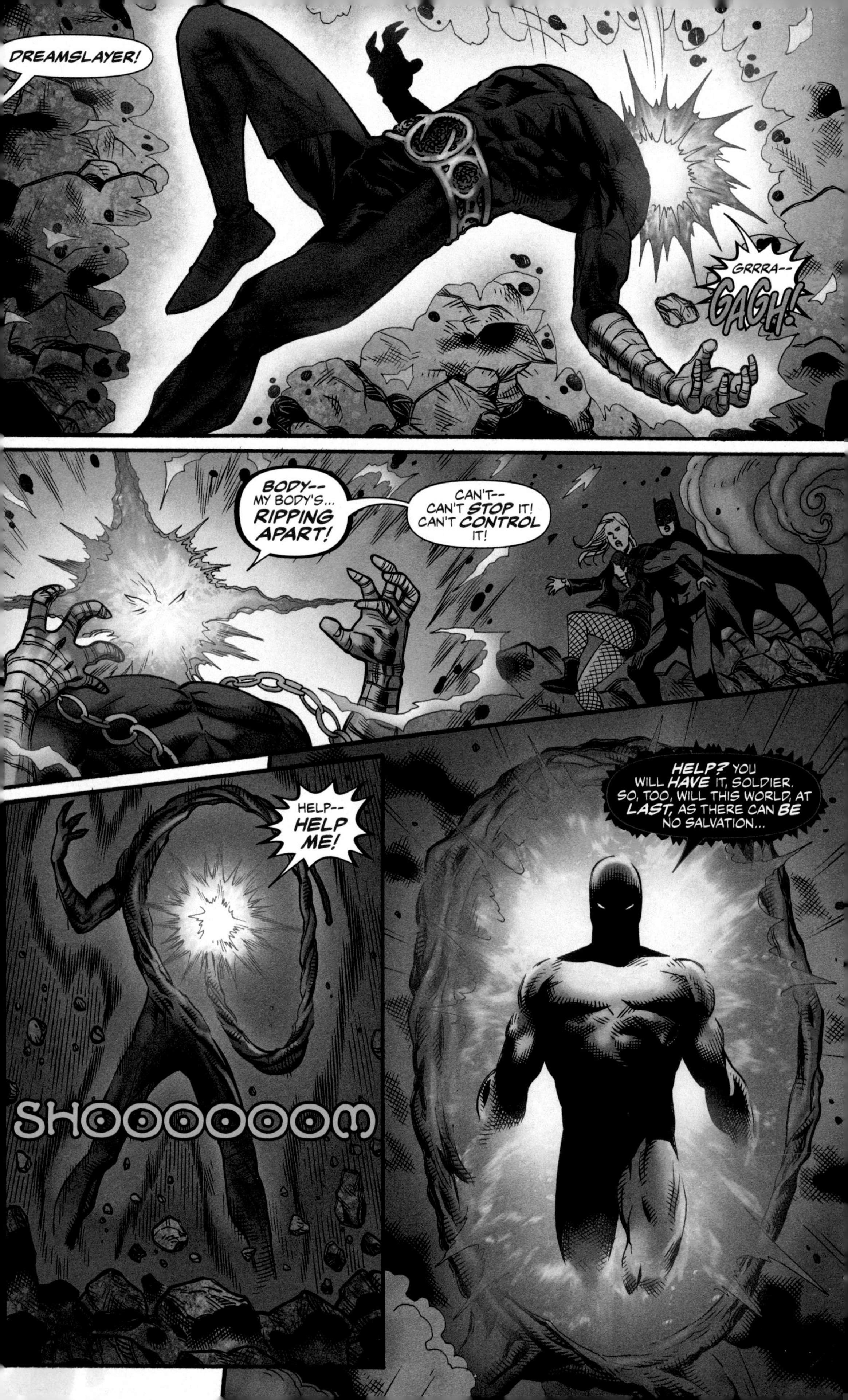
DREAMSLAYER!
GRRRA-- GAGH!
BODY-- MY BODY'S... RIPPING APART!
CAN'T-- CAN'T STOP IT! CAN'T CONTROL IT!
HELP-- HELP ME!
SHOOOOOOOM
HELP? YOU WILL HAVE IT, SOLDIER. SO, TOO, WILL THIS WORLD, AT LAST, AS THERE CAN BE NO SALVATION...

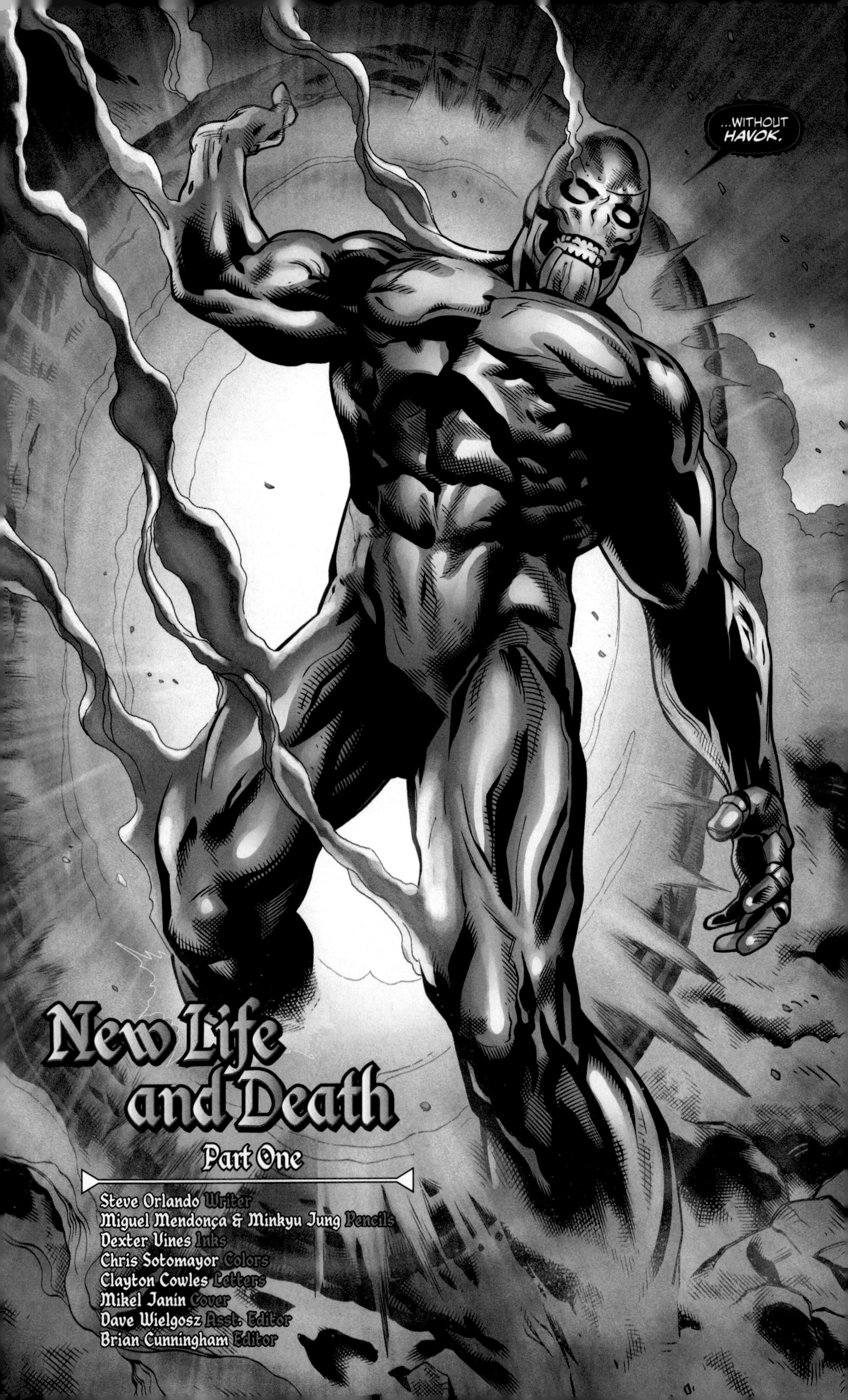
...WITHOUT HAVOK.
New Life and Death
Part One
Steve Orlando Writer
Miguel Mendonça & Minkyu Jung Pencils
Dexter Vines Inks
Chris Sotomayor Colors
Clayton Cowles Letters
Mikel Janín Cover
Dave Wielgosz Asst. Editor
Brian Cunningham Editor

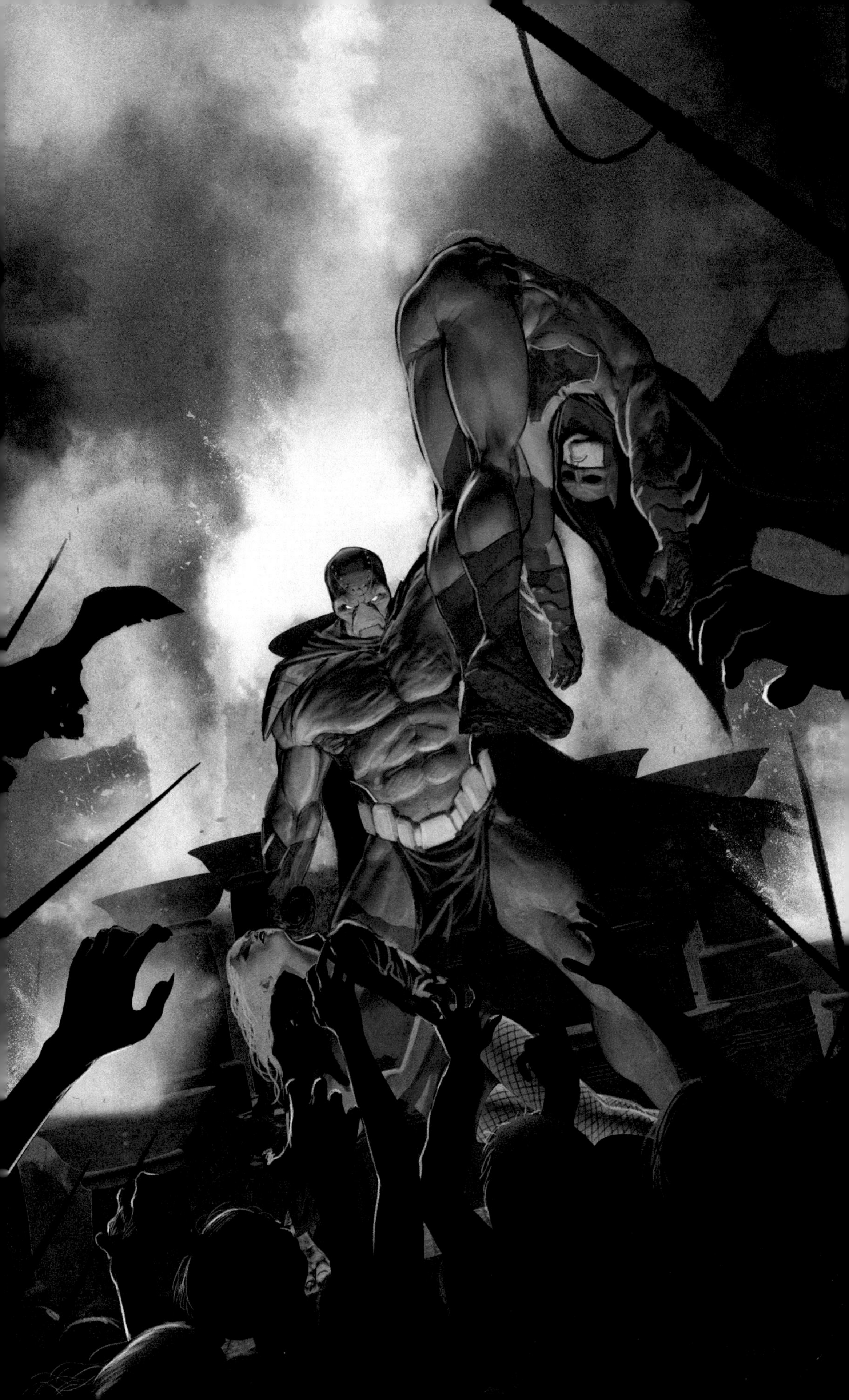

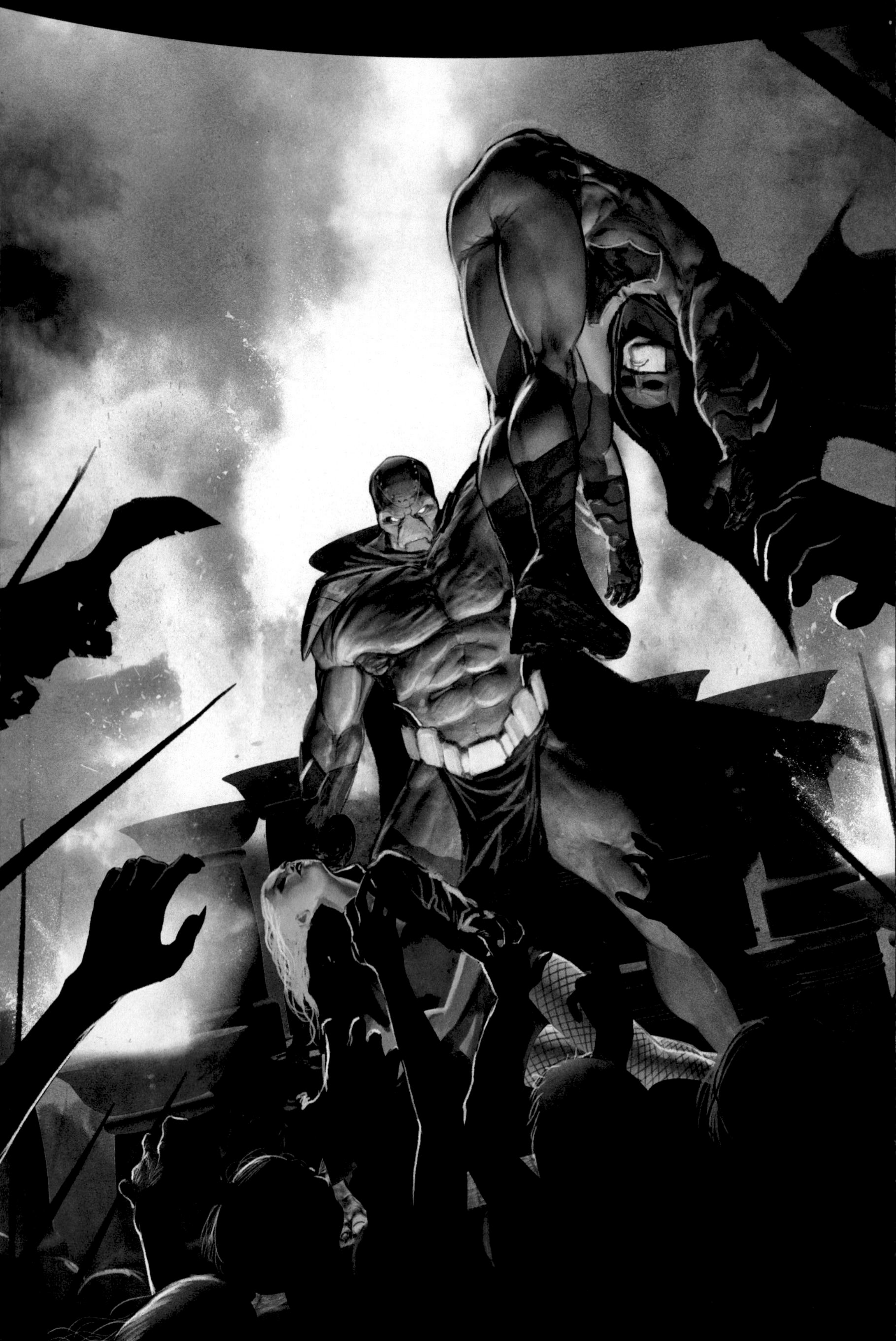

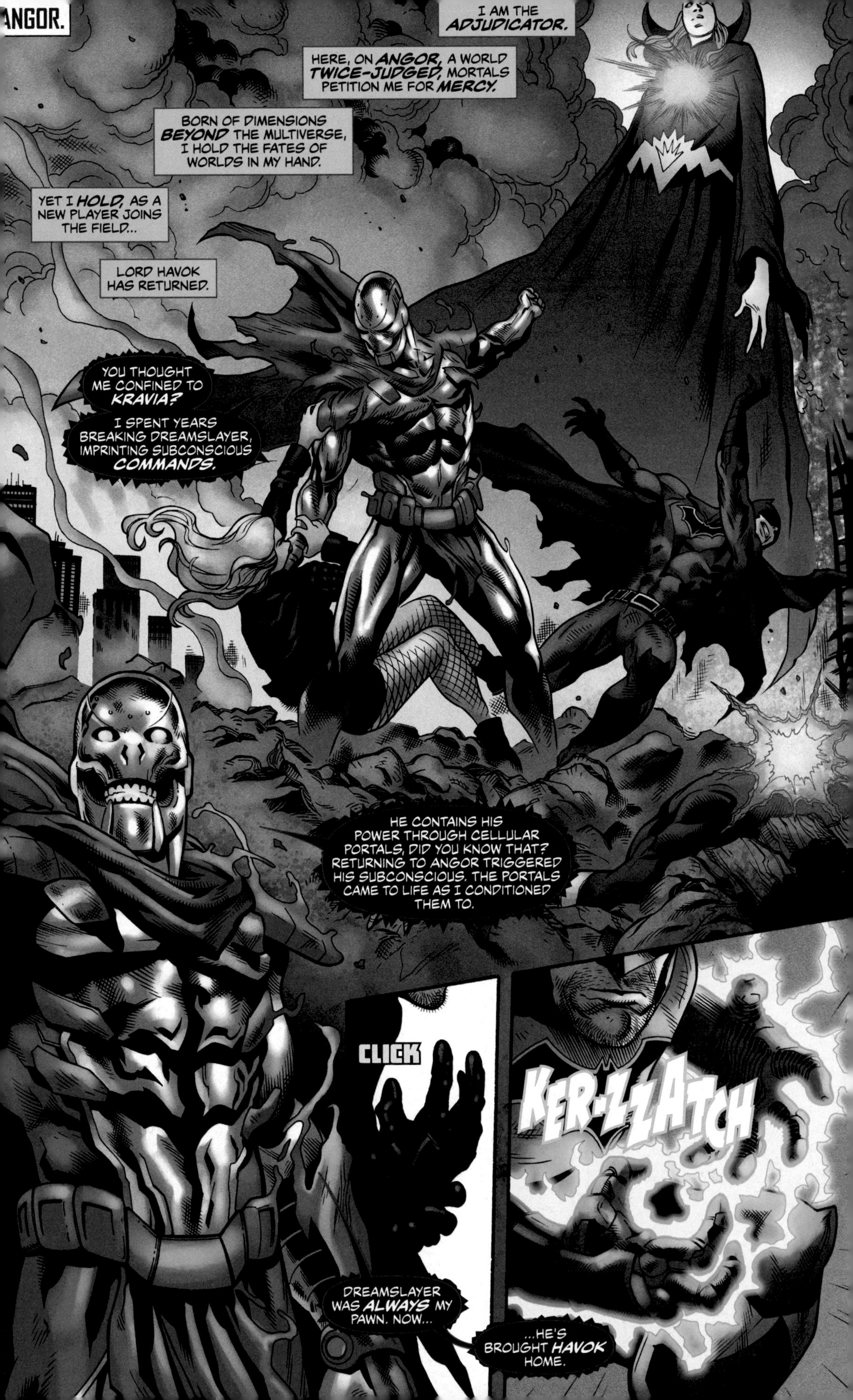

ANGOR.
I AM THE ADJUDICATOR.
HERE, ON ANGOR, A WORLD TWICE-JUDGED, MORTALS PETITION ME FOR MERCY.
BORN OF DIMENSIONS BEYOND THE MULTIVERSE, I HOLD THE FATES OF WORLDS IN MY HAND.
YET I HOLD, AS A NEW PLAYER JOINS THE FIELD...
LORD HAVOK HAS RETURNED.
YOU THOUGHT ME CONFINED TO KRAVIA?
I SPENT YEARS BREAKING DREAMSLAYER, IMPRINTING SUBCONSCIOUS COMMANDS.
HE CONTAINS HIS POWER THROUGH CELLULAR PORTALS, DID YOU KNOW THAT? RETURNING TO ANGOR TRIGGERED HIS SUBCONSCIOUS. THE PORTALS CAME TO LIFE AS I CONDITIONED THEM TO.
CLICK
KER-ZZATCH
DREAMSLAYER WAS ALWAYS MY PAWN. NOW...
...HE'S BROUGHT HAVOK HOME.

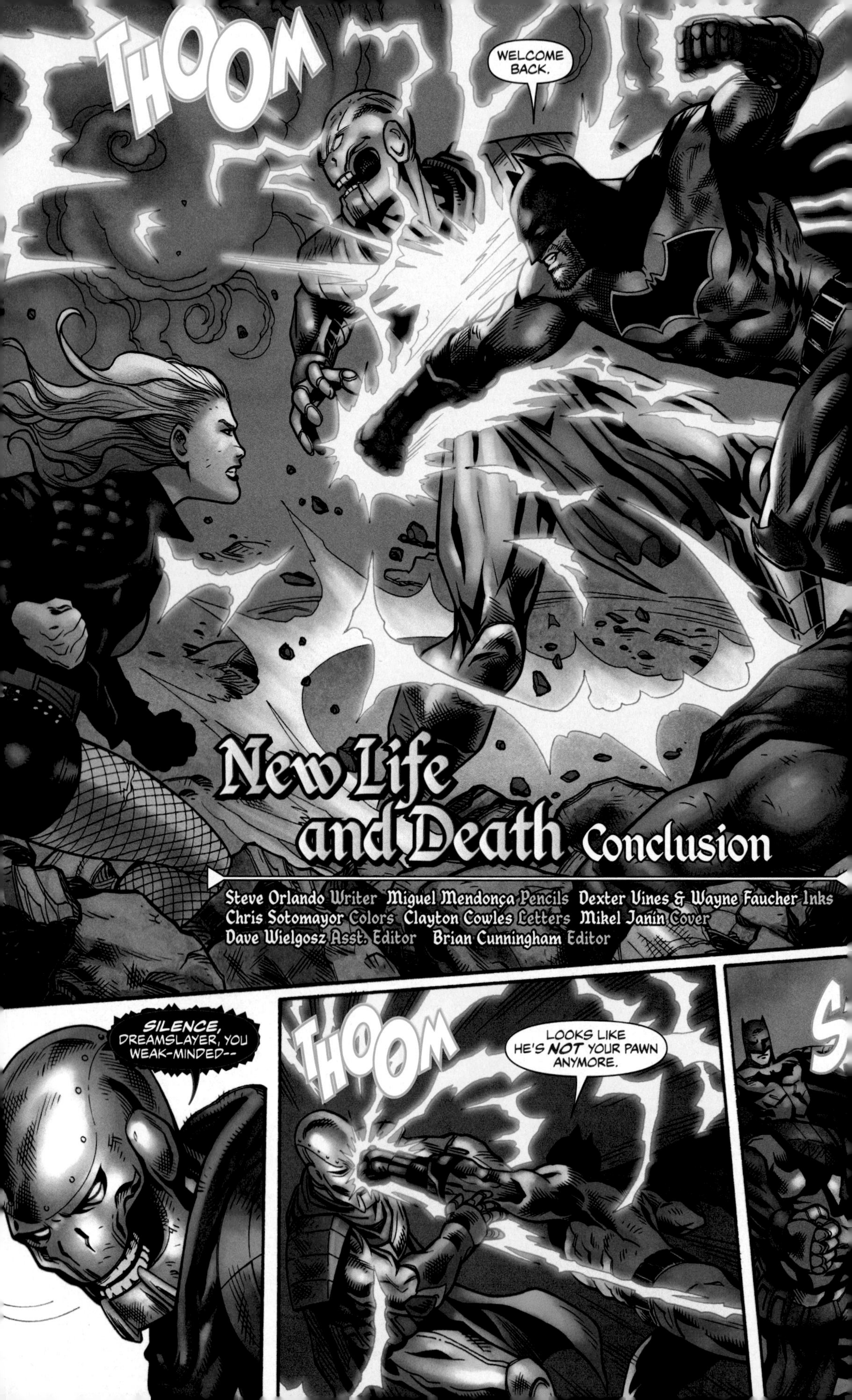
THOOM
WELCOME BACK.
New Life and Death Conclusion
Steve Orlando Writer Miguel Mendonça Pencils Dexter Vines & Wayne Faucher Inks
Chris Sotomayor Colors Clayton Cowles Letters Mikel Janín Cover
Dave Wielgosz Asst. Editor Brian Cunningham Editor
SILENCE, DREAMSLAYER, YOU WEAK-MINDED--
THOOM
LOOKS LIKE HE'S NOT YOUR PAWN ANYMORE.

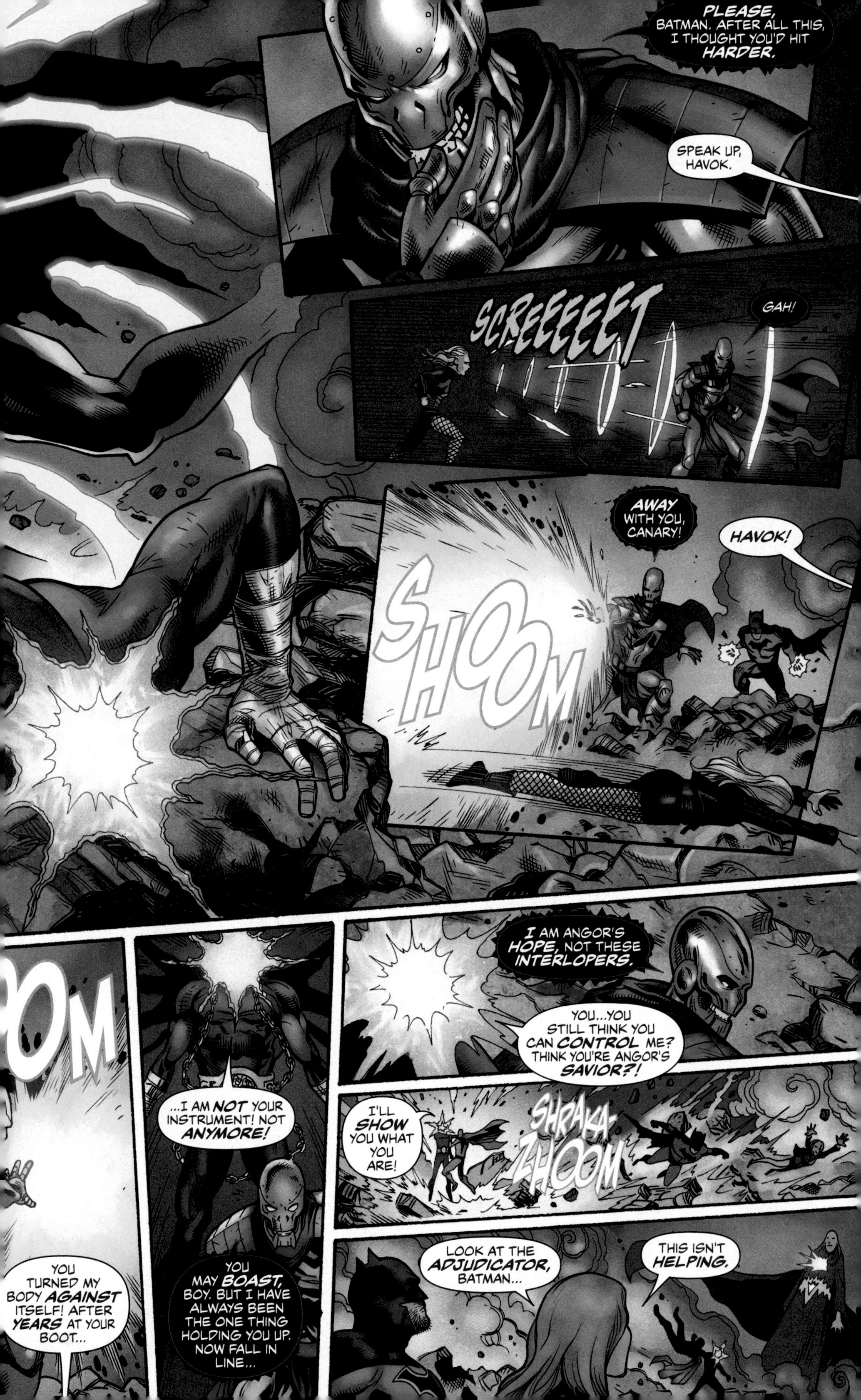
PLEASE, BATMAN. AFTER ALL THIS, I THOUGHT YOU'D HIT HARDER.
SPEAK UP, HAVOK.
SCREEEEEET
GAH!
AWAY WITH YOU, CANARY!
HAVOK!
SHOOOM
...I AM NOT YOUR INSTRUMENT! NOT ANYMORE!
YOU TURNED MY BODY AGAINST ITSELF! AFTER YEARS AT YOUR BOOT...
YOU MAY BOAST, BOY. BUT I HAVE ALWAYS BEEN THE ONE THING HOLDING YOU UP. NOW FALL IN LINE...
I AM ANGOR'S HOPE, NOT THESE INTERLOPERS.
YOU...YOU STILL THINK YOU CAN CONTROL ME? THINK YOU'RE ANGOR'S SAVIOR?!
I'LL SHOW YOU WHAT YOU ARE!
SHRAKA-ZHOOM
LOOK AT THE ADJUDICATOR, BATMAN...
THIS ISN'T HELPING.

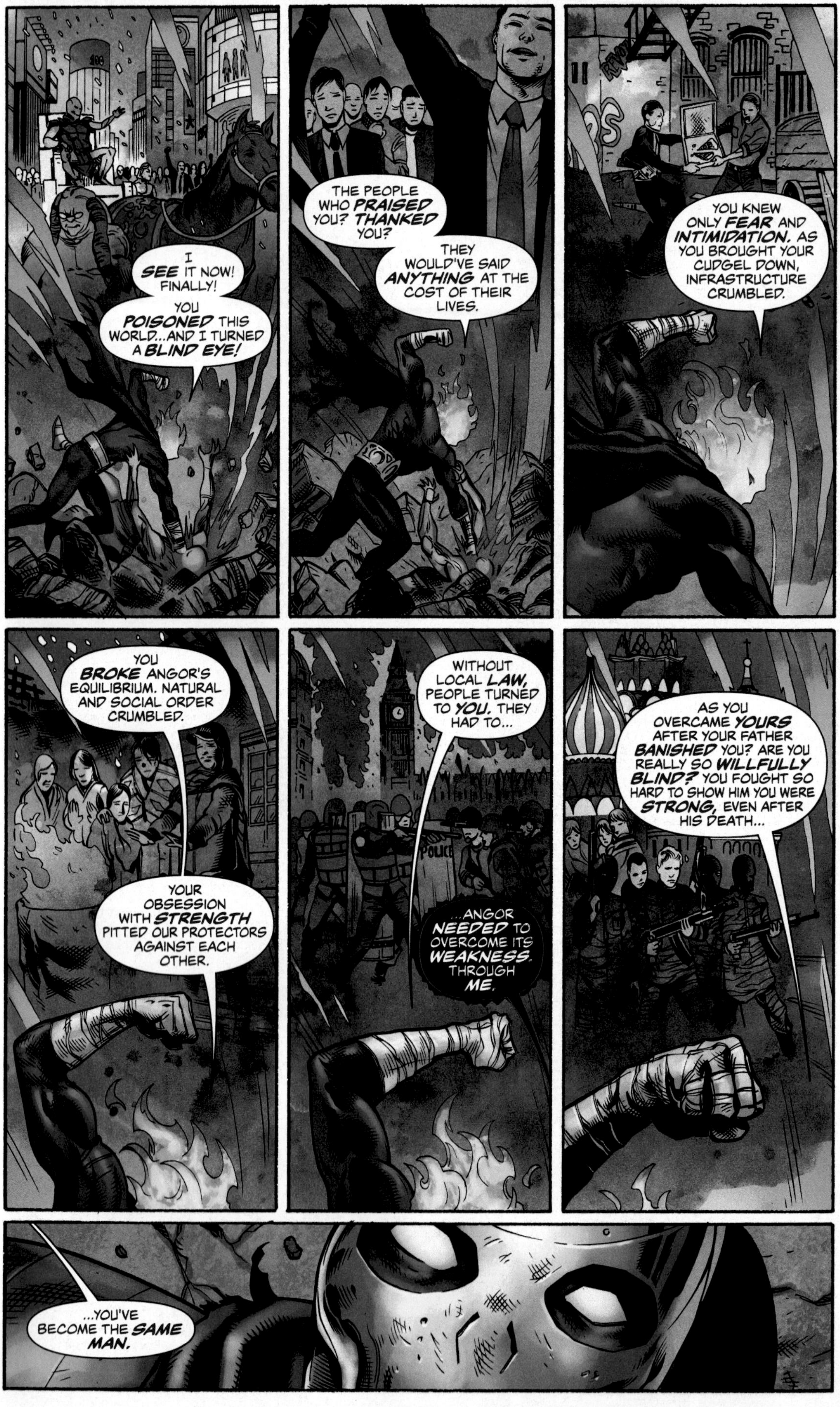
I SEE IT NOW! FINALLY!
YOU POISONED THIS WORLD...AND I TURNED A BLIND EYE!
THE PEOPLE WHO PRAISED YOU? THANKED YOU?
THEY WOULD'VE SAID ANYTHING AT THE COST OF THEIR LIVES.
YOU KNEW ONLY FEAR AND INTIMIDATION. AS YOU BROUGHT YOUR CUDGEL DOWN, INFRASTRUCTURE CRUMBLED.
YOU BROKE ANGOR'S EQUILIBRIUM. NATURAL AND SOCIAL ORDER CRUMBLED.
YOUR OBSESSION WITH STRENGTH PITTED OUR PROTECTORS AGAINST EACH OTHER.
WITHOUT LOCAL LAW, PEOPLE TURNED TO YOU. THEY HAD TO...
...ANGOR NEEDED TO OVERCOME ITS WEAKNESS. THROUGH ME.
AS YOU OVERCAME YOURS AFTER YOUR FATHER BANISHED YOU? ARE YOU REALLY SO WILLFULLY BLIND? YOU FOUGHT SO HARD TO SHOW HIM YOU WERE STRONG, EVEN AFTER HIS DEATH...
...YOU'VE BECOME THE SAME MAN.

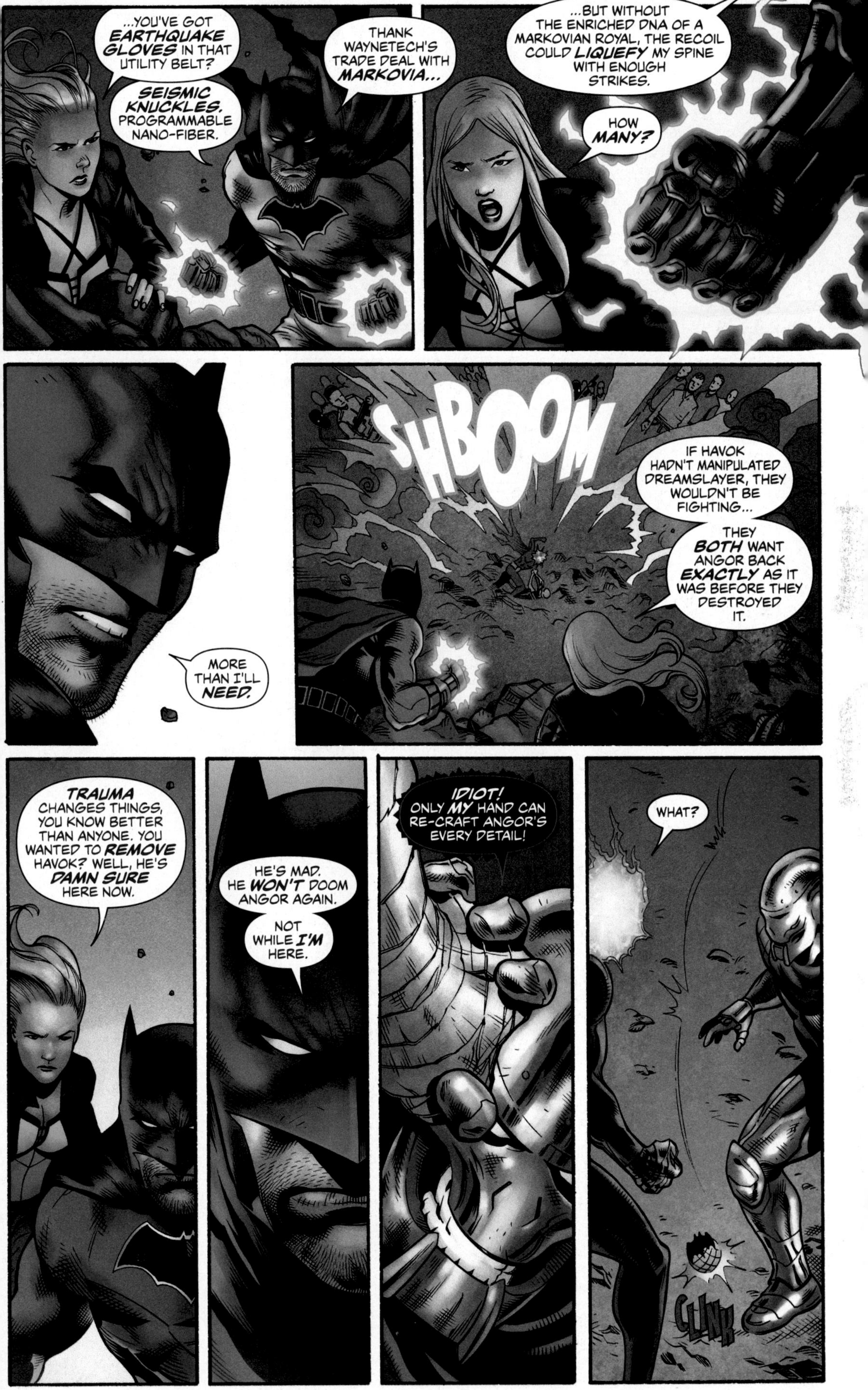
...YOU'VE GOT EARTHQUAKE GLOVES IN THAT UTILITY BELT?
SEISMIC KNUCKLES. PROGRAMMABLE NANO-FIBER.
THANK WAYNETECH'S TRADE DEAL WITH MARKOVIA...
...BUT WITHOUT THE ENRICHED DNA OF A MARKOVIAN ROYAL, THE RECOIL COULD LIQUEFY MY SPINE WITH ENOUGH STRIKES.
HOW MANY?
MORE THAN I'LL NEED.
SHBOOM
IF HAVOK HADN'T MANIPULATED DREAMSLAYER, THEY WOULDN'T BE FIGHTING...
THEY BOTH WANT ANGOR BACK EXACTLY AS IT WAS BEFORE THEY DESTROYED IT.
TRAUMA CHANGES THINGS, YOU KNOW BETTER THAN ANYONE. YOU WANTED TO REMOVE HAVOK? WELL, HE'S DAMN SURE HERE NOW.
HE'S MAD. HE WON'T DOOM ANGOR AGAIN.
NOT WHILE I'M HERE.
IDIOT! ONLY MY HAND CAN RE-CRAFT ANGOR'S EVERY DETAIL!
WHAT?
CLINK

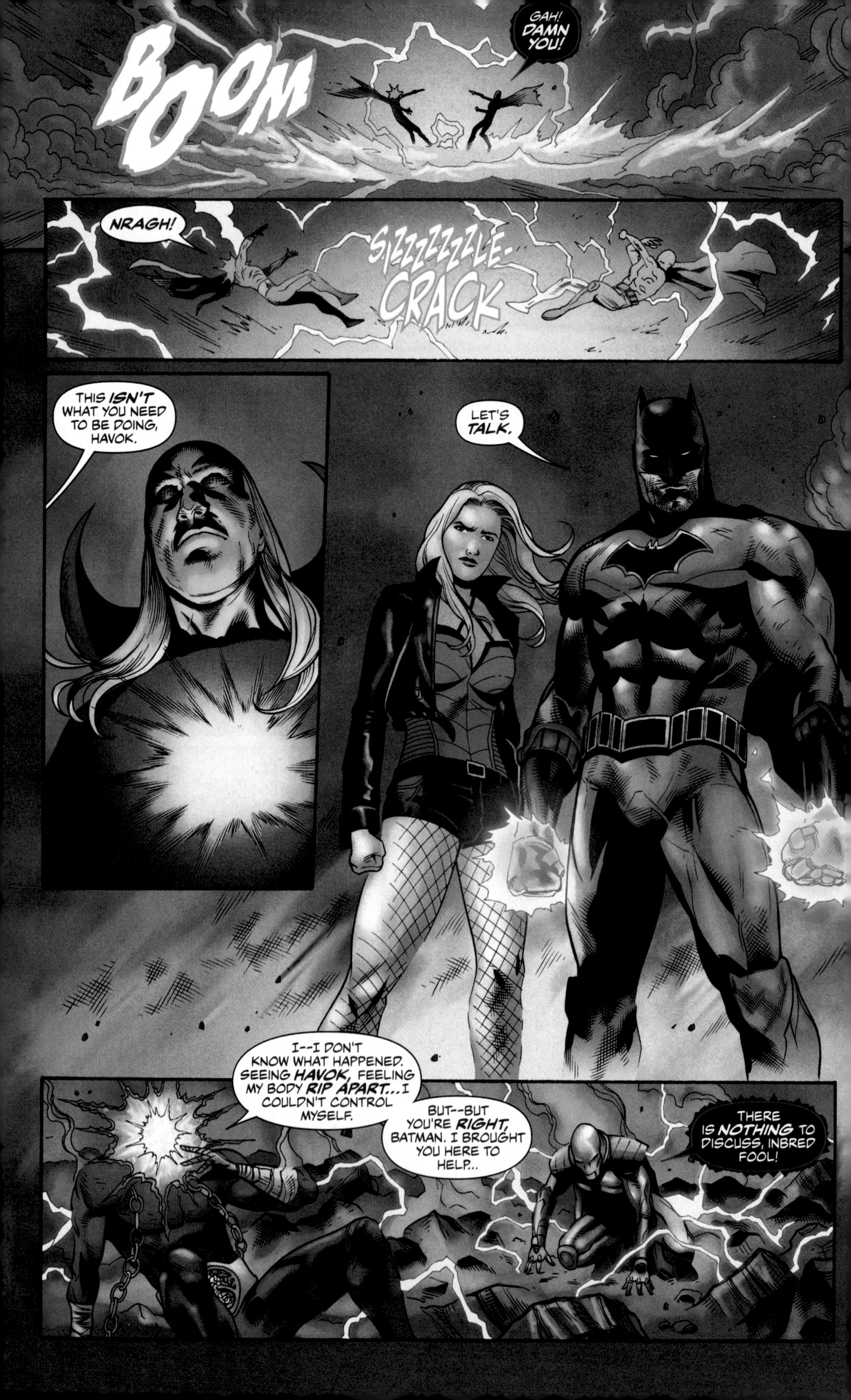
BOOM
GAH! DAMN YOU!
NRAGH!
SIZZZZZZZLE-CRACK
THIS ISN'T WHAT YOU NEED TO BE DOING, HAVOK.
LET'S TALK.
I--I DON'T KNOW WHAT HAPPENED. SEEING HAVOK, FEELING MY BODY RIP APART...I COULDN'T CONTROL MYSELF.
BUT--BUT YOU'RE RIGHT, BATMAN. I BROUGHT YOU HERE TO HELP...
THERE IS NOTHING TO DISCUSS, INBRED FOOL!

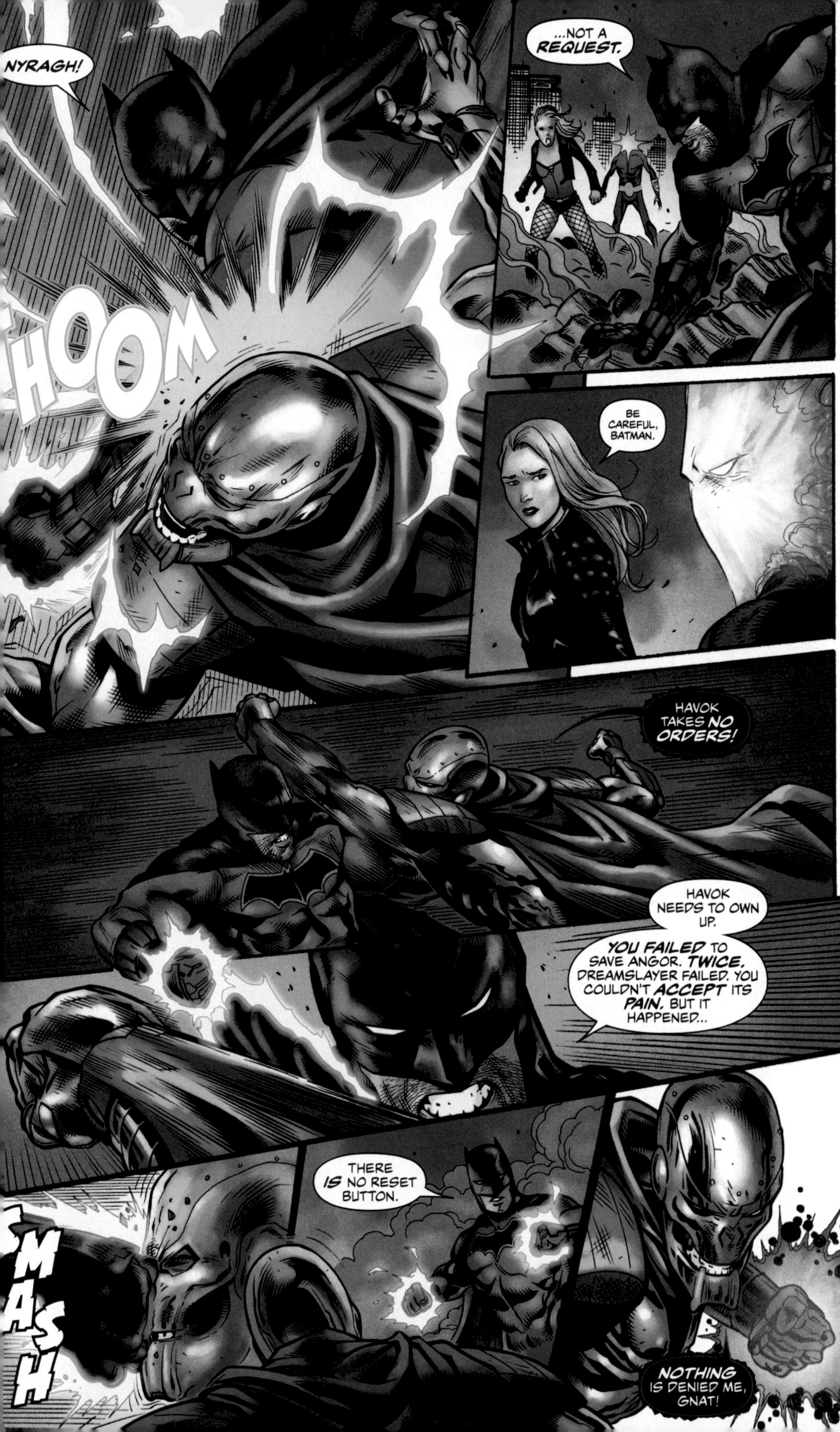
NYRAGH!
...NOT A REQUEST.
WHOOM
BE CAREFUL, BATMAN.
HAVOK TAKES NO ORDERS!
HAVOK NEEDS TO OWN UP.
YOU FAILED TO SAVE ANGOR. TWICE. DREAMSLAYER FAILED. YOU COULDN'T ACCEPT ITS PAIN. BUT IT HAPPENED...
THERE IS NO RESET BUTTON.
SMASH
NOTHING IS DENIED ME, GNAT!

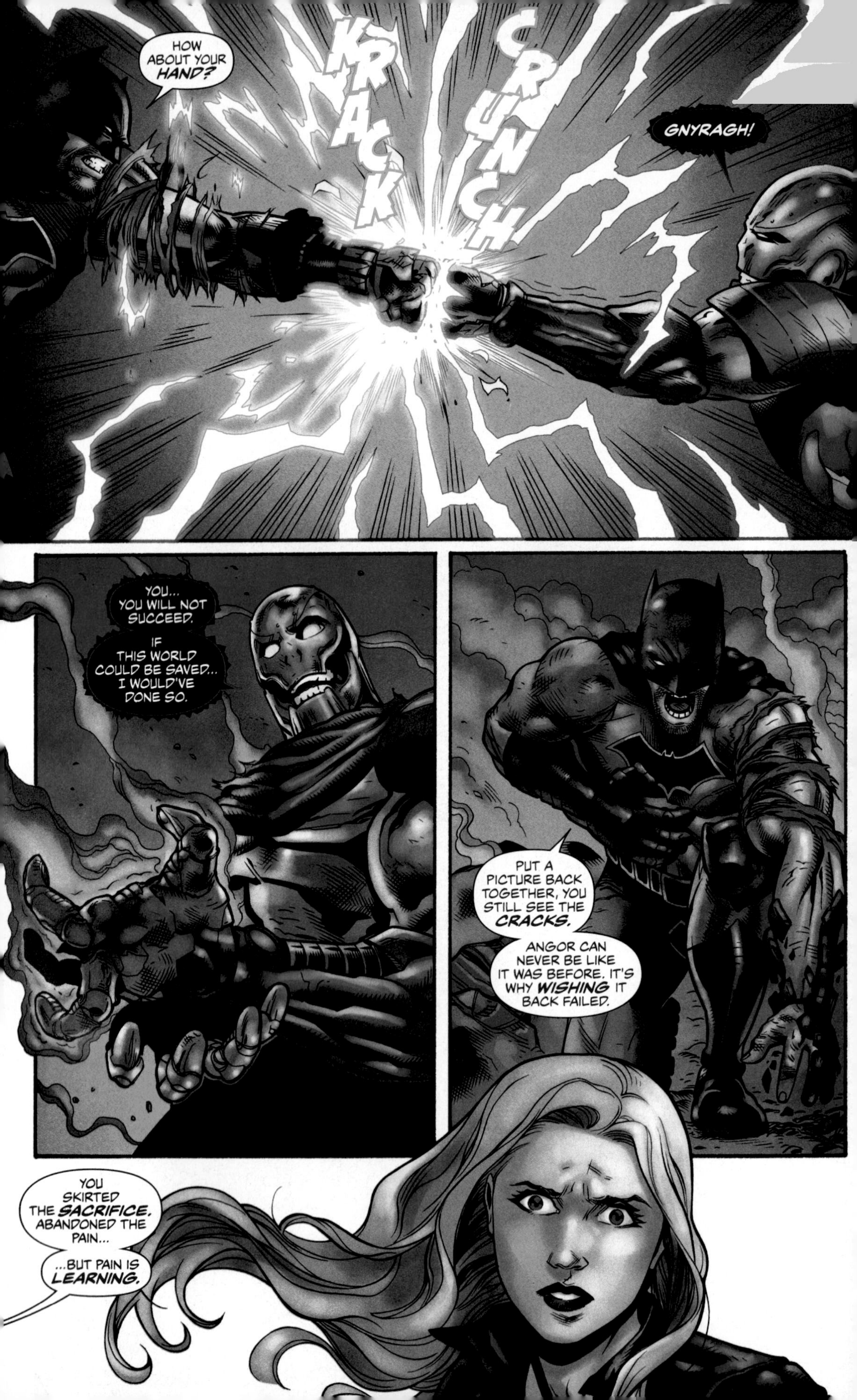

HOW ABOUT YOUR HAND?
KRACK
CRUNCH
GNYRAGH!
YOU... YOU WILL NOT SUCCEED.
IF THIS WORLD COULD BE SAVED... I WOULD'VE DONE SO.
PUT A PICTURE BACK TOGETHER, YOU STILL SEE THE CRACKS.
ANGOR CAN NEVER BE LIKE IT WAS BEFORE. IT'S WHY WISHING IT BACK FAILED.
YOU SKIRTED THE SACRIFICE. ABANDONED THE PAIN...
...BUT PAIN IS LEARNING.

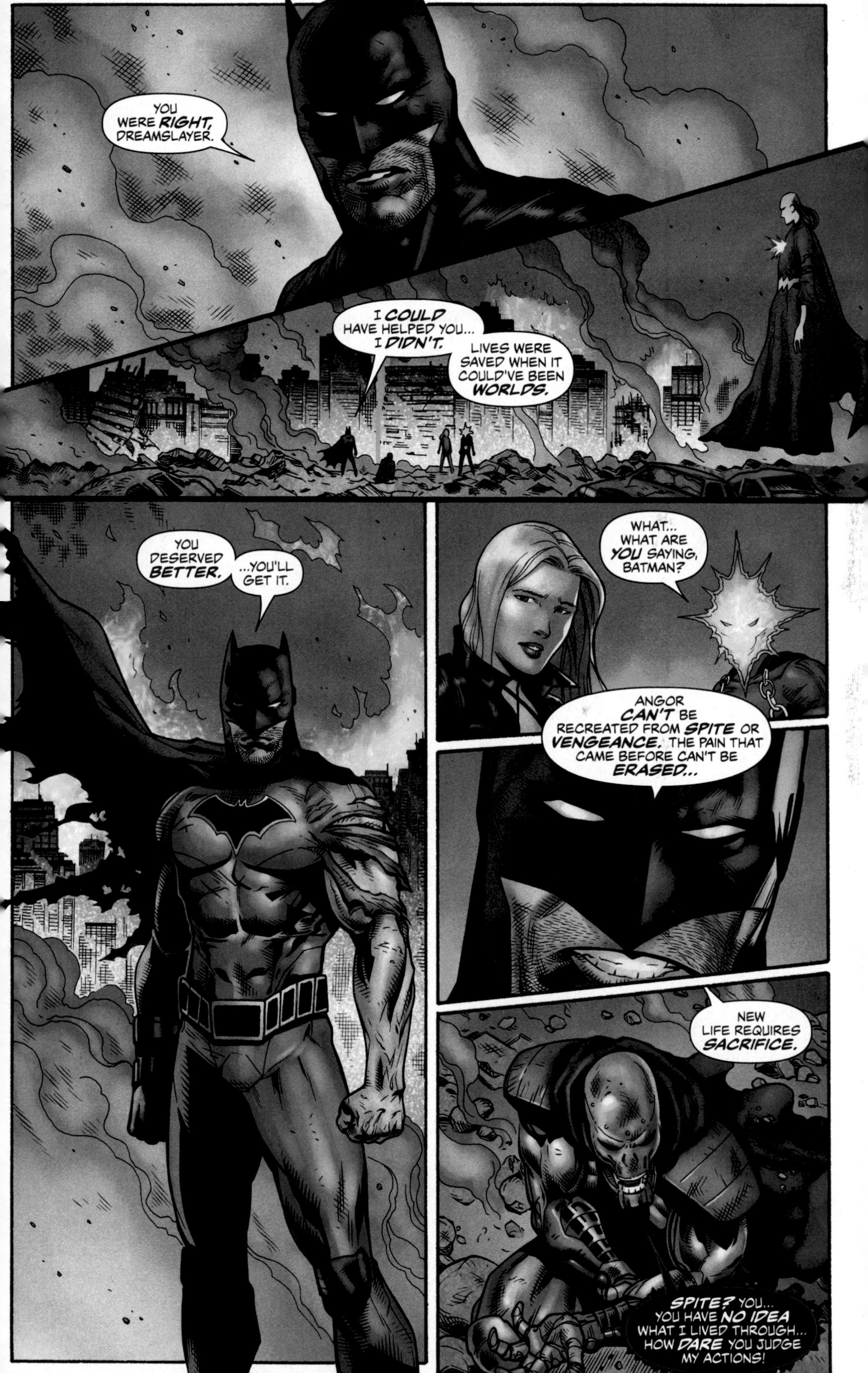
YOU WERE RIGHT, DREAMSLAYER.
I COULD HAVE HELPED YOU... I DIDN'T.
LIVES WERE SAVED WHEN IT COULD'VE BEEN WORLDS.
YOU DESERVED BETTER.
...YOU'LL GET IT.
WHAT... WHAT ARE YOU SAYING, BATMAN?
ANGOR CAN'T BE RECREATED FROM SPITE OR VENGEANCE. THE PAIN THAT CAME BEFORE CAN'T BE ERASED...
NEW LIFE REQUIRES SACRIFICE.
SPITE? YOU... YOU HAVE NO IDEA WHAT I LIVED THROUGH... HOW DARE YOU JUDGE MY ACTIONS!

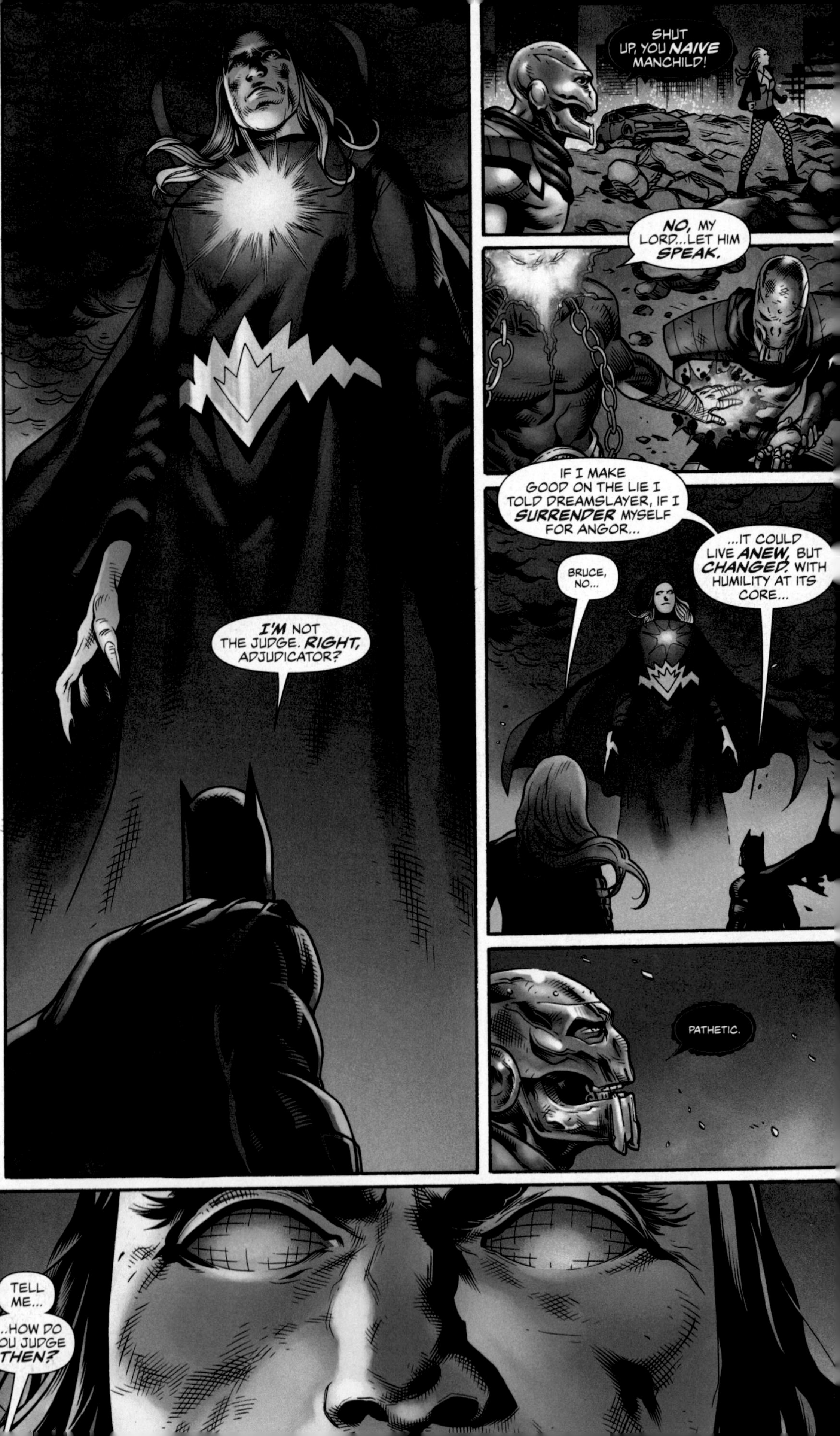
I'M NOT THE JUDGE. RIGHT, ADJUDICATOR?
SHUT UP, YOU NAIVE MANCHILD!
NO, MY LORD...LET HIM SPEAK.
IF I MAKE GOOD ON THE LIE I TOLD DREAMSLAYER, IF I SURRENDER MYSELF FOR ANGOR...
...IT COULD LIVE ANEW, BUT CHANGED. WITH HUMILITY AT ITS CORE...
BRUCE, NO...
PATHETIC.
TELL ME...
...HOW DO YOU JUDGE THEN?

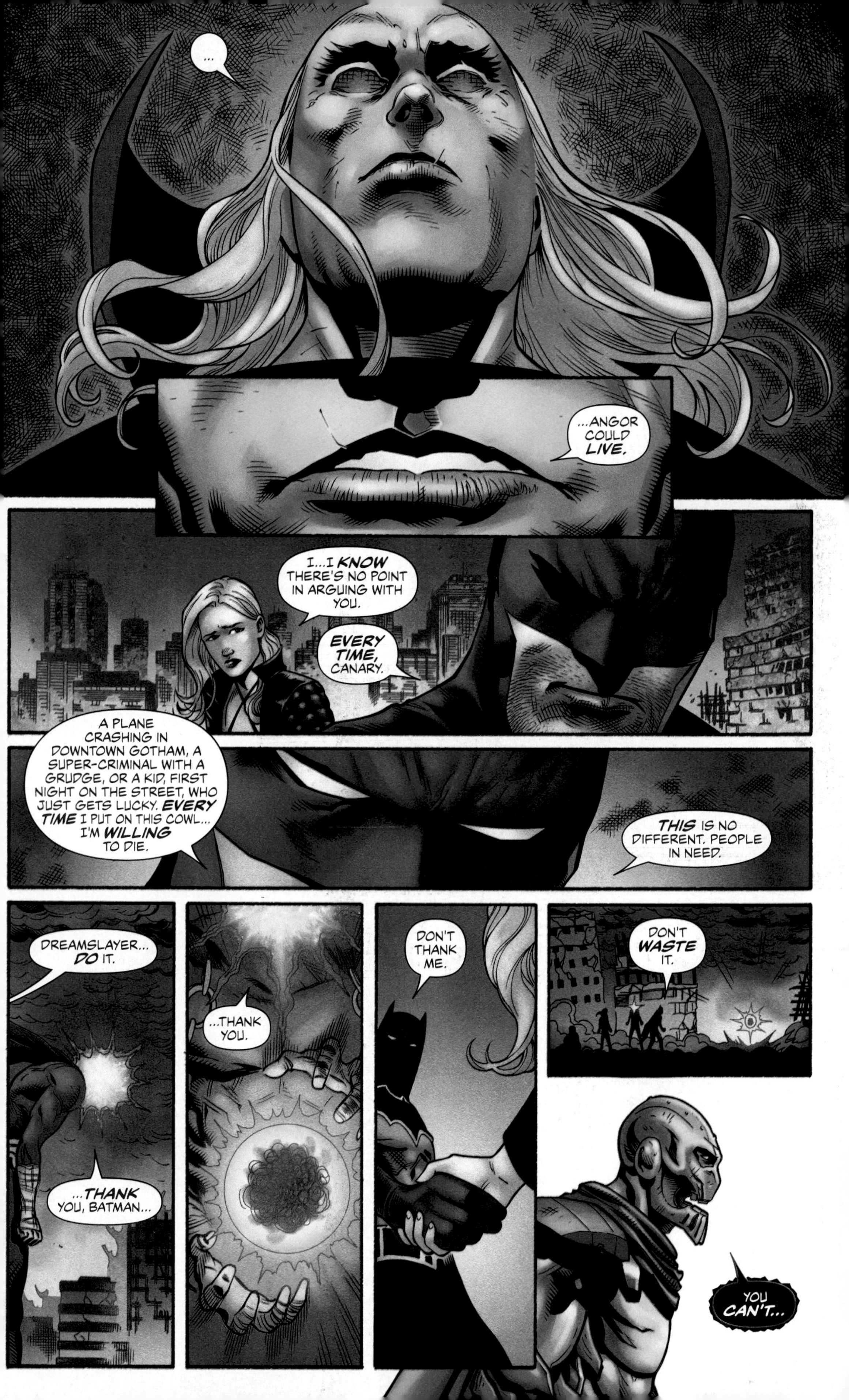
...
...ANGOR COULD LIVE.
I...I KNOW THERE'S NO POINT IN ARGUING WITH YOU.
EVERY TIME, CANARY.
A PLANE CRASHING IN DOWNTOWN GOTHAM, A SUPER-CRIMINAL WITH A GRUDGE, OR A KID, FIRST NIGHT ON THE STREET, WHO JUST GETS LUCKY. EVERY TIME I PUT ON THIS COWL... I'M WILLING TO DIE.
THIS IS NO DIFFERENT. PEOPLE IN NEED.
DREAMSLAYER... DO IT.
...THANK YOU, BATMAN...
...THANK YOU.
DON'T THANK ME.
DON'T WASTE IT.
YOU CAN'T...

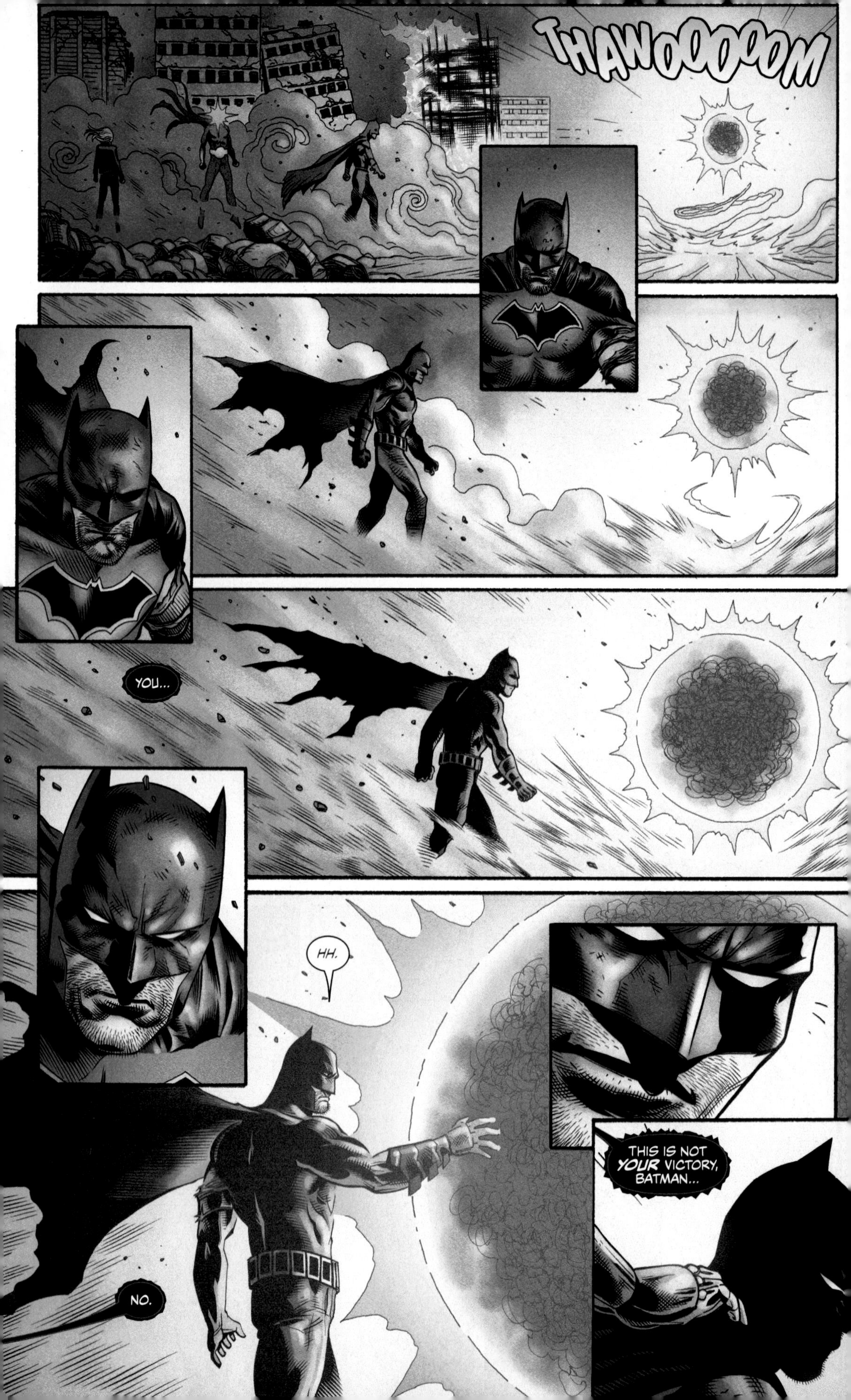
THAWOOOOOM
YOU...
HH.
NO.
THIS IS NOT YOUR VICTORY, BATMAN...

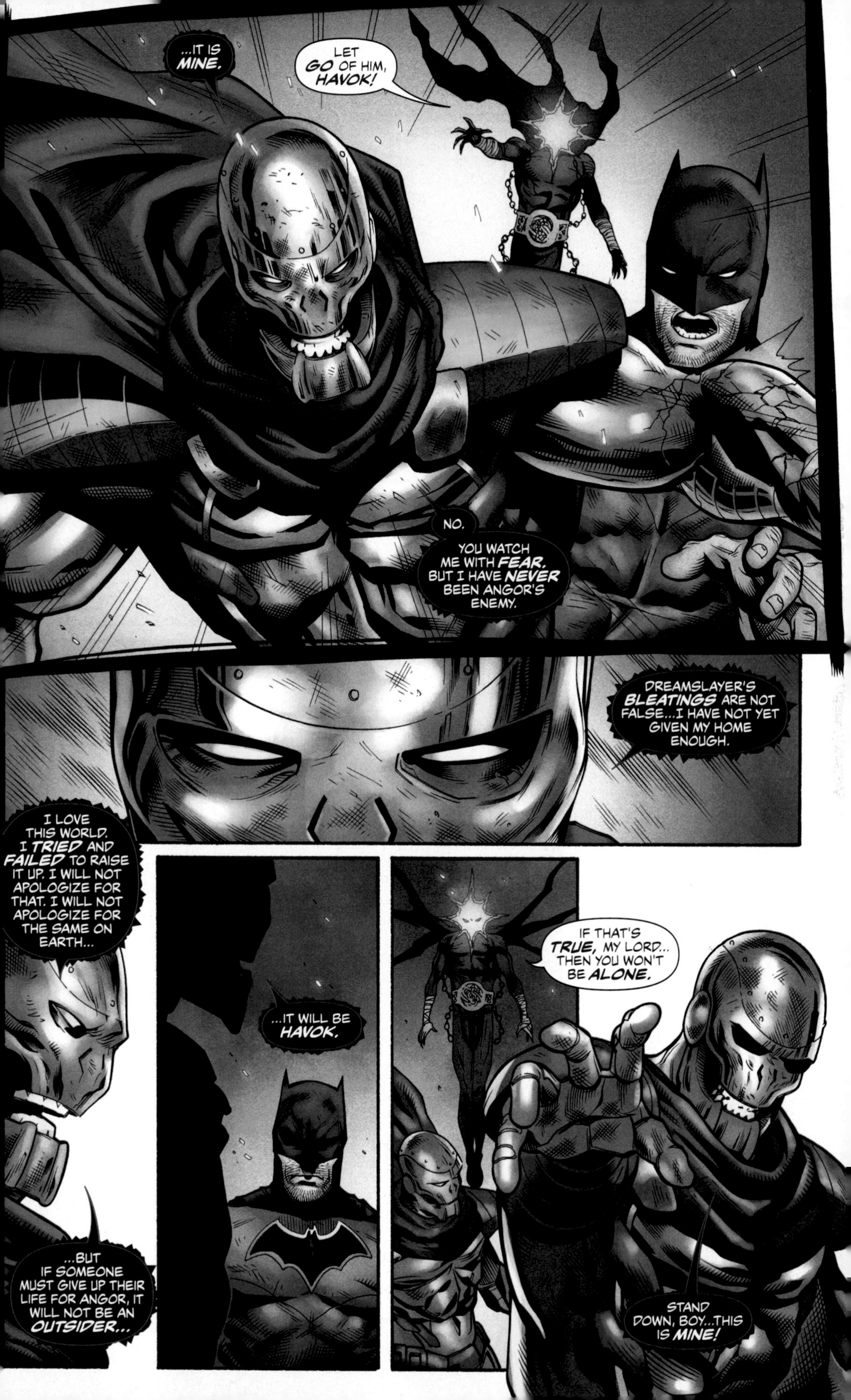
...IT IS MINE.
LET GO OF HIM, HAVOK!
NO.
YOU WATCH ME WITH FEAR. BUT I HAVE NEVER BEEN ANGOR'S ENEMY.
DREAMSLAYER'S BLEATINGS ARE NOT FALSE...I HAVE NOT YET GIVEN MY HOME ENOUGH.
I LOVE THIS WORLD. I TRIED AND FAILED TO RAISE IT UP. I WILL NOT APOLOGIZE FOR THAT. I WILL NOT APOLOGIZE FOR THE SAME ON EARTH...
...BUT IF SOMEONE MUST GIVE UP THEIR LIFE FOR ANGOR, IT WILL NOT BE AN OUTSIDER...
...IT WILL BE HAVOK.
IF THAT'S TRUE, MY LORD... THEN YOU WON'T BE ALONE.
STAND DOWN, BOY...THIS IS MINE!

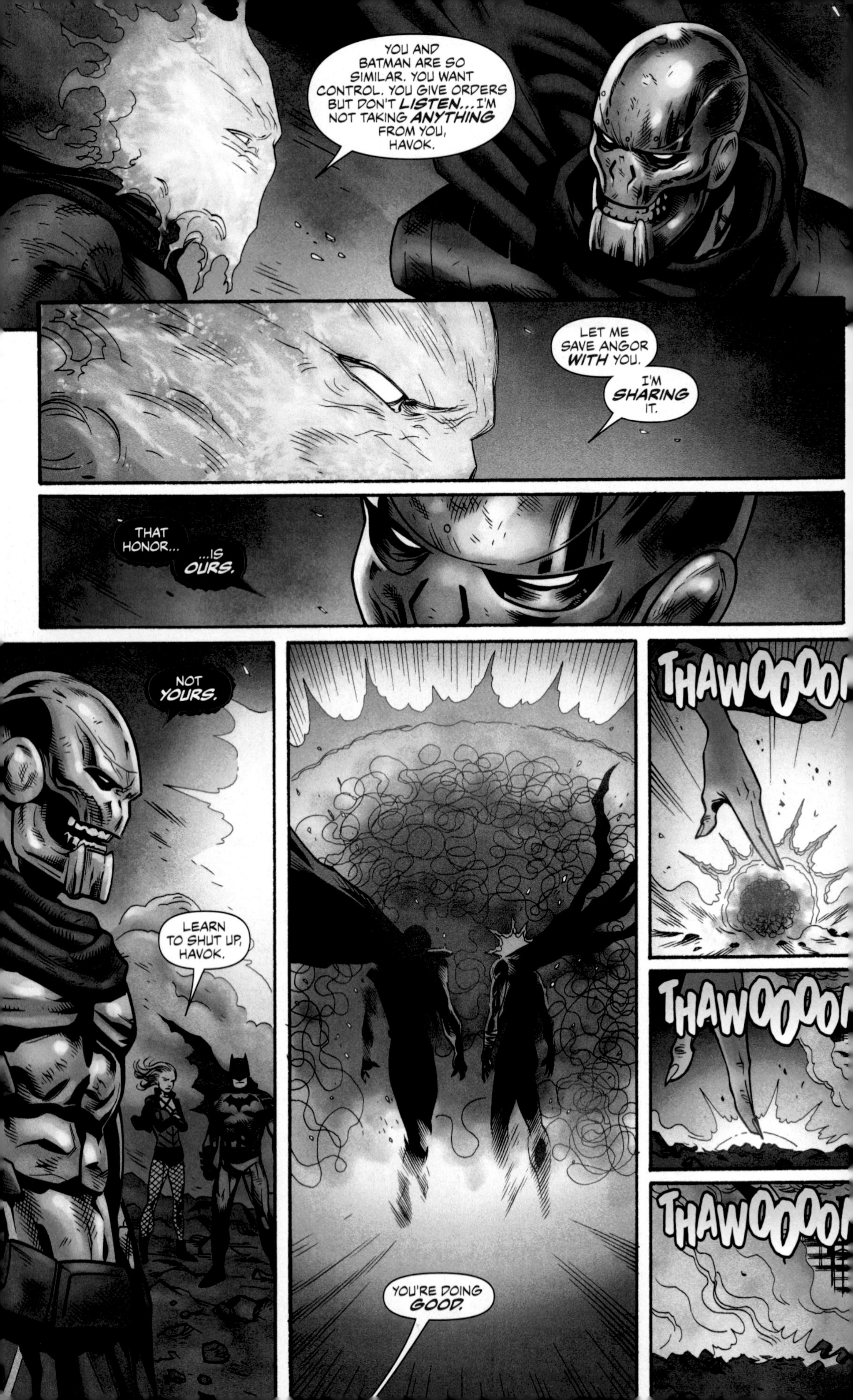
YOU AND BATMAN ARE SO SIMILAR. YOU WANT CONTROL. YOU GIVE ORDERS BUT DON'T LISTEN... I'M NOT TAKING ANYTHING FROM YOU, HAVOK.
LET ME SAVE ANGOR WITH YOU.
I'M SHARING IT.
THAT HONOR...
...IS OURS.
NOT YOURS.
LEARN TO SHUT UP, HAVOK.
YOU'RE DOING GOOD.
THAWOOOOO
THAWOOOOO
THAWOOOOO

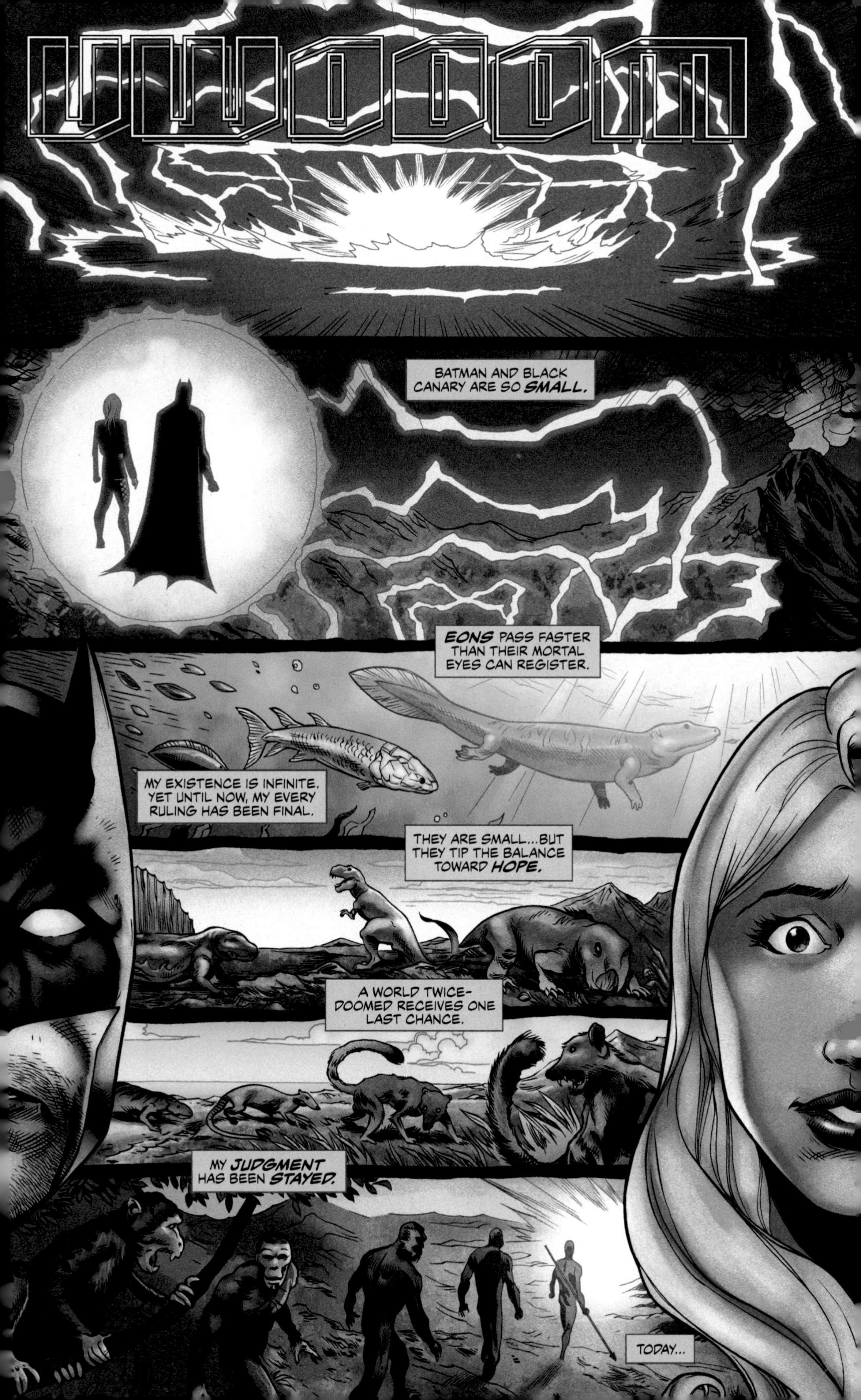

UNDOOOM
BATMAN AND BLACK CANARY ARE SO SMALL.
EONS PASS FASTER THAN THEIR MORTAL EYES CAN REGISTER.
MY EXISTENCE IS INFINITE. YET UNTIL NOW, MY EVERY RULING HAS BEEN FINAL.
THEY ARE SMALL...BUT THEY TIP THE BALANCE TOWARD HOPE.
A WORLD TWICE-DOOMED RECEIVES ONE LAST CHANCE.
MY JUDGMENT HAS BEEN STAYED.
TODAY...

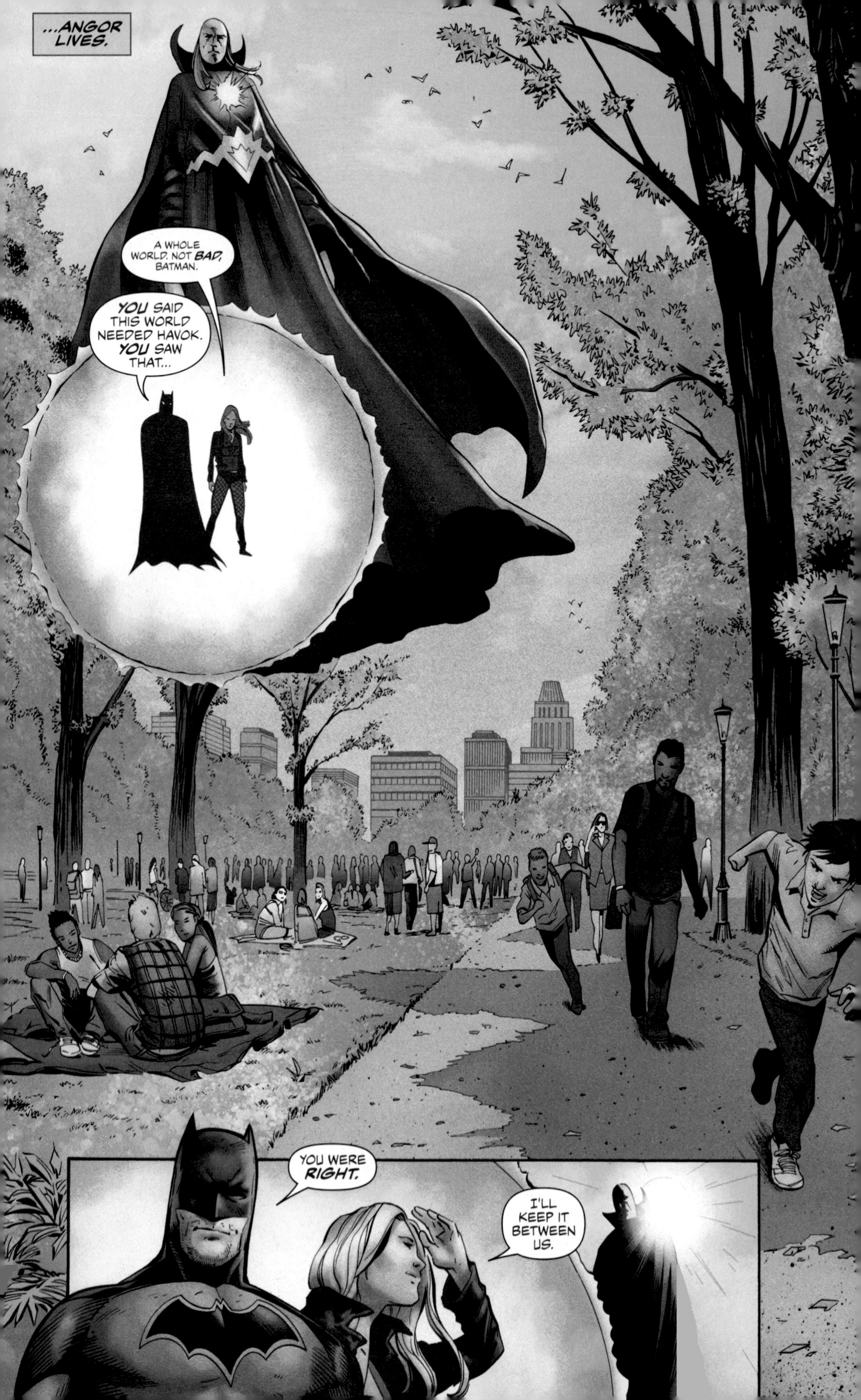
...ANGOR LIVES.
A WHOLE WORLD. NOT BAD, BATMAN.
YOU SAID THIS WORLD NEEDED HAVOK. YOU SAW THAT...
YOU WERE RIGHT.
I'LL KEEP IT BETWEEN US.

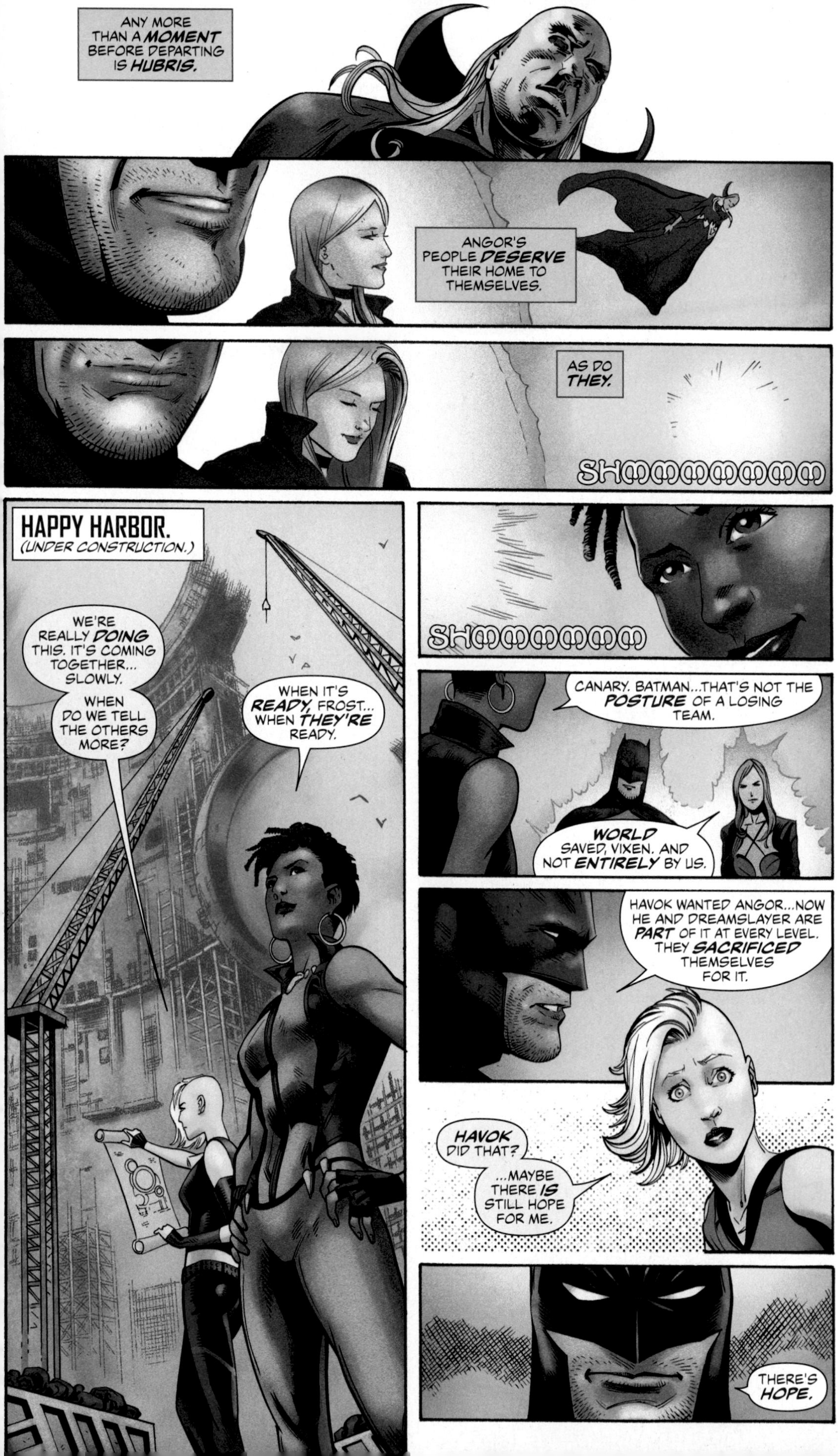
ANY MORE THAN A MOMENT BEFORE DEPARTING IS HUBRIS.
ANGOR'S PEOPLE DESERVE THEIR HOME TO THEMSELVES.
AS DO THEY.
SHMMMMMMMM
HAPPY HARBOR. (UNDER CONSTRUCTION.)
WE'RE REALLY DOING THIS. IT'S COMING TOGETHER... SLOWLY.
WHEN DO WE TELL THE OTHERS MORE?
WHEN IT'S READY, FROST... WHEN THEY'RE READY.
SHMMMMMMM
CANARY. BATMAN...THAT'S NOT THE POSTURE OF A LOSING TEAM.
WORLD SAVED, VIXEN. AND NOT ENTIRELY BY US.
HAVOK WANTED ANGOR...NOW HE AND DREAMSLAYER ARE PART OF IT AT EVERY LEVEL. THEY SACRIFICED THEMSELVES FOR IT.
HAVOK DID THAT?
...MAYBE THERE IS STILL HOPE FOR ME.
THERE'S HOPE.

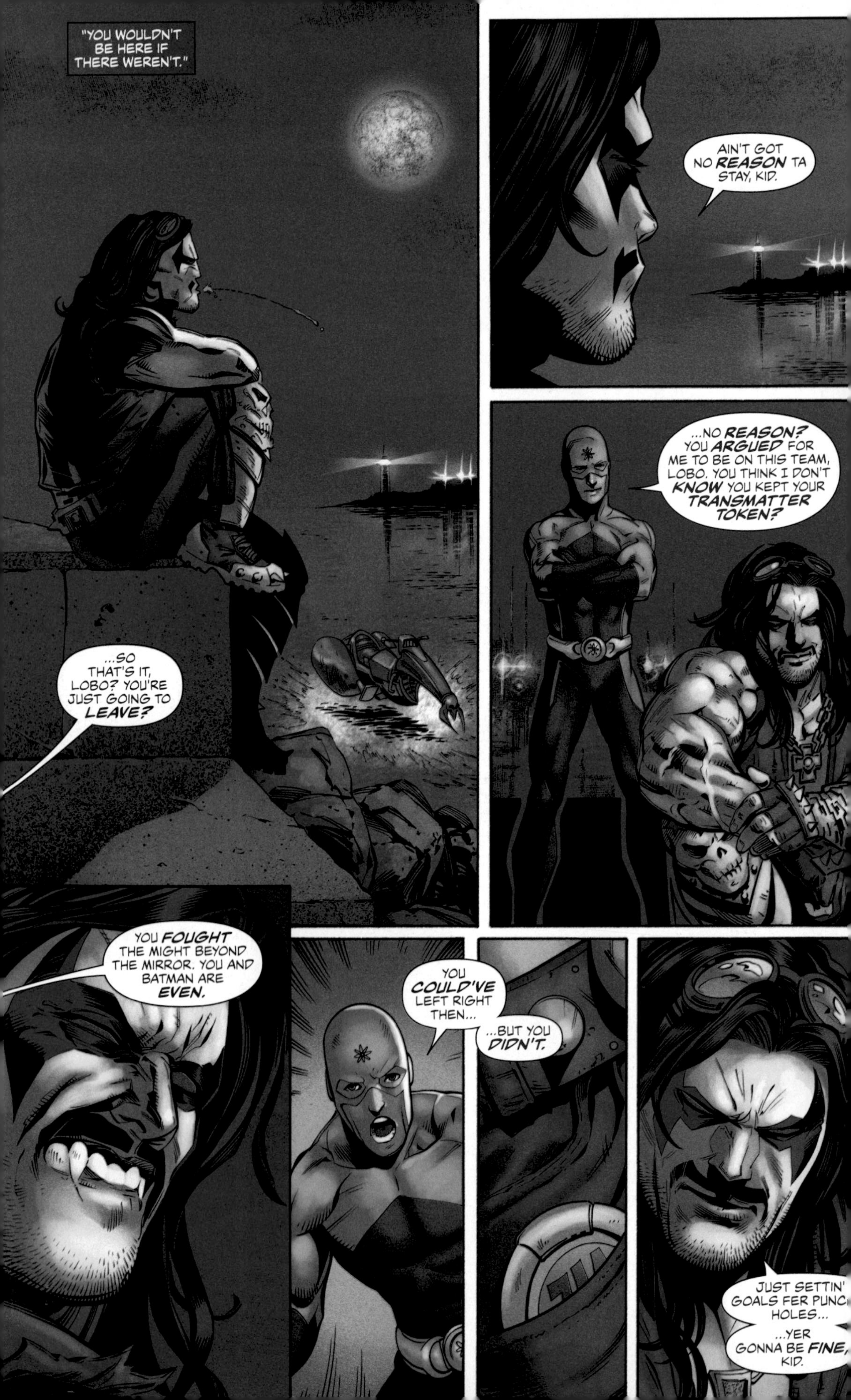
"YOU WOULDN'T BE HERE IF THERE WEREN'T."
...SO THAT'S IT, LOBO? YOU'RE JUST GOING TO LEAVE?
AIN'T GOT NO REASON TA STAY, KID.
...NO REASON? YOU ARGUED FOR ME TO BE ON THIS TEAM, LOBO. YOU THINK I DON'T KNOW YOU KEPT YOUR TRANSMATTER TOKEN?
YOU FOUGHT THE MIGHT BEYOND THE MIRROR. YOU AND BATMAN ARE EVEN.
YOU COULD'VE LEFT RIGHT THEN...
...BUT YOU DIDN'T.
JUST SETTIN' GOALS FER PUNC HOLES...
...YER GONNA BE FINE, KID.

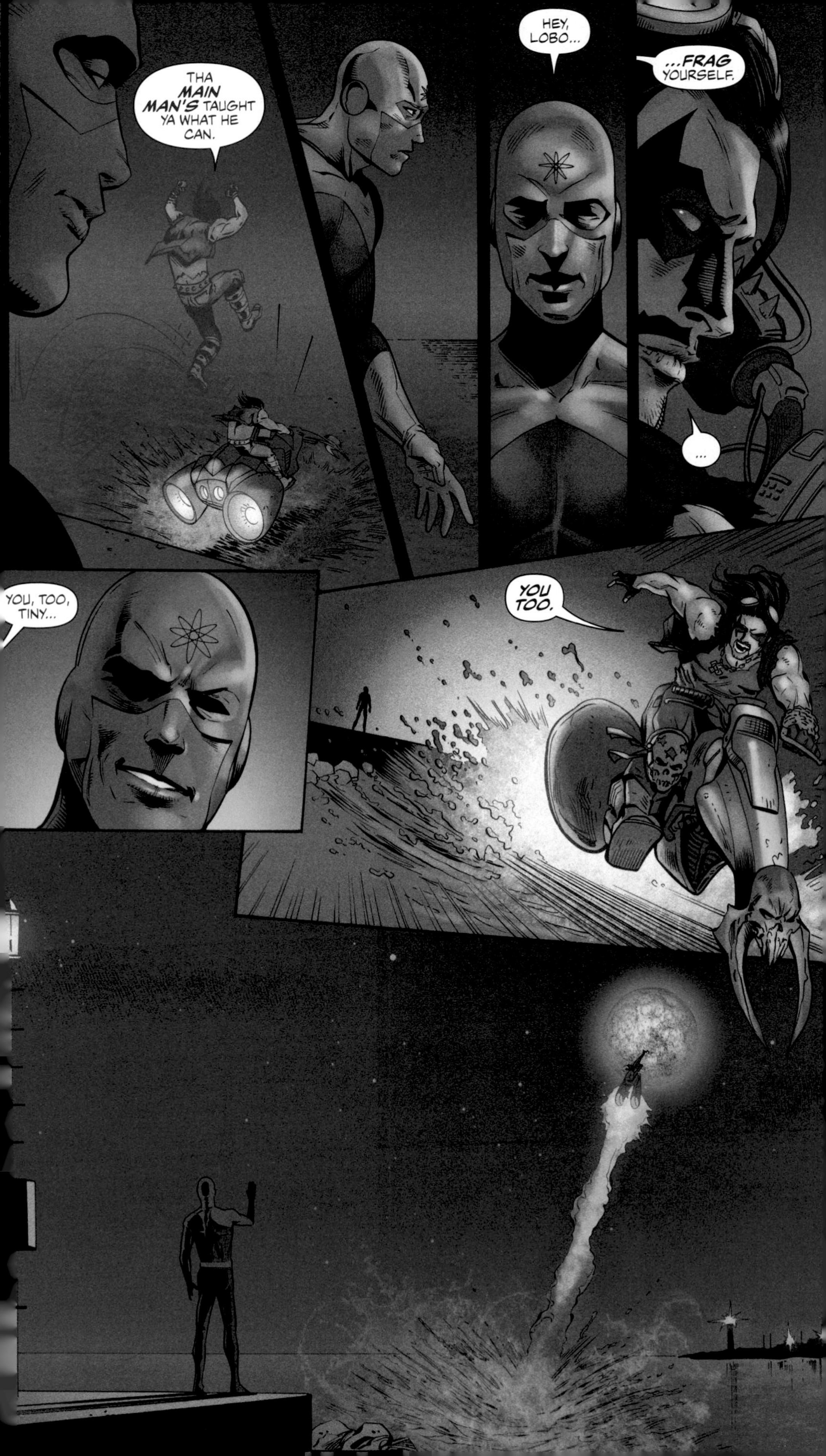
THA MAIN MAN'S TAUGHT YA WHAT HE CAN.
HEY, LOBO...
...FRAG YOURSELF.
...
YOU, TOO, TINY...
YOU TOO.

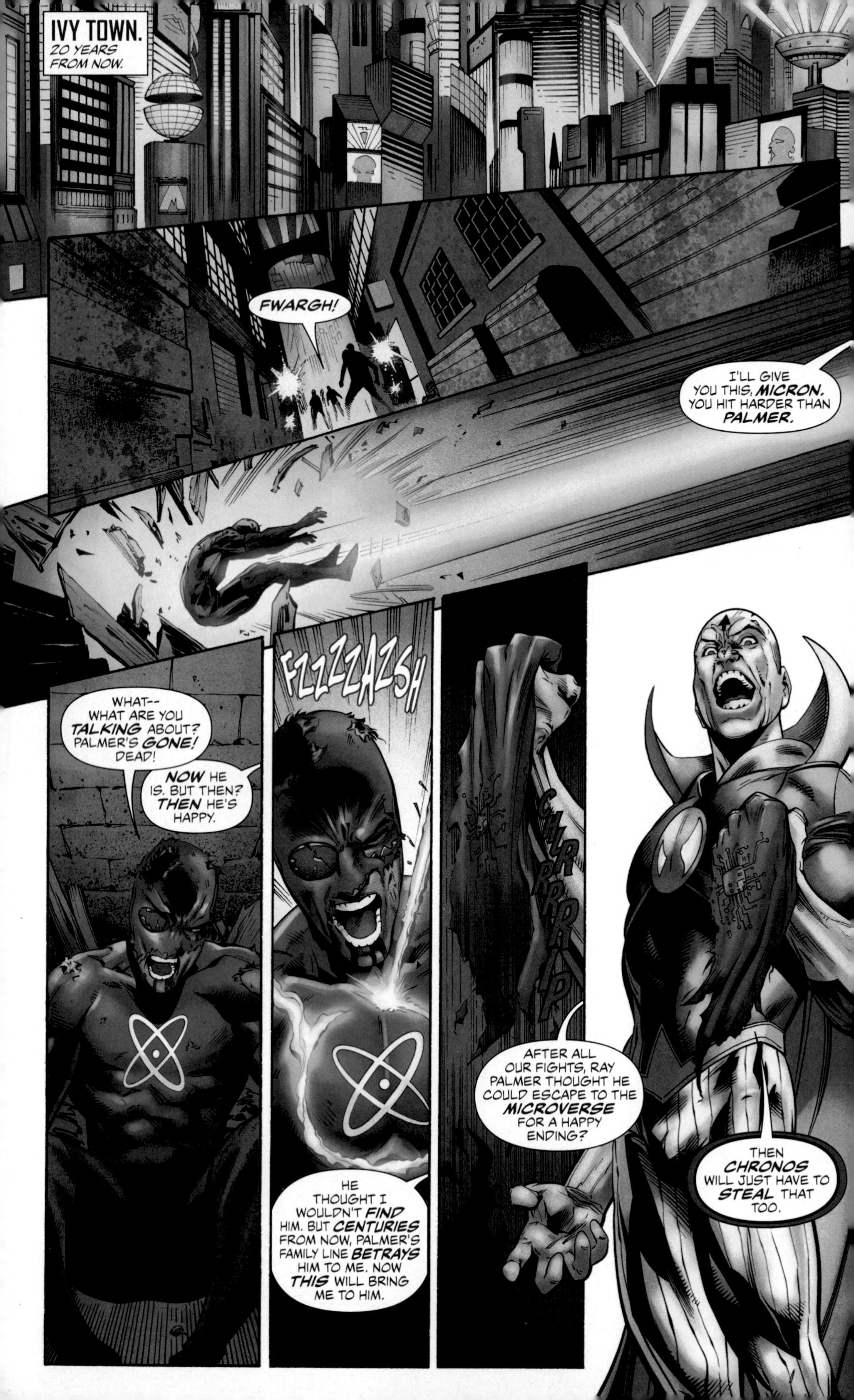
IVY TOWN. 20 YEARS FROM NOW.
FWARGH!
I'LL GIVE YOU THIS, MICRON. YOU HIT HARDER THAN PALMER.
WHAT-- WHAT ARE YOU TALKING ABOUT? PALMER'S GONE! DEAD!
NOW HE IS. BUT THEN? THEN HE'S HAPPY.
FZZZZAZSH
HE THOUGHT I WOULDN'T FIND HIM. BUT CENTURIES FROM NOW, PALMER'S FAMILY LINE BETRAYS HIM TO ME. NOW THIS WILL BRING ME TO HIM.
CHRRRRRIP
AFTER ALL OUR FIGHTS, RAY PALMER THOUGHT HE COULD ESCAPE TO THE MICROVERSE FOR A HAPPY ENDING?
THEN CHRONOS WILL JUST HAVE TO STEAL THAT TOO.

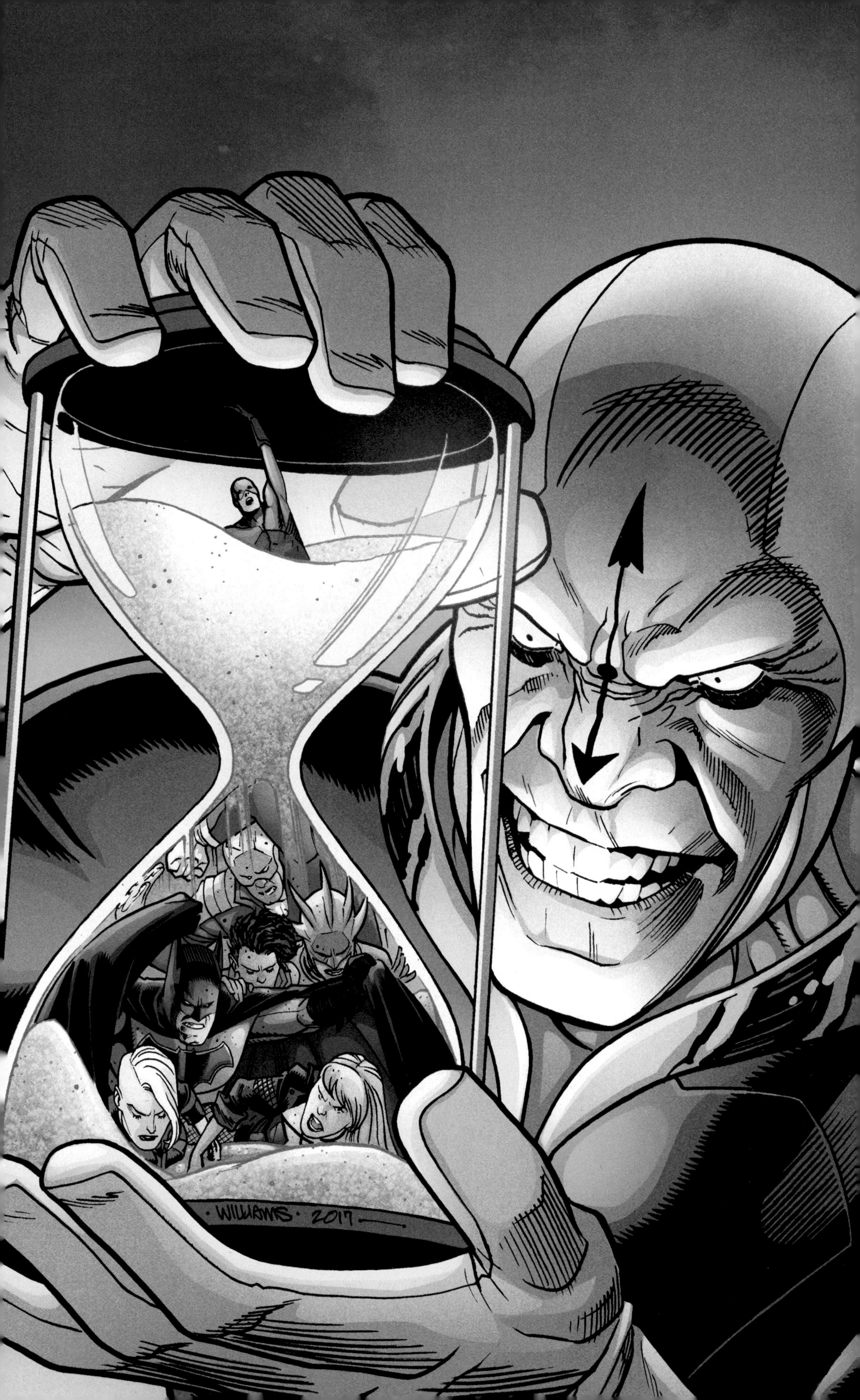
WILLIAMS 2017

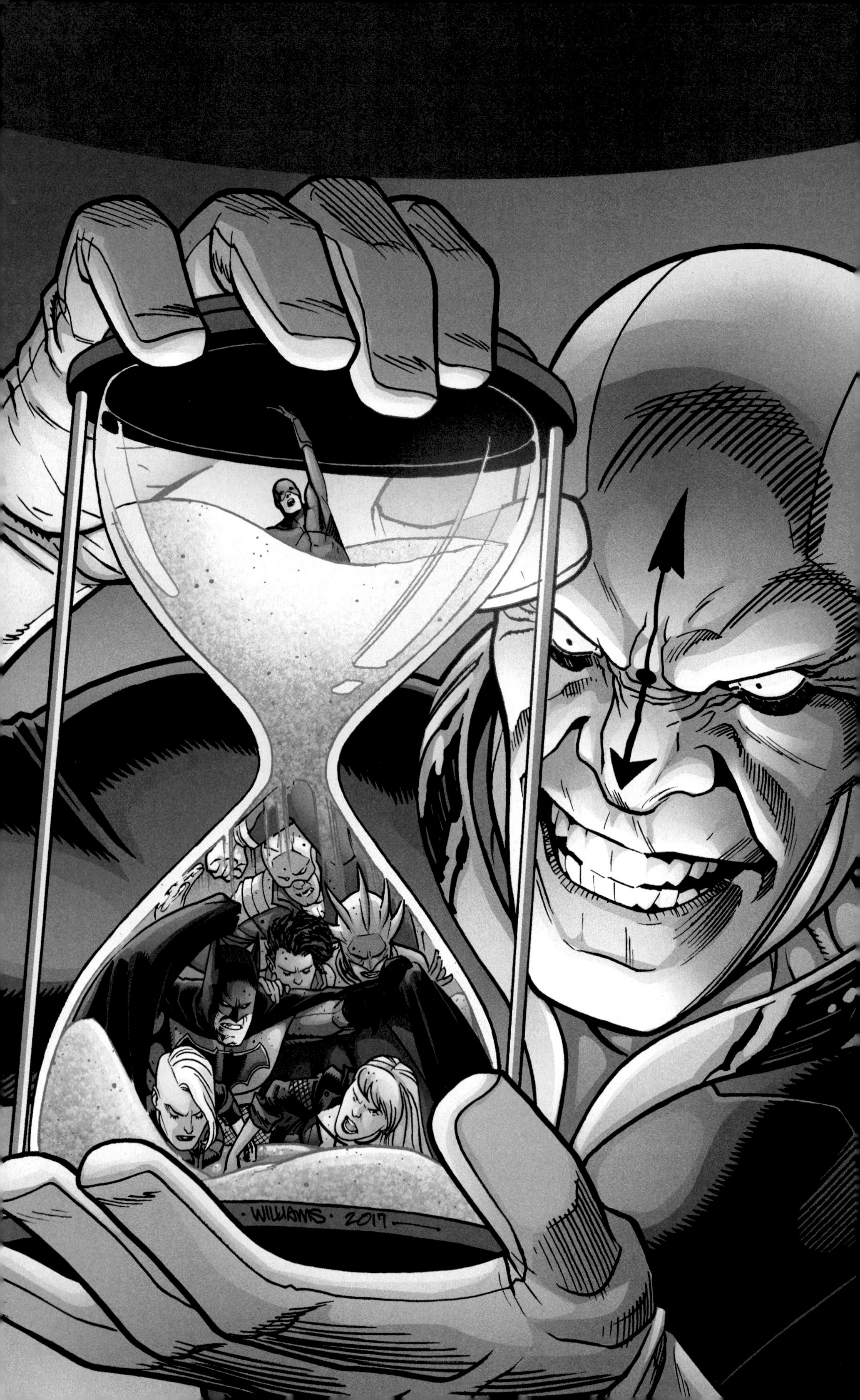
WILLIAMS 2017

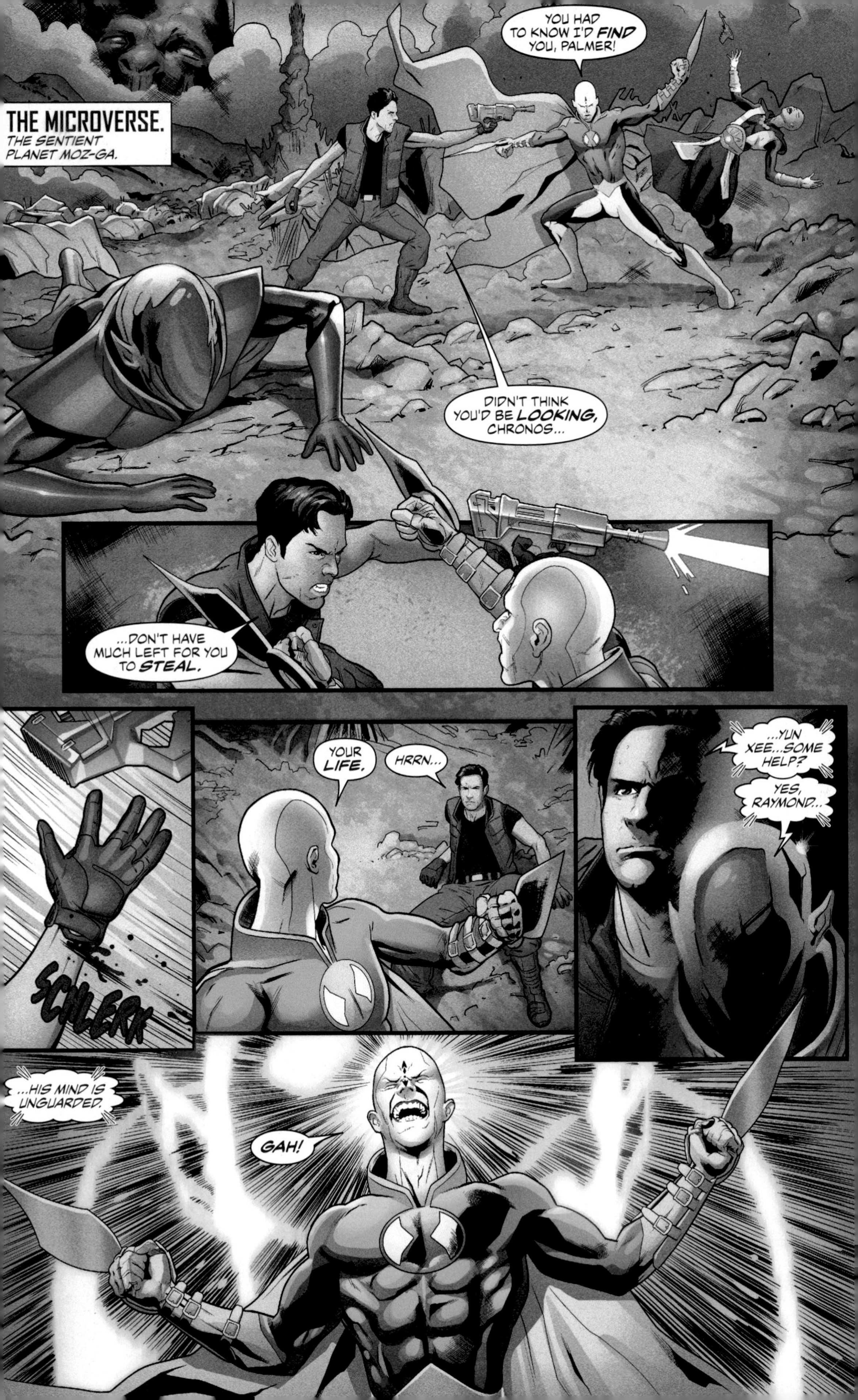
THE MICROVERSE.
THE SENTIENT PLANET MOZ-GA.
YOU HAD TO KNOW I'D FIND YOU, PALMER!
DIDN'T THINK YOU'D BE LOOKING, CHRONOS...
...DON'T HAVE MUCH LEFT FOR YOU TO STEAL.
SCHLERK
YOUR LIFE.
HRRN...
...YUN XEE...SOME HELP?
YES, RAYMOND...
...HIS MIND IS UNGUARDED.
GAH!

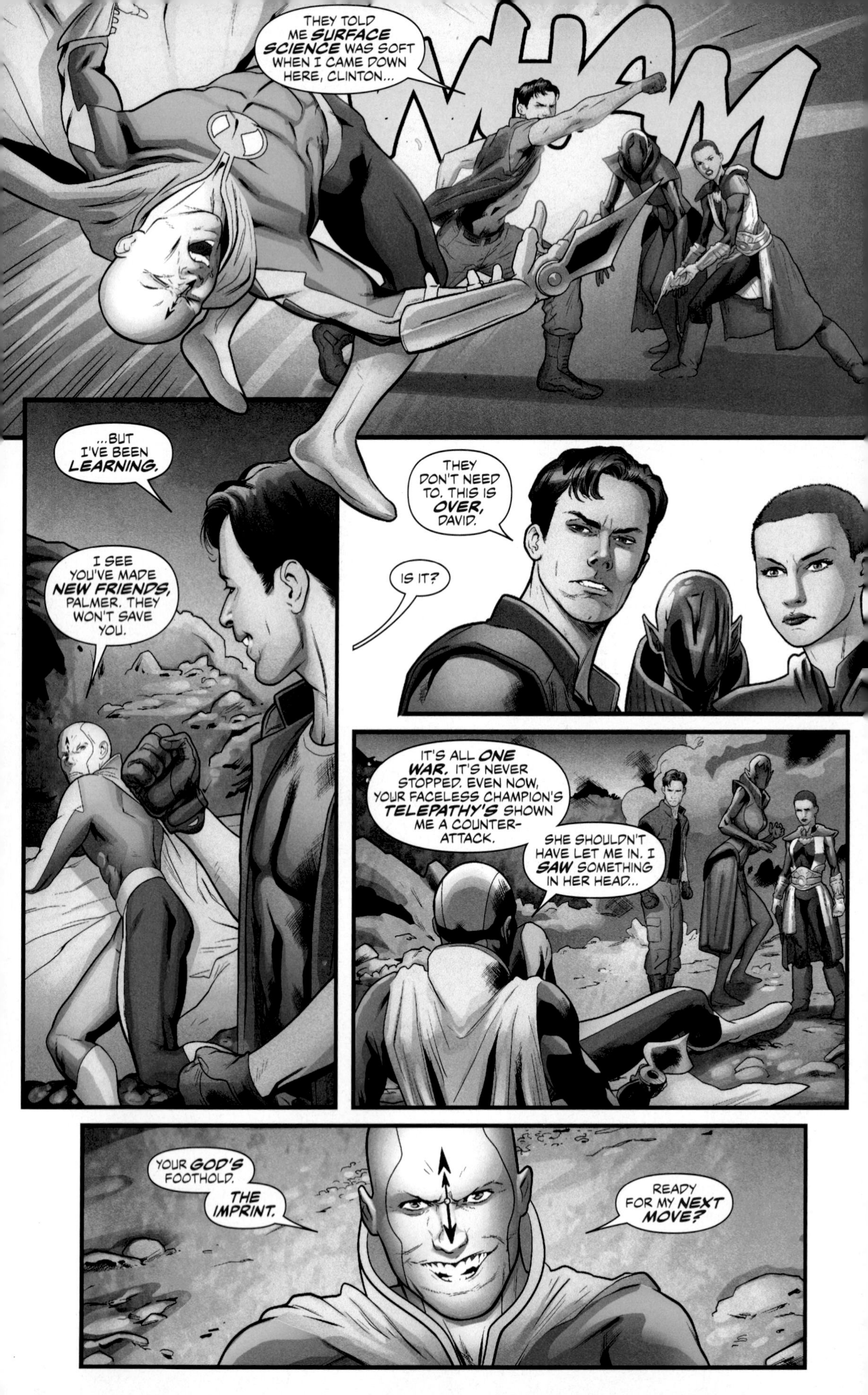
THEY TOLD ME SURFACE SCIENCE WAS SOFT WHEN I CAME DOWN HERE, CLINTON...
WHAM
...BUT I'VE BEEN LEARNING.
I SEE YOU'VE MADE NEW FRIENDS, PALMER. THEY WON'T SAVE YOU.
THEY DON'T NEED TO. THIS IS OVER, DAVID.
IS IT?
IT'S ALL ONE WAR. IT'S NEVER STOPPED. EVEN NOW, YOUR FACELESS CHAMPION'S TELEPATHY'S SHOWN ME A COUNTER-ATTACK.
SHE SHOULDN'T HAVE LET ME IN. I SAW SOMETHING IN HER HEAD...
YOUR GOD'S FOOTHOLD. THE IMPRINT.
READY FOR MY NEXT MOVE?

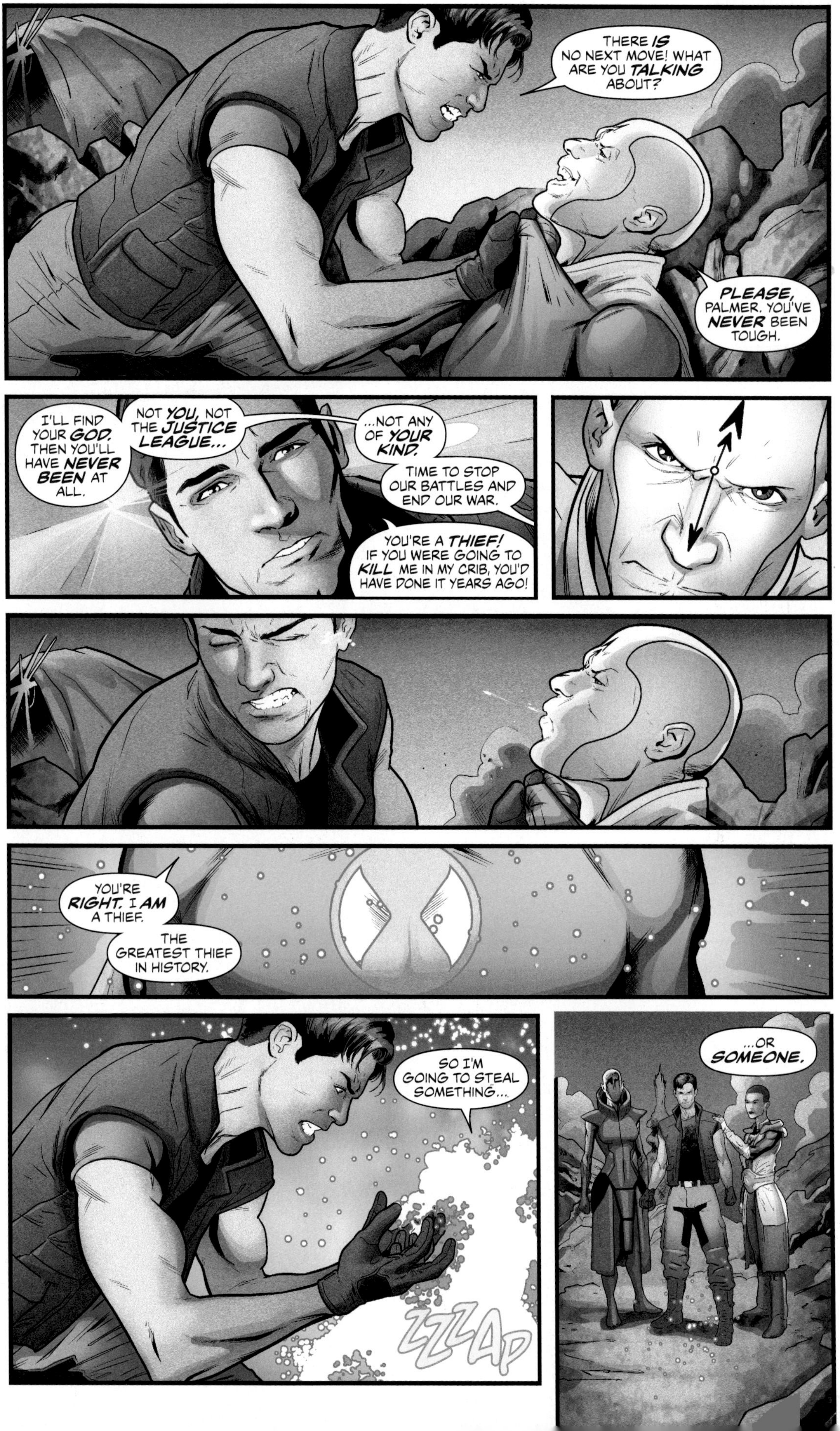
THERE IS NO NEXT MOVE! WHAT ARE YOU TALKING ABOUT?
PLEASE, PALMER. YOU'VE NEVER BEEN TOUGH.
I'LL FIND YOUR GOD. THEN YOU'LL HAVE NEVER BEEN AT ALL.
NOT YOU, NOT THE JUSTICE LEAGUE...
...NOT ANY OF YOUR KIND.
TIME TO STOP OUR BATTLES AND END OUR WAR.
YOU'RE A THIEF! IF YOU WERE GOING TO KILL ME IN MY CRIB, YOU'D HAVE DONE IT YEARS AGO!
YOU'RE RIGHT. I AM A THIEF.
THE GREATEST THIEF IN HISTORY.
SO I'M GOING TO STEAL SOMETHING...
ZZZAP
...OR SOMEONE.

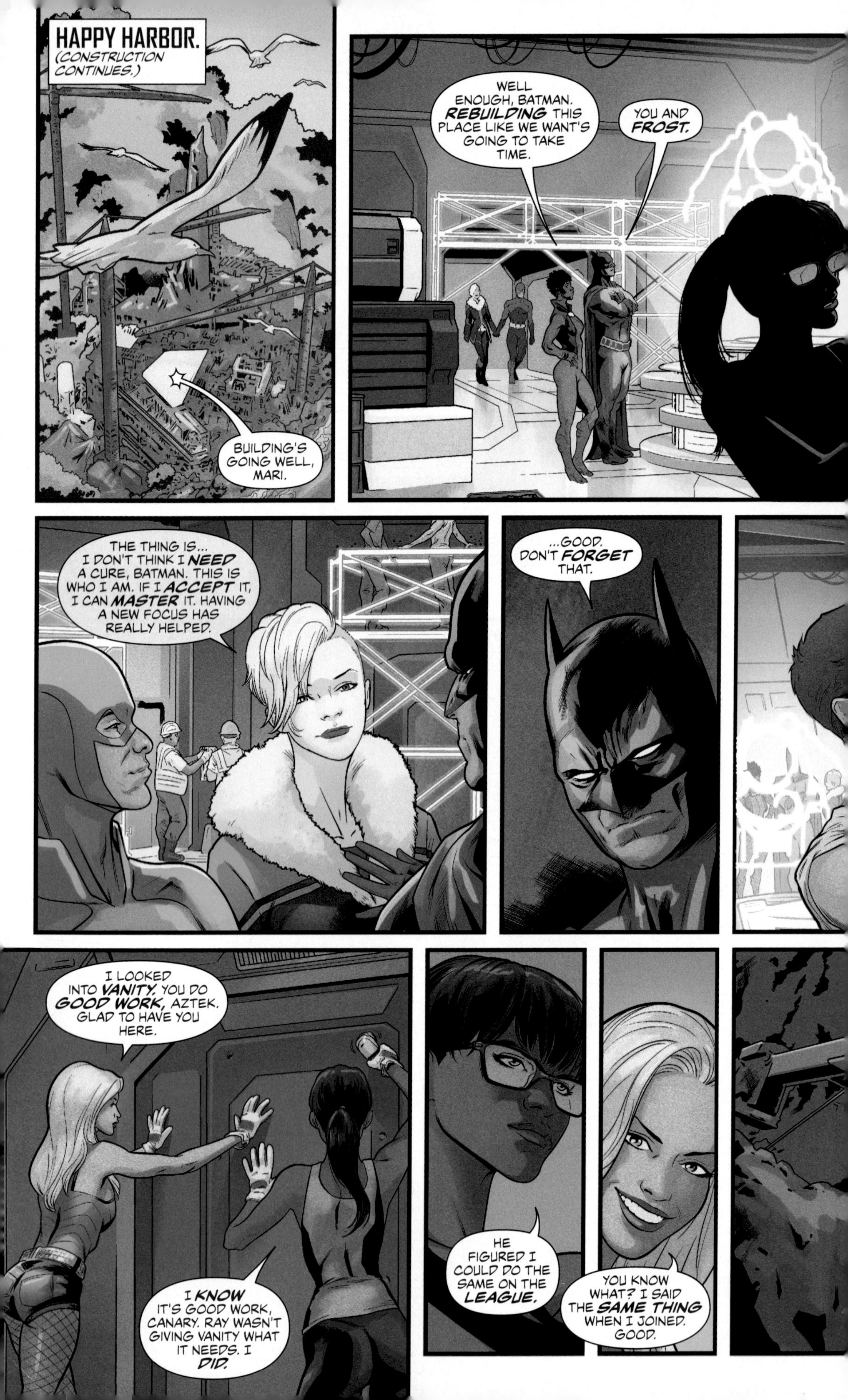
HAPPY HARBOR.
(CONSTRUCTION CONTINUES.)
BUILDING'S GOING WELL, MARI.
WELL ENOUGH, BATMAN. REBUILDING THIS PLACE LIKE WE WANT'S GOING TO TAKE TIME.
YOU AND FROST.
THE THING IS... I DON'T THINK I NEED A CURE, BATMAN. THIS IS WHO I AM. IF I ACCEPT IT, I CAN MASTER IT. HAVING A NEW FOCUS HAS REALLY HELPED.
...GOOD. DON'T FORGET THAT.
I LOOKED INTO VANITY. YOU DO GOOD WORK, AZTEK. GLAD TO HAVE YOU HERE.
I KNOW IT'S GOOD WORK, CANARY. RAY WASN'T GIVING VANITY WHAT IT NEEDS. I DID.
HE FIGURED I COULD DO THE SAME ON THE LEAGUE.
YOU KNOW WHAT? I SAID THE SAME THING WHEN I JOINED. GOOD.

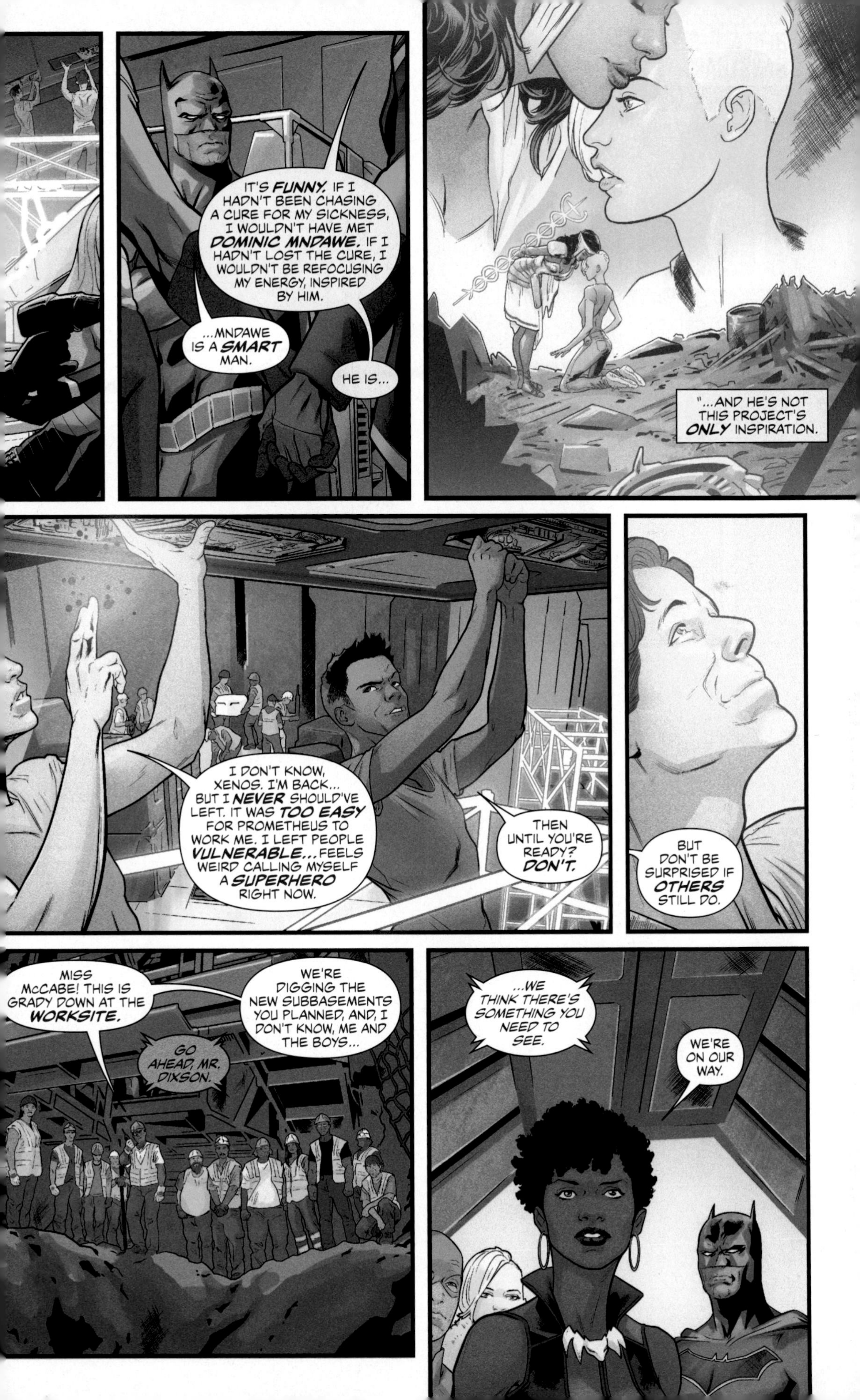
IT'S FUNNY. IF I HADN'T BEEN CHASING A CURE FOR MY SICKNESS, I WOULDN'T HAVE MET DOMINIC MNDAWE. IF I HADN'T LOST THE CURE, I WOULDN'T BE REFOCUSING MY ENERGY, INSPIRED BY HIM.
...MNDAWE IS A SMART MAN.
HE IS...
"...AND HE'S NOT THIS PROJECT'S ONLY INSPIRATION.
I DON'T KNOW, XENOS. I'M BACK... BUT I NEVER SHOULD'VE LEFT. IT WAS TOO EASY FOR PROMETHEUS TO WORK ME. I LEFT PEOPLE VULNERABLE... FEELS WEIRD CALLING MYSELF A SUPERHERO RIGHT NOW.
THEN UNTIL YOU'RE READY? DON'T.
BUT DON'T BE SURPRISED IF OTHERS STILL DO.
MISS McCABE! THIS IS GRADY DOWN AT THE WORKSITE.
WE'RE DIGGING THE NEW SUBBASEMENTS YOU PLANNED, AND, I DON'T KNOW, ME AND THE BOYS...
GO AHEAD, MR. DIXSON.
...WE THINK THERE'S SOMETHING YOU NEED TO SEE.
WE'RE ON OUR WAY.

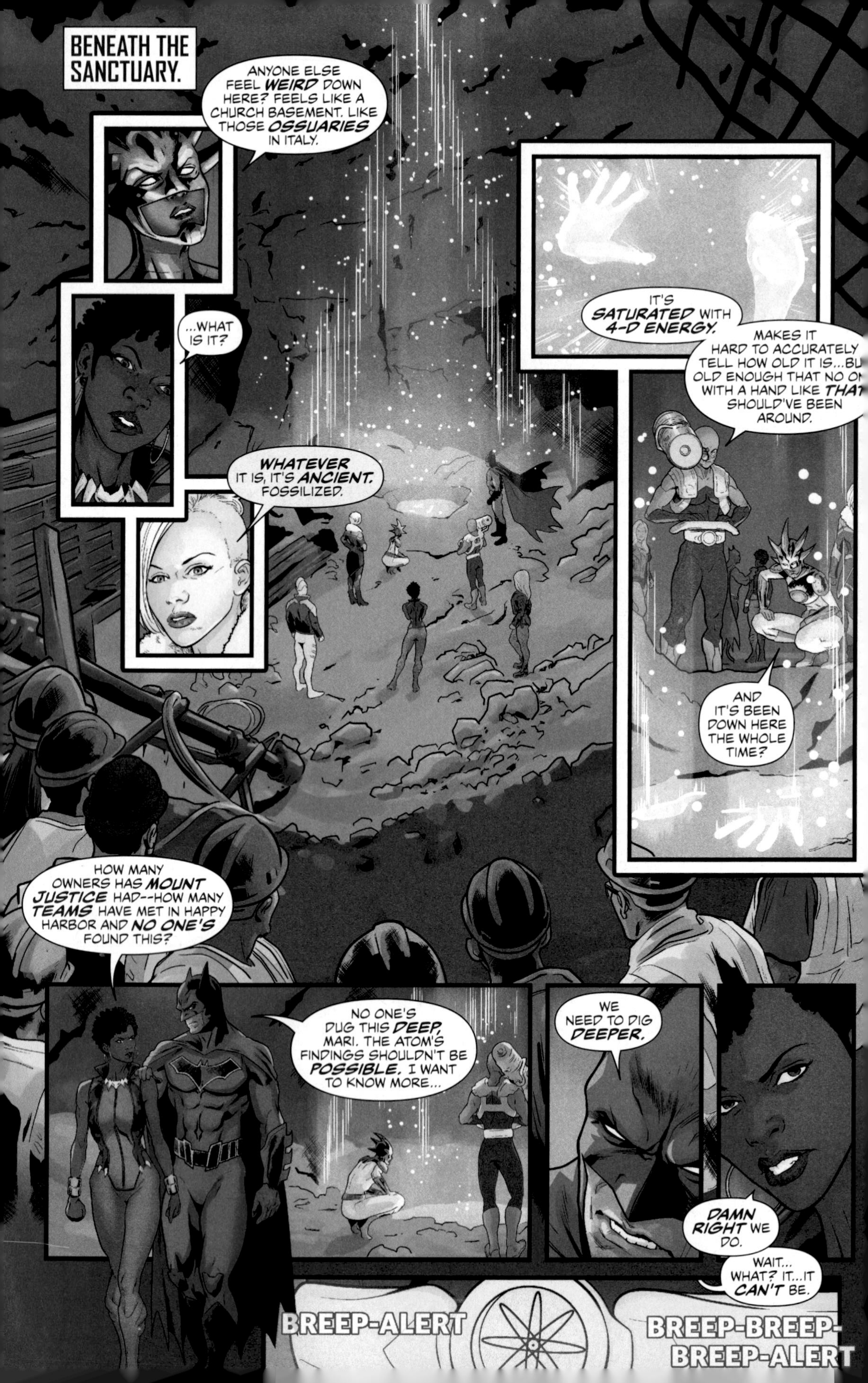
BENEATH THE SANCTUARY.
ANYONE ELSE FEEL WEIRD DOWN HERE? FEELS LIKE A CHURCH BASEMENT. LIKE THOSE OSSUARIES IN ITALY.
...WHAT IS IT?
WHATEVER IT IS, IT'S ANCIENT. FOSSILIZED.
IT'S SATURATED WITH 4-D ENERGY.
MAKES IT HARD TO ACCURATELY TELL HOW OLD IT IS...BU OLD ENOUGH THAT NO O WITH A HAND LIKE THAT SHOULD'VE BEEN AROUND.
AND IT'S BEEN DOWN HERE THE WHOLE TIME?
HOW MANY OWNERS HAS MOUNT JUSTICE HAD--HOW MANY TEAMS HAVE MET IN HAPPY HARBOR AND NO ONE'S FOUND THIS?
NO ONE'S DUG THIS DEEP, MARI. THE ATOM'S FINDINGS SHOULDN'T BE POSSIBLE. I WANT TO KNOW MORE...
WE NEED TO DIG DEEPER.
DAMN RIGHT WE DO.
WAIT... WHAT? IT...IT CAN'T BE.
BREEP-ALERT
BREEP-BREEP-BREEP-ALERT

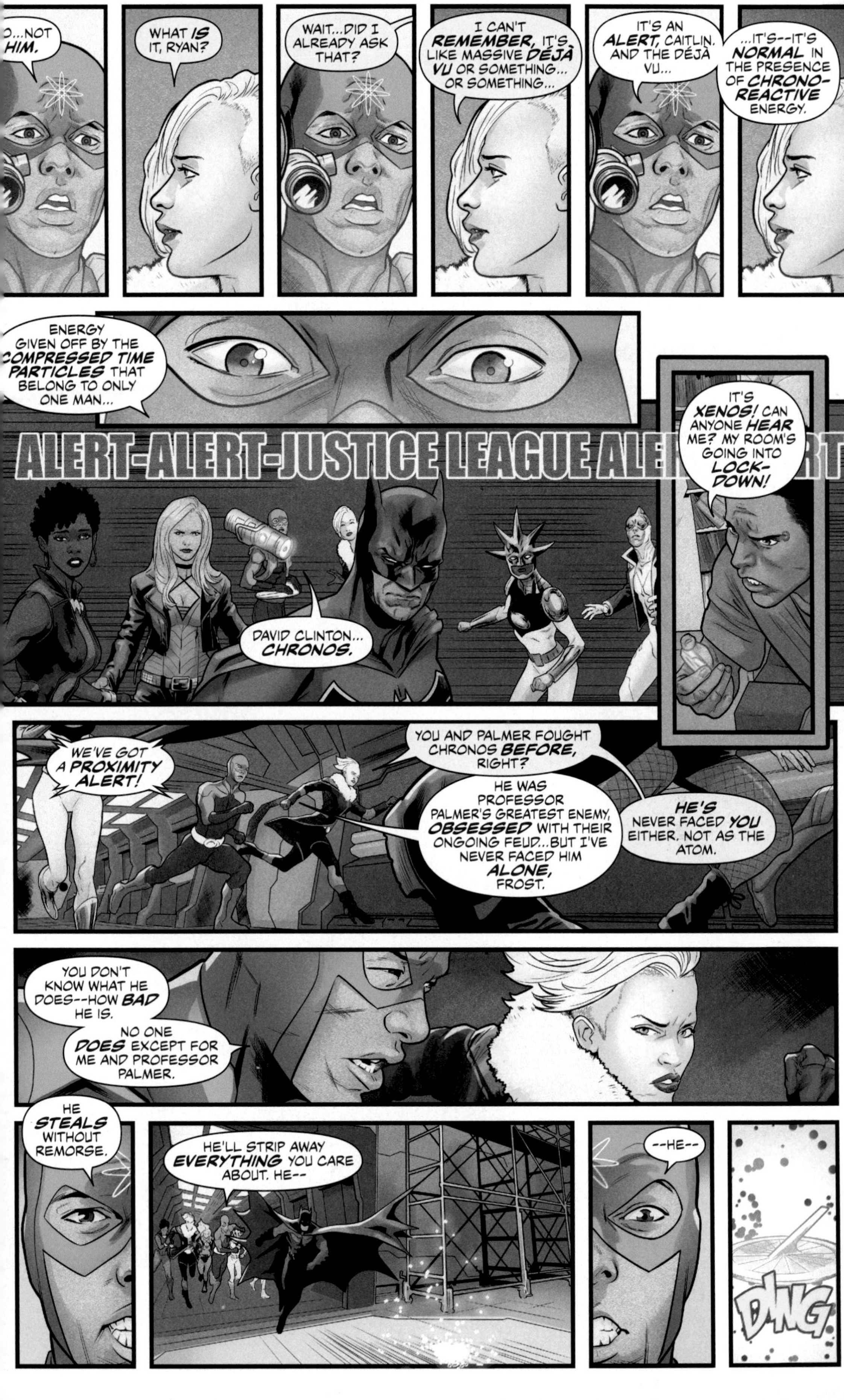

...NOT HIM.
WHAT IS IT, RYAN?
WAIT...DID I ALREADY ASK THAT?
I CAN'T REMEMBER, IT'S LIKE MASSIVE DÉJÀ VU OR SOMETHING... OR SOMETHING...
IT'S AN ALERT, CAITLIN. AND THE DÉJÀ VU...
...IT'S--IT'S NORMAL IN THE PRESENCE OF CHRONO-REACTIVE ENERGY.
ENERGY GIVEN OFF BY THE COMPRESSED TIME PARTICLES THAT BELONG TO ONLY ONE MAN...
ALERT-ALERT-JUSTICE LEAGUE ALE RT
DAVID CLINTON... CHRONOS.
IT'S XENOS! CAN ANYONE HEAR ME? MY ROOM'S GOING INTO LOCK-DOWN!
WE'VE GOT A PROXIMITY ALERT!
YOU AND PALMER FOUGHT CHRONOS BEFORE, RIGHT?
HE WAS PROFESSOR PALMER'S GREATEST ENEMY, OBSESSED WITH THEIR ONGOING FEUD...BUT I'VE NEVER FACED HIM ALONE, FROST.
HE'S NEVER FACED YOU EITHER. NOT AS THE ATOM.
YOU DON'T KNOW WHAT HE DOES--HOW BAD HE IS.
NO ONE DOES EXCEPT FOR ME AND PROFESSOR PALMER.
HE STEALS WITHOUT REMORSE.
HE'LL STRIP AWAY EVERYTHING YOU CARE ABOUT. HE--
--HE--
DING

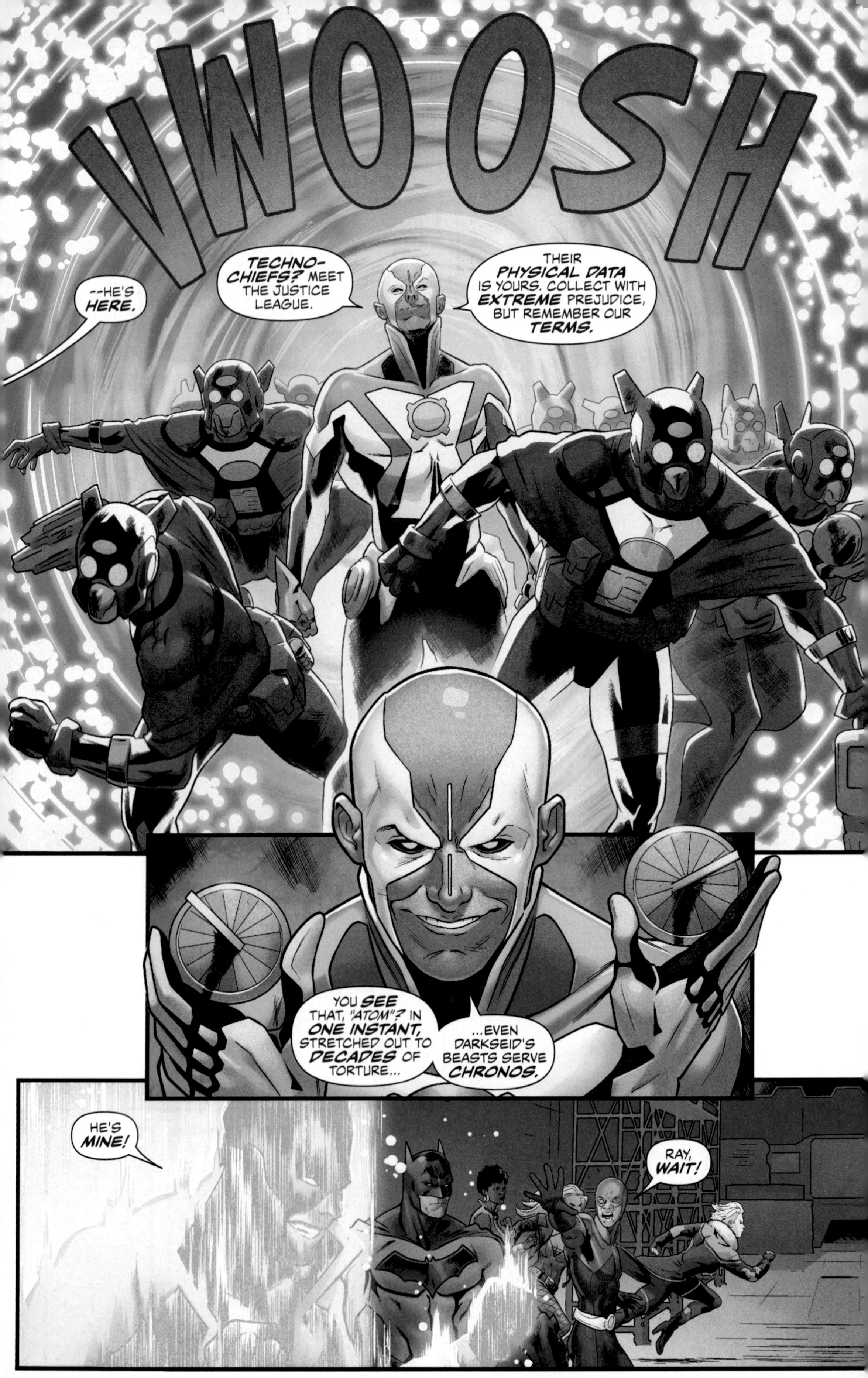
VWOOSH
--HE'S HERE.
TECHNO-CHIEFS? MEET THE JUSTICE LEAGUE.
THEIR PHYSICAL DATA IS YOURS. COLLECT WITH EXTREME PREJUDICE, BUT REMEMBER OUR TERMS.
YOU SEE THAT, "ATOM"? IN ONE INSTANT, STRETCHED OUT TO DECADES OF TORTURE...
...EVEN DARKSEID'S BEASTS SERVE CHRONOS.
HE'S MINE!
RAY, WAIT!

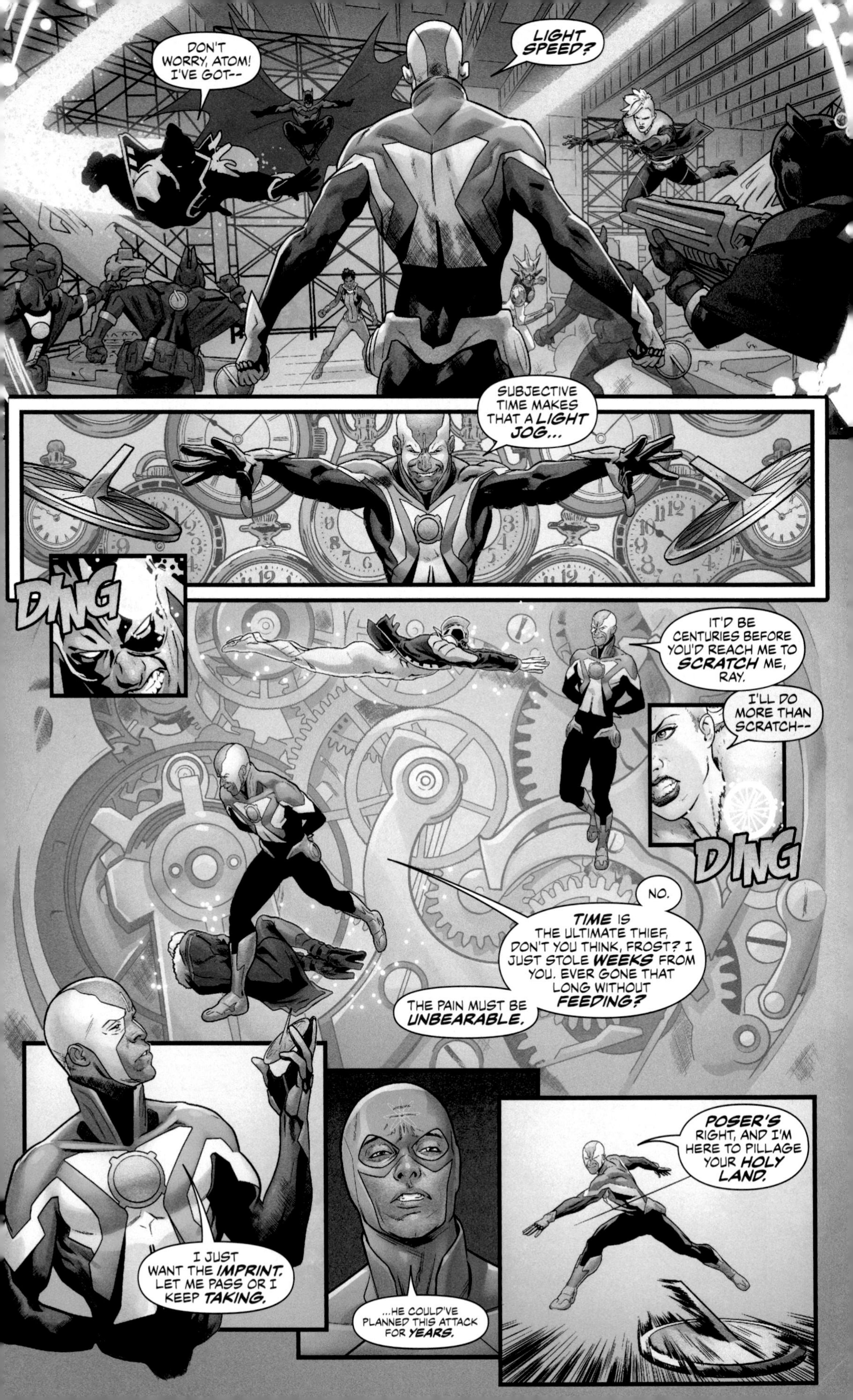
DON'T WORRY, ATOM! I'VE GOT--
LIGHT SPEED?
SUBJECTIVE TIME MAKES THAT A LIGHT JOG...
DING
IT'D BE CENTURIES BEFORE YOU'D REACH ME TO SCRATCH ME, RAY.
I'LL DO MORE THAN SCRATCH--
DING
NO.
TIME IS THE ULTIMATE THIEF, DON'T YOU THINK, FROST? I JUST STOLE WEEKS FROM YOU. EVER GONE THAT LONG WITHOUT FEEDING?
THE PAIN MUST BE UNBEARABLE.
I JUST WANT THE IMPRINT. LET ME PASS OR I KEEP TAKING.
...HE COULD'VE PLANNED THIS ATTACK FOR YEARS.
POSER'S RIGHT, AND I'M HERE TO PILLAGE YOUR HOLY LAND.

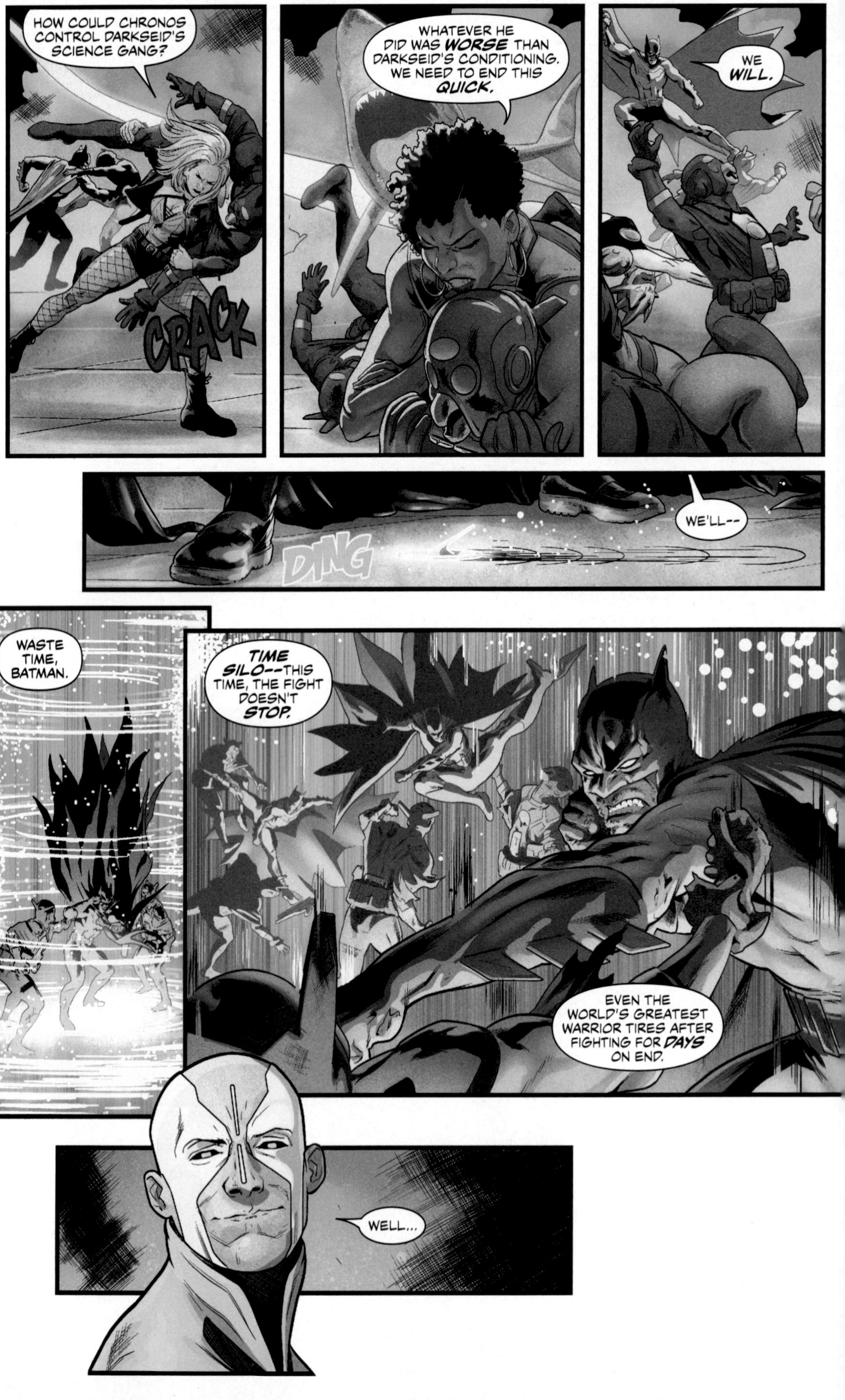
HOW COULD CHRONOS CONTROL DARKSEID'S SCIENCE GANG?
CRACK
WHATEVER HE DID WAS WORSE THAN DARKSEID'S CONDITIONING. WE NEED TO END THIS QUICK.
WE WILL.
DING
WE'LL--
WASTE TIME, BATMAN.
TIME SILO--THIS TIME, THE FIGHT DOESN'T STOP.
EVEN THE WORLD'S GREATEST WARRIOR TIRES AFTER FIGHTING FOR DAYS ON END.
WELL...

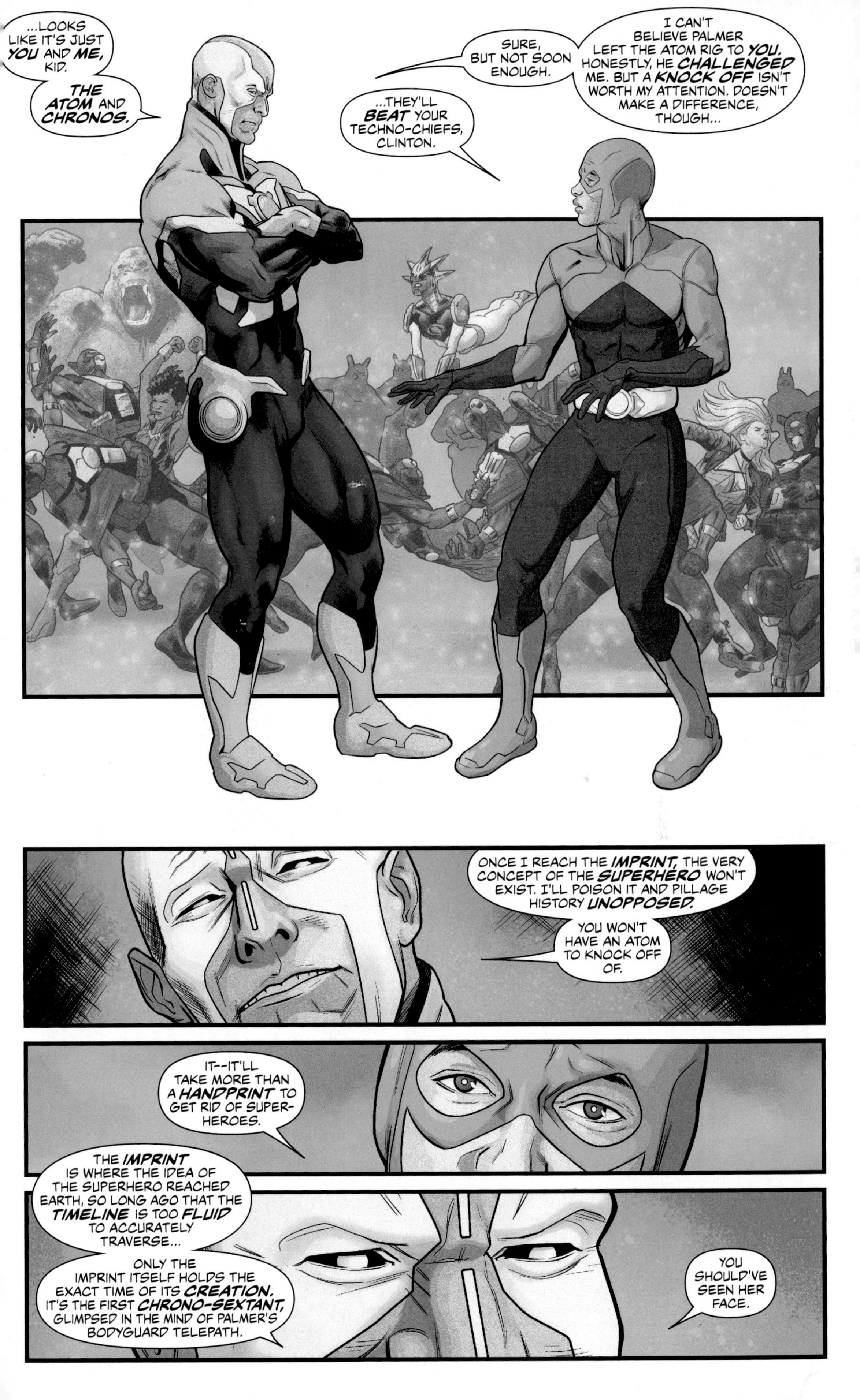
...LOOKS LIKE IT'S JUST YOU AND ME, KID.
THE ATOM AND CHRONOS.
SURE, BUT NOT SOON ENOUGH.
I CAN'T BELIEVE PALMER LEFT THE ATOM RIG TO YOU. HONESTLY, HE CHALLENGED ME. BUT A KNOCK OFF ISN'T WORTH MY ATTENTION. DOESN'T MAKE A DIFFERENCE, THOUGH...
...THEY'LL BEAT YOUR TECHNO-CHIEFS, CLINTON.
ONCE I REACH THE IMPRINT, THE VERY CONCEPT OF THE SUPERHERO WON'T EXIST. I'LL POISON IT AND PILLAGE HISTORY UNOPPOSED.
YOU WON'T HAVE AN ATOM TO KNOCK OFF OF.
IT--IT'LL TAKE MORE THAN A HANDPRINT TO GET RID OF SUPER-HEROES.
THE IMPRINT IS WHERE THE IDEA OF THE SUPERHERO REACHED EARTH, SO LONG AGO THAT THE TIMELINE IS TOO FLUID TO ACCURATELY TRAVERSE...
ONLY THE IMPRINT ITSELF HOLDS THE EXACT TIME OF ITS CREATION. IT'S THE FIRST CHRONO-SEXTANT, GLIMPSED IN THE MIND OF PALMER'S BODYGUARD TELEPATH.
YOU SHOULD'VE SEEN HER FACE.

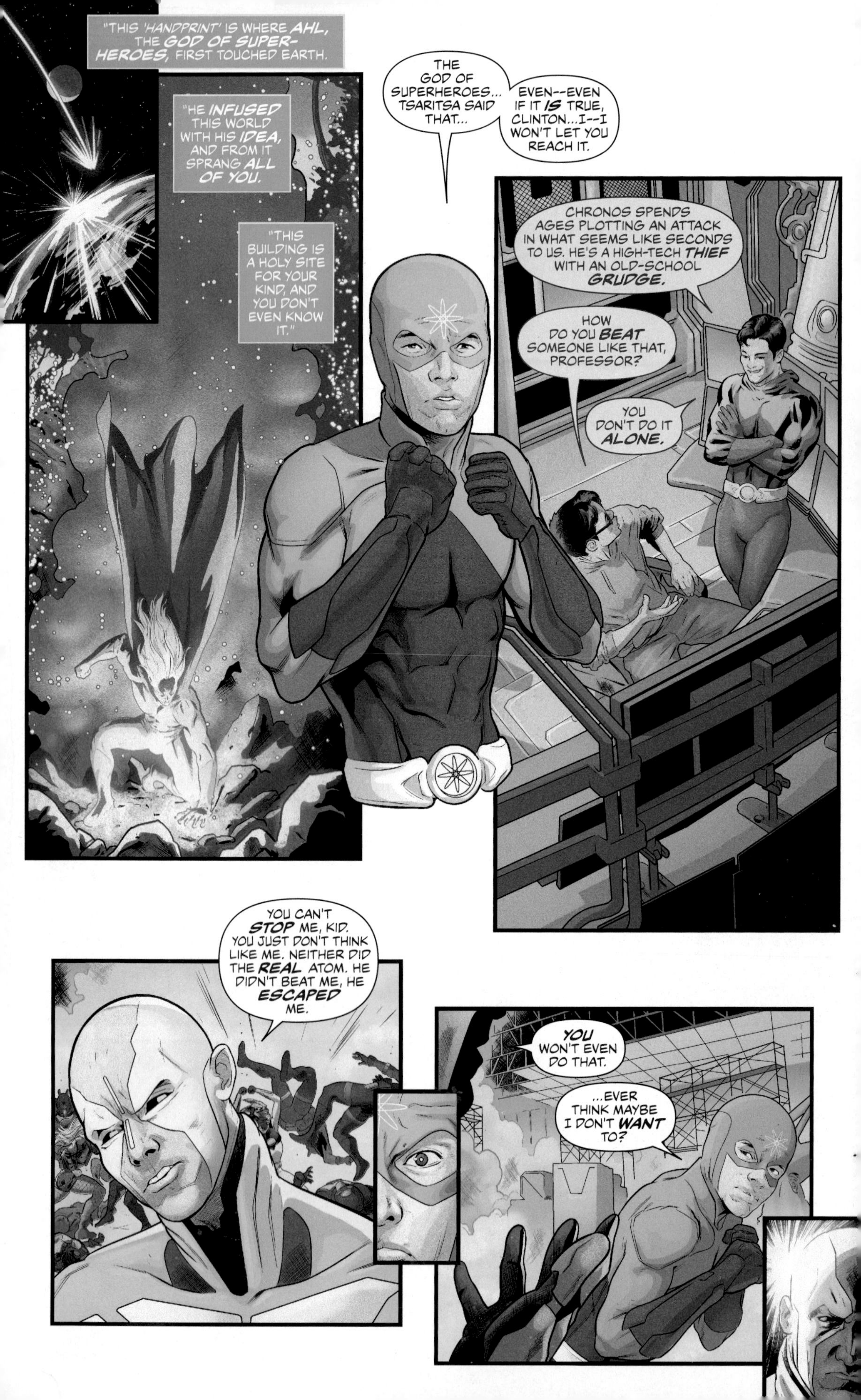
"THIS 'HANDPRINT' IS WHERE AHL, THE GOD OF SUPER-HEROES, FIRST TOUCHED EARTH.
"HE INFUSED THIS WORLD WITH HIS IDEA, AND FROM IT SPRANG ALL OF YOU.
"THIS BUILDING IS A HOLY SITE FOR YOUR KIND, AND YOU DON'T EVEN KNOW IT."
THE GOD OF SUPERHEROES... TSARITSA SAID THAT...
EVEN--EVEN IF IT IS TRUE, CLINTON...I--I WON'T LET YOU REACH IT.
CHRONOS SPENDS AGES PLOTTING AN ATTACK IN WHAT SEEMS LIKE SECONDS TO US. HE'S A HIGH-TECH THIEF WITH AN OLD-SCHOOL GRUDGE.
HOW DO YOU BEAT SOMEONE LIKE THAT, PROFESSOR?
YOU DON'T DO IT ALONE.
YOU CAN'T STOP ME, KID. YOU JUST DON'T THINK LIKE ME. NEITHER DID THE REAL ATOM. HE DIDN'T BEAT ME, HE ESCAPED ME.
YOU WON'T EVEN DO THAT.
...EVER THINK MAYBE I DON'T WANT TO?

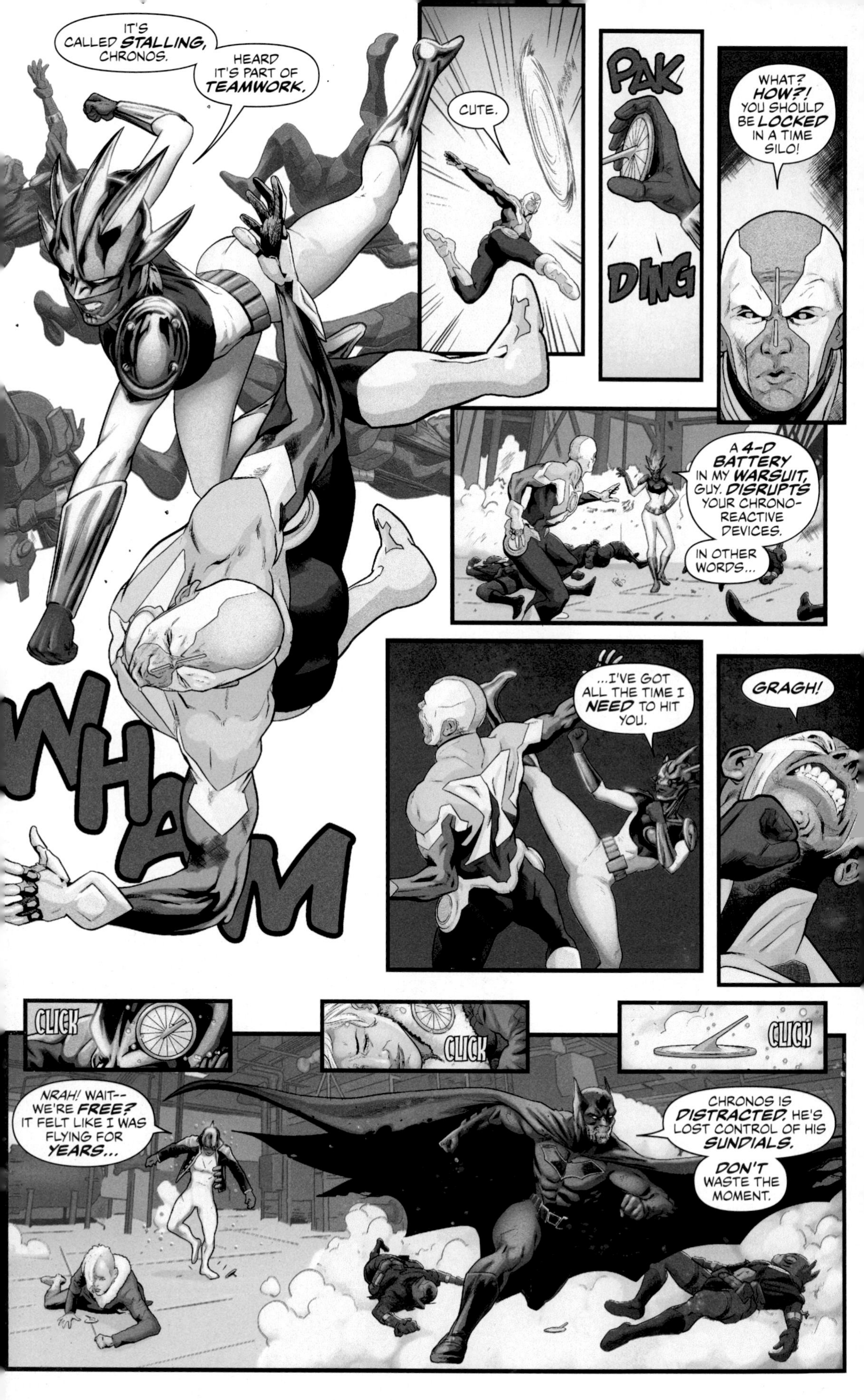
IT'S CALLED STALLING, CHRONOS.
HEARD IT'S PART OF TEAMWORK.
WHAM
CUTE.
PAK
DING
WHAT? HOW?! YOU SHOULD BE LOCKED IN A TIME SILO!
A 4-D BATTERY IN MY WARSUIT, GUY. DISRUPTS YOUR CHRONO-REACTIVE DEVICES.
IN OTHER WORDS...
...I'VE GOT ALL THE TIME I NEED TO HIT YOU.
GRAGH!
CLICK
CLICK
CLICK
NRAH! WAIT-- WE'RE FREE? IT FELT LIKE I WAS FLYING FOR YEARS...
CHRONOS IS DISTRACTED. HE'S LOST CONTROL OF HIS SUNDIALS.
DON'T WASTE THE MOMENT.

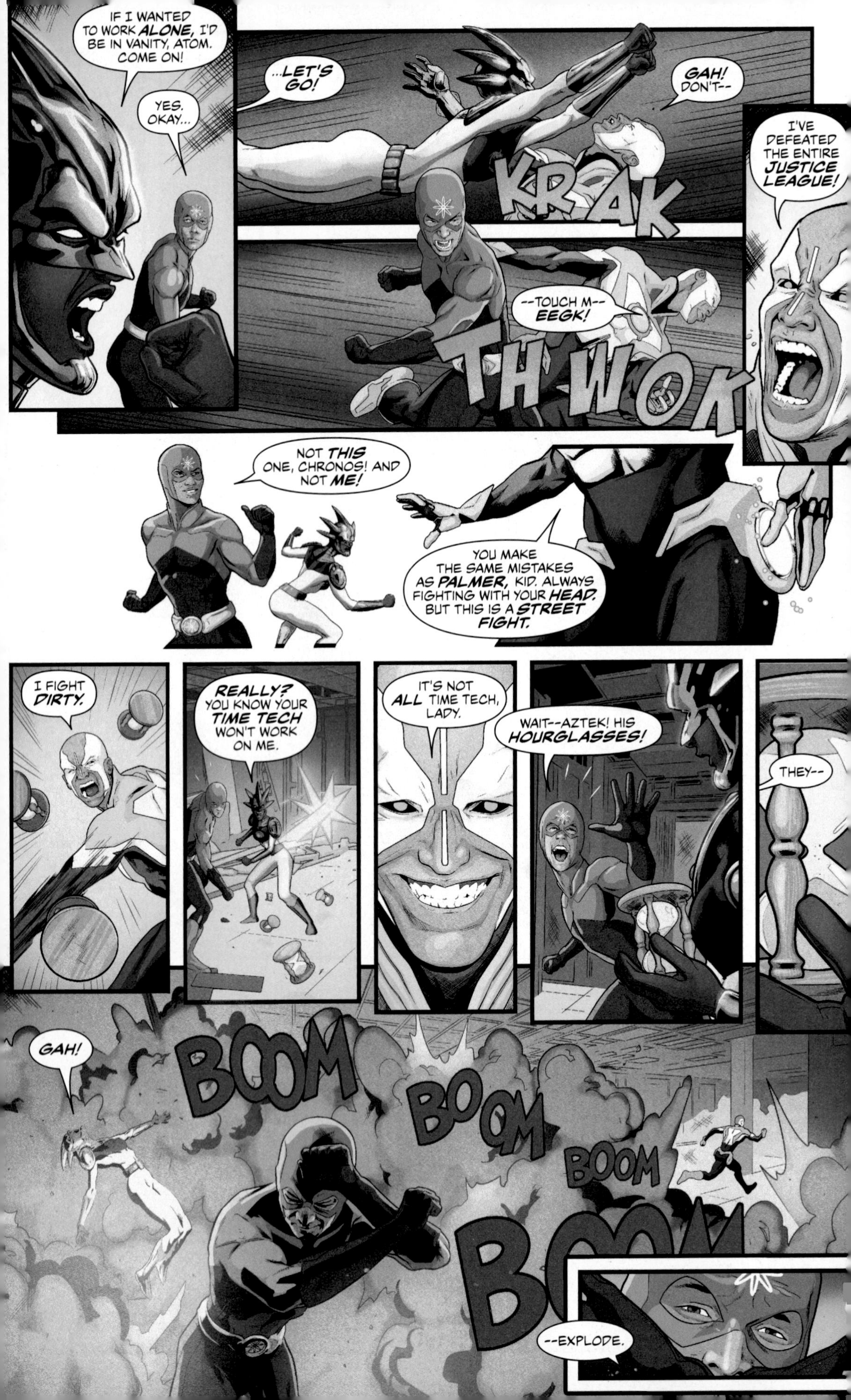
IF I WANTED TO WORK ALONE, I'D BE IN VANITY, ATOM. COME ON!
YES. OKAY...
...LET'S GO!
GAH! DON'T--
KRAK
--TOUCH M-- EEGK!
THWOK
I'VE DEFEATED THE ENTIRE JUSTICE LEAGUE!
NOT THIS ONE, CHRONOS! AND NOT ME!
YOU MAKE THE SAME MISTAKES AS PALMER, KID. ALWAYS FIGHTING WITH YOUR HEAD. BUT THIS IS A STREET FIGHT.
I FIGHT DIRTY.
REALLY? YOU KNOW YOUR TIME TECH WON'T WORK ON ME.
IT'S NOT ALL TIME TECH, LADY.
WAIT--AZTEK! HIS HOURGLASSES!
THEY--
GAH!
BOOM
BOOM
BOOM
BOOM
--EXPLODE.

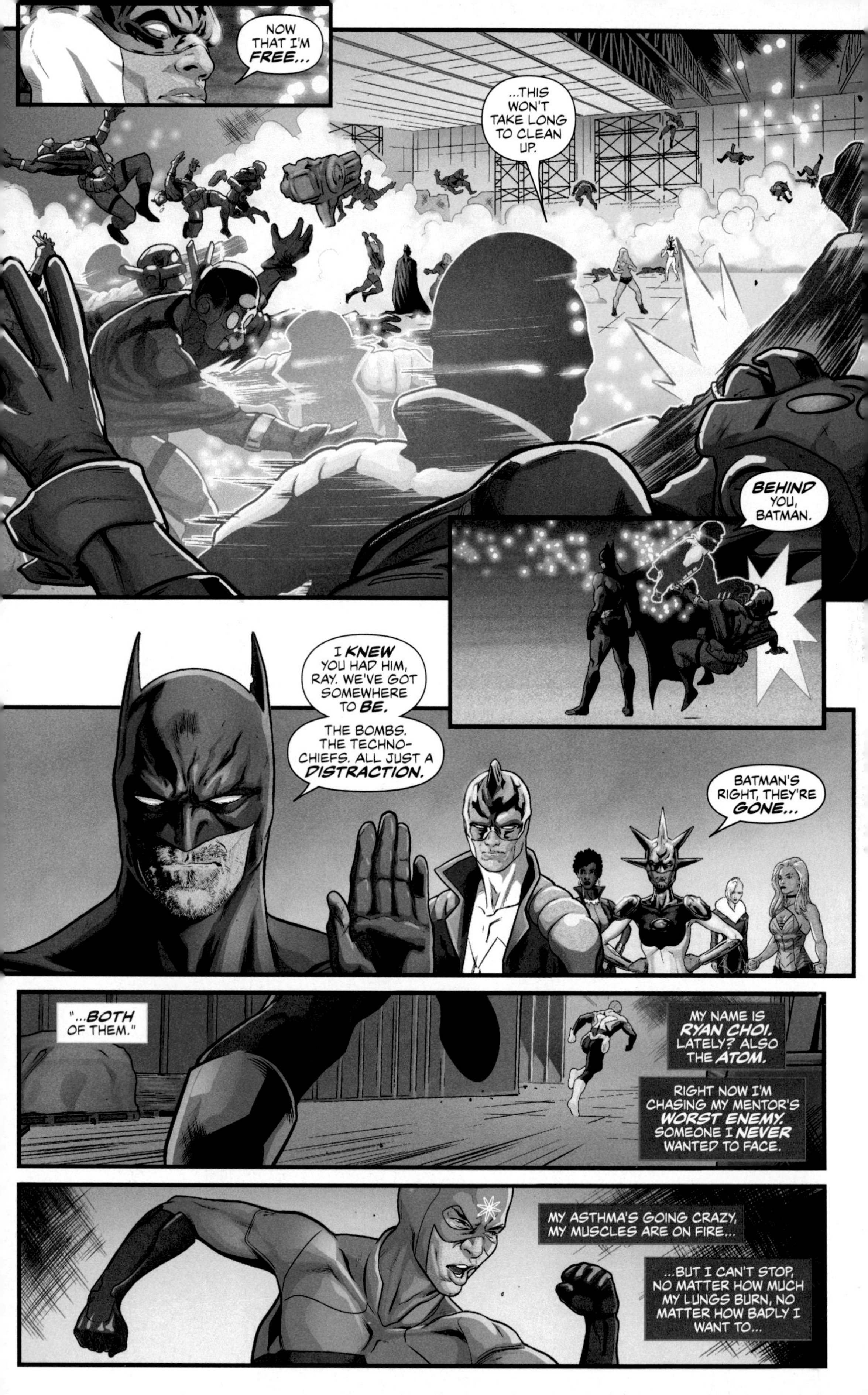
NOW THAT I'M FREE...
...THIS WON'T TAKE LONG TO CLEAN UP.
BEHIND YOU, BATMAN.
I KNEW YOU HAD HIM, RAY. WE'VE GOT SOMEWHERE TO BE.
THE BOMBS. THE TECHNO-CHIEFS. ALL JUST A DISTRACTION.
BATMAN'S RIGHT, THEY'RE GONE...
"...BOTH OF THEM."
MY NAME IS RYAN CHOI. LATELY? ALSO THE ATOM.
RIGHT NOW I'M CHASING MY MENTOR'S WORST ENEMY. SOMEONE I NEVER WANTED TO FACE.
MY ASTHMA'S GOING CRAZY, MY MUSCLES ARE ON FIRE...
...BUT I CAN'T STOP, NO MATTER HOW MUCH MY LUNGS BURN, NO MATTER HOW BADLY I WANT TO...

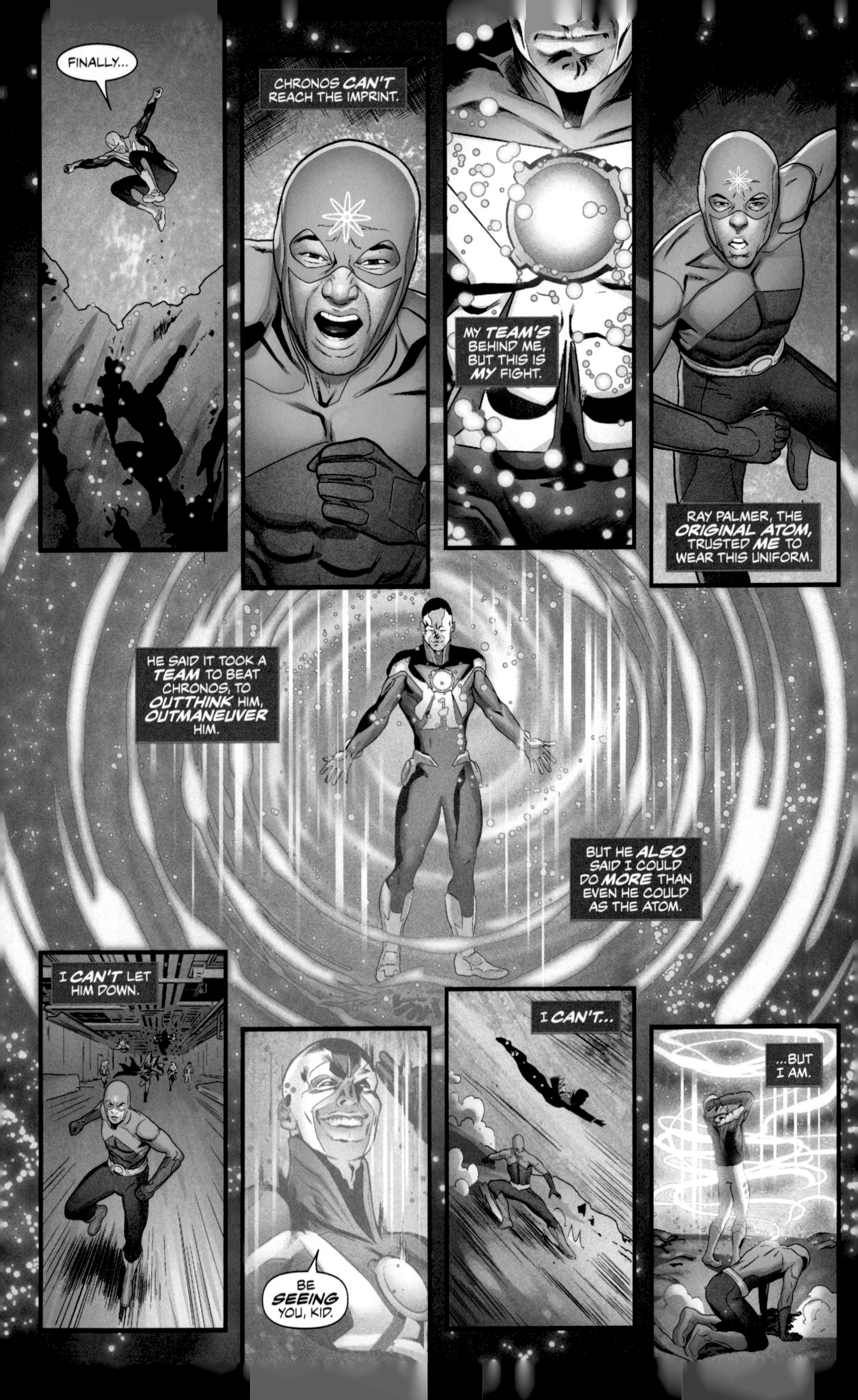
FINALLY...
CHRONOS CAN'T REACH THE IMPRINT.
MY TEAM'S BEHIND ME, BUT THIS IS MY FIGHT.
RAY PALMER, THE ORIGINAL ATOM, TRUSTED ME TO WEAR THIS UNIFORM.
HE SAID IT TOOK A TEAM TO BEAT CHRONOS, TO OUTTHINK HIM, OUTMANEUVER HIM.
BUT HE ALSO SAID I COULD DO MORE THAN EVEN HE COULD AS THE ATOM.
I CAN'T LET HIM DOWN.
BE SEEING YOU, KID.
I CAN'T...
...BUT I AM.

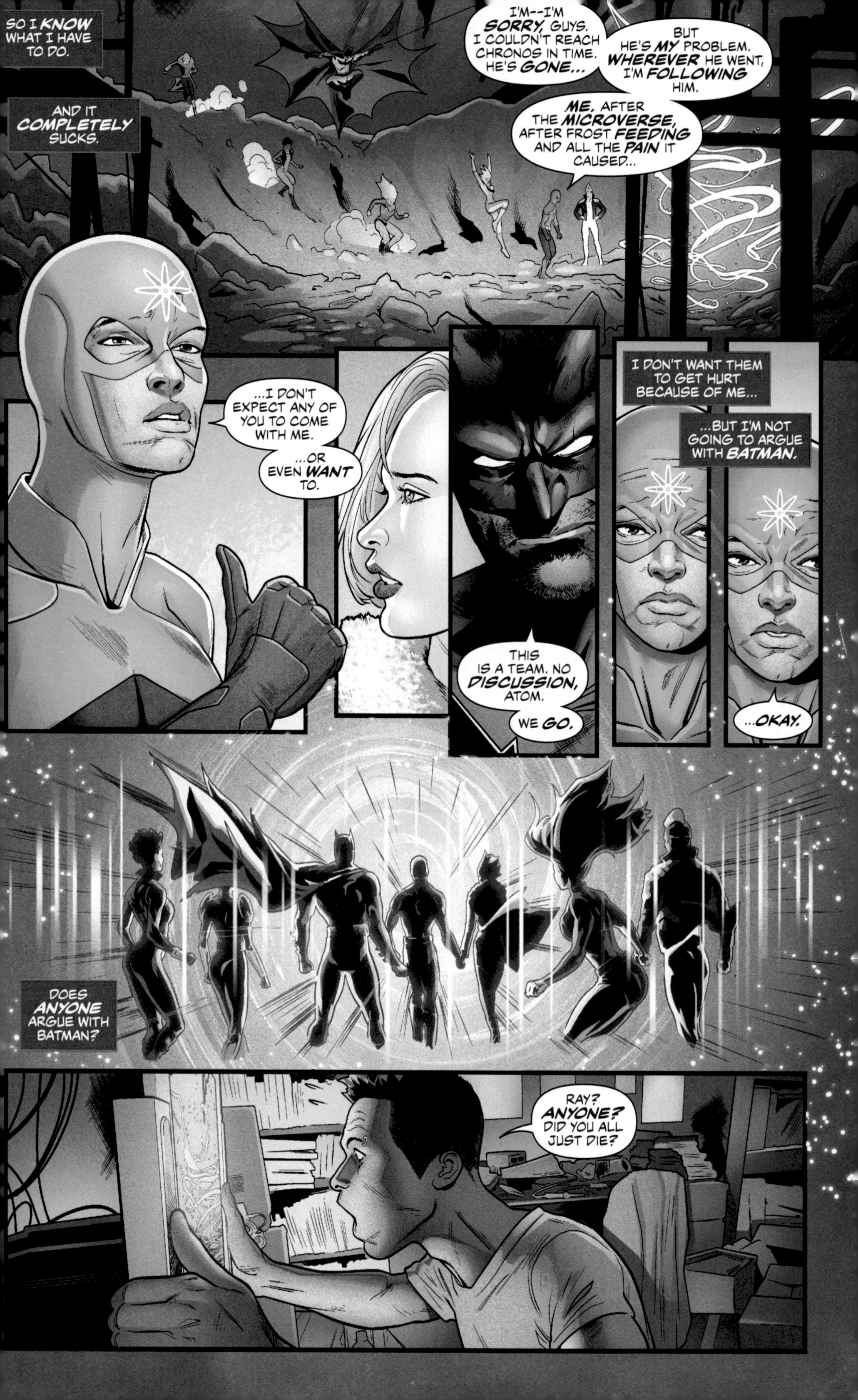
SO I KNOW WHAT I HAVE TO DO.
AND IT COMPLETELY SUCKS.
I'M--I'M SORRY, GUYS. I COULDN'T REACH CHRONOS IN TIME. HE'S GONE...
BUT HE'S MY PROBLEM. WHEREVER HE WENT, I'M FOLLOWING HIM.
ME. AFTER THE MICROVERSE, AFTER FROST FEEDING AND ALL THE PAIN IT CAUSED...
...I DON'T EXPECT ANY OF YOU TO COME WITH ME.
...OR EVEN WANT TO.
THIS IS A TEAM. NO DISCUSSION, ATOM.
WE GO.
I DON'T WANT THEM TO GET HURT BECAUSE OF ME...
...BUT I'M NOT GOING TO ARGUE WITH BATMAN.
...OKAY.
DOES ANYONE ARGUE WITH BATMAN?
RAY? ANYONE? DID YOU ALL JUST DIE?

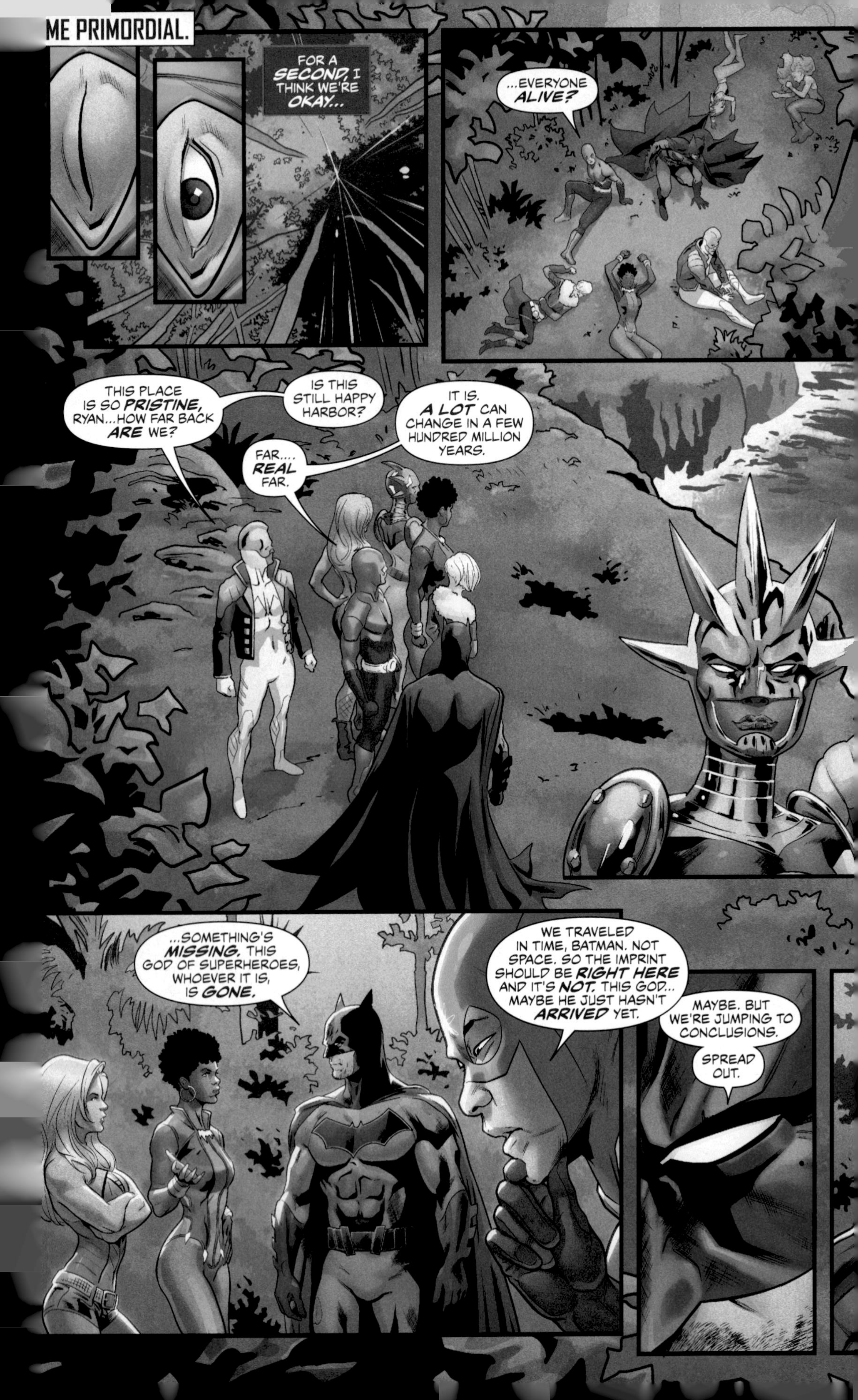
ME PRIMORDIAL.
FOR A SECOND, I THINK WE'RE OKAY...
...EVERYONE ALIVE?
THIS PLACE IS SO PRISTINE, RYAN...HOW FAR BACK ARE WE?
IS THIS STILL HAPPY HARBOR?
FAR.... REAL FAR.
IT IS. A LOT CAN CHANGE IN A FEW HUNDRED MILLION YEARS.
...SOMETHING'S MISSING. THIS GOD OF SUPERHEROES, WHOEVER IT IS, IS GONE.
WE TRAVELED IN TIME, BATMAN. NOT SPACE. SO THE IMPRINT SHOULD BE RIGHT HERE AND IT'S NOT. THIS GOD... MAYBE HE JUST HASN'T ARRIVED YET.
MAYBE. BUT WE'RE JUMPING TO CONCLUSIONS.
SPREAD OUT.

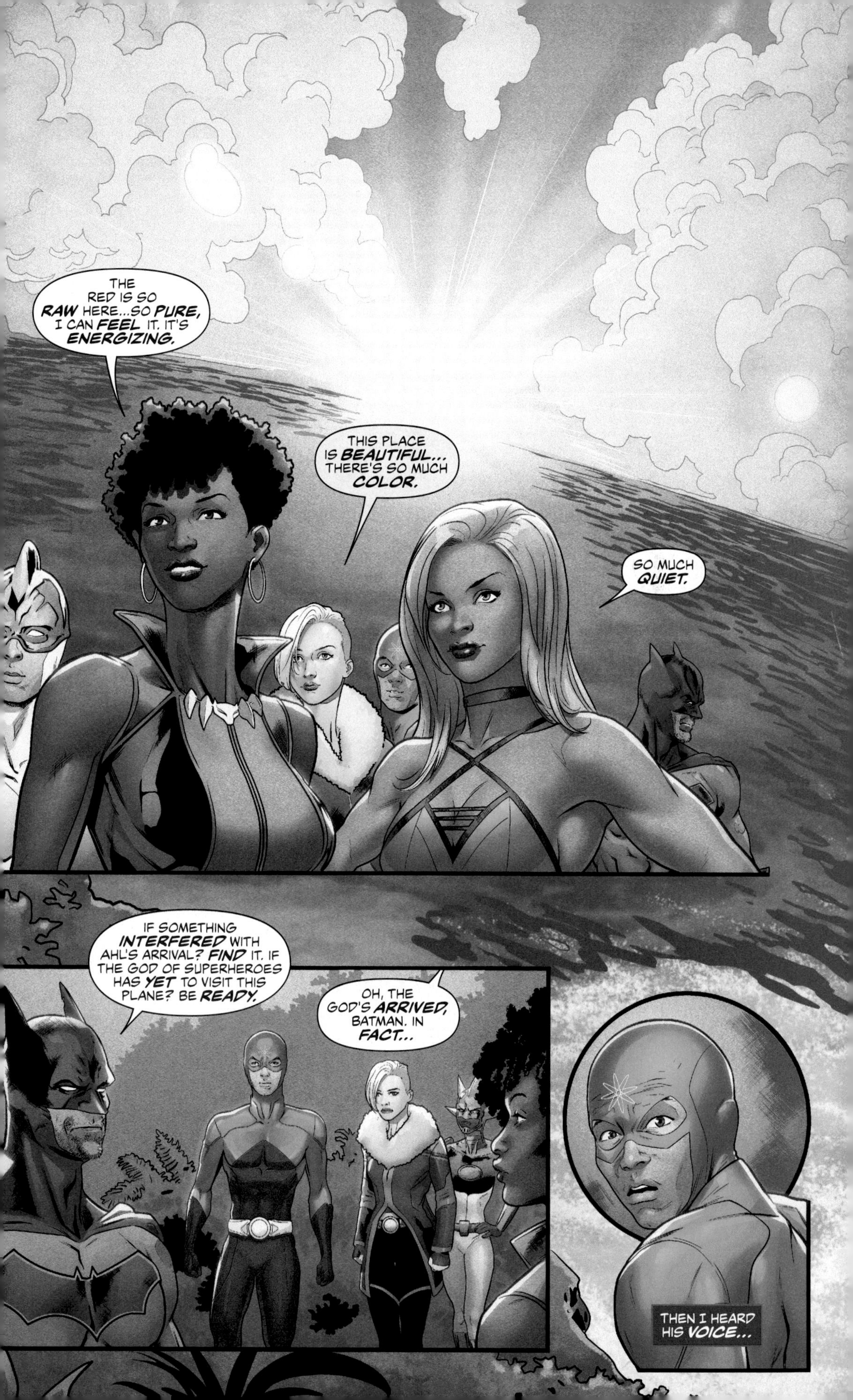
THE RED IS SO RAW HERE...SO PURE, I CAN FEEL IT. IT'S ENERGIZING.
THIS PLACE IS BEAUTIFUL... THERE'S SO MUCH COLOR.
SO MUCH QUIET.
IF SOMETHING INTERFERED WITH AHL'S ARRIVAL? FIND IT. IF THE GOD OF SUPERHEROES HAS YET TO VISIT THIS PLANE? BE READY.
OH, THE GOD'S ARRIVED, BATMAN. IN FACT...
THEN I HEARD HIS VOICE...

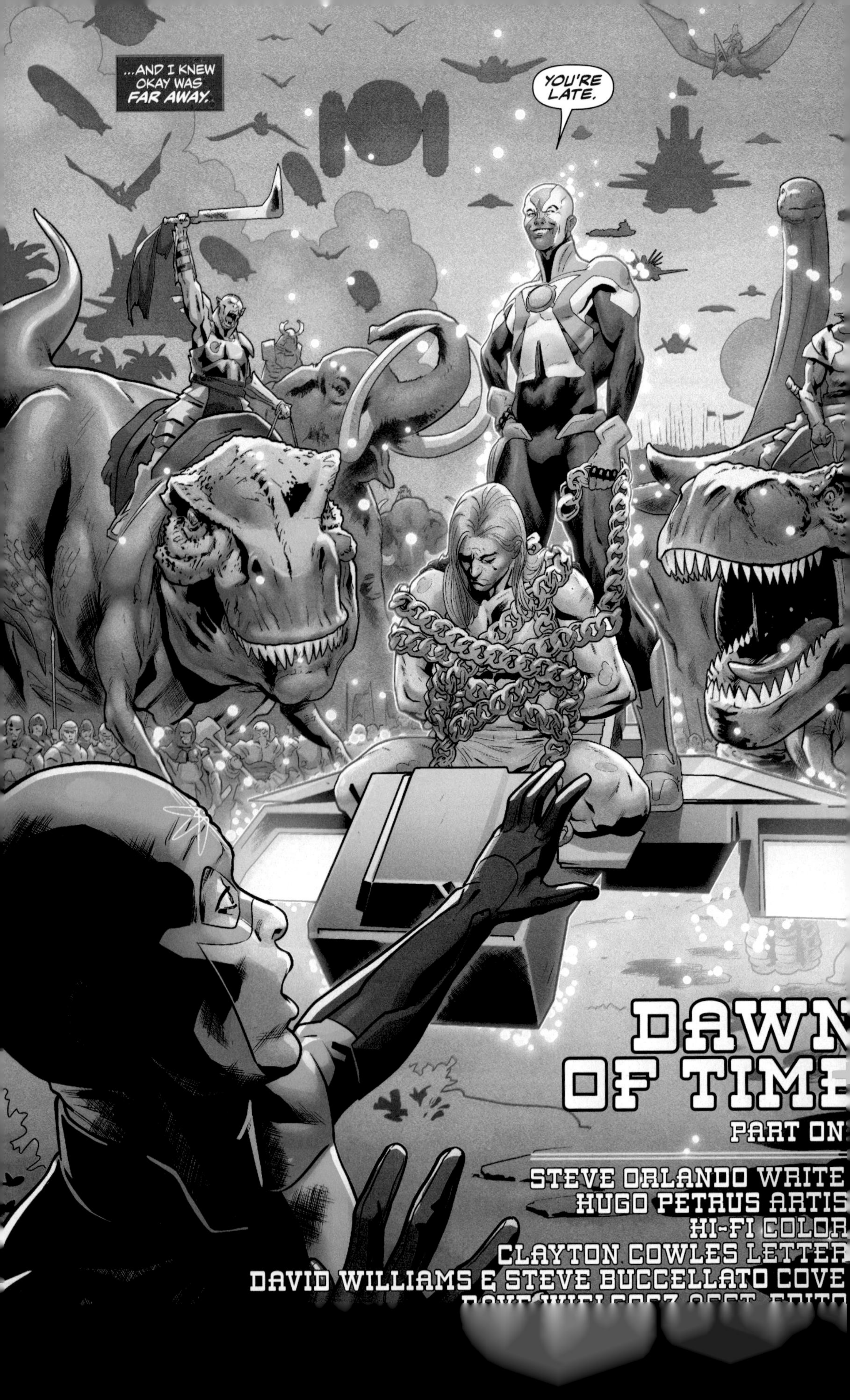
...AND I KNEW
OKAY WAS
FAR AWAY.
YOU'RE
LATE.
DAWN
OF TIME
PART ON
STEVE ORLANDO WRITE
HUGO PETRUS ARTIS
HI-FI COLOR
CLAYTON COWLES LETTER
DAVID WILLIAMS & STEVE BUCCELLATO COVE

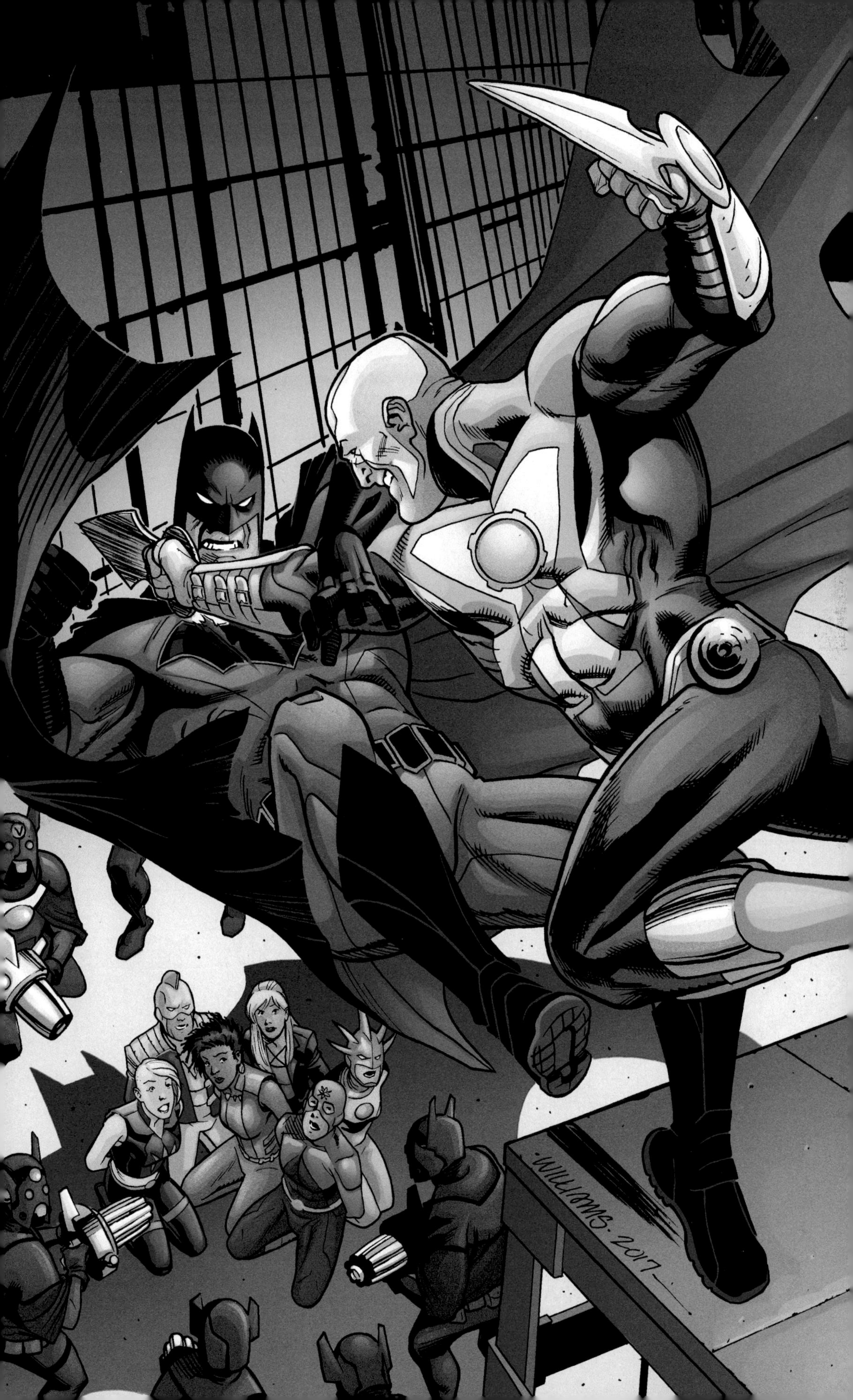
WILLIAMS. 2017

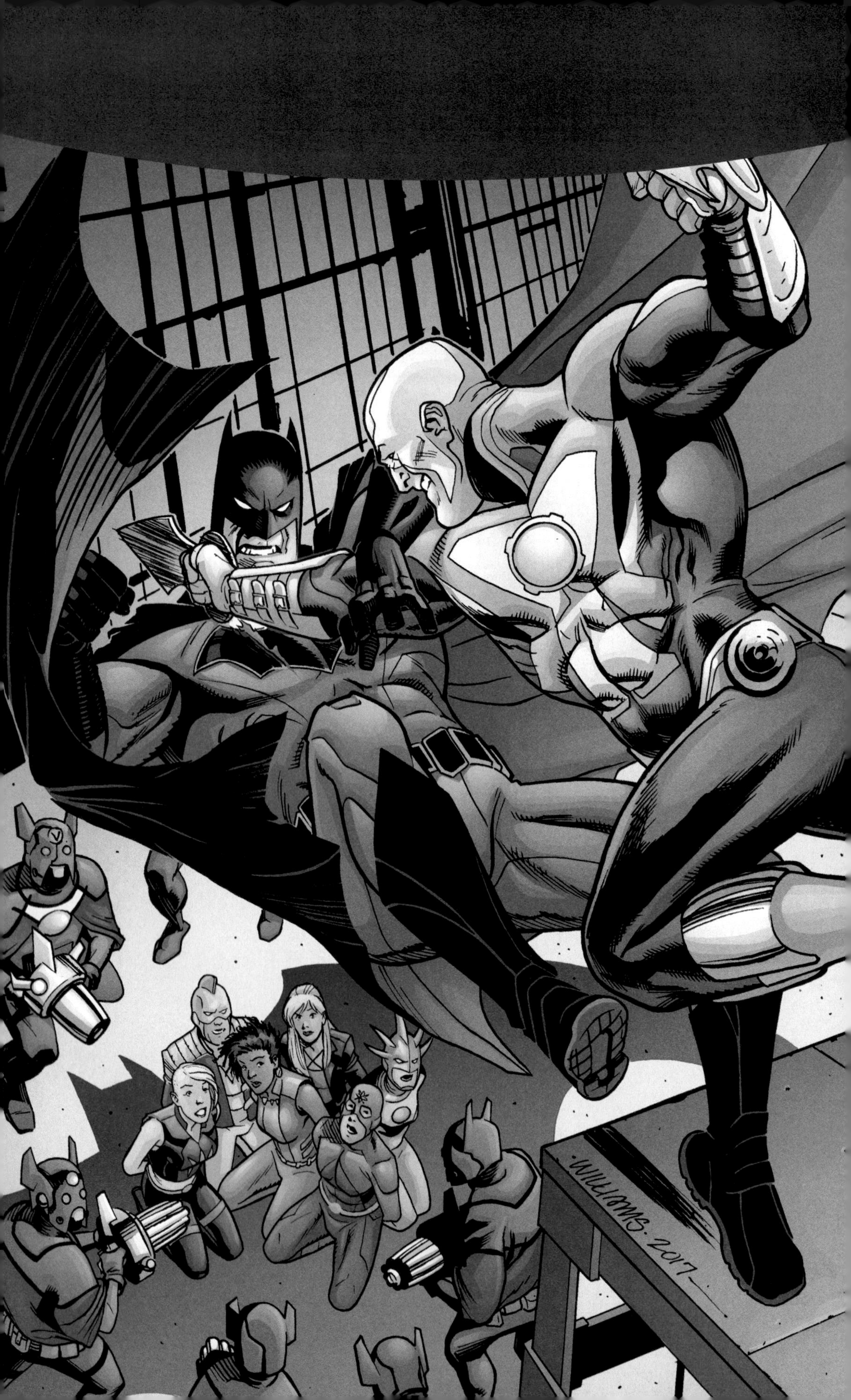
WILLIAMS. 2017

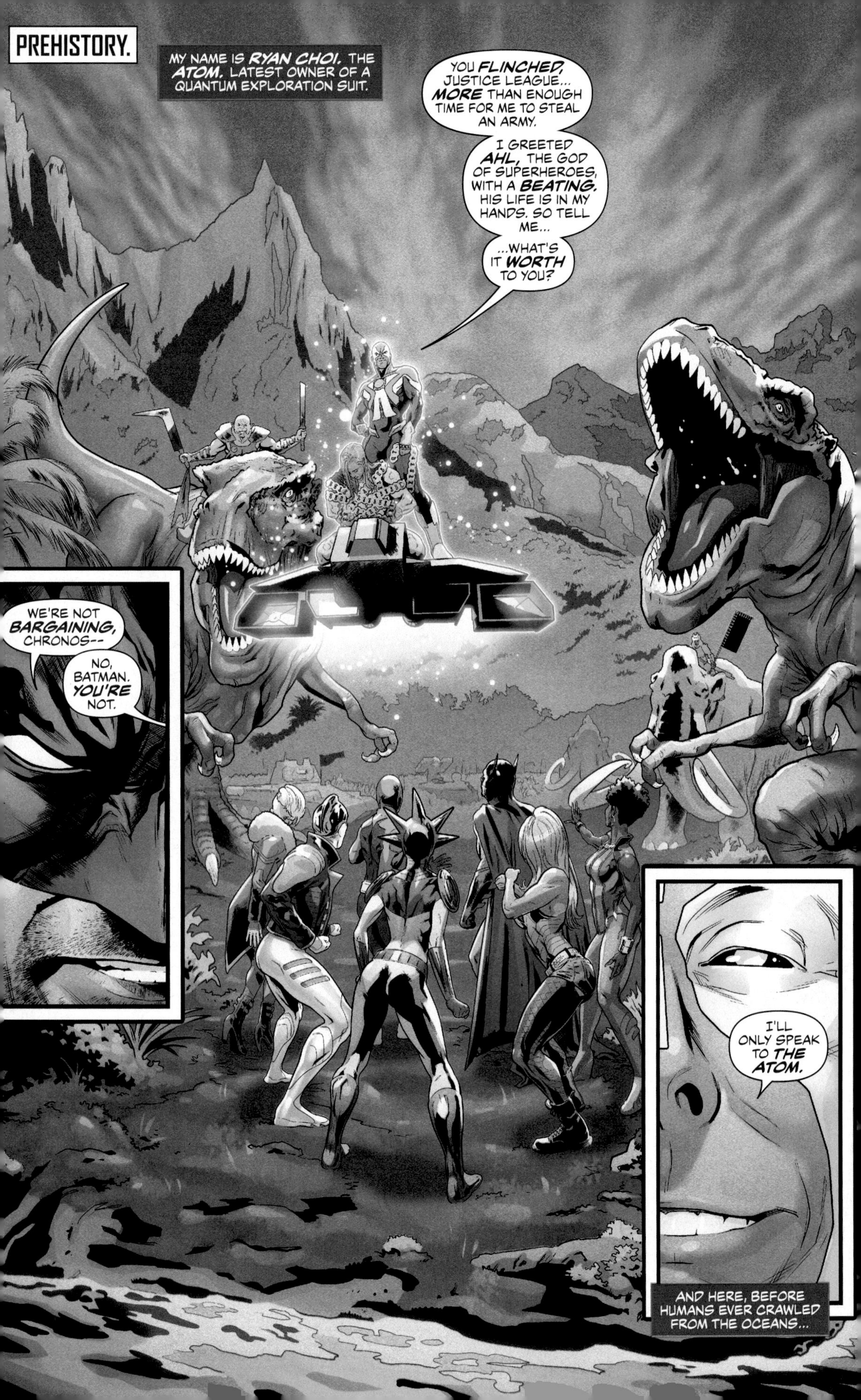
PREHISTORY.
MY NAME IS RYAN CHOI. THE ATOM. LATEST OWNER OF A QUANTUM EXPLORATION SUIT.
YOU FLINCHED, JUSTICE LEAGUE... MORE THAN ENOUGH TIME FOR ME TO STEAL AN ARMY.
I GREETED AHL, THE GOD OF SUPERHEROES, WITH A BEATING. HIS LIFE IS IN MY HANDS. SO TELL ME...
...WHAT'S IT WORTH TO YOU?
WE'RE NOT BARGAINING, CHRONOS--
NO, BATMAN. YOU'RE NOT.
I'LL ONLY SPEAK TO THE ATOM.
AND HERE, BEFORE HUMANS EVER CRAWLED FROM THE OCEANS...

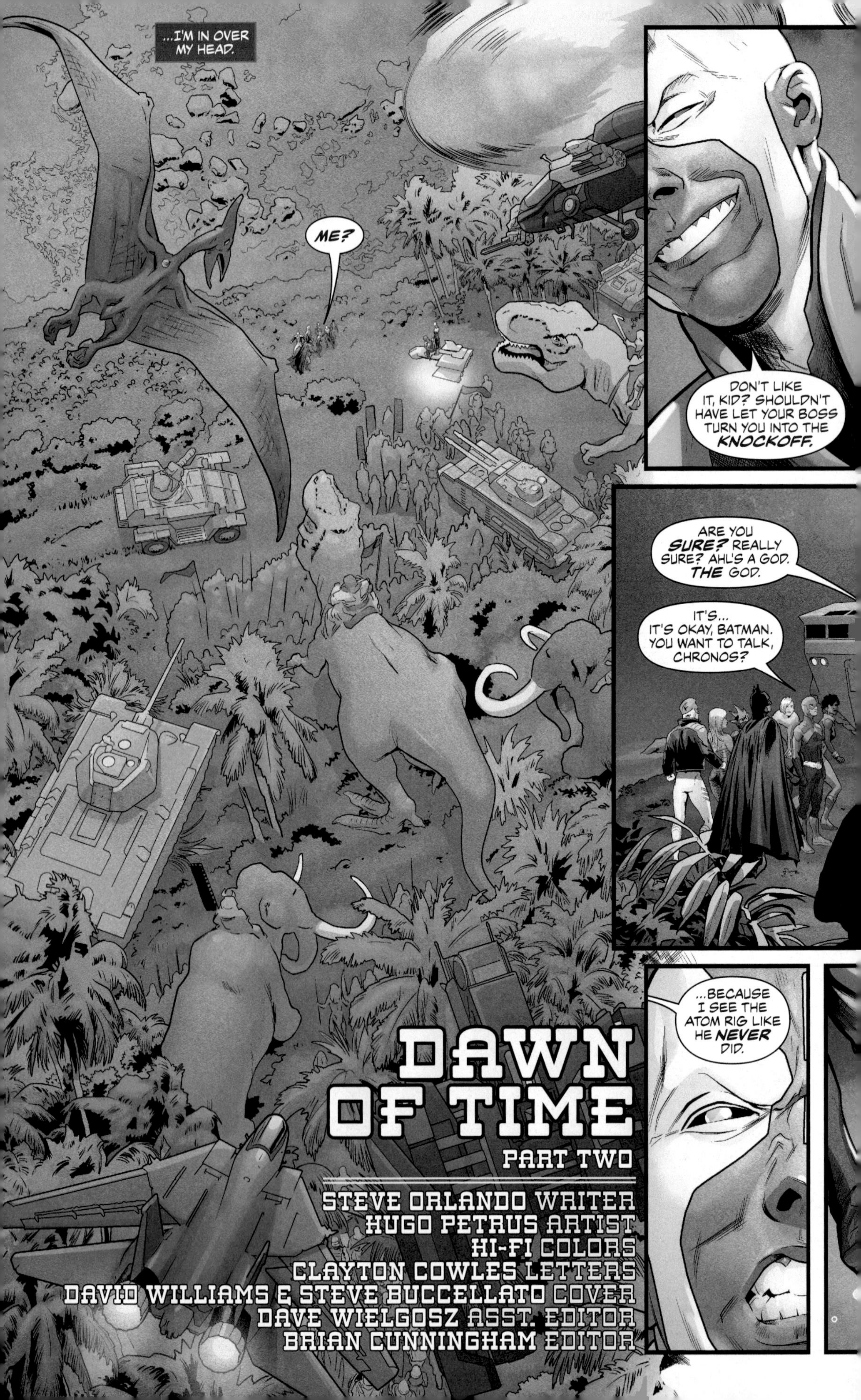
...I'M IN OVER MY HEAD.
ME?
DON'T LIKE IT, KID? SHOULDN'T HAVE LET YOUR BOSS TURN YOU INTO THE KNOCKOFF.
ARE YOU SURE? REALLY SURE? AHL'S A GOD. THE GOD.
IT'S... IT'S OKAY, BATMAN. YOU WANT TO TALK, CHRONOS?
...BECAUSE I SEE THE ATOM RIG LIKE HE NEVER DID.
DAWN OF TIME
PART TWO
STEVE ORLANDO WRITER
HUGO PETRUS ARTIST
HI-FI COLORS
CLAYTON COWLES LETTERS
DAVID WILLIAMS & STEVE BUCCELLATO COVER
DAVE WIELGOSZ ASST. EDITOR
BRIAN CUNNINGHAM EDITOR

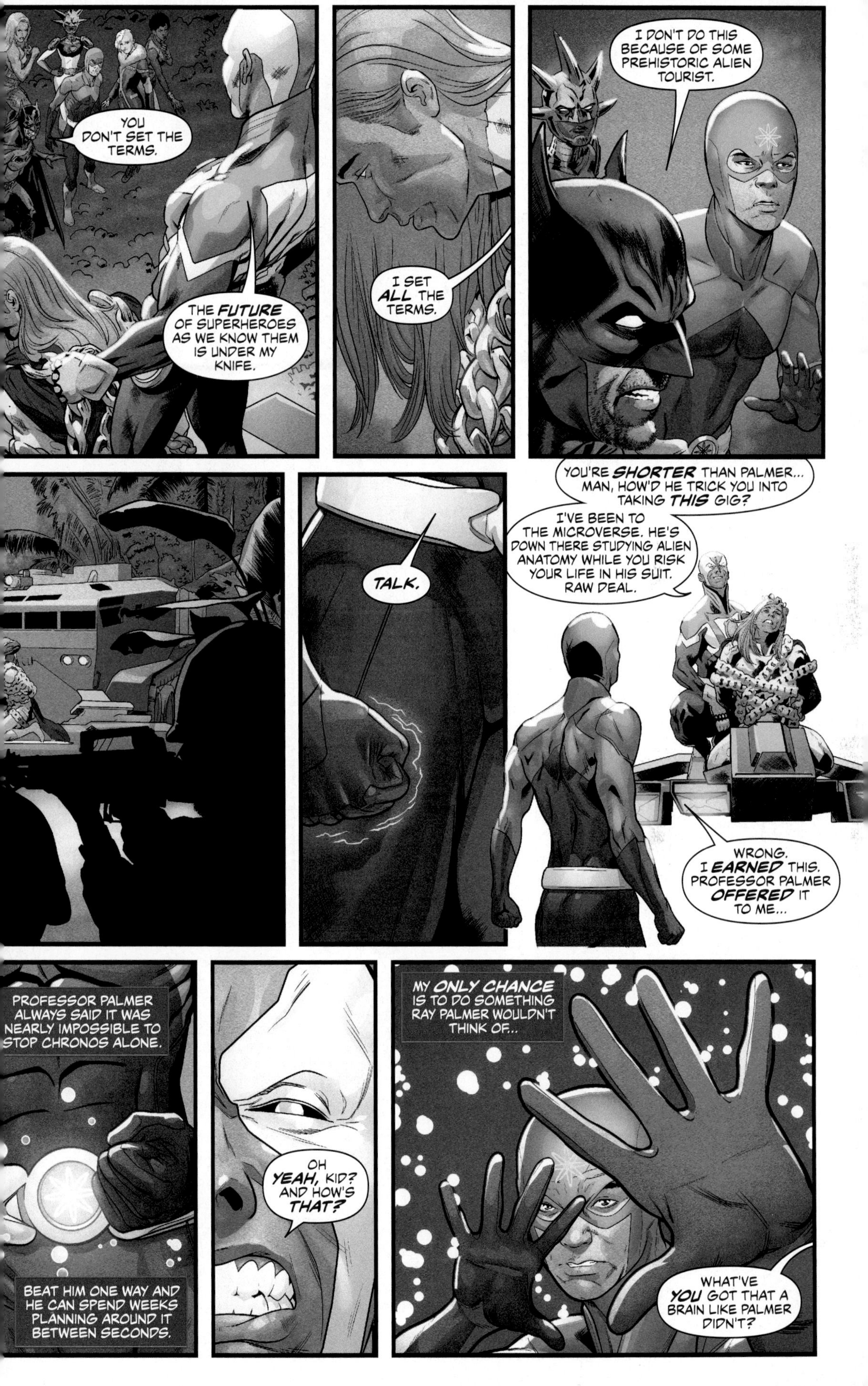
YOU DON'T SET THE TERMS.
THE FUTURE OF SUPERHEROES AS WE KNOW THEM IS UNDER MY KNIFE.
I SET ALL THE TERMS.
I DON'T DO THIS BECAUSE OF SOME PREHISTORIC ALIEN TOURIST.
TALK.
YOU'RE SHORTER THAN PALMER... MAN, HOW'D HE TRICK YOU INTO TAKING THIS GIG?
I'VE BEEN TO THE MICROVERSE. HE'S DOWN THERE STUDYING ALIEN ANATOMY WHILE YOU RISK YOUR LIFE IN HIS SUIT. RAW DEAL.
WRONG. I EARNED THIS. PROFESSOR PALMER OFFERED IT TO ME...
PROFESSOR PALMER ALWAYS SAID IT WAS NEARLY IMPOSSIBLE TO STOP CHRONOS ALONE.
BEAT HIM ONE WAY AND HE CAN SPEND WEEKS PLANNING AROUND IT BETWEEN SECONDS.
OH YEAH, KID? AND HOW'S THAT?
MY ONLY CHANCE IS TO DO SOMETHING RAY PALMER WOULDN'T THINK OF...
WHAT'VE YOU GOT THAT A BRAIN LIKE PALMER DIDN'T?

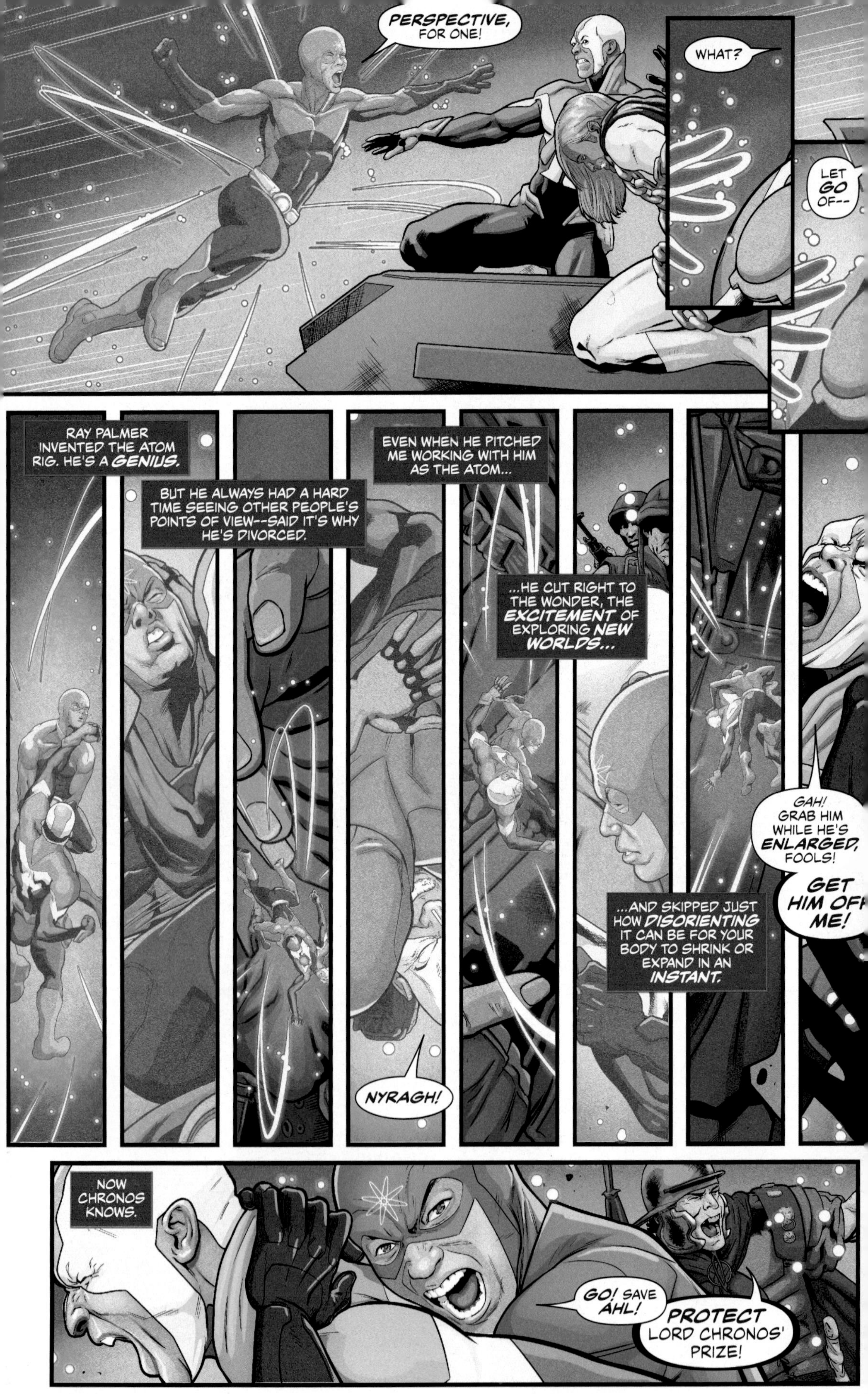
PERSPECTIVE, FOR ONE!
WHAT?
LET GO OF--
RAY PALMER INVENTED THE ATOM RIG. HE'S A GENIUS.
BUT HE ALWAYS HAD A HARD TIME SEEING OTHER PEOPLE'S POINTS OF VIEW--SAID IT'S WHY HE'S DIVORCED.
EVEN WHEN HE PITCHED ME WORKING WITH HIM AS THE ATOM...
...HE CUT RIGHT TO THE WONDER, THE EXCITEMENT OF EXPLORING NEW WORLDS...
NYRAGH!
...AND SKIPPED JUST HOW DISORIENTING IT CAN BE FOR YOUR BODY TO SHRINK OR EXPAND IN AN INSTANT.
GAH! GRAB HIM WHILE HE'S ENLARGED, FOOLS!
GET HIM OFF ME!
NOW CHRONOS KNOWS.
GO! SAVE AHL!
PROTECT LORD CHRONOS' PRIZE!

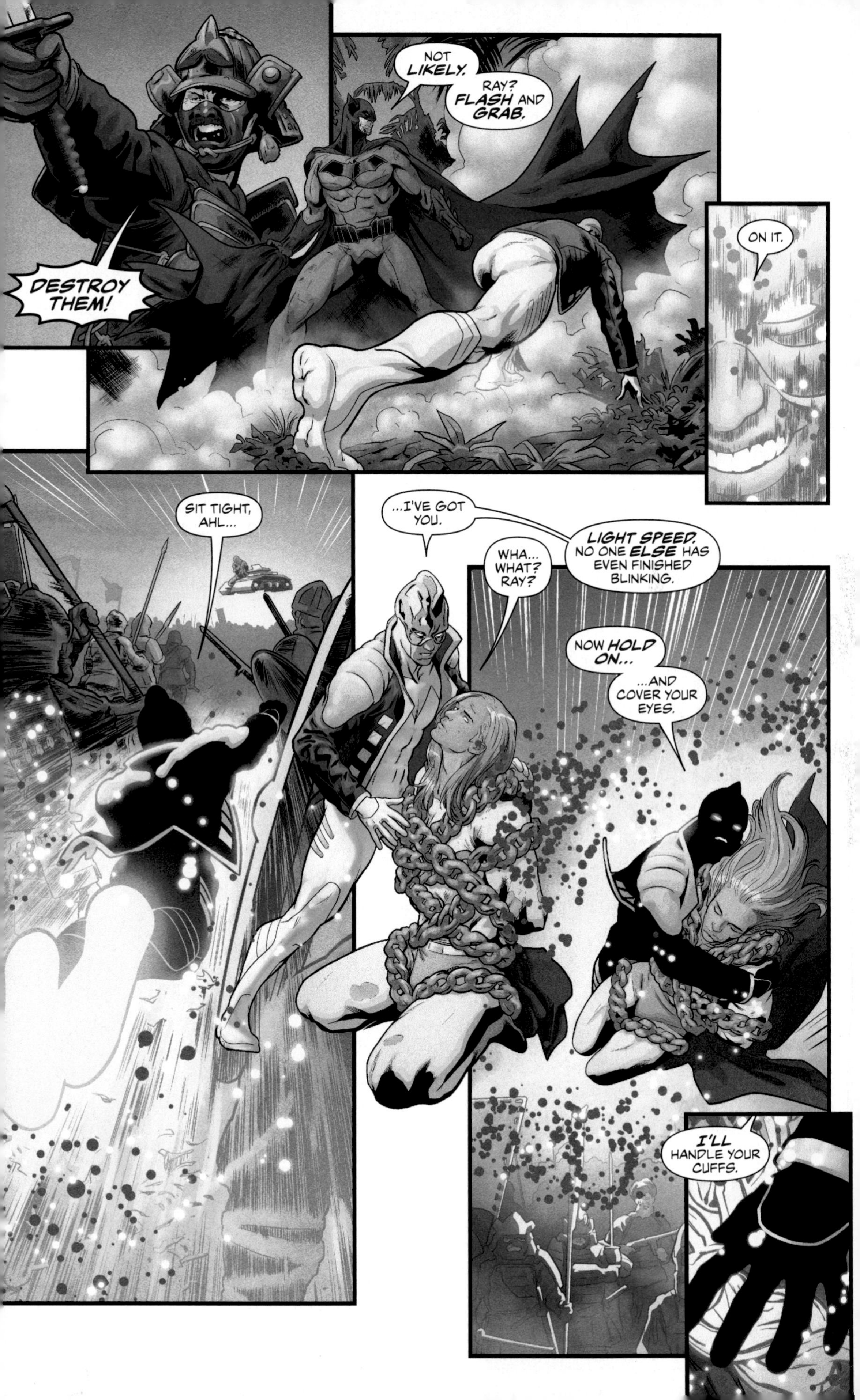
NOT LIKELY.
RAY? FLASH AND GRAB.
DESTROY THEM!
ON IT.
SIT TIGHT, AHL...
...I'VE GOT YOU.
LIGHT SPEED. NO ONE ELSE HAS EVEN FINISHED BLINKING.
WHA... WHAT? RAY?
NOW HOLD ON...
...AND COVER YOUR EYES.
I'LL HANDLE YOUR CUFFS.

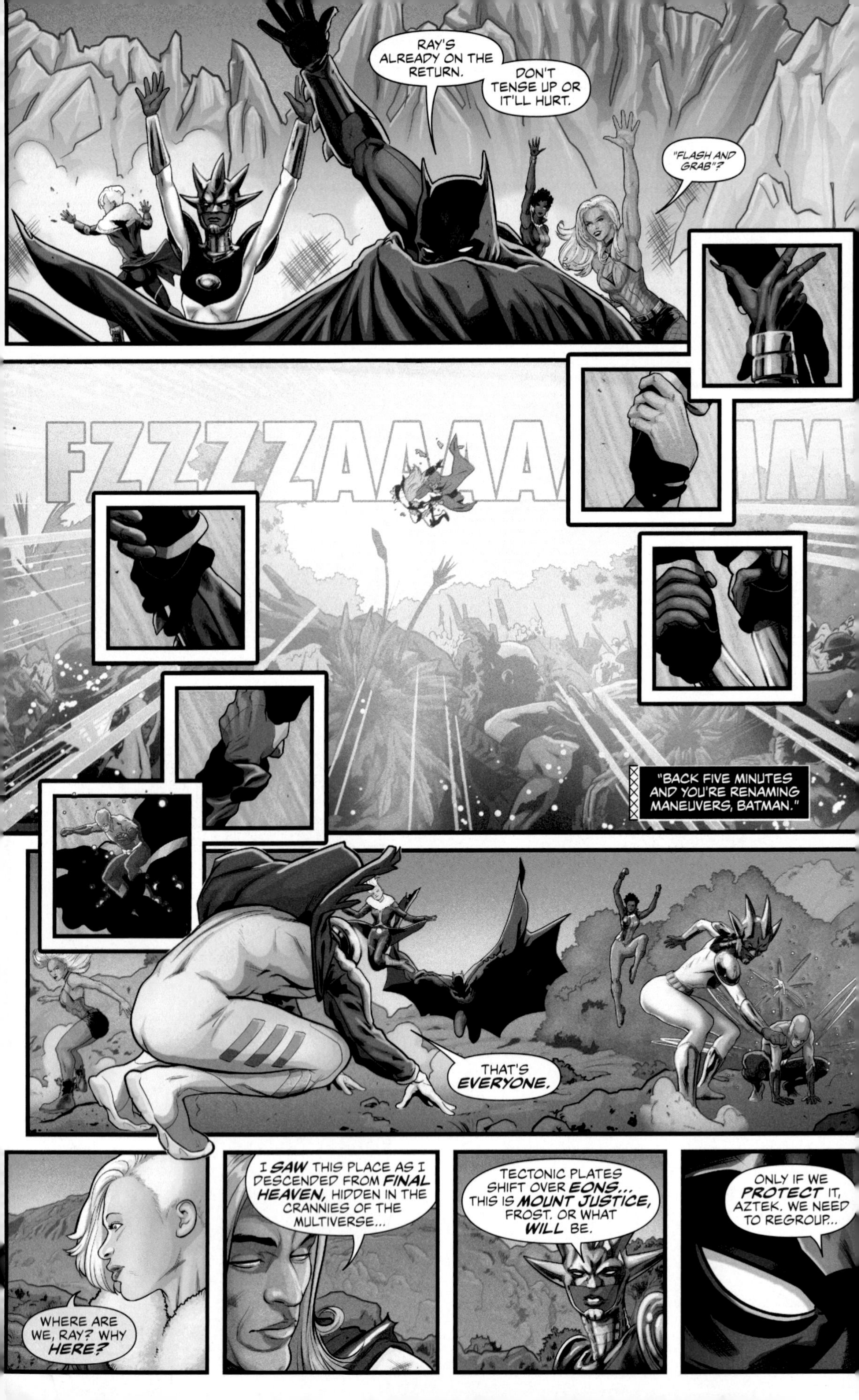
RAY'S ALREADY ON THE RETURN.
DON'T TENSE UP OR IT'LL HURT.
"FLASH AND GRAB"?
FZZZZAAAAAMM
"BACK FIVE MINUTES AND YOU'RE RENAMING MANEUVERS, BATMAN."
THAT'S EVERYONE.
WHERE ARE WE, RAY? WHY HERE?
I SAW THIS PLACE AS I DESCENDED FROM FINAL HEAVEN, HIDDEN IN THE CRANNIES OF THE MULTIVERSE...
TECTONIC PLATES SHIFT OVER EONS... THIS IS MOUNT JUSTICE, FROST. OR WHAT WILL BE.
ONLY IF WE PROTECT IT, AZTEK. WE NEED TO REGROUP...

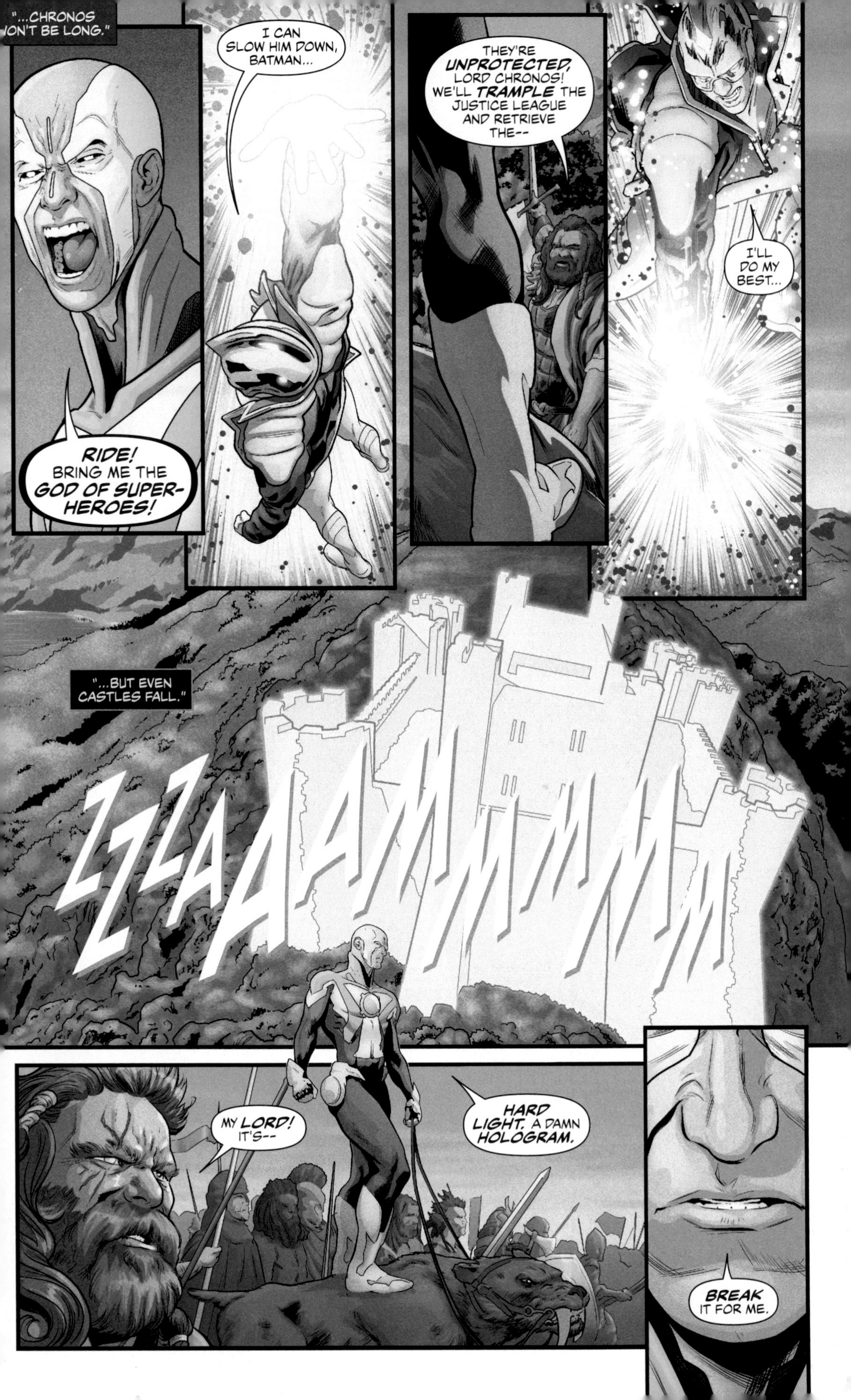

"...CHRONOS WON'T BE LONG."
RIDE! BRING ME THE GOD OF SUPER-HEROES!
I CAN SLOW HIM DOWN, BATMAN...
THEY'RE UNPROTECTED, LORD CHRONOS! WE'LL TRAMPLE THE JUSTICE LEAGUE AND RETRIEVE THE--
I'LL DO MY BEST...
"...BUT EVEN CASTLES FALL."
ZZZAAAMMMMMM
MY LORD! IT'S--
HARD LIGHT. A DAMN HOLOGRAM.
BREAK IT FOR ME.

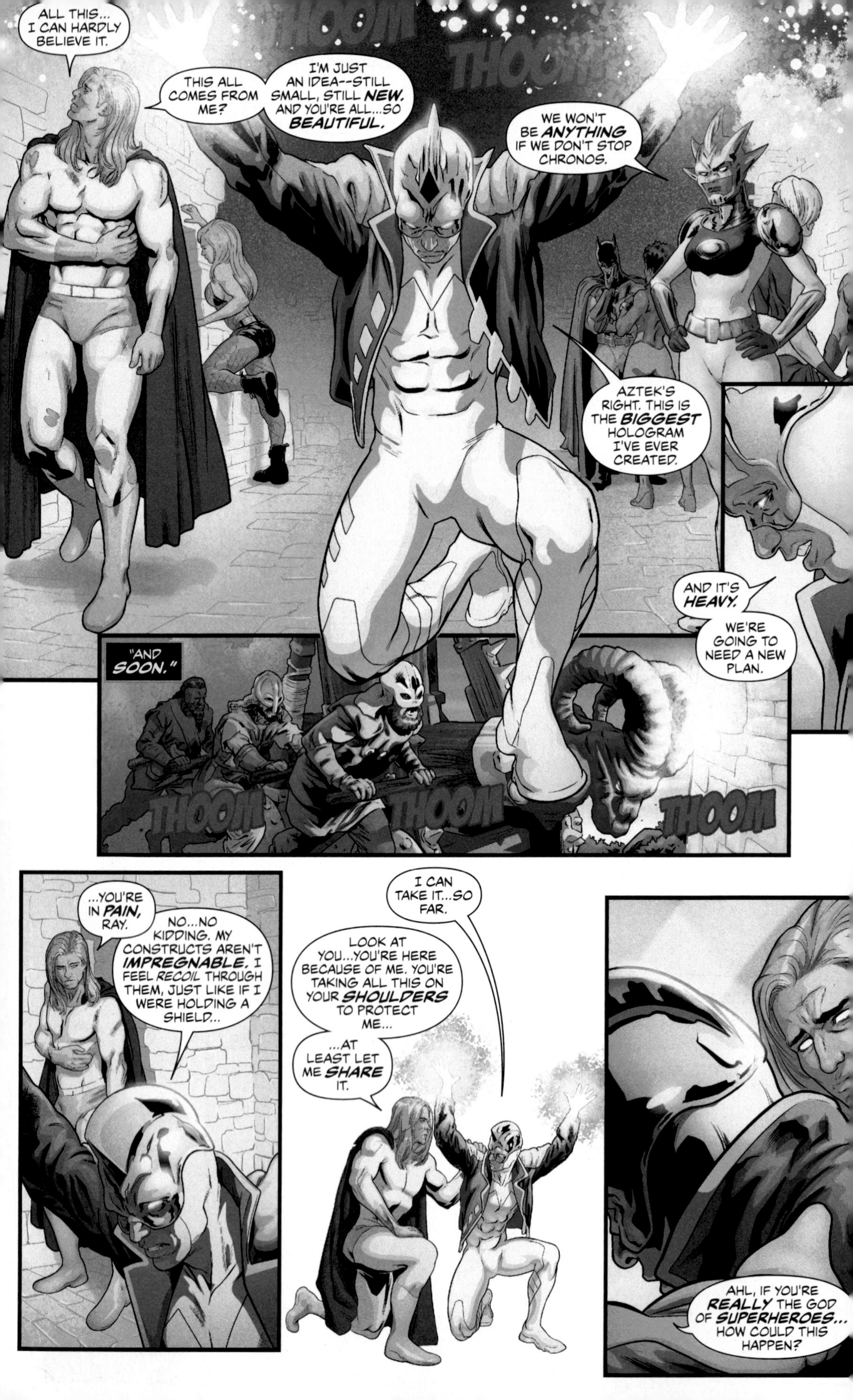
ALL THIS... I CAN HARDLY BELIEVE IT.
THIS ALL COMES FROM ME?
I'M JUST AN IDEA--STILL SMALL, STILL NEW. AND YOU'RE ALL...SO BEAUTIFUL.
THOOM
THOOM
WE WON'T BE ANYTHING IF WE DON'T STOP CHRONOS.
AZTEK'S RIGHT. THIS IS THE BIGGEST HOLOGRAM I'VE EVER CREATED.
AND IT'S HEAVY.
WE'RE GOING TO NEED A NEW PLAN.
"AND SOON."
THOOM
THOOM
THOOM
...YOU'RE IN PAIN, RAY.
NO...NO KIDDING. MY CONSTRUCTS AREN'T IMPREGNABLE. I FEEL RECOIL THROUGH THEM, JUST LIKE IF I WERE HOLDING A SHIELD...
I CAN TAKE IT...SO FAR.
LOOK AT YOU...YOU'RE HERE BECAUSE OF ME. YOU'RE TAKING ALL THIS ON YOUR SHOULDERS TO PROTECT ME...
...AT LEAST LET ME SHARE IT.
AHL, IF YOU'RE REALLY THE GOD OF SUPERHEROES... HOW COULD THIS HAPPEN?

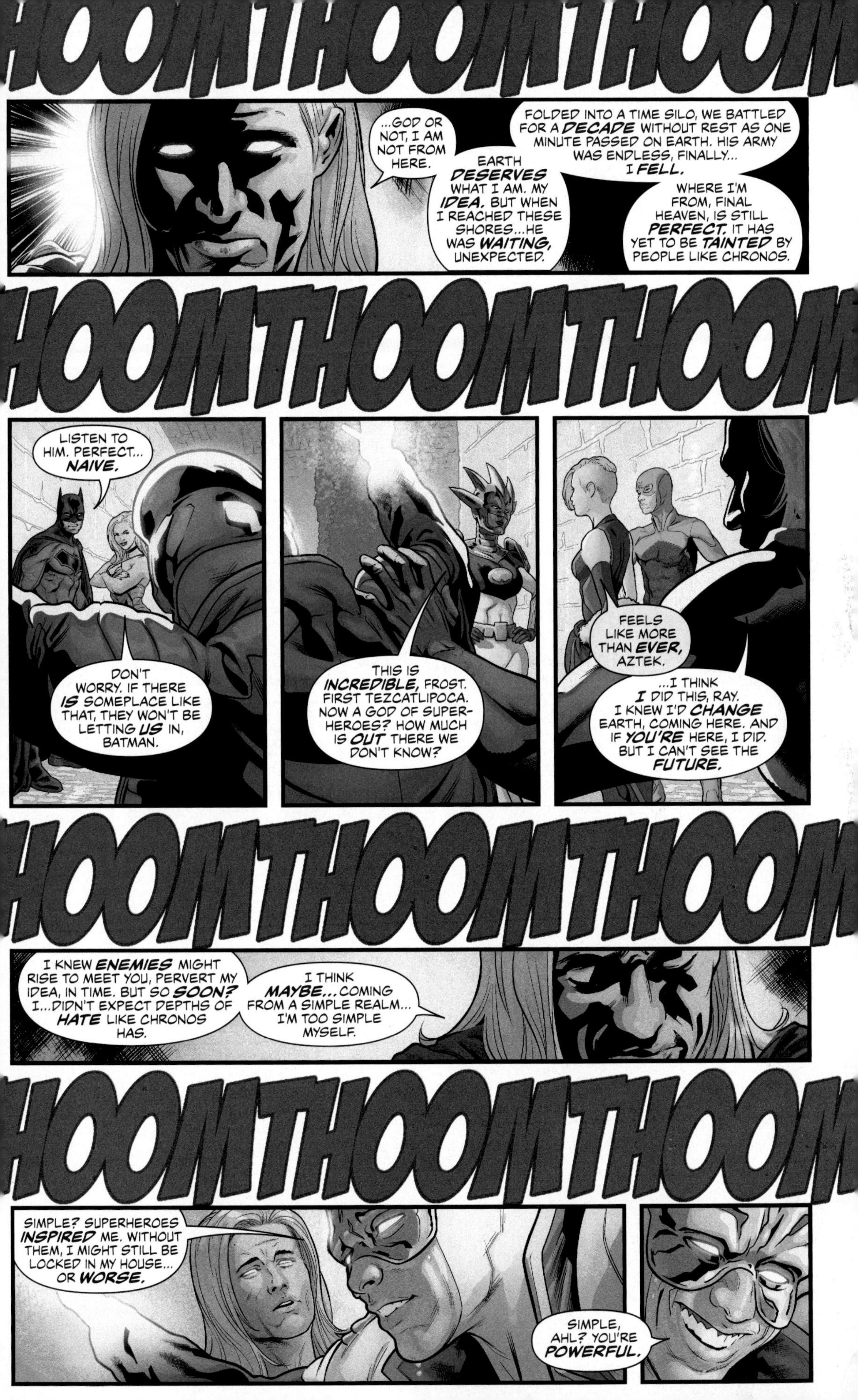

THOOM THOOM
...GOD OR NOT, I AM NOT FROM HERE.
EARTH DESERVES WHAT I AM. MY IDEA. BUT WHEN I REACHED THESE SHORES...HE WAS WAITING, UNEXPECTED.
FOLDED INTO A TIME SILO, WE BATTLED FOR A DECADE WITHOUT REST AS ONE MINUTE PASSED ON EARTH. HIS ARMY WAS ENDLESS, FINALLY... I FELL.
WHERE I'M FROM, FINAL HEAVEN, IS STILL PERFECT. IT HAS YET TO BE TAINTED BY PEOPLE LIKE CHRONOS.
THOOM THOOM
LISTEN TO HIM. PERFECT... NAIVE.
DON'T WORRY. IF THERE IS SOMEPLACE LIKE THAT, THEY WON'T BE LETTING US IN, BATMAN.
THIS IS INCREDIBLE, FROST. FIRST TEZCATLIPOCA. NOW A GOD OF SUPER-HEROES? HOW MUCH IS OUT THERE WE DON'T KNOW?
FEELS LIKE MORE THAN EVER, AZTEK.
...I THINK I DID THIS, RAY. I KNEW I'D CHANGE EARTH, COMING HERE. AND IF YOU'RE HERE, I DID. BUT I CAN'T SEE THE FUTURE.
THOOM THOOM
I KNEW ENEMIES MIGHT RISE TO MEET YOU, PERVERT MY IDEA, IN TIME. BUT SO SOON? I...DIDN'T EXPECT DEPTHS OF HATE LIKE CHRONOS HAS.
I THINK MAYBE... COMING FROM A SIMPLE REALM... I'M TOO SIMPLE MYSELF.
THOOM THOOM
SIMPLE? SUPERHEROES INSPIRED ME. WITHOUT THEM, I MIGHT STILL BE LOCKED IN MY HOUSE... OR WORSE.
SIMPLE, AHL? YOU'RE POWERFUL.

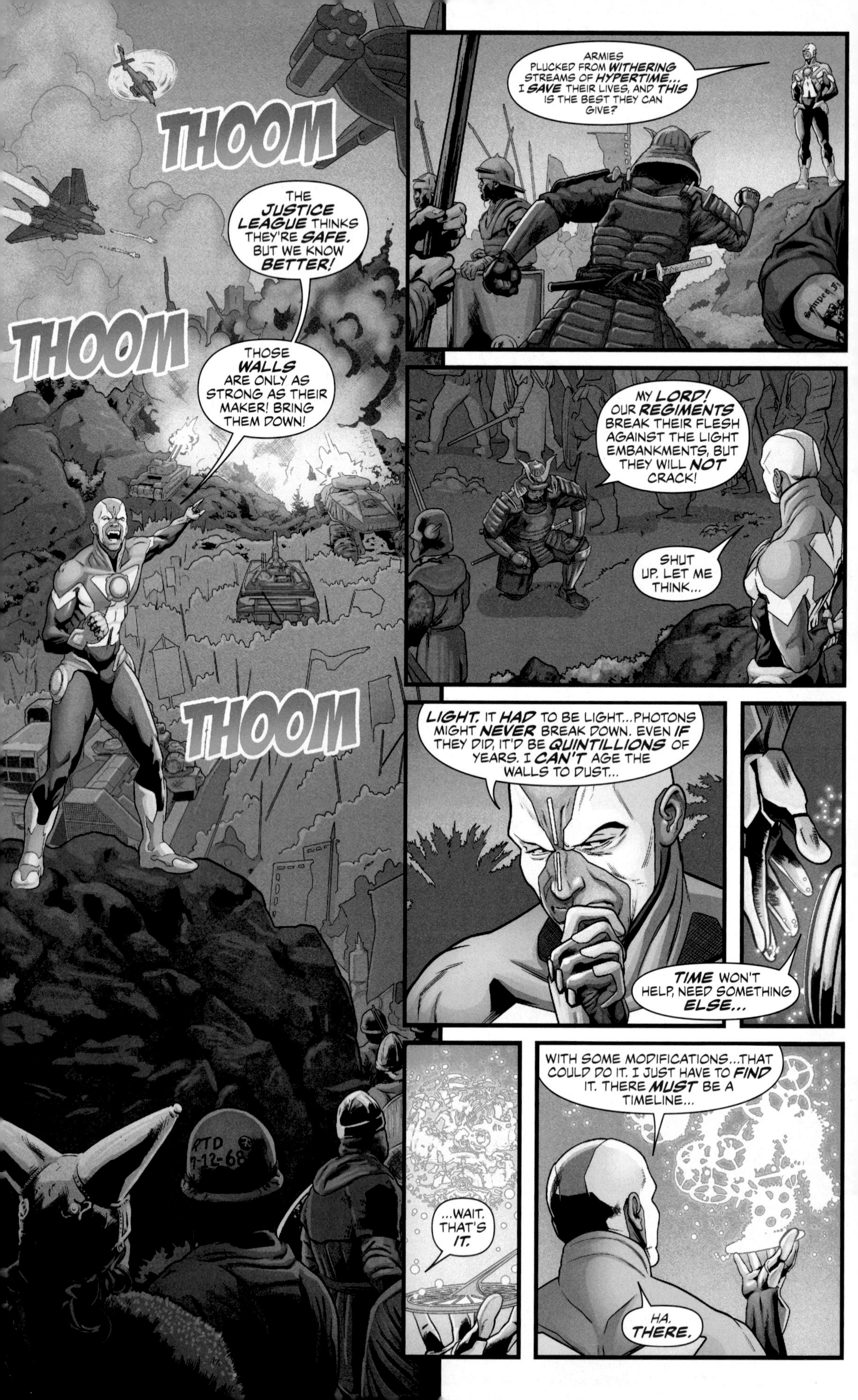
THOOM
THE JUSTICE LEAGUE THINKS THEY'RE SAFE. BUT WE KNOW BETTER!
THOOM
THOSE WALLS ARE ONLY AS STRONG AS THEIR MAKER! BRING THEM DOWN!
THOOM
ARMIES PLUCKED FROM WITHERING STREAMS OF HYPERTIME... I SAVE THEIR LIVES, AND THIS IS THE BEST THEY CAN GIVE?
MY LORD! OUR REGIMENTS BREAK THEIR FLESH AGAINST THE LIGHT EMBANKMENTS, BUT THEY WILL NOT CRACK!
SHUT UP. LET ME THINK...
LIGHT. IT HAD TO BE LIGHT...PHOTONS MIGHT NEVER BREAK DOWN. EVEN IF THEY DID, IT'D BE QUINTILLIONS OF YEARS. I CAN'T AGE THE WALLS TO DUST...
TIME WON'T HELP, NEED SOMETHING ELSE...
...WAIT. THAT'S IT.
WITH SOME MODIFICATIONS...THAT COULD DO IT. I JUST HAVE TO FIND IT. THERE MUST BE A TIMELINE...
HA. THERE.

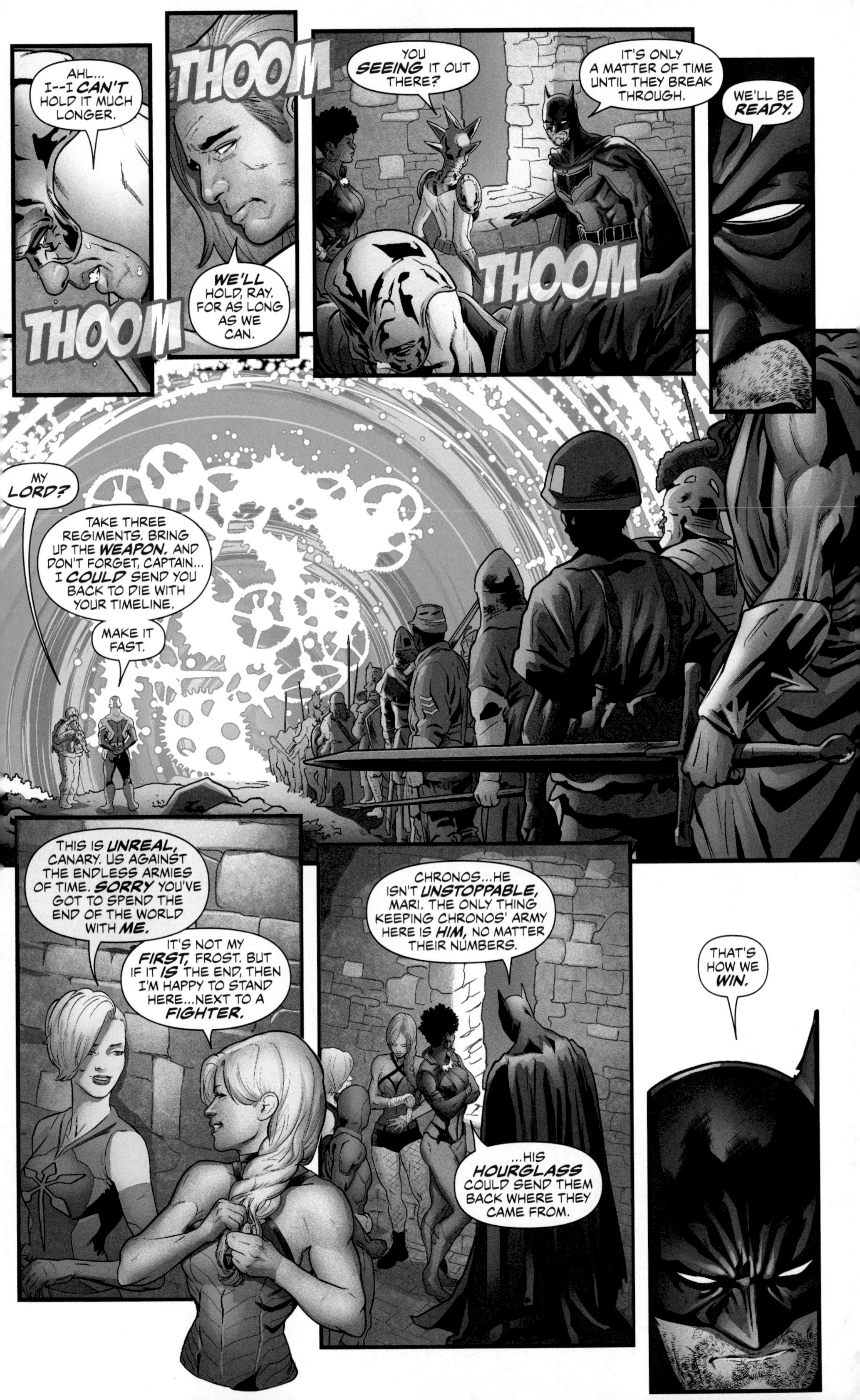
AHL... I--I CAN'T HOLD IT MUCH LONGER.
THOOM
THOOM
WE'LL HOLD, RAY. FOR AS LONG AS WE CAN.
YOU SEEING IT OUT THERE?
IT'S ONLY A MATTER OF TIME UNTIL THEY BREAK THROUGH.
THOOM
WE'LL BE READY.
MY LORD?
TAKE THREE REGIMENTS. BRING UP THE WEAPON. AND DON'T FORGET, CAPTAIN... I COULD SEND YOU BACK TO DIE WITH YOUR TIMELINE.
MAKE IT FAST.
THIS IS UNREAL, CANARY. US AGAINST THE ENDLESS ARMIES OF TIME. SORRY YOU'VE GOT TO SPEND THE END OF THE WORLD WITH ME.
IT'S NOT MY FIRST, FROST. BUT IF IT IS THE END, THEN I'M HAPPY TO STAND HERE...NEXT TO A FIGHTER.
CHRONOS...HE ISN'T UNSTOPPABLE, MARI. THE ONLY THING KEEPING CHRONOS' ARMY HERE IS HIM, NO MATTER THEIR NUMBERS.
...HIS HOURGLASS COULD SEND THEM BACK WHERE THEY CAME FROM.
THAT'S HOW WE WIN.

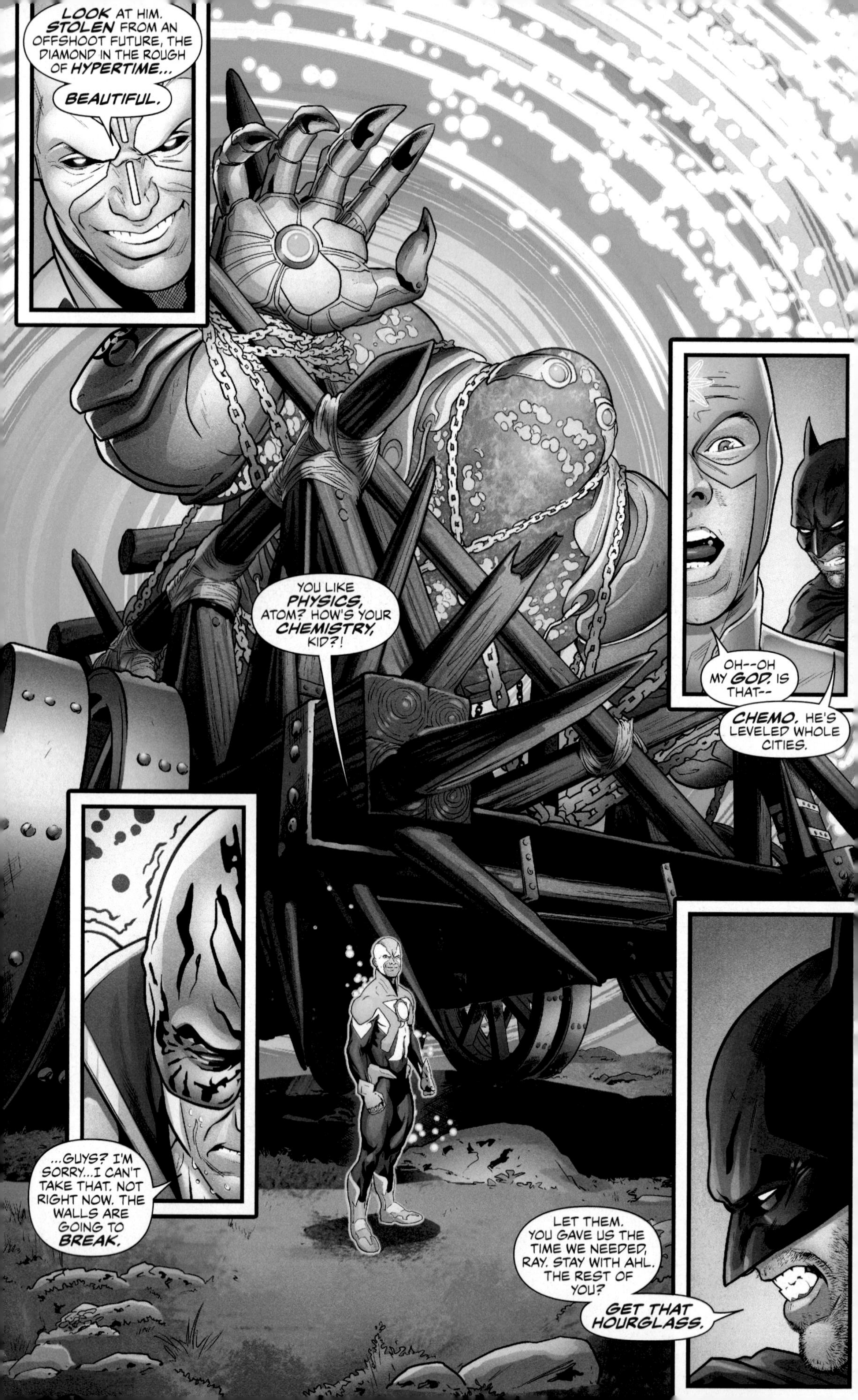
LOOK AT HIM. STOLEN FROM AN OFFSHOOT FUTURE, THE DIAMOND IN THE ROUGH OF HYPERTIME...
BEAUTIFUL.
YOU LIKE PHYSICS, ATOM? HOW'S YOUR CHEMISTRY, KID?!
OH--OH MY GOD. IS THAT--
CHEMO. HE'S LEVELED WHOLE CITIES.
...GUYS? I'M SORRY...I CAN'T TAKE THAT. NOT RIGHT NOW. THE WALLS ARE GOING TO BREAK.
LET THEM. YOU GAVE US THE TIME WE NEEDED, RAY. STAY WITH AHL. THE REST OF YOU?
GET THAT HOURGLASS.

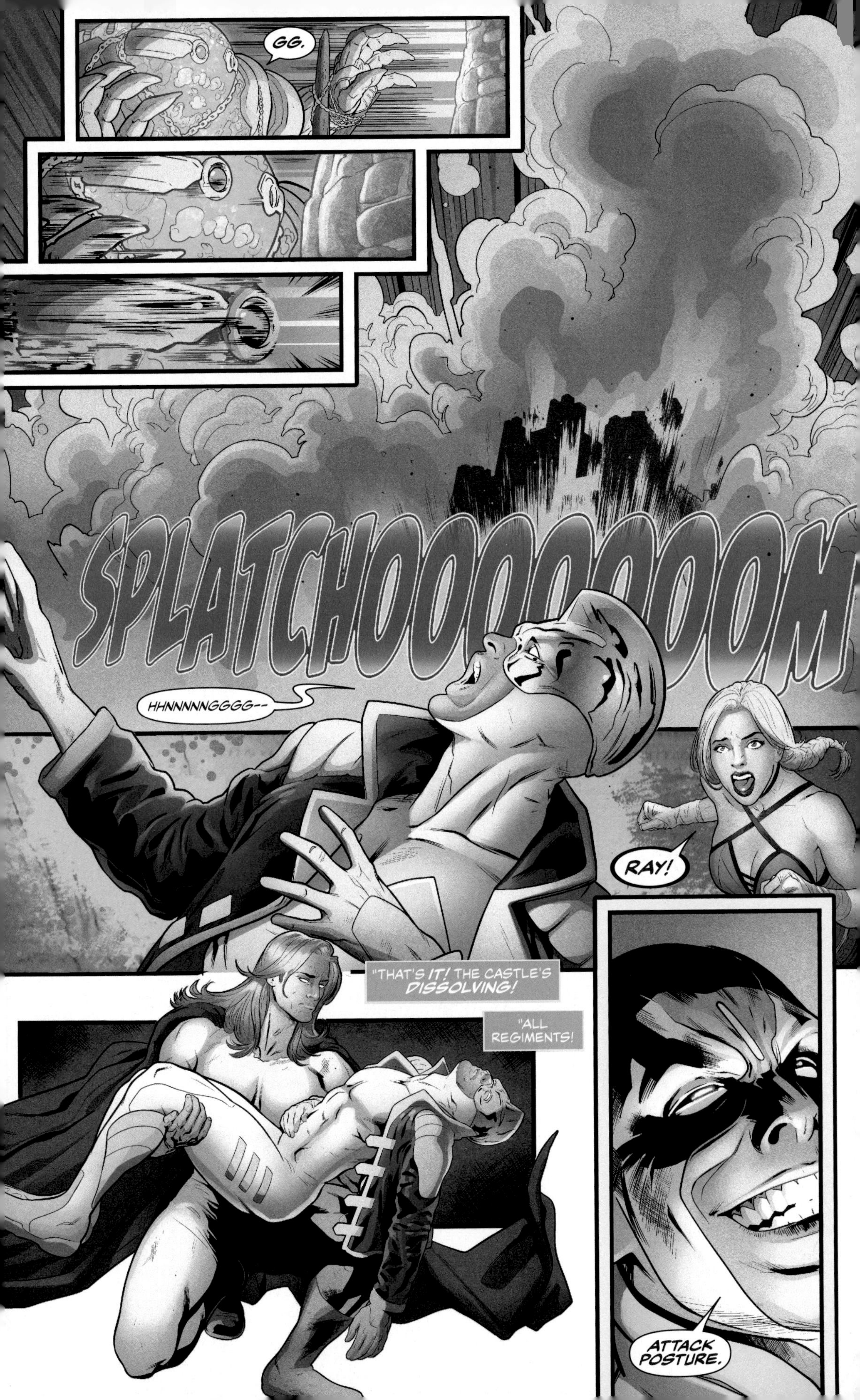
GG.
SPLATCHOOOOOOOOM
HHNNNNNGGGG--
RAY!
"THAT'S IT! THE CASTLE'S DISSOLVING!
"ALL REGIMENTS!
ATTACK POSTURE.

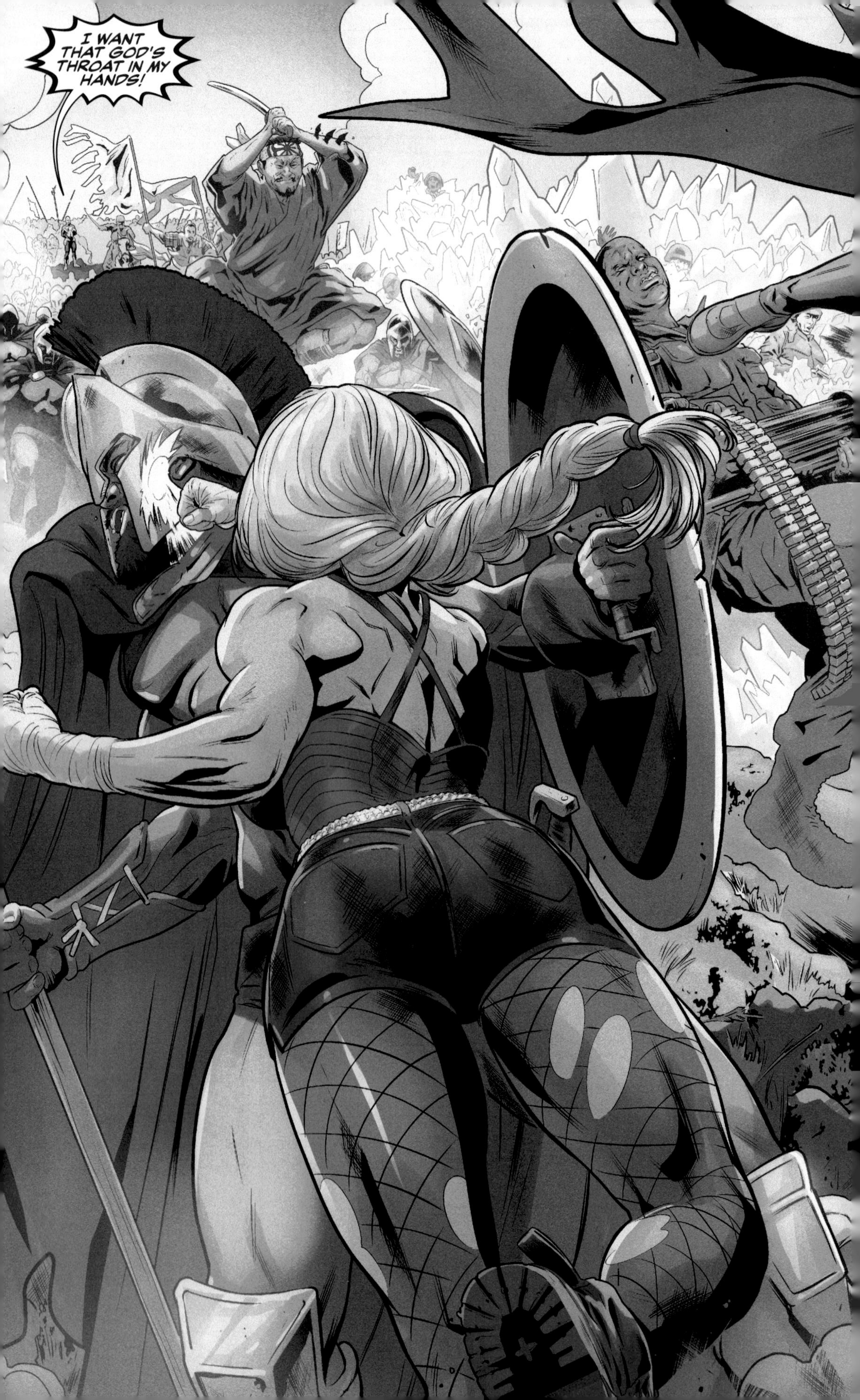
I WANT THAT GOD'S THROAT IN MY HANDS!

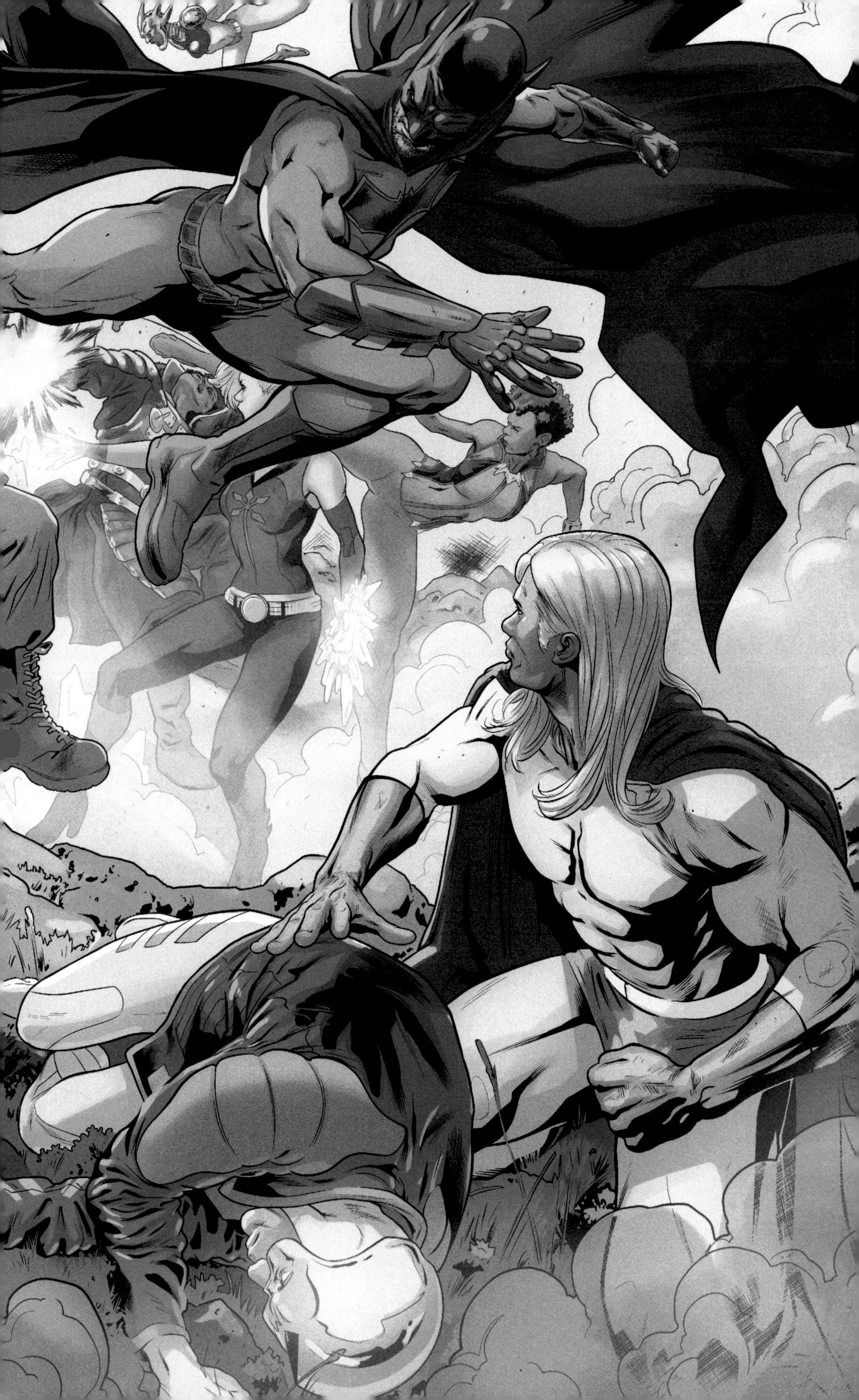

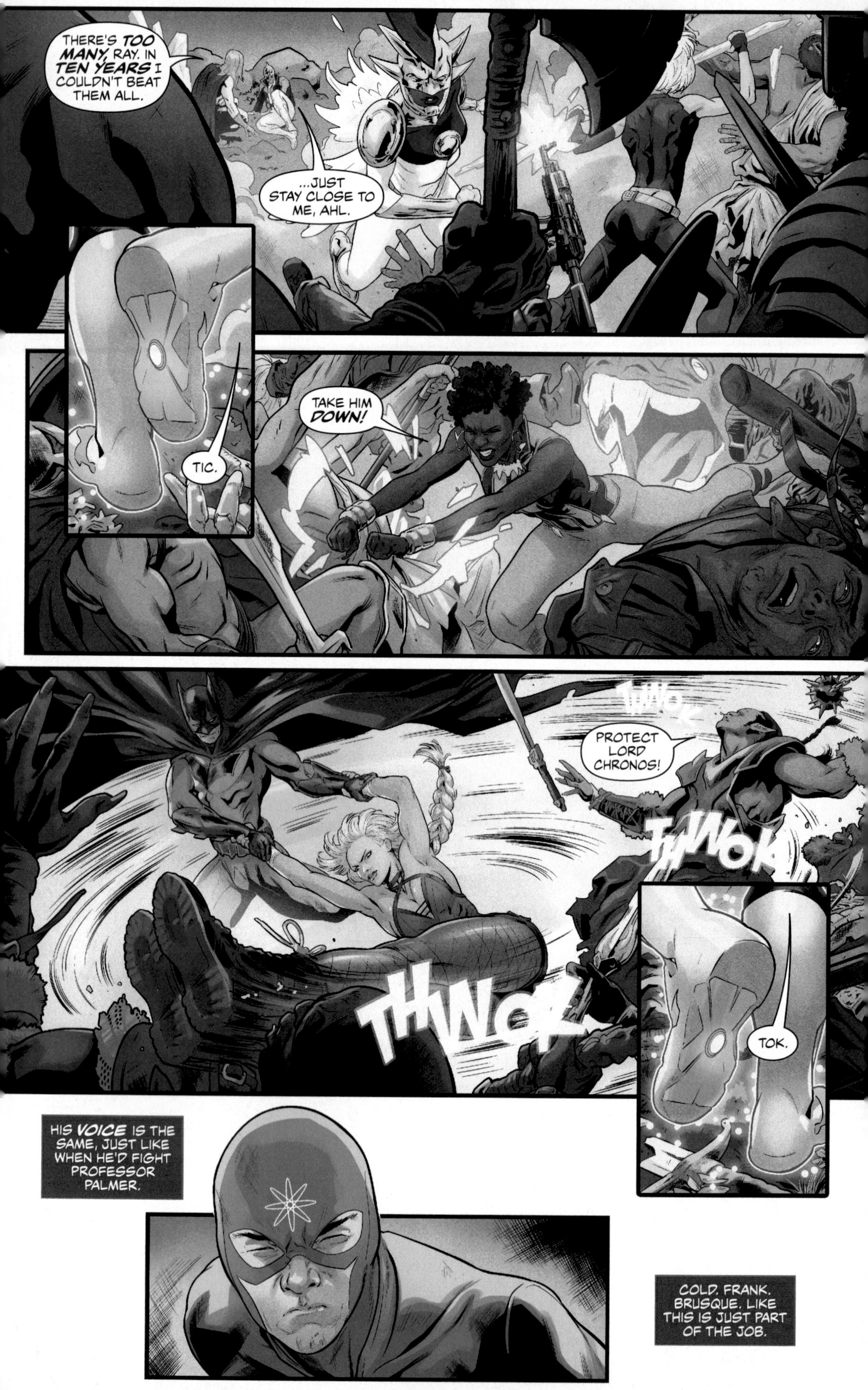

THERE'S TOO MANY, RAY. IN TEN YEARS I COULDN'T BEAT THEM ALL.
...JUST STAY CLOSE TO ME, AHL.
TIC.
TAKE HIM DOWN!
THWOK
PROTECT LORD CHRONOS!
THWOK
THWOK
TOK.
HIS VOICE IS THE SAME, JUST LIKE WHEN HE'D FIGHT PROFESSOR PALMER.
COLD. FRANK. BRUSQUE. LIKE THIS IS JUST PART OF THE JOB.

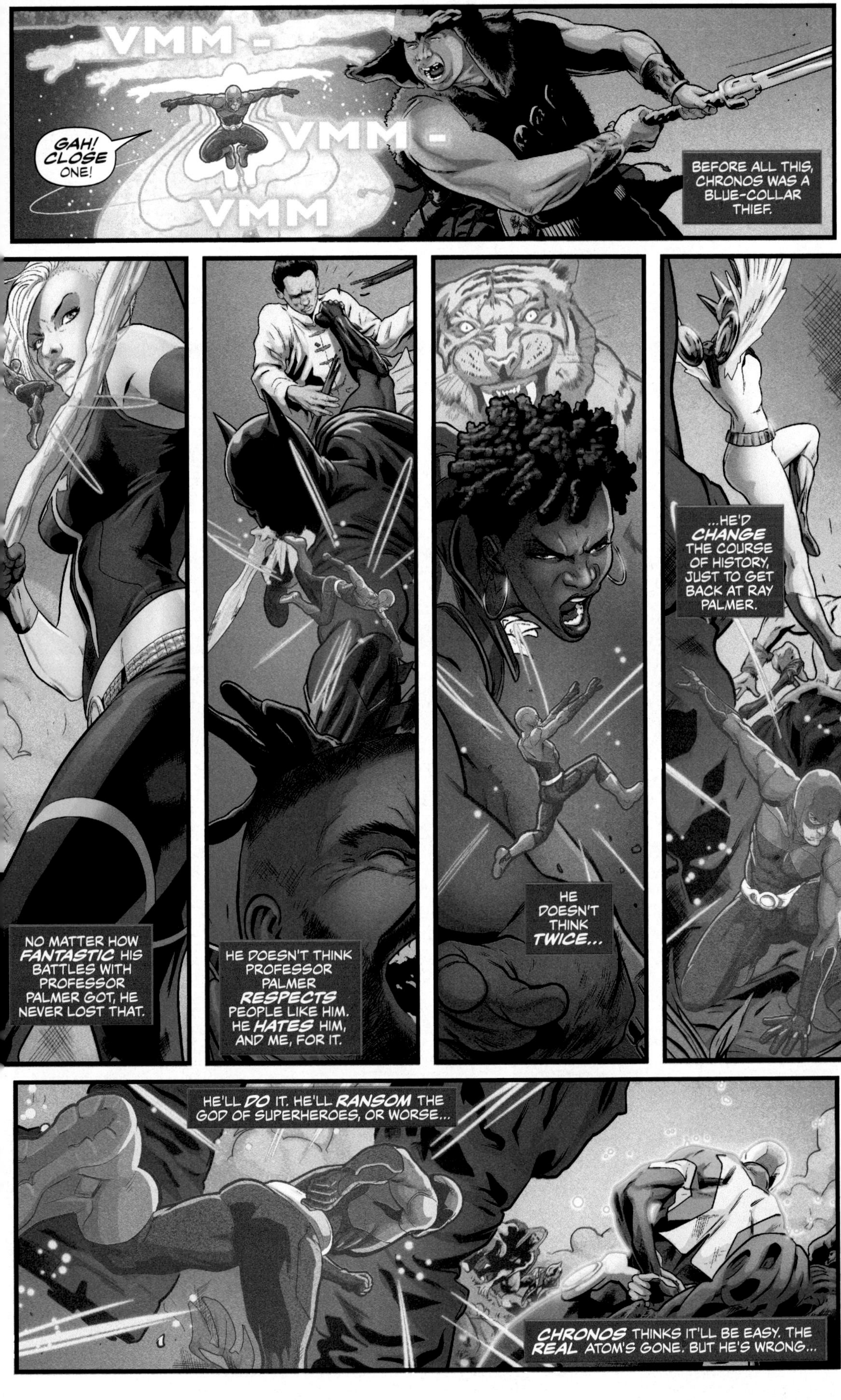
VMM - VMM - VMM
GAH! CLOSE ONE!
BEFORE ALL THIS, CHRONOS WAS A BLUE-COLLAR THIEF.
NO MATTER HOW FANTASTIC HIS BATTLES WITH PROFESSOR PALMER GOT, HE NEVER LOST THAT.
HE DOESN'T THINK PROFESSOR PALMER RESPECTS PEOPLE LIKE HIM. HE HATES HIM, AND ME, FOR IT.
HE DOESN'T THINK TWICE...
...HE'D CHANGE THE COURSE OF HISTORY, JUST TO GET BACK AT RAY PALMER.
HE'LL DO IT. HE'LL RANSOM THE GOD OF SUPERHEROES, OR WORSE...
CHRONOS THINKS IT'LL BE EASY. THE REAL ATOM'S GONE. BUT HE'S WRONG...

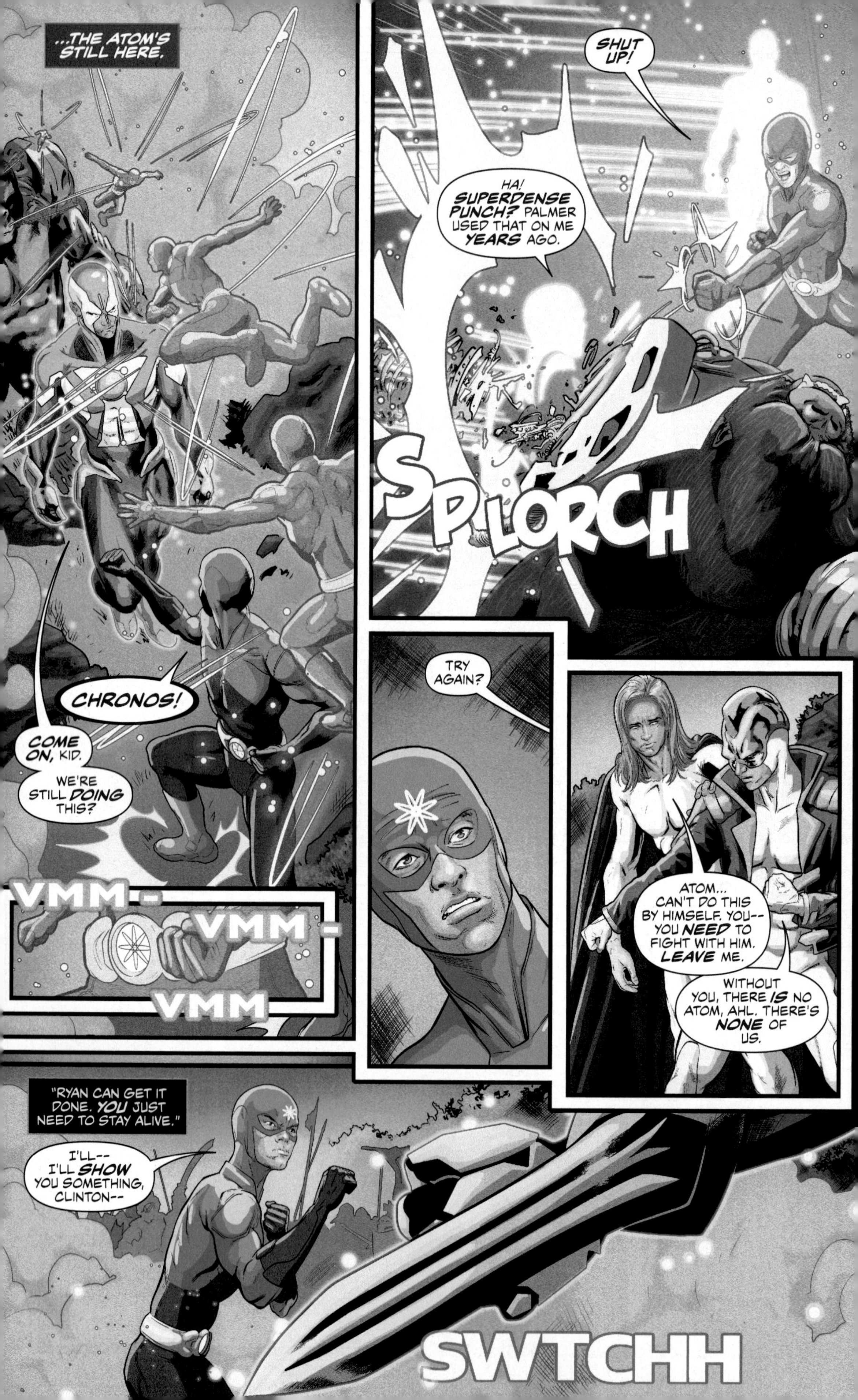
...THE ATOM'S STILL HERE.
SHUT UP!
HA! SUPERDENSE PUNCH? PALMER USED THAT ON ME YEARS AGO.
SPLORCH
CHRONOS!
COME ON, KID.
WE'RE STILL DOING THIS?
VMM - VMM - VMM
TRY AGAIN?
ATOM... CAN'T DO THIS BY HIMSELF. YOU-- YOU NEED TO FIGHT WITH HIM. LEAVE ME.
WITHOUT YOU, THERE IS NO ATOM, AHL. THERE'S NONE OF US.
"RYAN CAN GET IT DONE. YOU JUST NEED TO STAY ALIVE."
I'LL-- I'LL SHOW YOU SOMETHING, CLINTON--
SWTCHH

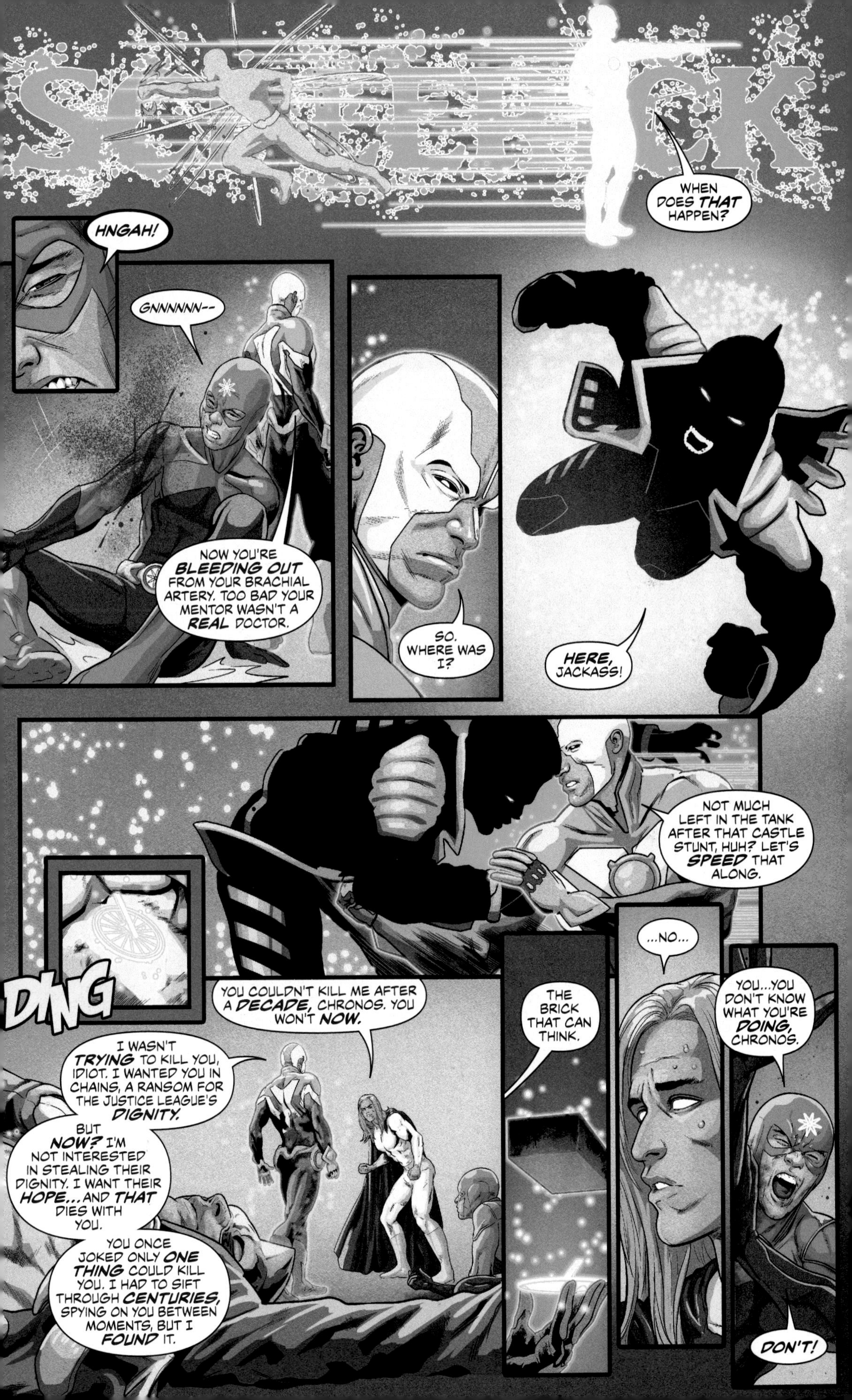
WHEN DOES THAT HAPPEN?
HNGAH!
GNNNNNN--
NOW YOU'RE BLEEDING OUT FROM YOUR BRACHIAL ARTERY. TOO BAD YOUR MENTOR WASN'T A REAL DOCTOR.
SO. WHERE WAS I?
HERE, JACKASS!
NOT MUCH LEFT IN THE TANK AFTER THAT CASTLE STUNT, HUH? LET'S SPEED THAT ALONG.
DING
YOU COULDN'T KILL ME AFTER A DECADE, CHRONOS. YOU WON'T NOW.
I WASN'T TRYING TO KILL YOU, IDIOT. I WANTED YOU IN CHAINS, A RANSOM FOR THE JUSTICE LEAGUE'S DIGNITY.
BUT NOW? I'M NOT INTERESTED IN STEALING THEIR DIGNITY. I WANT THEIR HOPE... AND THAT DIES WITH YOU.
YOU ONCE JOKED ONLY ONE THING COULD KILL YOU. I HAD TO SIFT THROUGH CENTURIES, SPYING ON YOU BETWEEN MOMENTS, BUT I FOUND IT.
THE BRICK THAT CAN THINK.
...NO...
YOU...YOU DON'T KNOW WHAT YOU'RE DOING, CHRONOS.
DON'T!

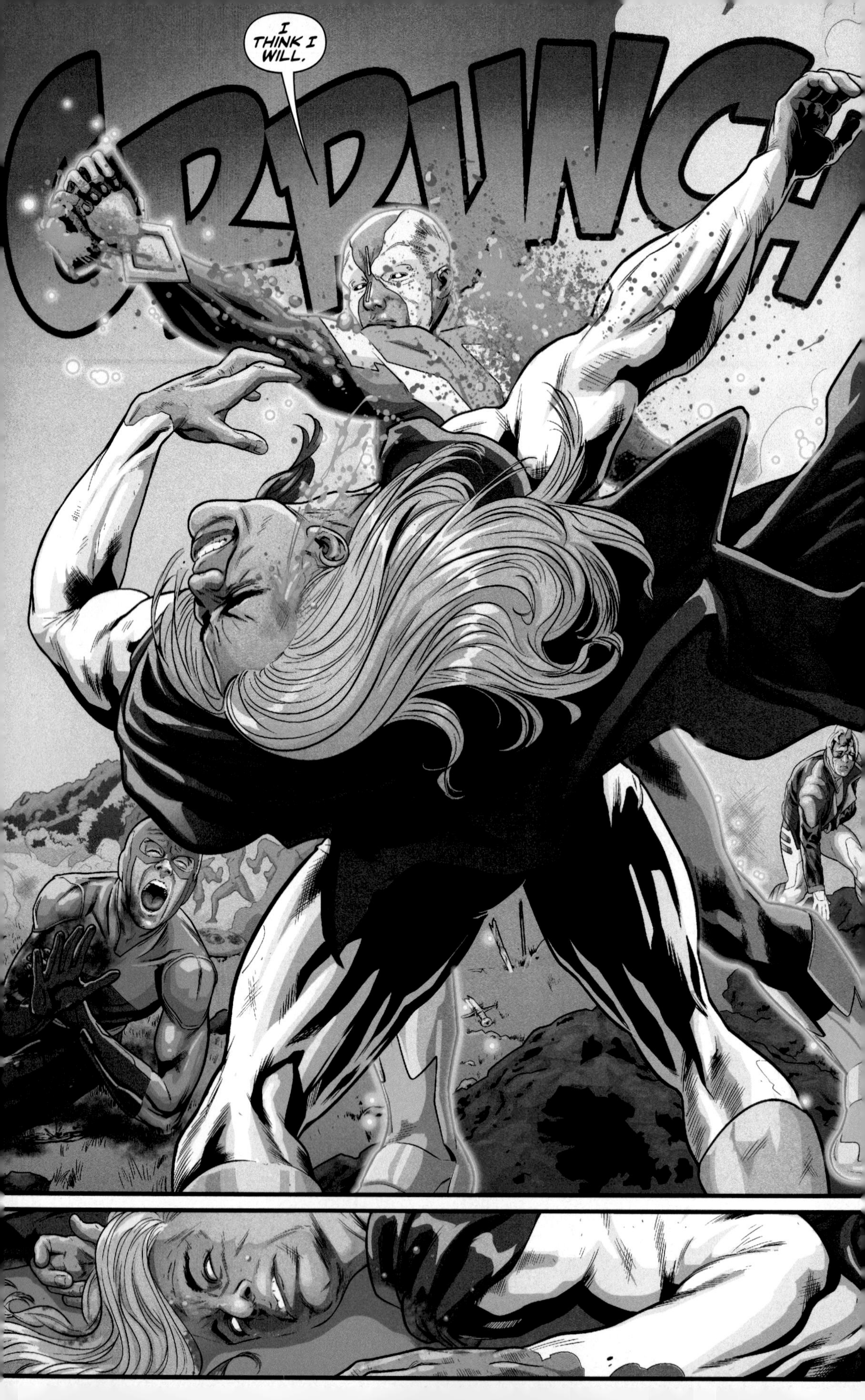
I THINK I WILL.
CRRUNCH

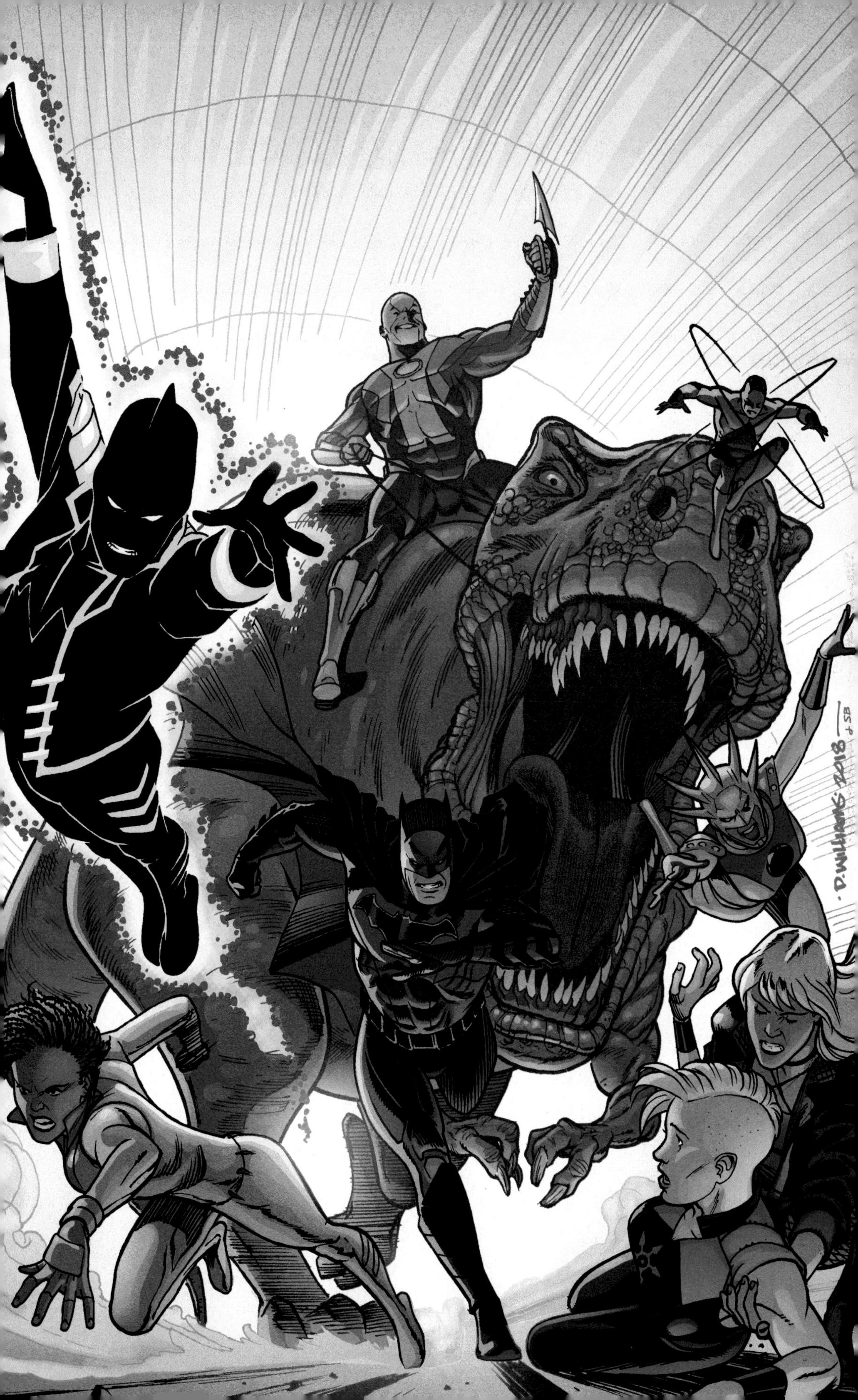
D.WILLIAMS 2018

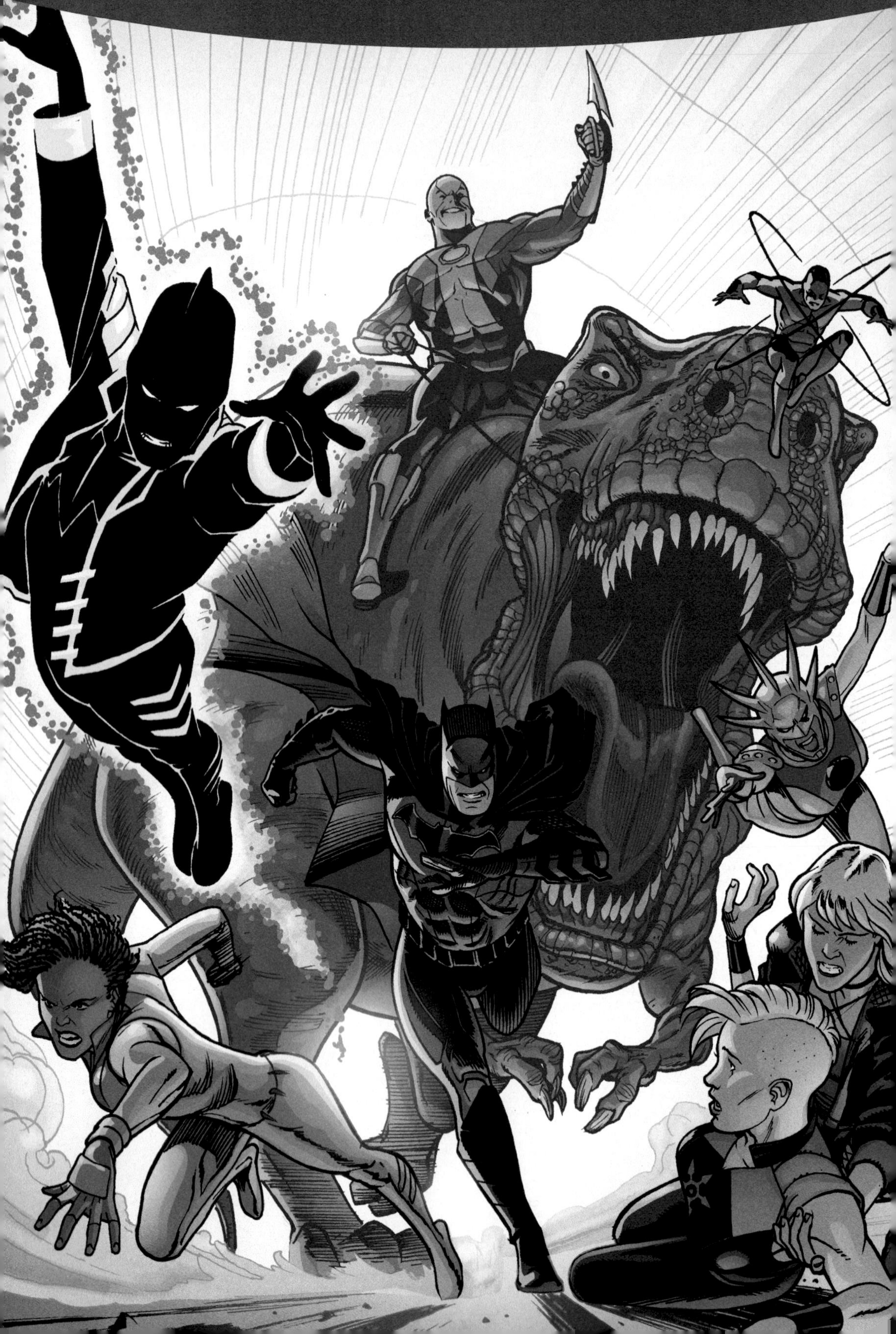

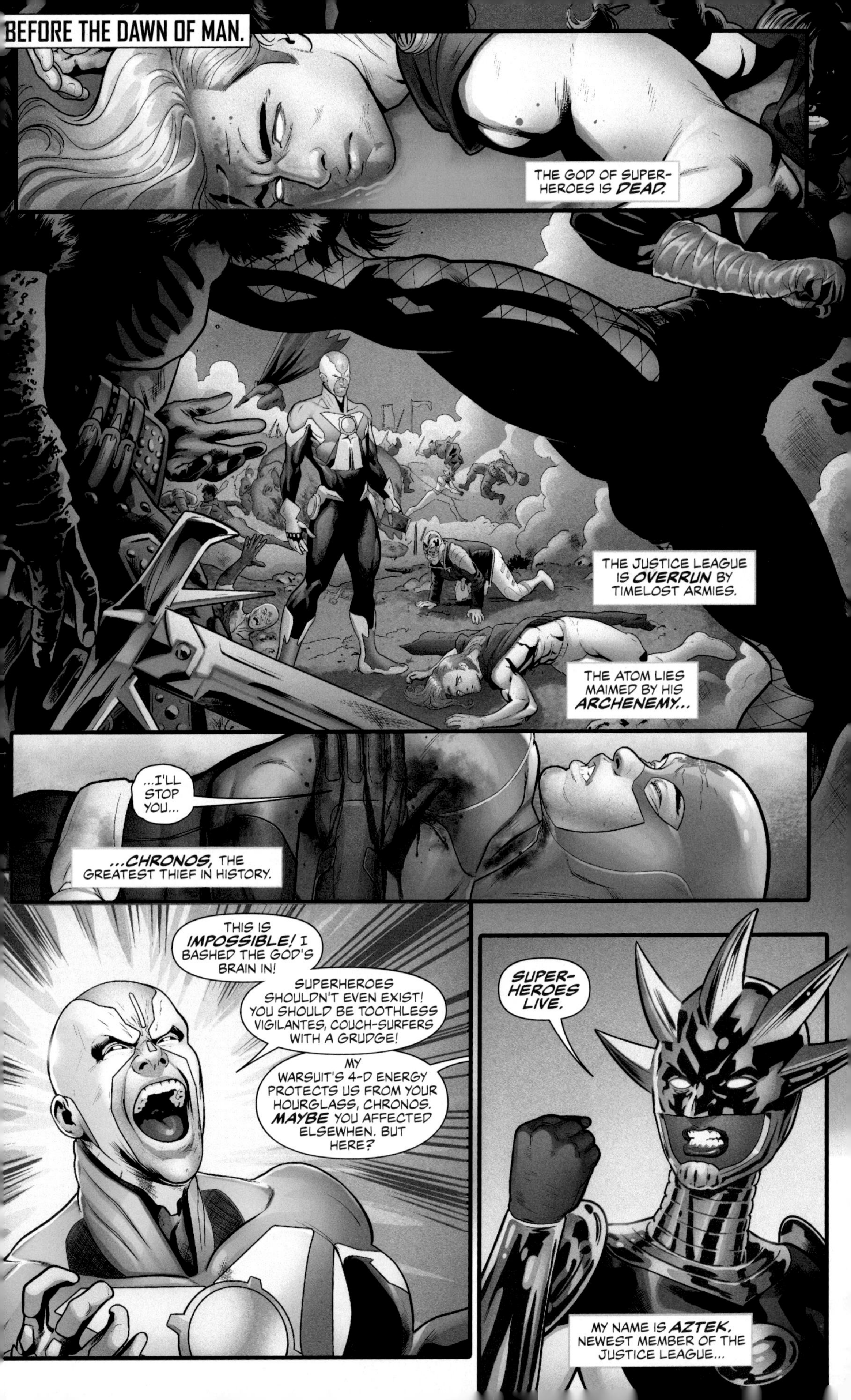
BEFORE THE DAWN OF MAN.
THE GOD OF SUPER-HEROES IS DEAD.
THE JUSTICE LEAGUE IS OVERRUN BY TIMELOST ARMIES.
THE ATOM LIES MAIMED BY HIS ARCHENEMY...
...I'LL STOP YOU...
...CHRONOS, THE GREATEST THIEF IN HISTORY.
THIS IS IMPOSSIBLE! I BASHED THE GOD'S BRAIN IN!
SUPERHEROES SHOULDN'T EVEN EXIST! YOU SHOULD BE TOOTHLESS VIGILANTES, COUCH-SURFERS WITH A GRUDGE!
MY WARSUIT'S 4-D ENERGY PROTECTS US FROM YOUR HOURGLASS, CHRONOS. MAYBE YOU AFFECTED ELSEWHEN. BUT HERE?
SUPER-HEROES LIVE.
MY NAME IS AZTEK, NEWEST MEMBER OF THE JUSTICE LEAGUE...

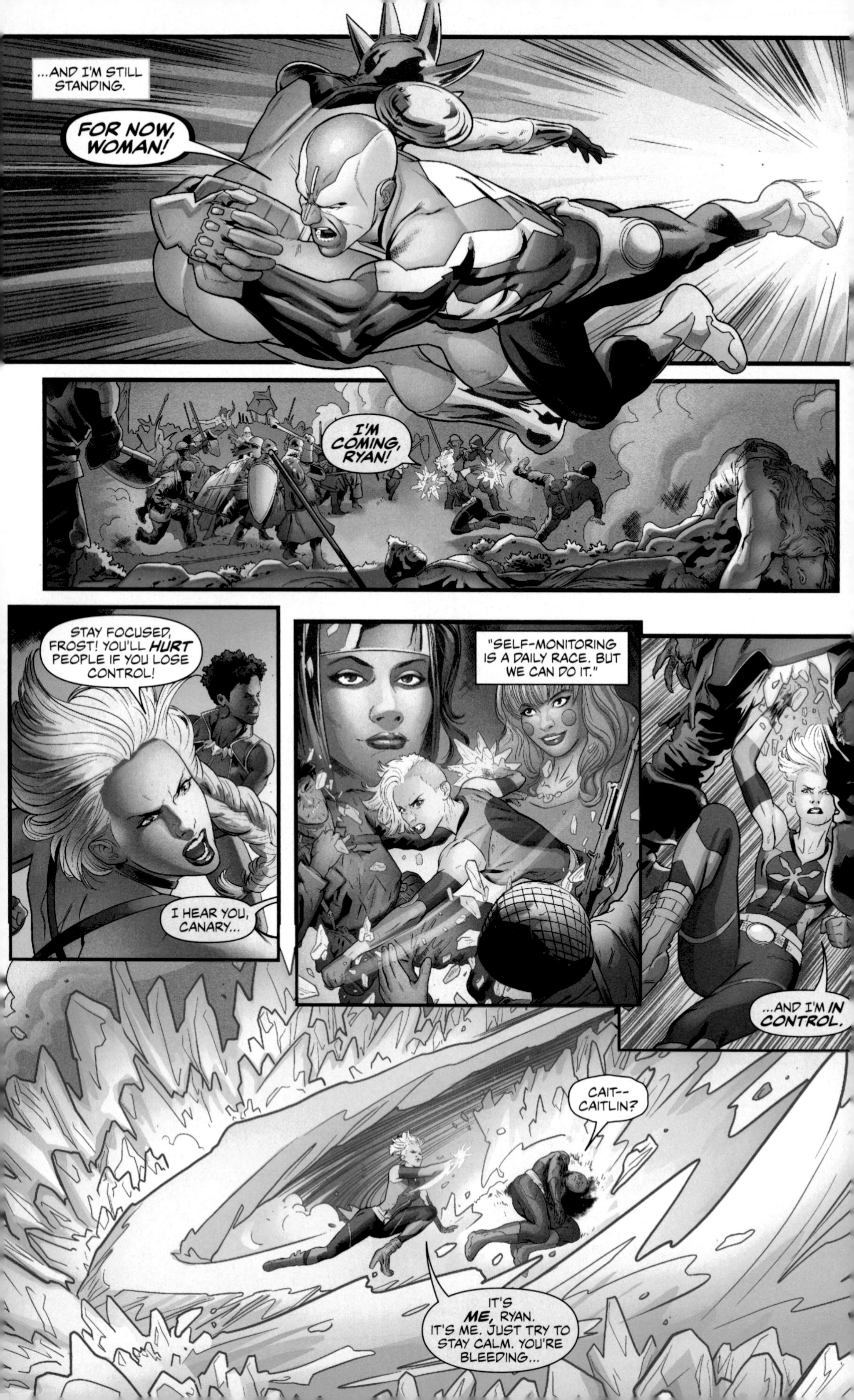
...AND I'M STILL STANDING.
FOR NOW, WOMAN!
I'M COMING, RYAN!
STAY FOCUSED, FROST! YOU'LL HURT PEOPLE IF YOU LOSE CONTROL!
I HEAR YOU, CANARY...
"SELF-MONITORING IS A DAILY RACE. BUT WE CAN DO IT."
...AND I'M IN CONTROL.
CAIT--CAITLIN?
IT'S ME, RYAN. IT'S ME. JUST TRY TO STAY CALM. YOU'RE BLEEDING...

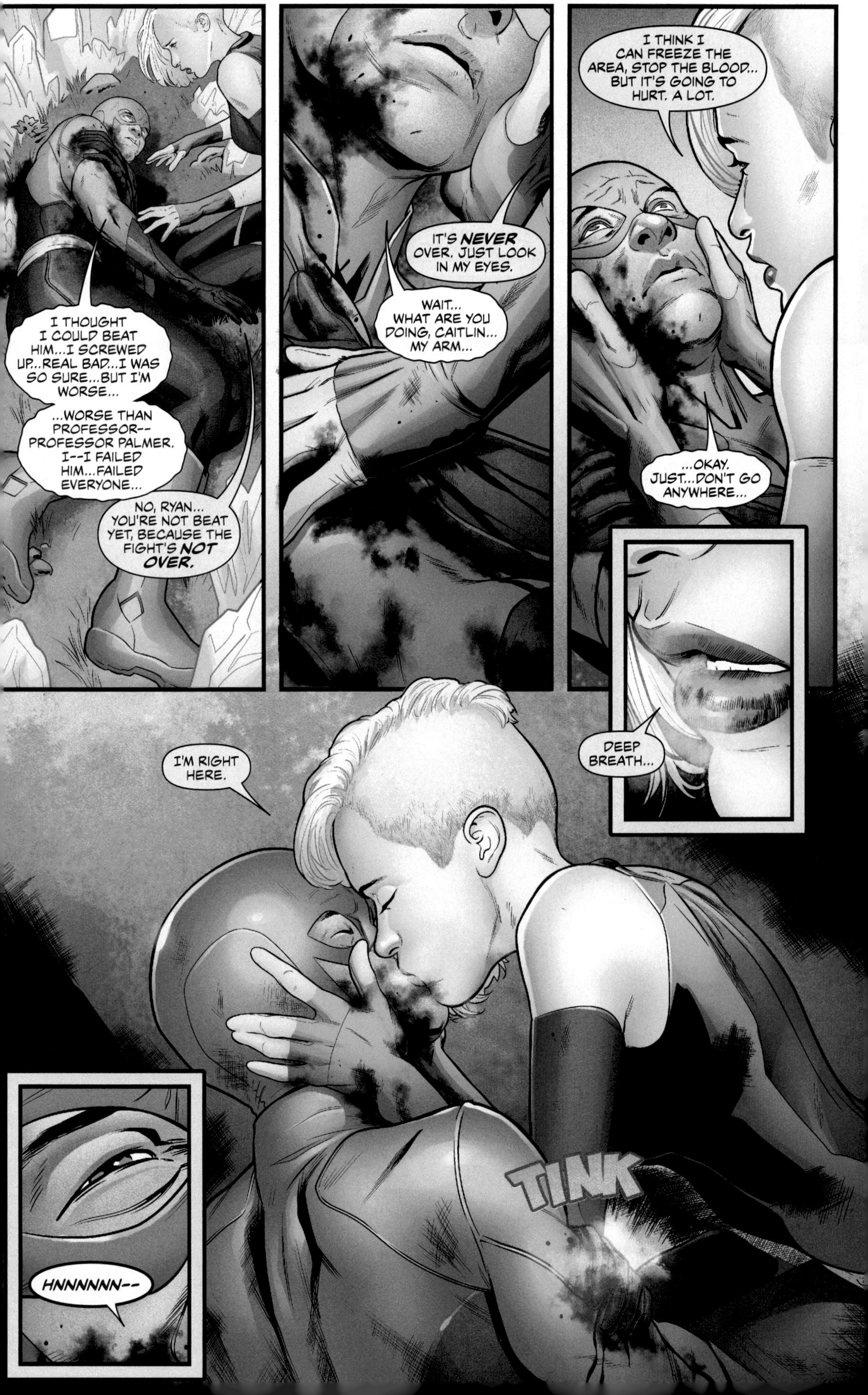
I THOUGHT I COULD BEAT HIM...I SCREWED UP...REAL BAD...I WAS SO SURE...BUT I'M WORSE...
...WORSE THAN PROFESSOR--PROFESSOR PALMER. I--I FAILED HIM...FAILED EVERYONE...
NO, RYAN... YOU'RE NOT BEAT YET, BECAUSE THE FIGHT'S NOT OVER.
IT'S NEVER OVER. JUST LOOK IN MY EYES.
WAIT... WHAT ARE YOU DOING, CAITLIN... MY ARM...
I THINK I CAN FREEZE THE AREA, STOP THE BLOOD... BUT IT'S GOING TO HURT. A LOT.
...OKAY. JUST...DON'T GO ANYWHERE...
DEEP BREATH...
I'M RIGHT HERE.
TINK
HNNNNNN--

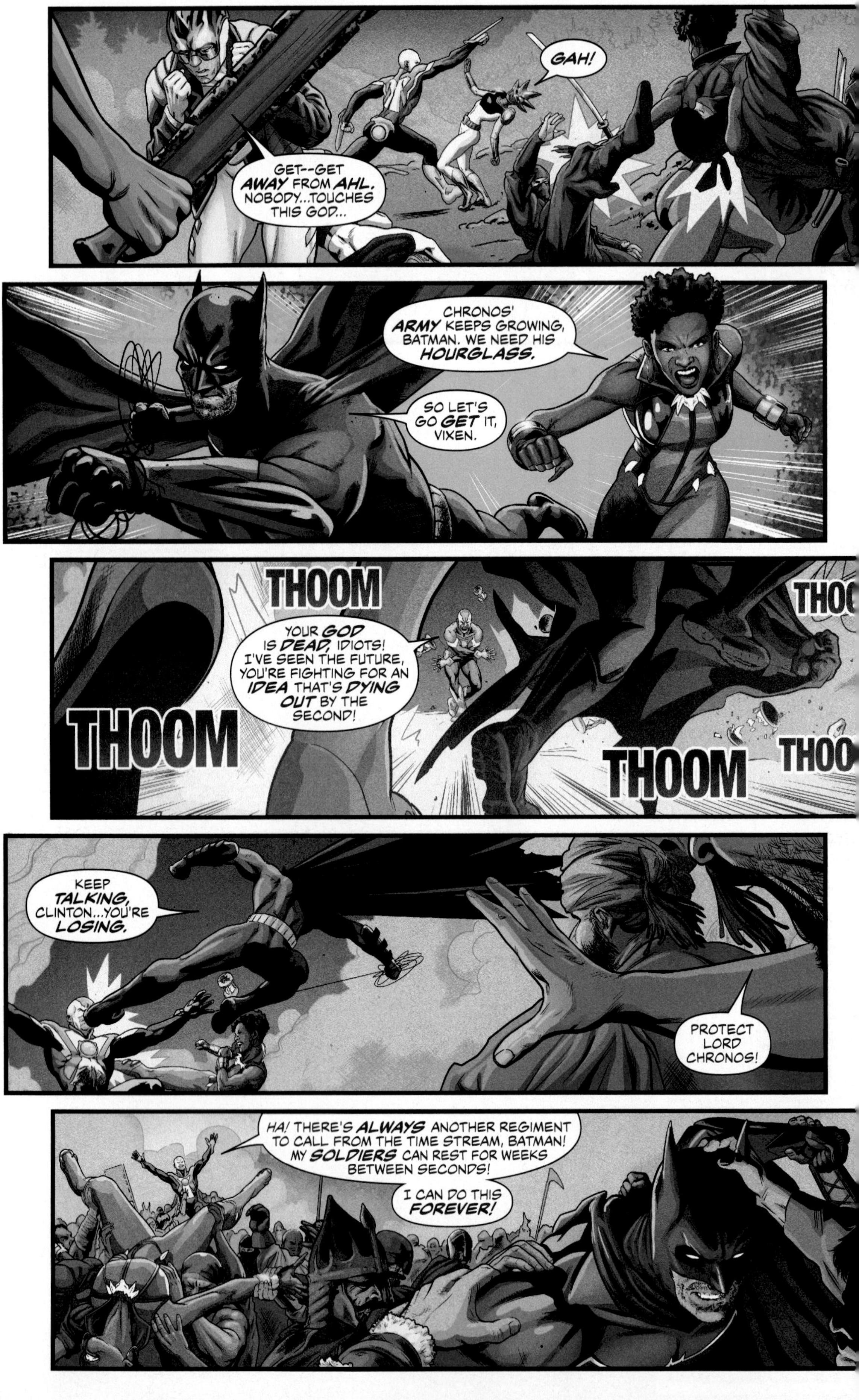
GAH!
GET--GET AWAY FROM AHL. NOBODY...TOUCHES THIS GOD...
CHRONOS' ARMY KEEPS GROWING, BATMAN. WE NEED HIS HOURGLASS.
SO LET'S GO GET IT, VIXEN.
THOOM
YOUR GOD IS DEAD, IDIOTS! I'VE SEEN THE FUTURE, YOU'RE FIGHTING FOR AN IDEA THAT'S DYING OUT BY THE SECOND!
THOOM
THOOM
KEEP TALKING, CLINTON...YOU'RE LOSING.
PROTECT LORD CHRONOS!
HA! THERE'S ALWAYS ANOTHER REGIMENT TO CALL FROM THE TIME STREAM, BATMAN! MY SOLDIERS CAN REST FOR WEEKS BETWEEN SECONDS!
I CAN DO THIS FOREVER!

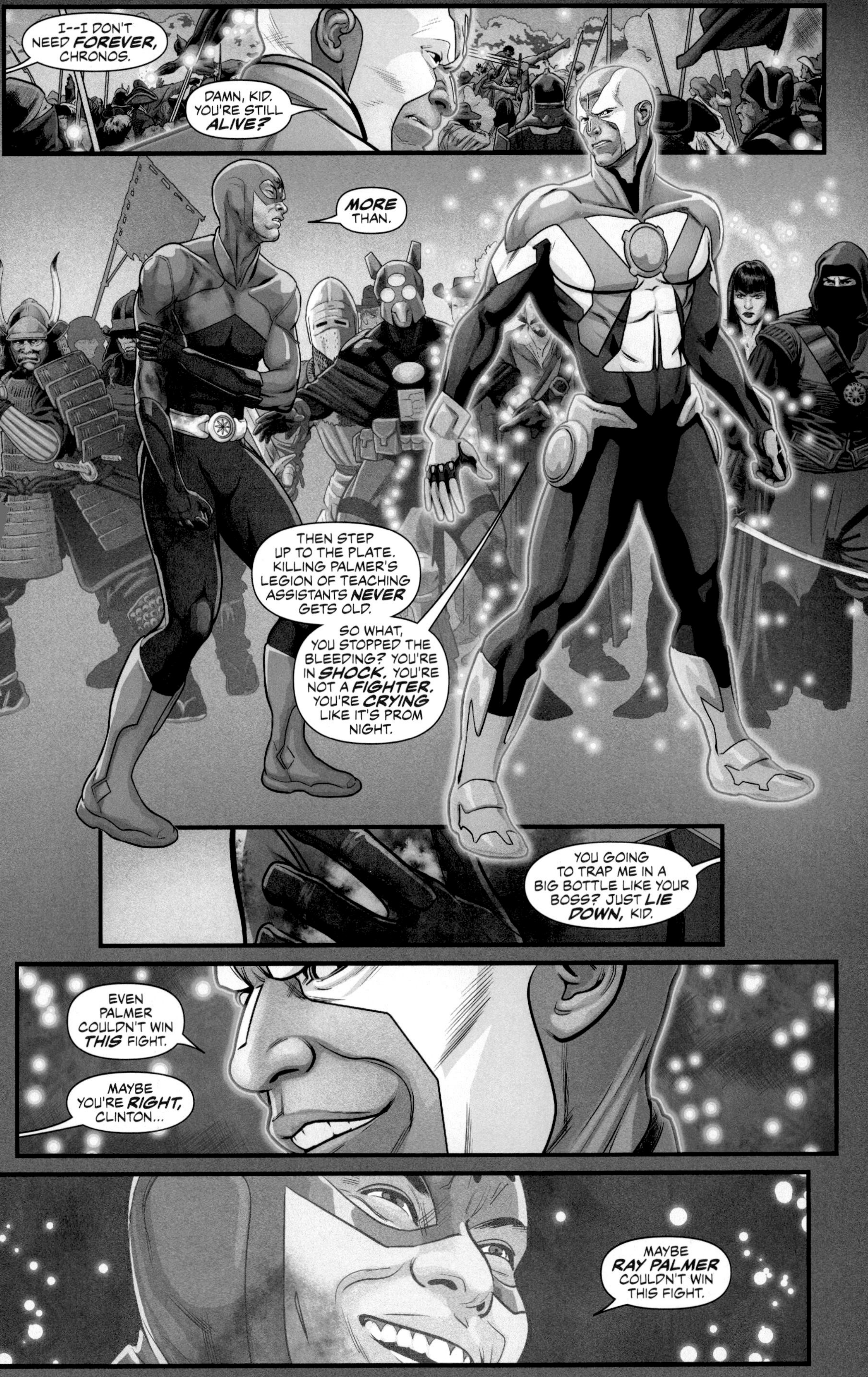
I--I DON'T NEED FOREVER, CHRONOS.
DAMN, KID. YOU'RE STILL ALIVE?
MORE THAN.
THEN STEP UP TO THE PLATE. KILLING PALMER'S LEGION OF TEACHING ASSISTANTS NEVER GETS OLD.
SO WHAT, YOU STOPPED THE BLEEDING? YOU'RE IN SHOCK. YOU'RE NOT A FIGHTER. YOU'RE CRYING LIKE IT'S PROM NIGHT.
YOU GOING TO TRAP ME IN A BIG BOTTLE LIKE YOUR BOSS? JUST LIE DOWN, KID.
EVEN PALMER COULDN'T WIN THIS FIGHT.
MAYBE YOU'RE RIGHT, CLINTON...
MAYBE RAY PALMER COULDN'T WIN THIS FIGHT.

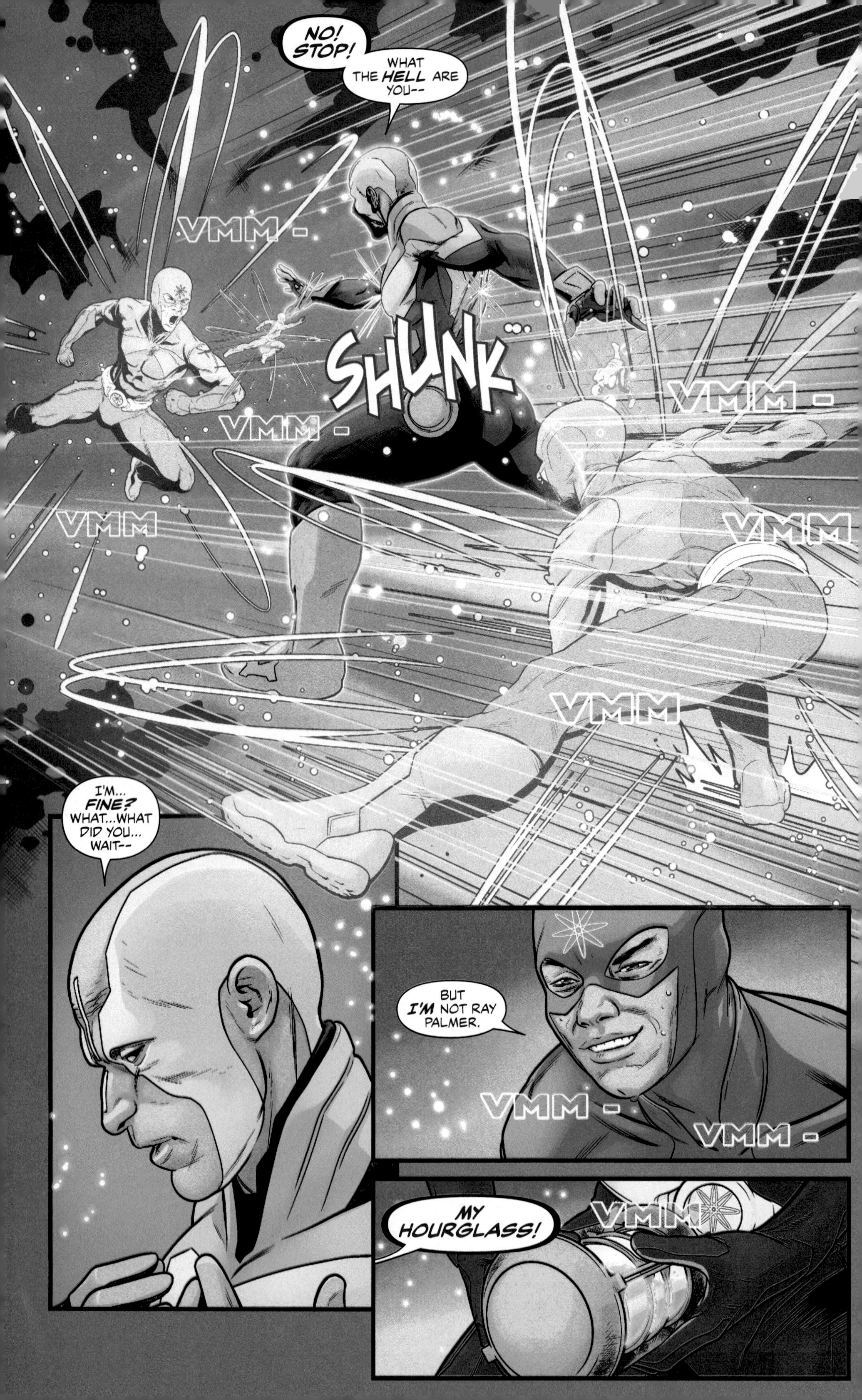
NO! STOP!
WHAT THE HELL ARE YOU--
VMM -
SHUNK
VMM -
VMM -
VMM
VMM
VMM
I'M... FINE? WHAT...WHAT DID YOU... WAIT--
BUT I'M NOT RAY PALMER.
VMM -
VMM -
VMM
MY HOURGLASS!

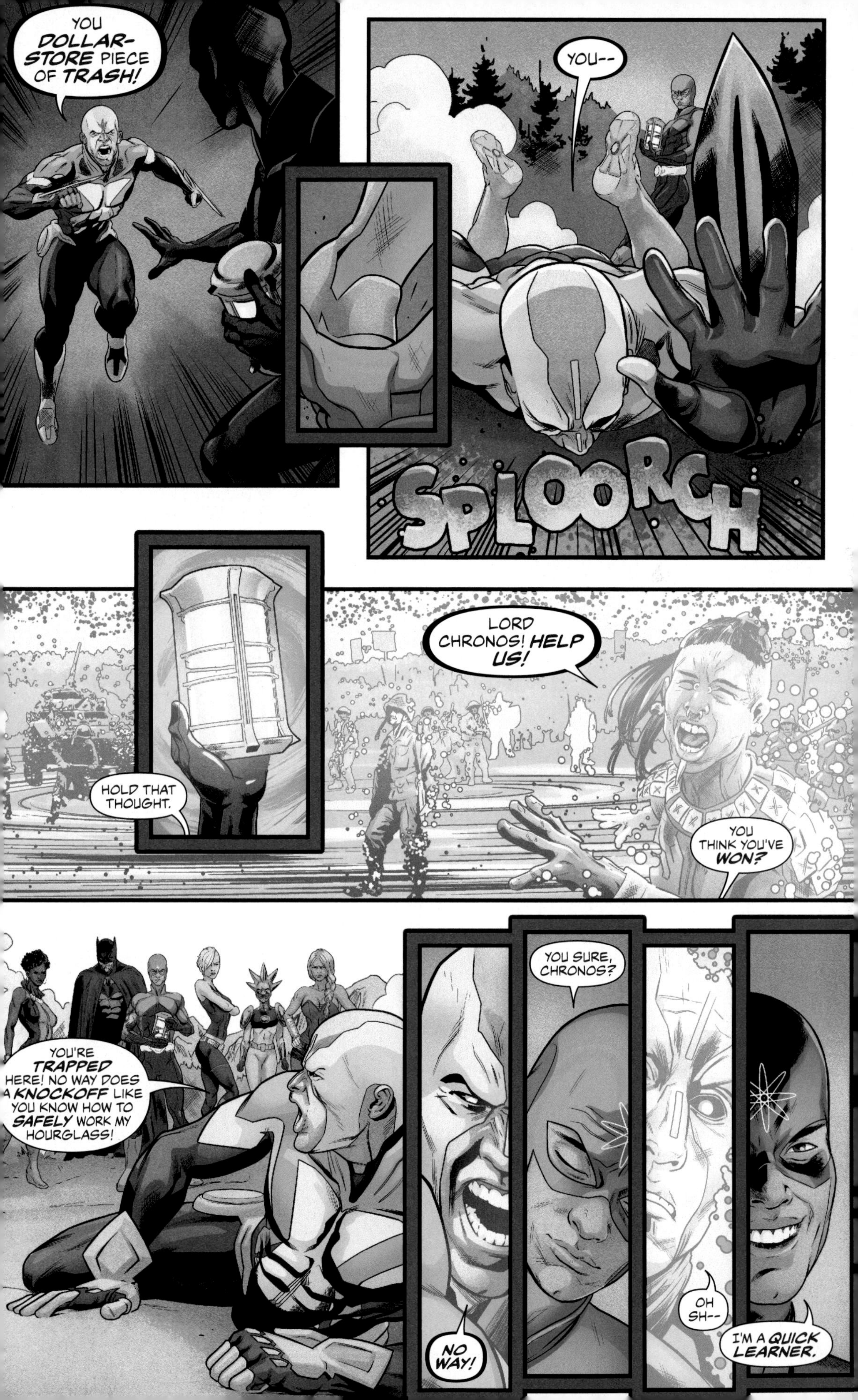
YOU DOLLAR-STORE PIECE OF TRASH!
YOU--
SPLOORCH
HOLD THAT THOUGHT.
LORD CHRONOS! HELP US!
YOU THINK YOU'VE WON?
YOU'RE TRAPPED HERE! NO WAY DOES A KNOCKOFF LIKE YOU KNOW HOW TO SAFELY WORK MY HOURGLASS!
YOU SURE, CHRONOS?
NO WAY!
OH SH--
I'M A QUICK LEARNER.

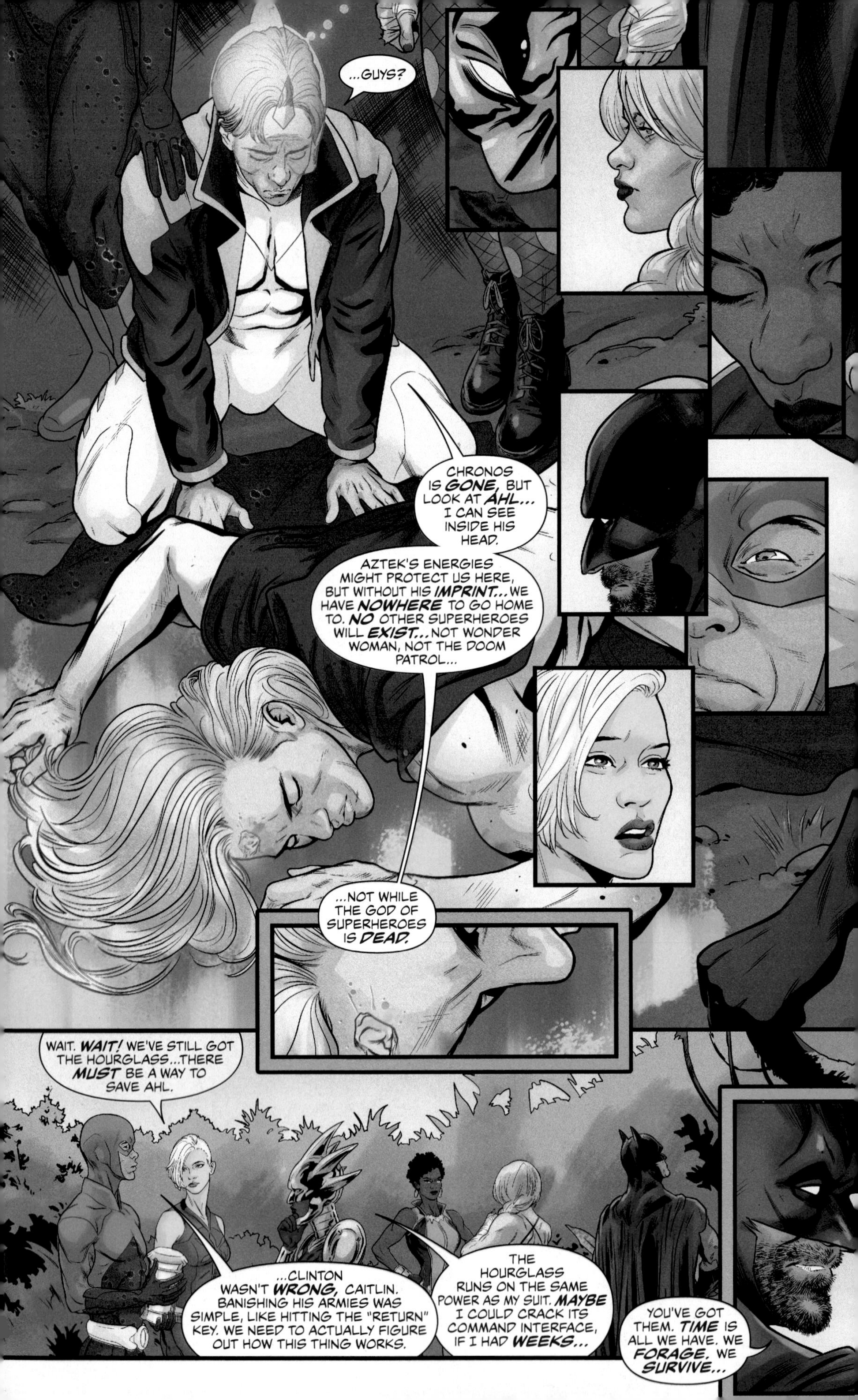
...GUYS?
CHRONOS IS GONE, BUT LOOK AT AHL... I CAN SEE INSIDE HIS HEAD.
AZTEK'S ENERGIES MIGHT PROTECT US HERE, BUT WITHOUT HIS IMPRINT... WE HAVE NOWHERE TO GO HOME TO. NO OTHER SUPERHEROES WILL EXIST... NOT WONDER WOMAN, NOT THE DOOM PATROL...
...NOT WHILE THE GOD OF SUPERHEROES IS DEAD.
WAIT. WAIT! WE'VE STILL GOT THE HOURGLASS...THERE MUST BE A WAY TO SAVE AHL.
...CLINTON WASN'T WRONG, CAITLIN. BANISHING HIS ARMIES WAS SIMPLE, LIKE HITTING THE "RETURN" KEY. WE NEED TO ACTUALLY FIGURE OUT HOW THIS THING WORKS.
THE HOURGLASS RUNS ON THE SAME POWER AS MY SUIT. MAYBE I COULD CRACK ITS COMMAND INTERFACE, IF I HAD WEEKS...
YOU'VE GOT THEM. TIME IS ALL WE HAVE. WE FORAGE. WE SURVIVE...

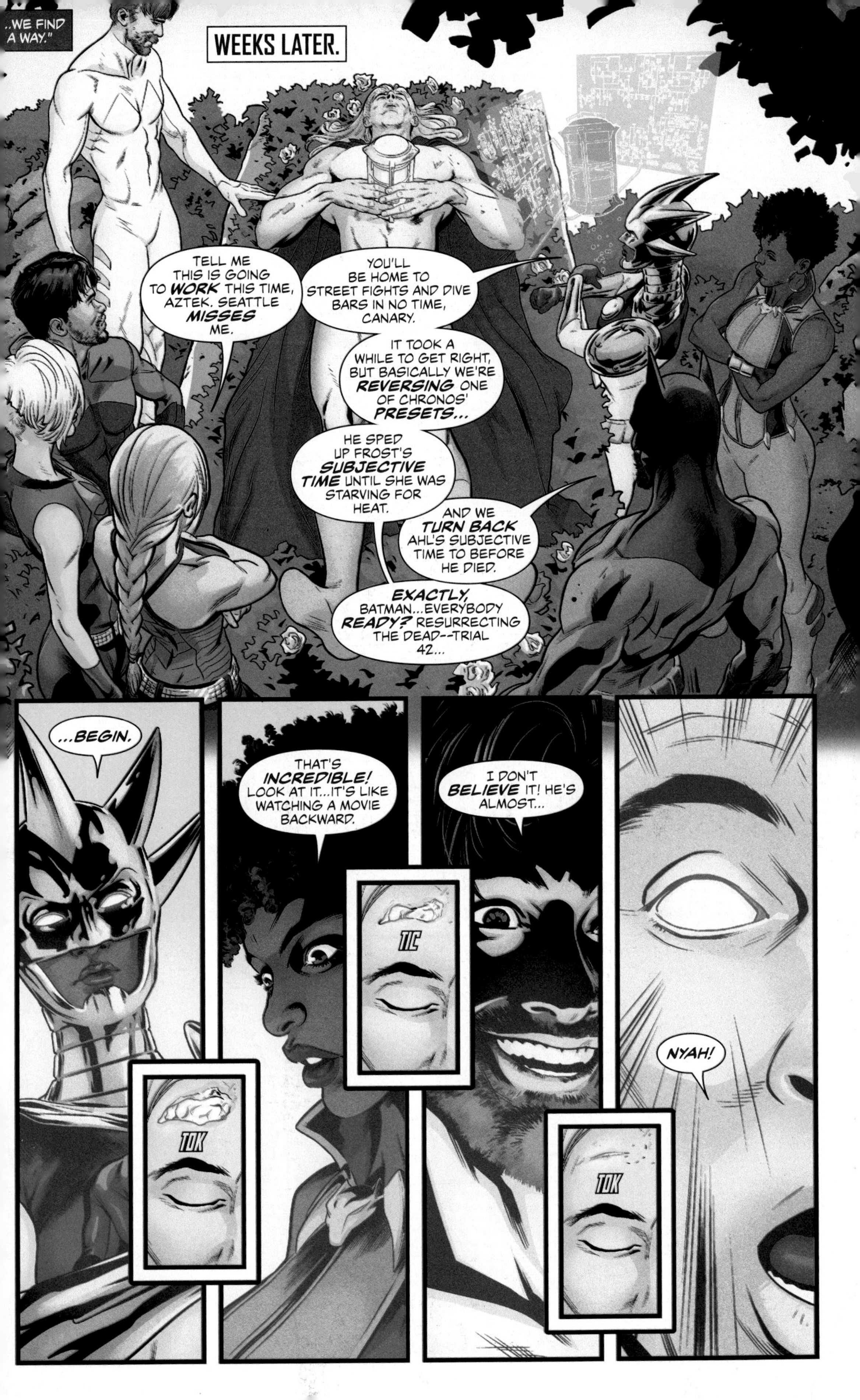

..WE FIND A WAY."
WEEKS LATER.
TELL ME THIS IS GOING TO WORK THIS TIME, AZTEK. SEATTLE MISSES ME.
YOU'LL BE HOME TO STREET FIGHTS AND DIVE BARS IN NO TIME, CANARY.
IT TOOK A WHILE TO GET RIGHT, BUT BASICALLY WE'RE REVERSING ONE OF CHRONOS' PRESETS...
HE SPED UP FROST'S SUBJECTIVE TIME UNTIL SHE WAS STARVING FOR HEAT.
AND WE TURN BACK AHL'S SUBJECTIVE TIME TO BEFORE HE DIED.
EXACTLY, BATMAN...EVERYBODY READY? RESURRECTING THE DEAD--TRIAL 42...
...BEGIN.
TOK
THAT'S INCREDIBLE! LOOK AT IT...IT'S LIKE WATCHING A MOVIE BACKWARD.
TIC
I DON'T BELIEVE IT! HE'S ALMOST...
TOK
NYAH!

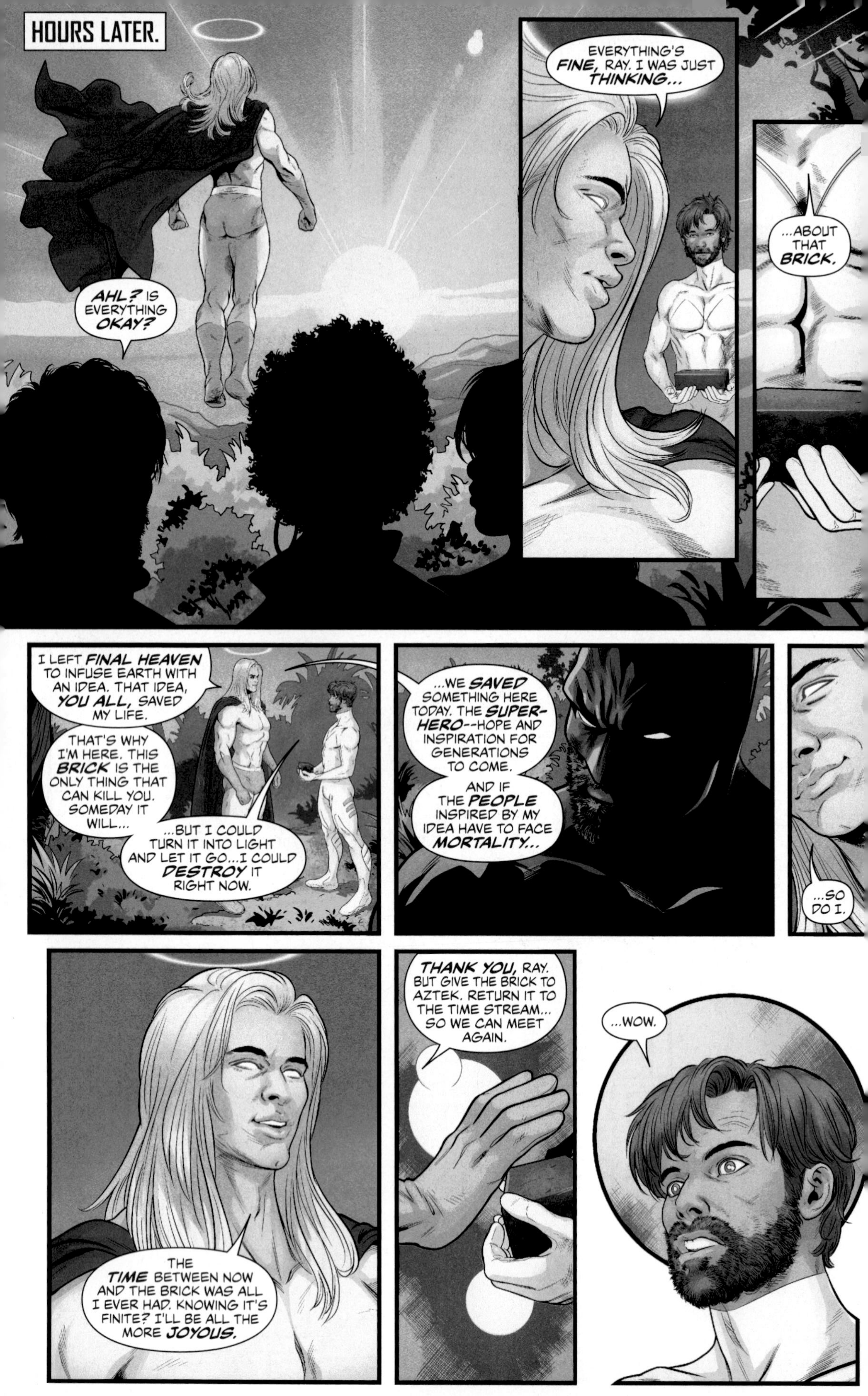
HOURS LATER.
AHL? IS EVERYTHING OKAY?
EVERYTHING'S FINE, RAY. I WAS JUST THINKING...
...ABOUT THAT BRICK.
I LEFT FINAL HEAVEN TO INFUSE EARTH WITH AN IDEA. THAT IDEA, YOU ALL, SAVED MY LIFE.
THAT'S WHY I'M HERE. THIS BRICK IS THE ONLY THING THAT CAN KILL YOU. SOMEDAY IT WILL...
...BUT I COULD TURN IT INTO LIGHT AND LET IT GO...I COULD DESTROY IT RIGHT NOW.
...WE SAVED SOMETHING HERE TODAY. THE SUPER-HERO--HOPE AND INSPIRATION FOR GENERATIONS TO COME.
AND IF THE PEOPLE INSPIRED BY MY IDEA HAVE TO FACE MORTALITY...
...SO DO I.
THE TIME BETWEEN NOW AND THE BRICK WAS ALL I EVER HAD. KNOWING IT'S FINITE? I'LL BE ALL THE MORE JOYOUS.
THANK YOU, RAY. BUT GIVE THE BRICK TO AZTEK. RETURN IT TO THE TIME STREAM... SO WE CAN MEET AGAIN.
...WOW.

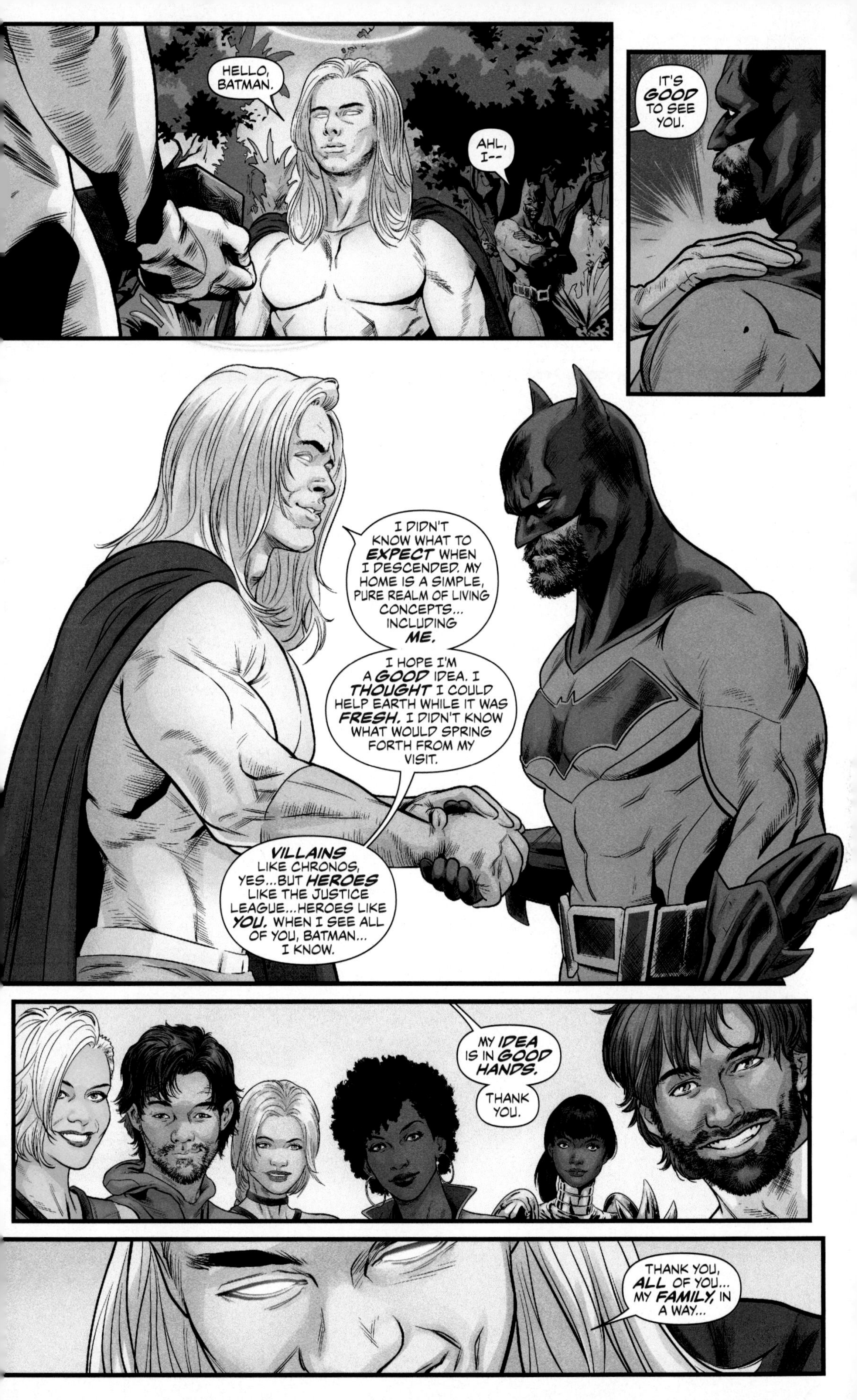
HELLO, BATMAN.
AHL, I--
IT'S GOOD TO SEE YOU.
I DIDN'T KNOW WHAT TO EXPECT WHEN I DESCENDED. MY HOME IS A SIMPLE, PURE REALM OF LIVING CONCEPTS... INCLUDING ME.
I HOPE I'M A GOOD IDEA. I THOUGHT I COULD HELP EARTH WHILE IT WAS FRESH. I DIDN'T KNOW WHAT WOULD SPRING FORTH FROM MY VISIT.
VILLAINS LIKE CHRONOS, YES...BUT HEROES LIKE THE JUSTICE LEAGUE...HEROES LIKE YOU. WHEN I SEE ALL OF YOU, BATMAN... I KNOW.
MY IDEA IS IN GOOD HANDS.
THANK YOU.
THANK YOU, ALL OF YOU... MY FAMILY, IN A WAY...

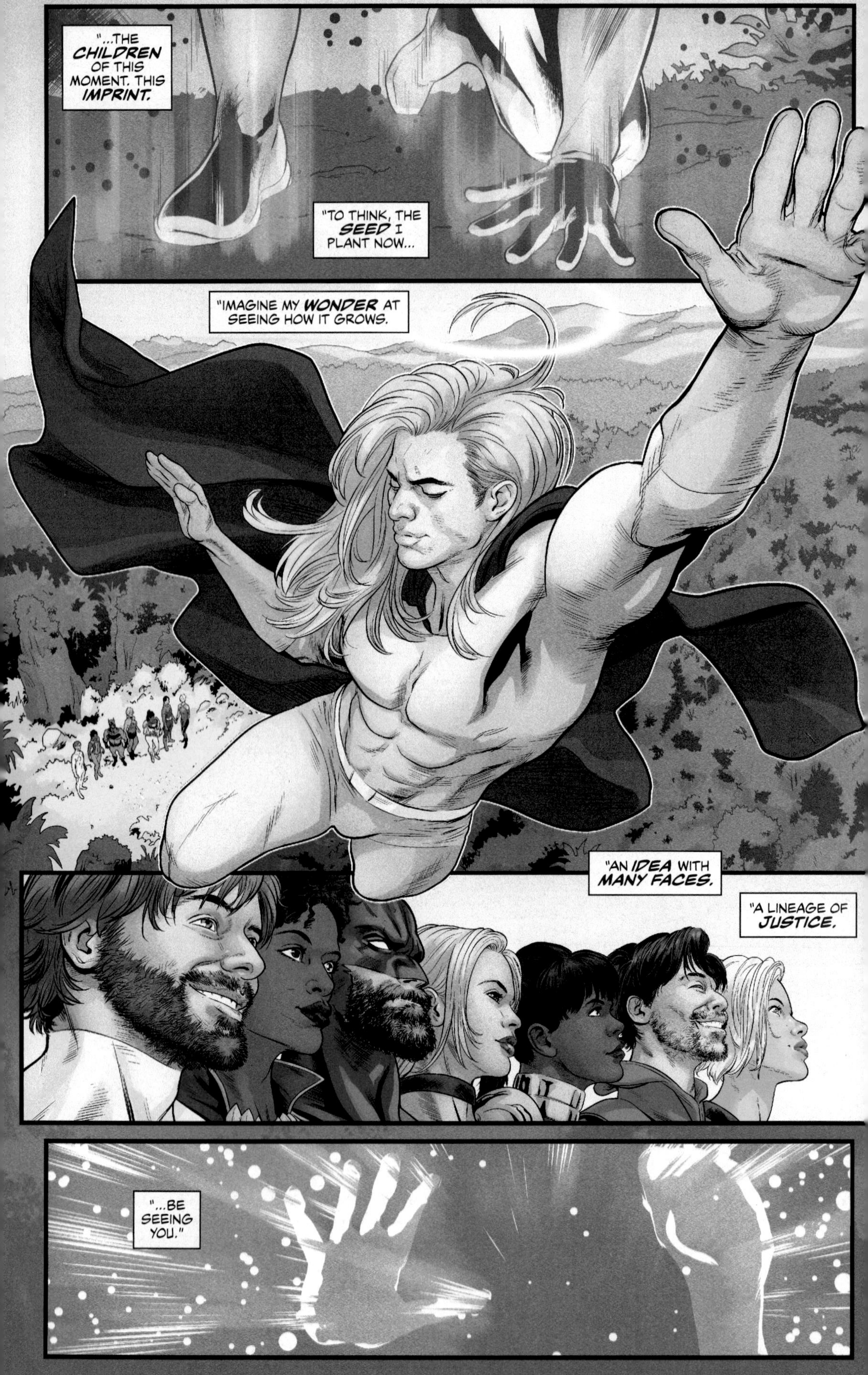
"...THE CHILDREN OF THIS MOMENT. THIS IMPRINT.
"TO THINK, THE SEED I PLANT NOW...
"IMAGINE MY WONDER AT SEEING HOW IT GROWS.
"AN IDEA WITH MANY FACES.
"A LINEAGE OF JUSTICE.
"...BE SEEING YOU."

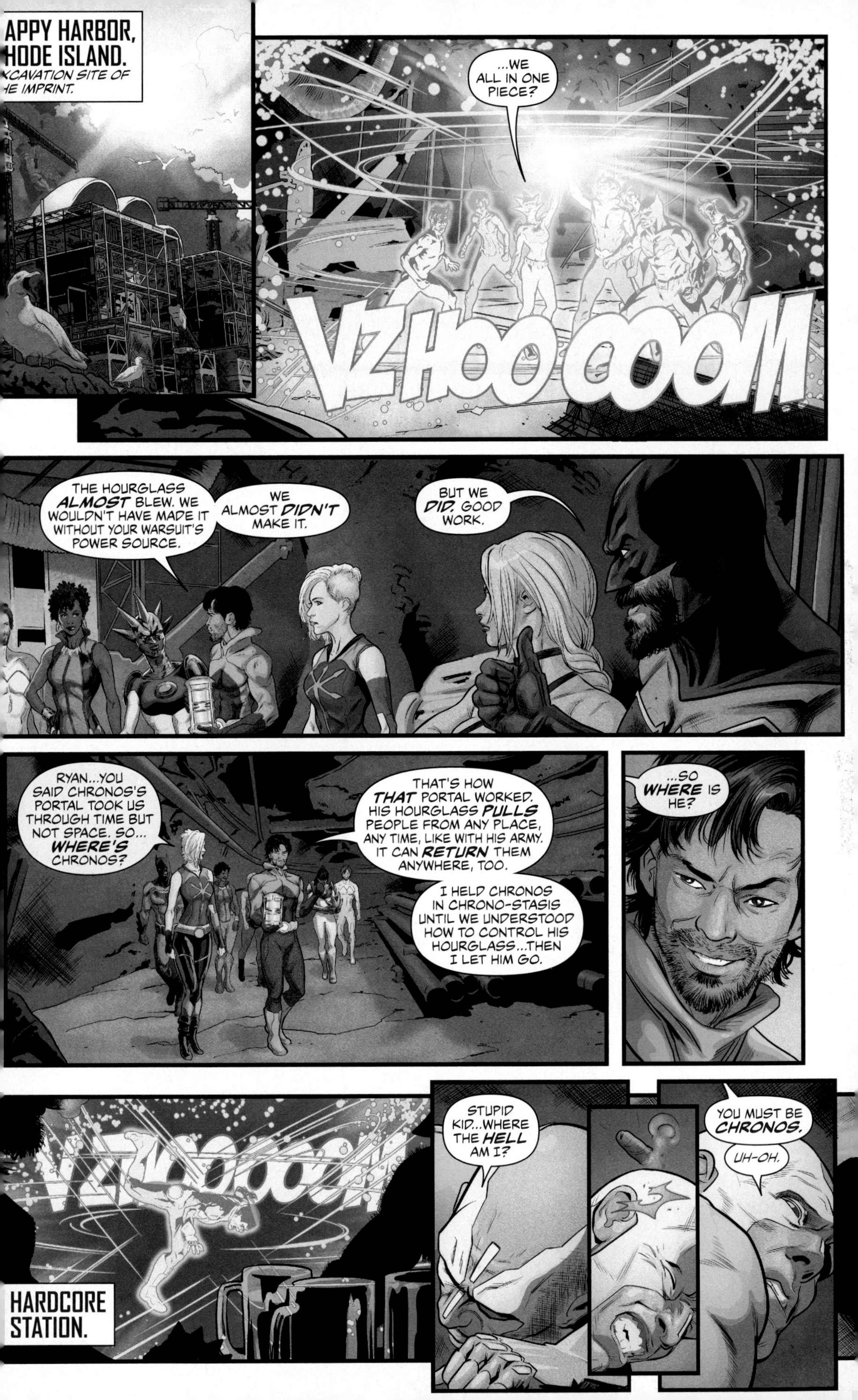
APPY HARBOR, HODE ISLAND.
XCAVATION SITE OF HE IMPRINT.
...WE ALL IN ONE PIECE?
VZHOOOOOM
THE HOURGLASS ALMOST BLEW. WE WOULDN'T HAVE MADE IT WITHOUT YOUR WARSUIT'S POWER SOURCE.
WE ALMOST DIDN'T MAKE IT.
BUT WE DID. GOOD WORK.
RYAN...YOU SAID CHRONOS'S PORTAL TOOK US THROUGH TIME BUT NOT SPACE. SO... WHERE'S CHRONOS?
THAT'S HOW THAT PORTAL WORKED. HIS HOURGLASS PULLS PEOPLE FROM ANY PLACE, ANY TIME, LIKE WITH HIS ARMY. IT CAN RETURN THEM ANYWHERE, TOO.
I HELD CHRONOS IN CHRONO-STASIS UNTIL WE UNDERSTOOD HOW TO CONTROL HIS HOURGLASS...THEN I LET HIM GO.
...SO WHERE IS HE?
HARDCORE STATION.
STUPID KID...WHERE THE HELL AM I?
YOU MUST BE CHRONOS.
UH-OH.

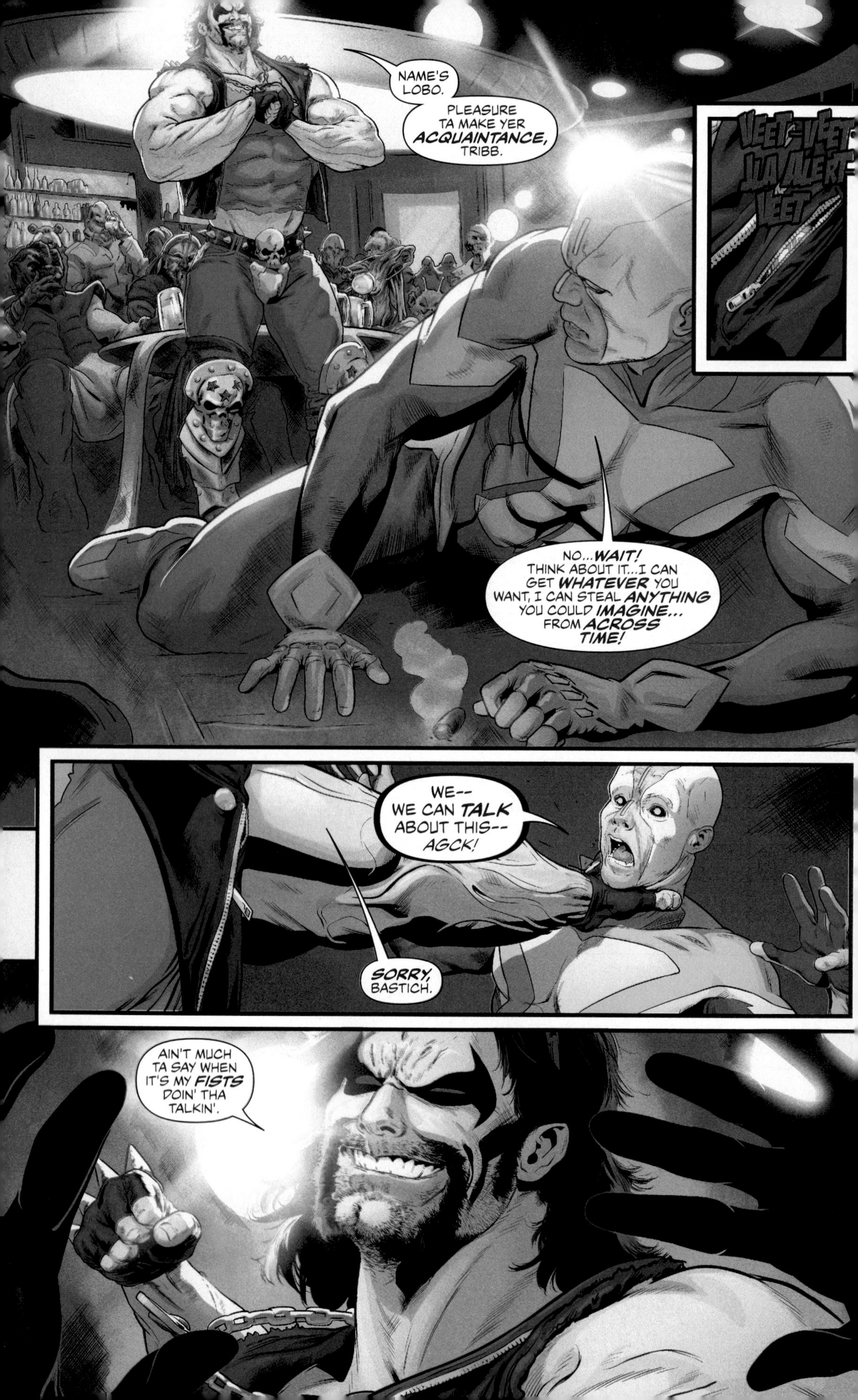
NAME'S LOBO.
PLEASURE TA MAKE YER ACQUAINTANCE, TRIBB.
VEET-VEET JLA ALERT VEET
NO...WAIT! THINK ABOUT IT...I CAN GET WHATEVER YOU WANT, I CAN STEAL ANYTHING YOU COULD IMAGINE... FROM ACROSS TIME!
WE-- WE CAN TALK ABOUT THIS-- AGCK!
SORRY, BASTICH.
AIN'T MUCH TA SAY WHEN IT'S MY FISTS DOIN' THA TALKIN'.

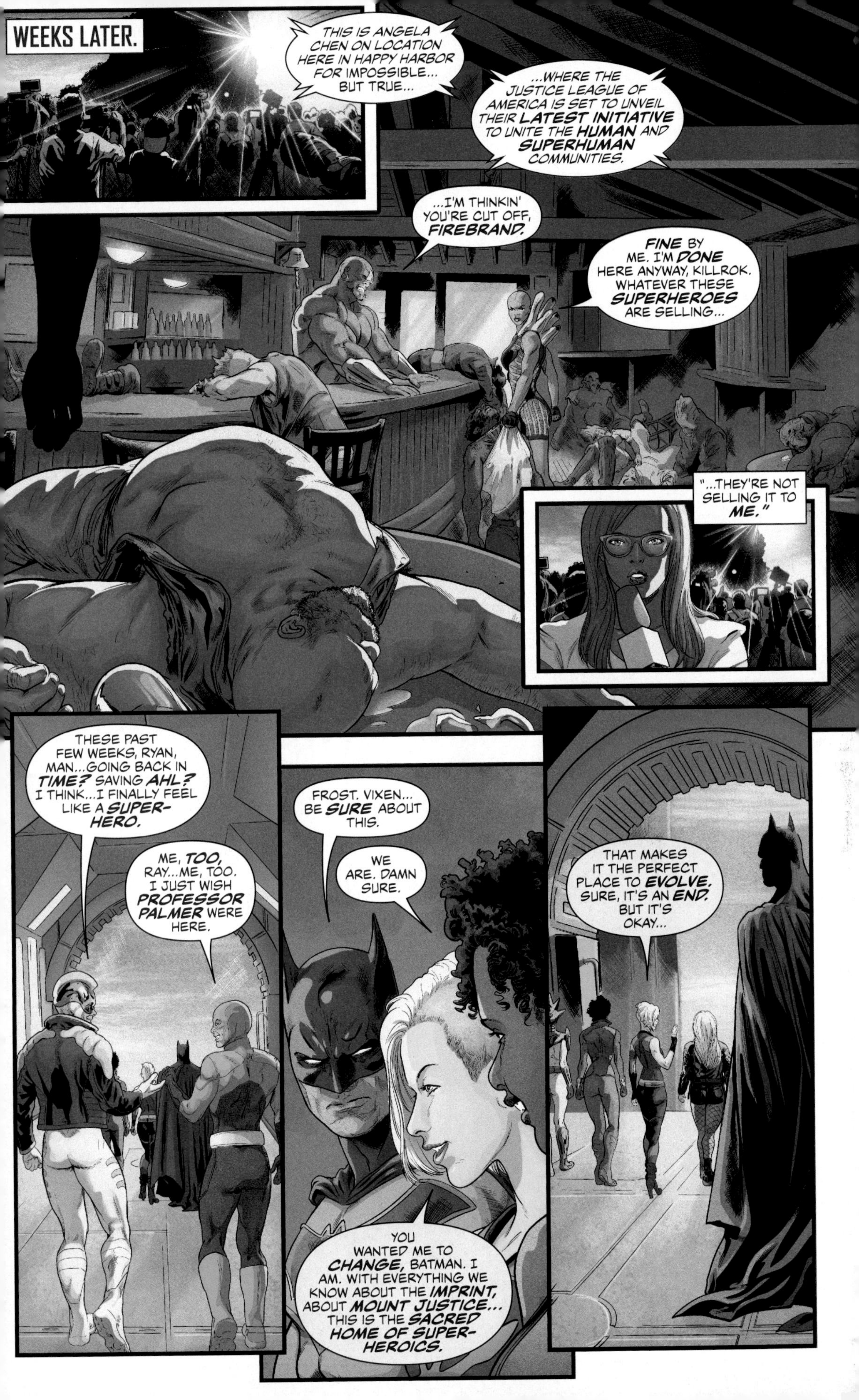
WEEKS LATER.
THIS IS ANGELA CHEN ON LOCATION HERE IN HAPPY HARBOR FOR IMPOSSIBLE... BUT TRUE...
...WHERE THE JUSTICE LEAGUE OF AMERICA IS SET TO UNVEIL THEIR LATEST INITIATIVE TO UNITE THE HUMAN AND SUPERHUMAN COMMUNITIES.
...I'M THINKIN' YOU'RE CUT OFF, FIREBRAND.
FINE BY ME. I'M DONE HERE ANYWAY, KILLROK. WHATEVER THESE SUPERHEROES ARE SELLING...
"...THEY'RE NOT SELLING IT TO ME."
THESE PAST FEW WEEKS, RYAN, MAN...GOING BACK IN TIME? SAVING AHL? I THINK...I FINALLY FEEL LIKE A SUPER-HERO.
ME, TOO, RAY...ME, TOO. I JUST WISH PROFESSOR PALMER WERE HERE.
FROST. VIXEN... BE SURE ABOUT THIS.
WE ARE. DAMN SURE.
YOU WANTED ME TO CHANGE, BATMAN. I AM. WITH EVERYTHING WE KNOW ABOUT THE IMPRINT, ABOUT MOUNT JUSTICE... THIS IS THE SACRED HOME OF SUPER-HEROICS.
THAT MAKES IT THE PERFECT PLACE TO EVOLVE. SURE, IT'S AN END. BUT IT'S OKAY...

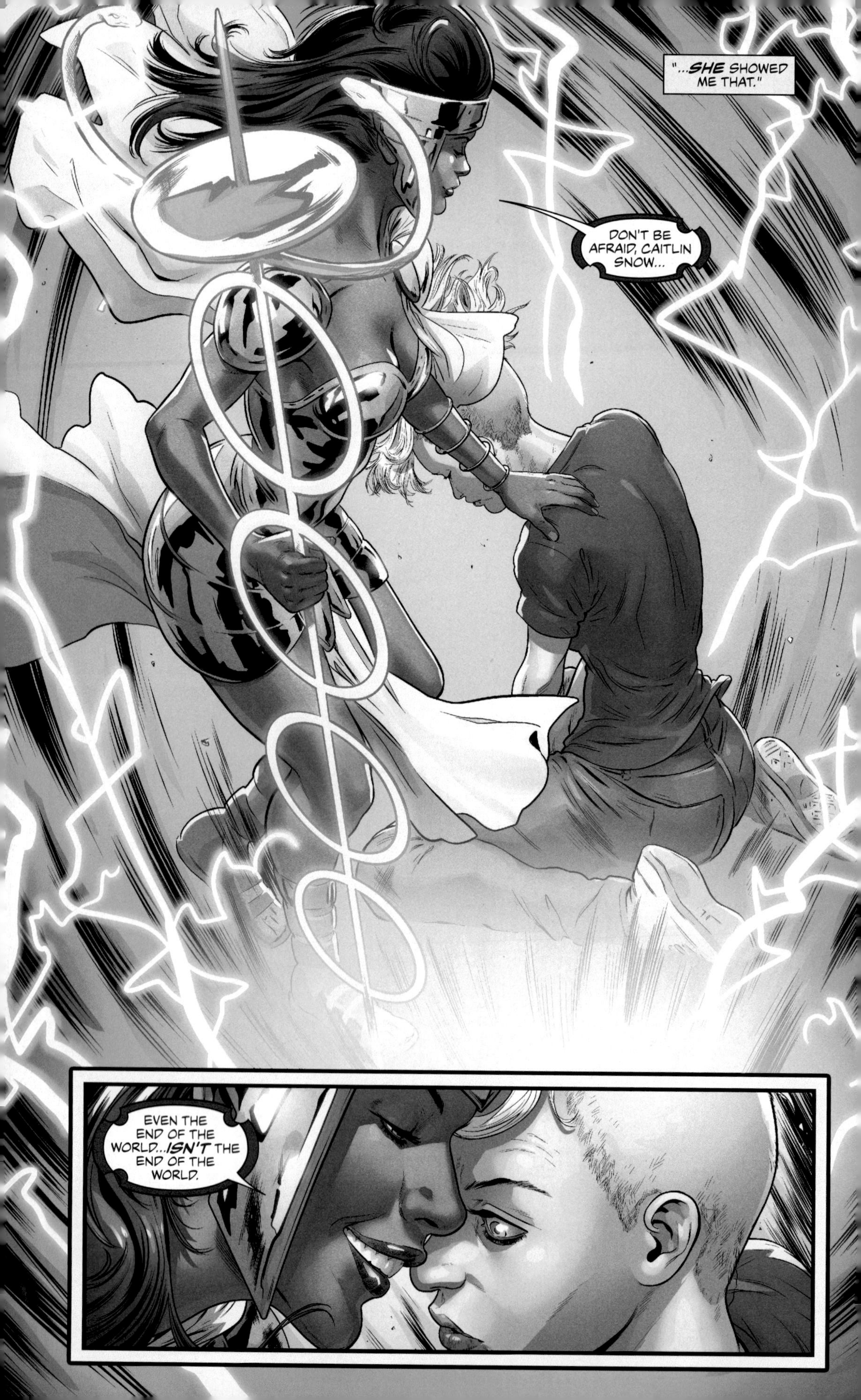
"...*SHE* SHOWED ME THAT."
DON'T BE AFRAID, CAITLIN SNOW...
EVEN THE END OF THE WORLD...*ISN'T* THE END OF THE WORLD.

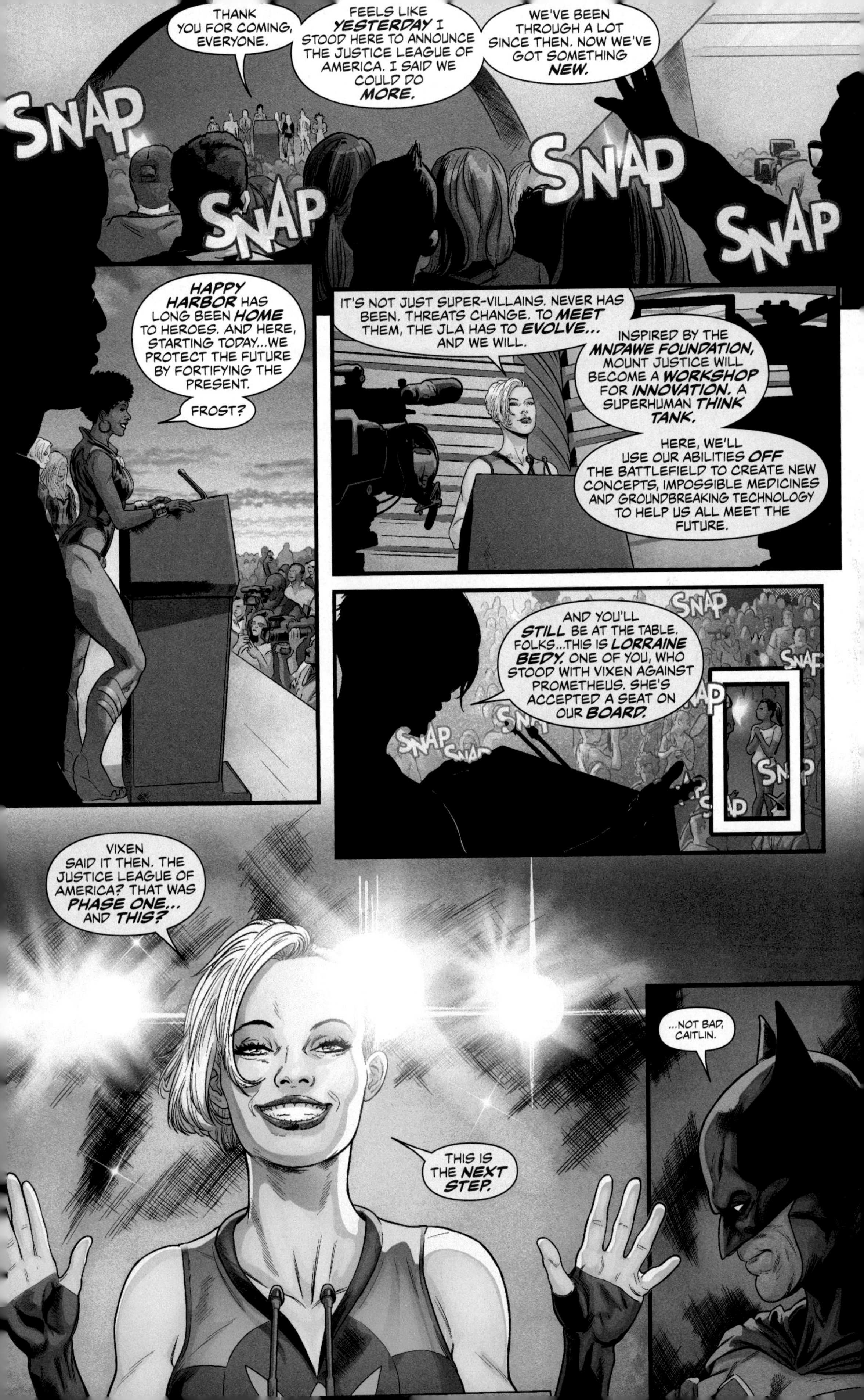
THANK YOU FOR COMING, EVERYONE.
FEELS LIKE YESTERDAY I STOOD HERE TO ANNOUNCE THE JUSTICE LEAGUE OF AMERICA. I SAID WE COULD DO MORE.
WE'VE BEEN THROUGH A LOT SINCE THEN. NOW WE'VE GOT SOMETHING NEW.
SNAP
SNAP
SNAP
SNAP
HAPPY HARBOR HAS LONG BEEN HOME TO HEROES. AND HERE, STARTING TODAY...WE PROTECT THE FUTURE BY FORTIFYING THE PRESENT.
FROST?
IT'S NOT JUST SUPER-VILLAINS. NEVER HAS BEEN. THREATS CHANGE. TO MEET THEM, THE JLA HAS TO EVOLVE... AND WE WILL.
INSPIRED BY THE MNDAWE FOUNDATION, MOUNT JUSTICE WILL BECOME A WORKSHOP FOR INNOVATION. A SUPERHUMAN THINK TANK.
HERE, WE'LL USE OUR ABILITIES OFF THE BATTLEFIELD TO CREATE NEW CONCEPTS, IMPOSSIBLE MEDICINES AND GROUNDBREAKING TECHNOLOGY TO HELP US ALL MEET THE FUTURE.
SNAP
AND YOU'LL STILL BE AT THE TABLE. FOLKS...THIS IS LORRAINE BEDY. ONE OF YOU, WHO STOOD WITH VIXEN AGAINST PROMETHEUS. SHE'S ACCEPTED A SEAT ON OUR BOARD.
SNAP
VIXEN SAID IT THEN. THE JUSTICE LEAGUE OF AMERICA? THAT WAS PHASE ONE... AND THIS?
THIS IS THE NEXT STEP.
...NOT BAD, CAITLIN.

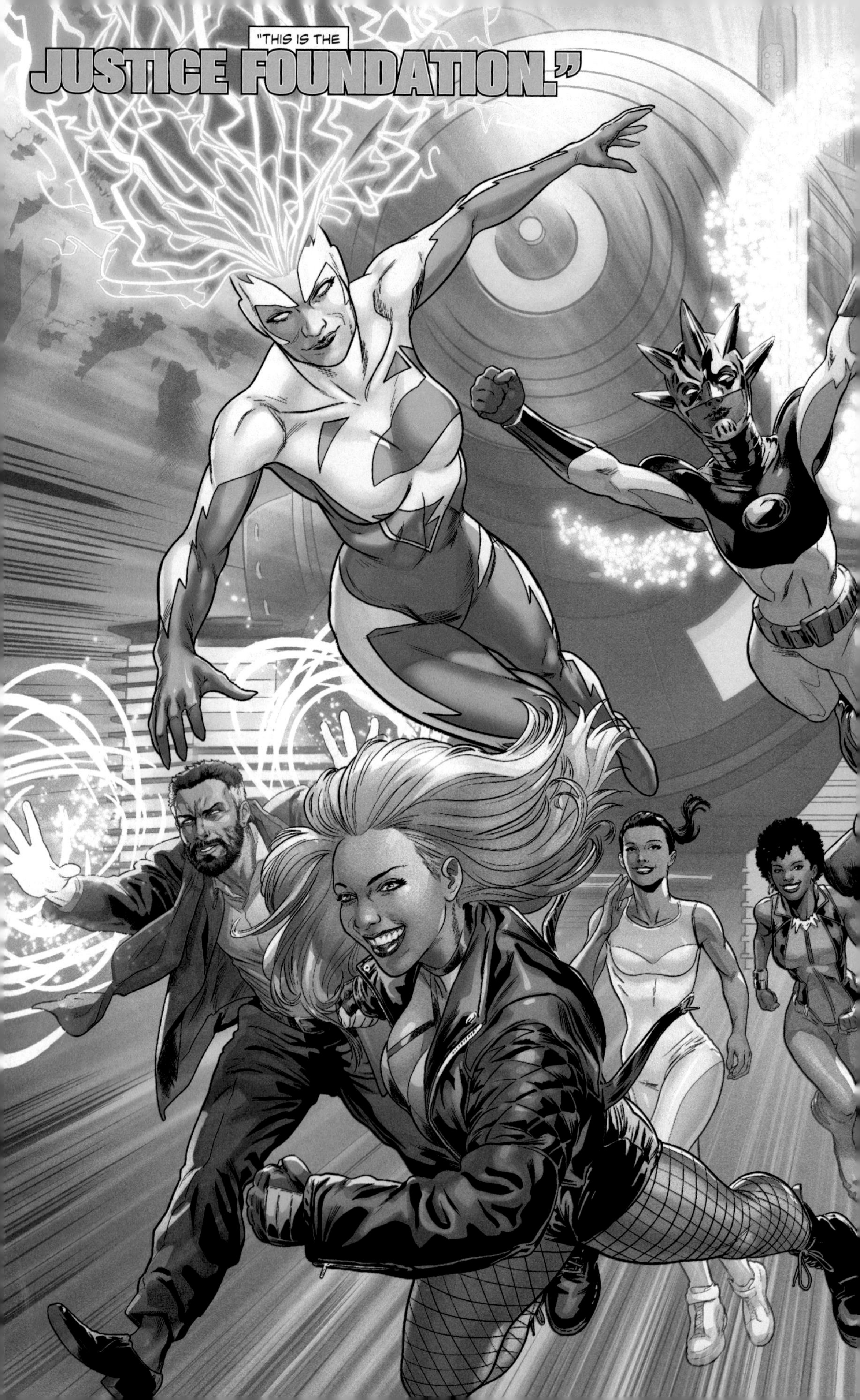
"THIS IS THE
JUSTICE FOUNDATION."

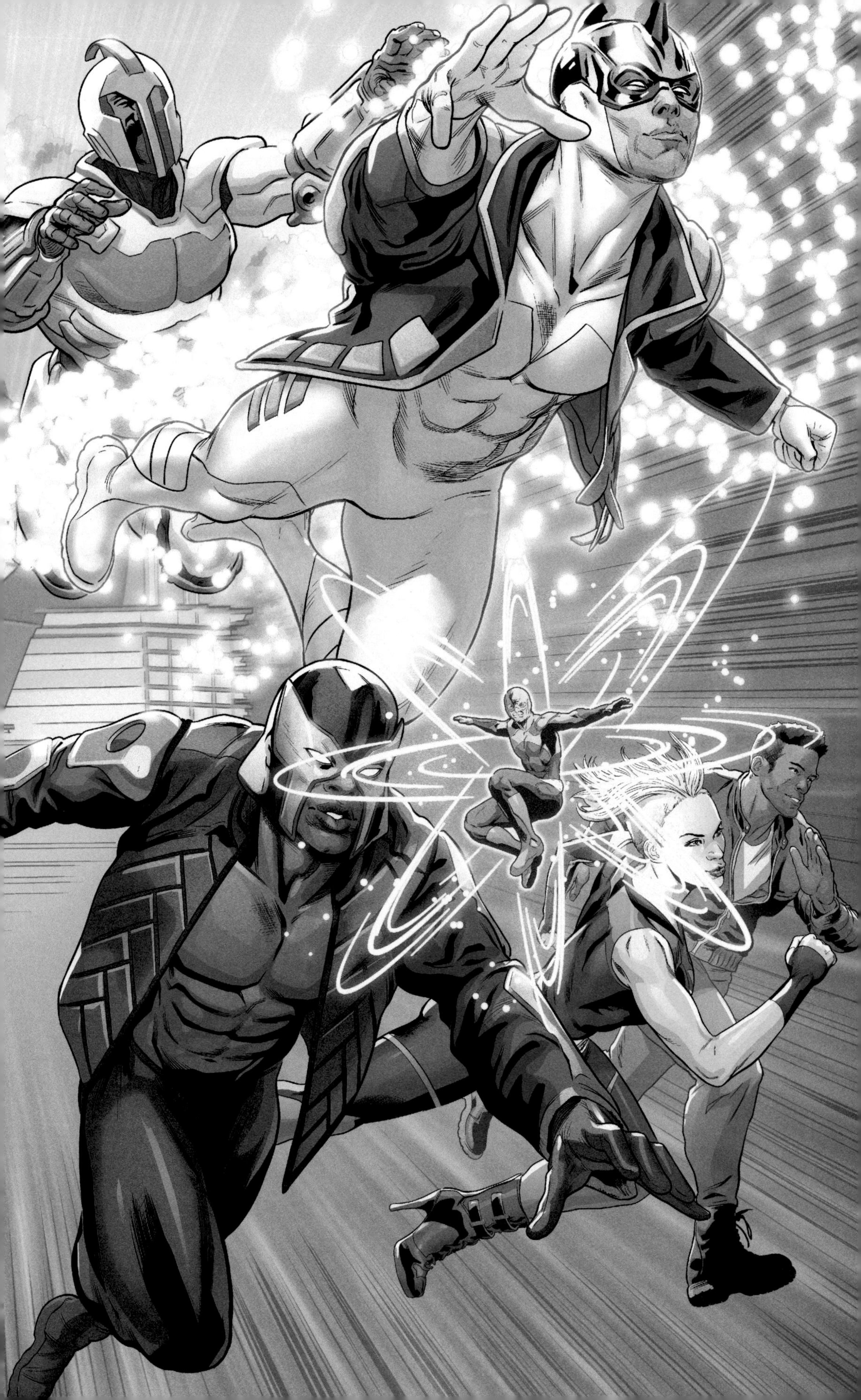

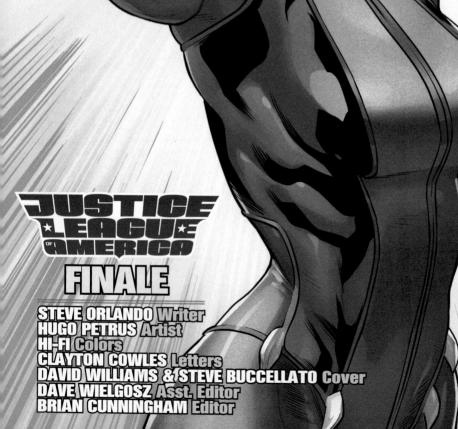

AND IT'S DAY ONE, PEOPLE.

JUSTICE LEAGUE OF AMERICA
FINALE

STEVE ORLANDO Writer
HUGO PETRUS Artist
HI-FI Colors
CLAYTON COWLES Letters
DAVID WILLIAMS & STEVE BUCCELLATO Cover
DAVE WIELGOSZ Asst. Editor
BRIAN CUNNINGHAM Editor

THE END.

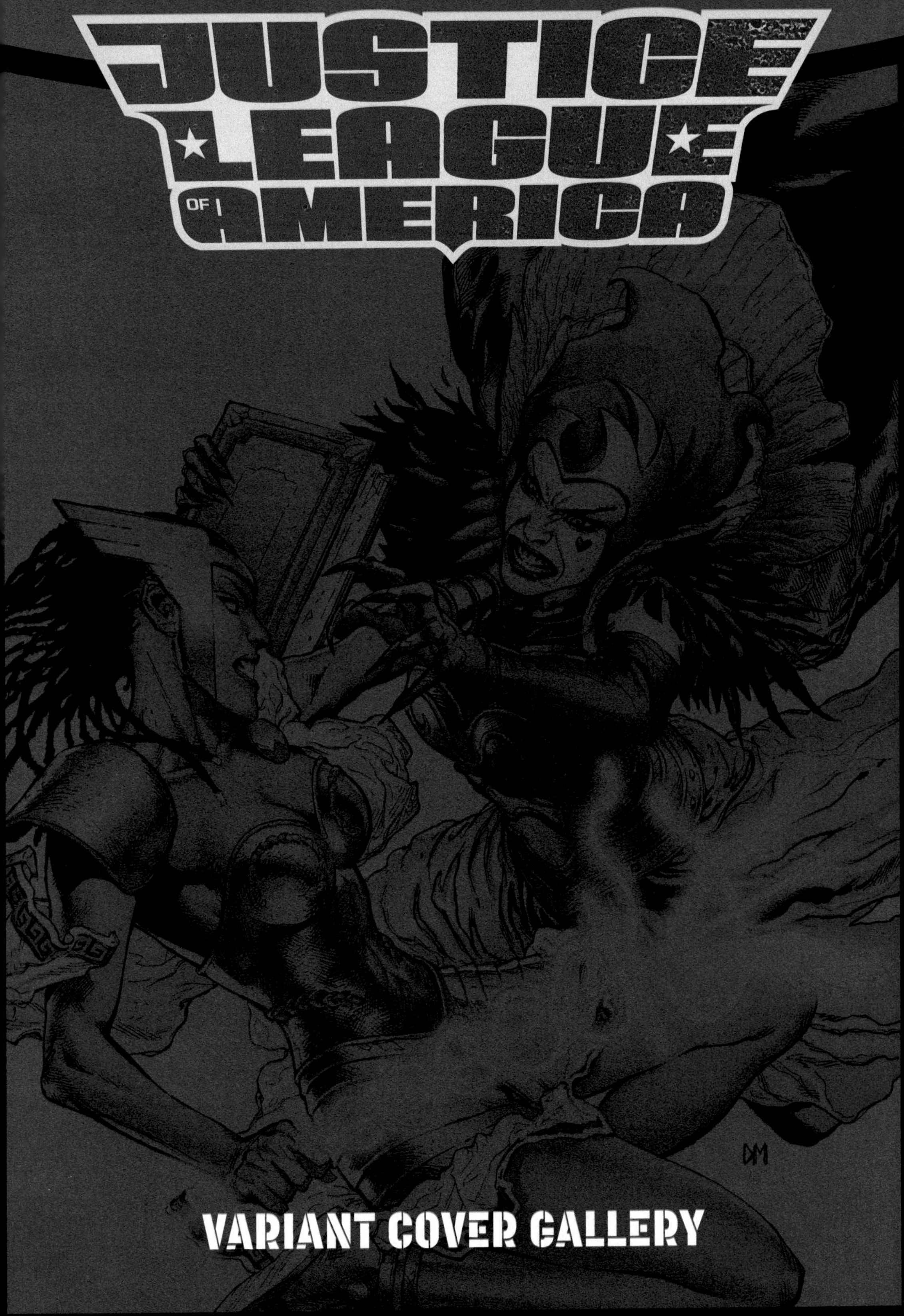
JUSTICE LEAGUE OF AMERICA

VARIANT COVER GALLERY

JUSTICE LEAGUE OF AMERICA #22 variant cover by DOUG MAHNKE and WIL QUINTANA

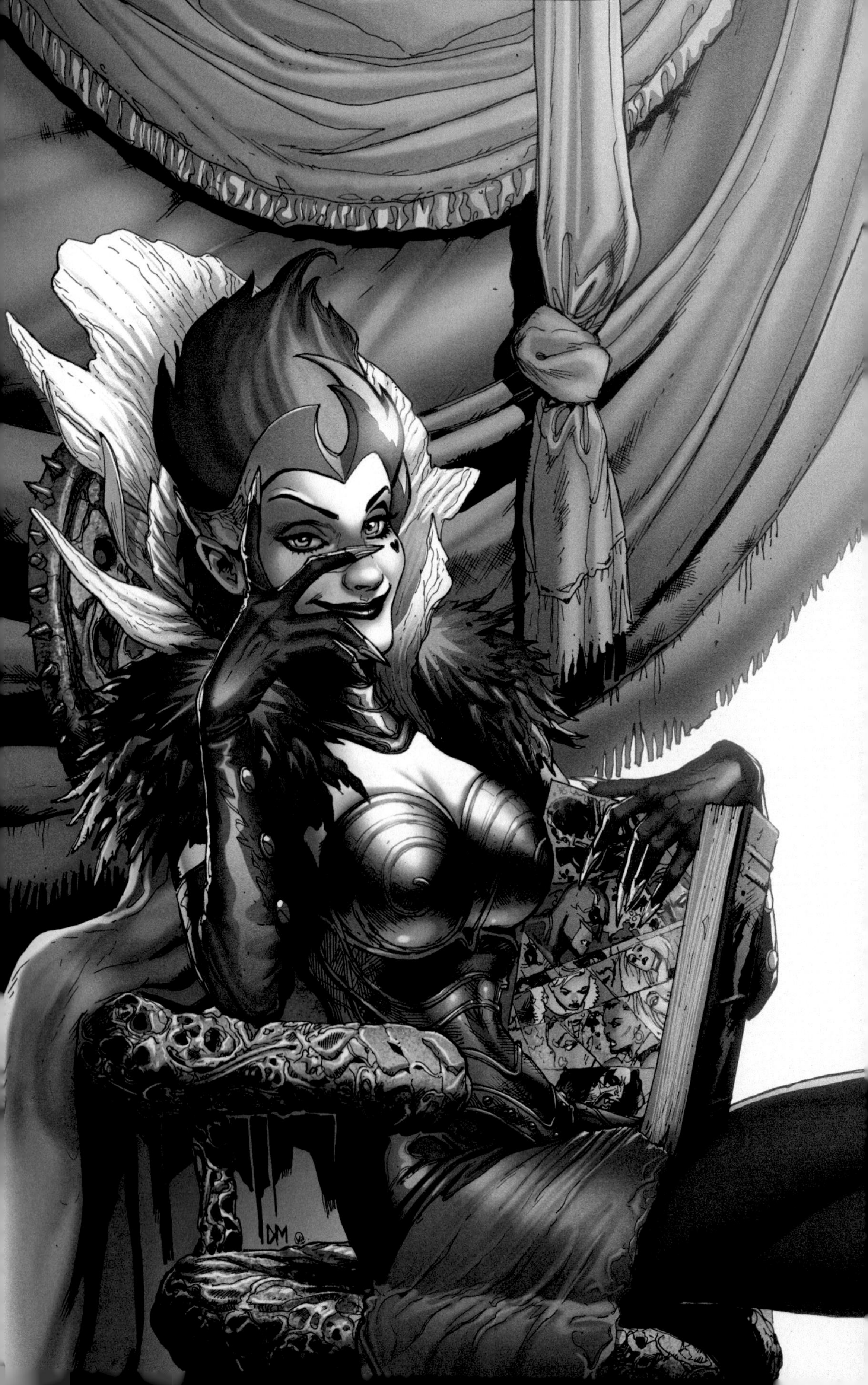

JUSTICE LEAGUE OF AMERICA #23 variant cover by DOUG MAHNKE and WIL QUINTANA

JUSTICE LEAGUE OF AMERICA #24 variant cover by DOUG MAHNKE and WIL QUINTANA

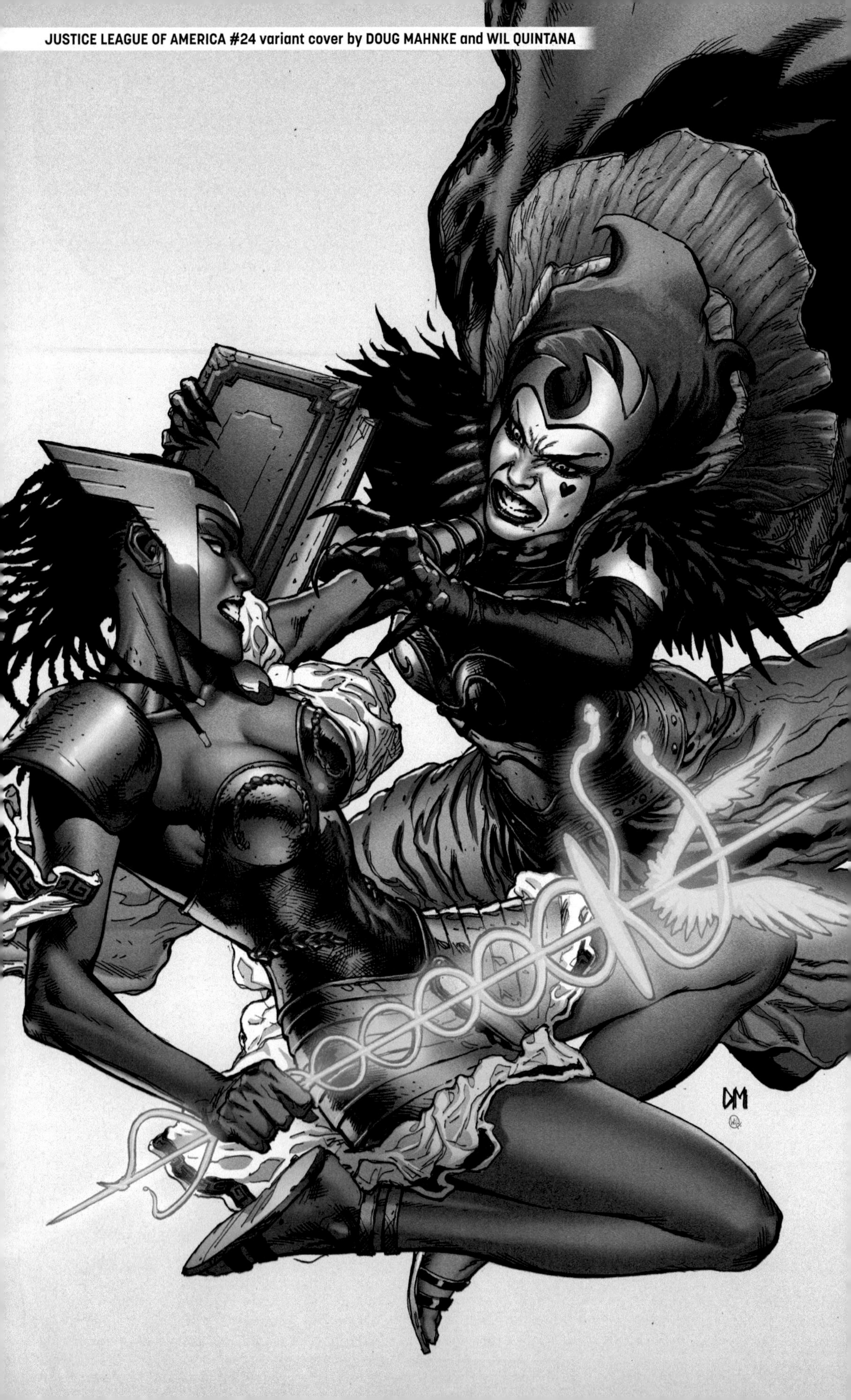

JUSTICE LEAGUE OF AMERICA #25 variant cover by DOUG MAHNKE and WIL QUINTANA

JUSTICE LEAGUE OF AMERICA #26 variant cover by FRANCESCO MATTINA

JUSTICE LEAGUE OF AMERICA #27 variant cover by FRANCESCO MATTINA

JUSTICE LEAGUE OF AMERICA #28 variant cover by FRANCESCO MATTINA

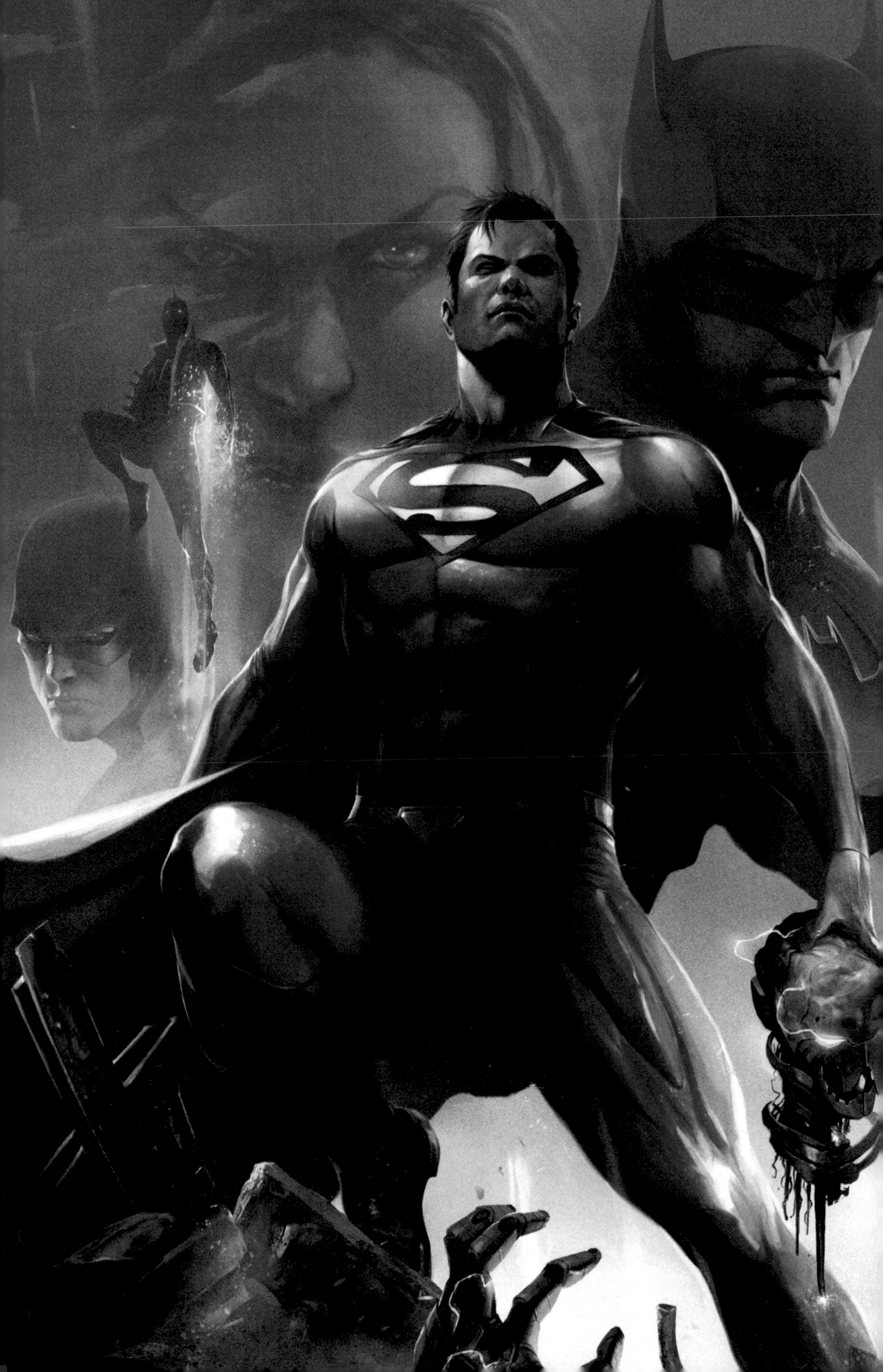

JUSTICE LEAGUE OF AMERICA #29 variant cover by FRANCESCO MATTINA

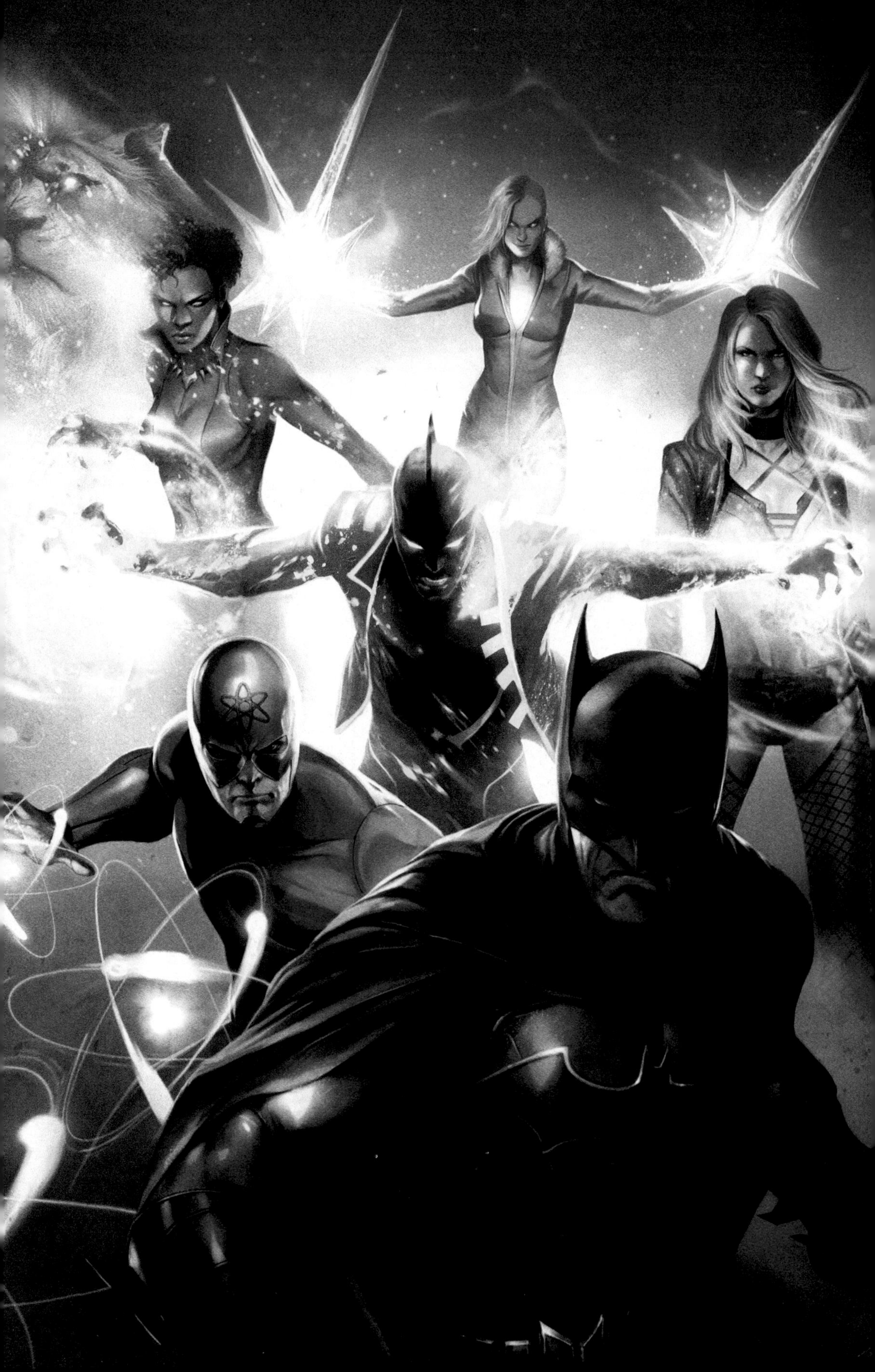

JUSTICE LEAGUE OF AMERICA #23 page 20 pencils by NEIL EDWARDS and inks by DANIEL HENRIQUES

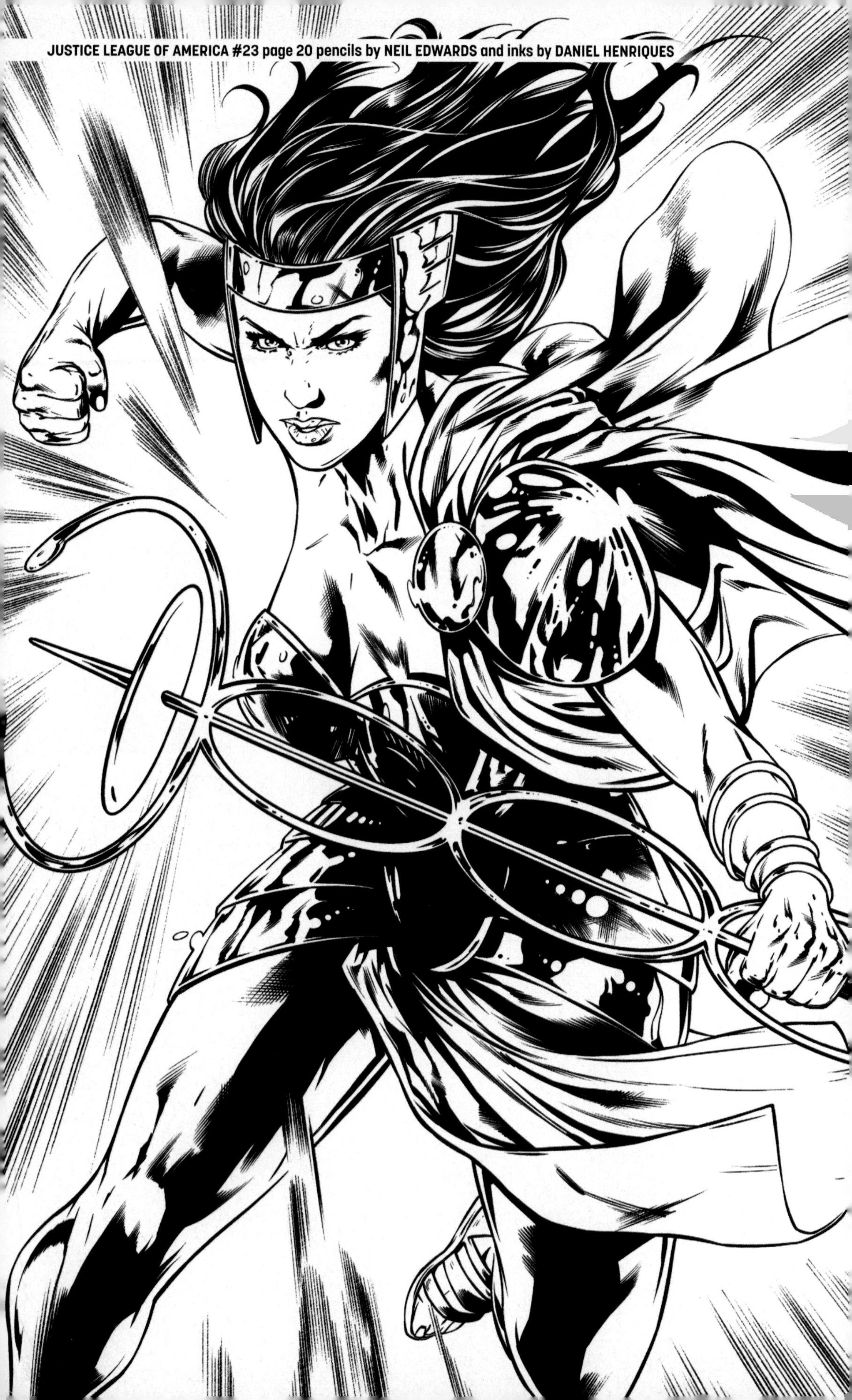

"A strong effort with good pacing, fun dialogue and beautiful art."
—PASTE MAGAZINE

"An excellent start to a brand new era."
—COMICOSITY

JUSTICE LEAGUE OF AMERICA
VOL. 1 THE EXTREMISTS
STEVE ORLANDO and IVAN REIS

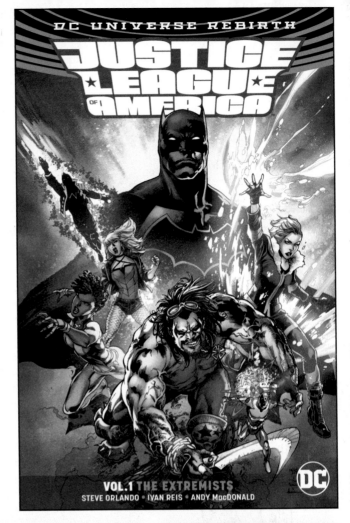

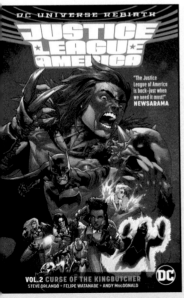

JUSTICE LEAGUE OF AMERICA VOL. 2: CURSE OF THE KINGBUTCHER

JUSTICE LEAGUE OF AMERICA VOL. 3: PANIC IN THE MICROVERSE

JUSTICE LEAGUE OF AMERICA: THE ROAD TO REBIRTH

Get more DC graphic novels wherever comics and books are sold!

"Some really thrilling artwork that establishes incredible scope and danger."
—IGN

DC UNIVERSE REBIRTH
JUSTICE LEAGUE
VOL. 1: The Extinction Machines
BRYAN HITCH
with TONY S. DANIEL

VOL.1 THE EXTINCTION MACHINES
BRYAN HITCH • TONY S. DANIEL • SANDU FLOREA • TOMEU MOREY

VOL.1 THE IMITATION OF LIFE
JOHN SEMPER JR. • PAUL PELLETIER • WILL CONRAD

**CYBORG VOL. 1:
THE IMITATION OF LIFE**

VOL.1 RAGE PLANET
SAM HUMPHRIES • ROBSON ROCHA • ETHAN VAN SCIVER • ED BENES

**GREEN LANTERNS VOL. 1:
RAGE PLANET**

VOL.1 THE DROWNING
DAN ABNETT • PHILIPPE BRIONES • SCOT EATON • BRAD WALKER

**AQUAMAN VOL. 1:
THE DROWNING**

Get more DC graphic novels wherever comics and books are sold!